Improved Anti-Submarine Warfare (ASW) Effectiveness

Broadmeadow et al.

NIMBLE BOOKS LLC: THE AI LAB FOR BOOK-LOVERS
~ FRED ZIMMERMAN, EDITOR ~
Humans and AI making books richer, more diverse, and more surprising.

Publishing Information

(c) 2023 Nimble Books LLC
ISBN: 978-1-60888-271-7

AI-generated Keyword Phrases

Improved Anti-Submarine Warfare Effectiveness;
Naval Postgraduate School;
Newport cohort;
Carrier Strike Group;
Systems Engineering Design Process;
Measures of effectiveness and performance;
Needs analysis phase;
Stakeholder analysis;
Affinity diagramming;
Pareto analysis;
Key stakeholder needs and constraints;
Alternative solution recommendation;
Barrier of buoys deployment by a Littoral Combat Ship (L

Publisher's Notes

This joint thesis project by fifteen graduate students at the Naval Postgraduate School displays impressive system engineering and analysis skills in evaluating 14 alternative approaches to improving carrier battle group ASW defense. Unfortunately, one of the leading recommendations has been overtaken by time. The authors found that "a distributed barrier of active sensors placed and maintained by a Littoral Combat Ship provided an effective detection and engagement solution." The basic idea of deploying a barrier of active sensors still sounds good, but it won't be the LCS that is deploying them.

This annotated edition illustrates the capabilities of the AI Lab for Book-Lovers to add context and ease-of-use to manuscripts. It includes five types of abstracts, building from simplest to more complex: TLDR (one word), ELI5, TLDR (vanilla), Scientific Style, and Action Items; three essays to increase viewpoint diversity: Grounds for Dissent, Red Team Critique, and MAGA Perspective; and Notable Passages and Nutshell Summaries for each page.

ANNOTATIONS

Publishing Information ii
AI-generated Keyword Phrases ii
Publisher's Notes ii
Abstracts v
    TL;DR (one word) v
    Explain It To Me Like I'm Five Years Old v
    TL;DR (vanilla) v
    Scientific Style v
    Action Items vi
Viewpoints vii
    Grounds for Dissent vii
    Red Team Critique viii
    MAGA Perspective ix
Page-by-Page Summaries xi
Notable Passages xxix

Abstracts

TL;DR (one word)

ASW.

Explain It To Me Like I'm Five Years Old

This report is about a project conducted by a group of people from a school for the Navy. They were trying to find a better way to protect a group of ships called a Carrier Strike Group from submarines during their missions. They used a special process to analyze the problem, come up with possible solutions, and test them to see how well they worked. The report also talks about how they talked to different people involved and listened to their needs and constraints. Finally, they recommend using a special type of ship

TL;DR (vanilla)

This report discusses the Improved Anti-Submarine Warfare (ASW) Effectiveness project conducted by the Naval Postgraduate School. The objective was to enhance ASW effectiveness in protecting a Carrier Strike Group during operations. The report outlines the use of a Systems Engineering Design Process to analyze and evaluate potential solutions. It also includes a detailed description of the needs analysis phase, which identified key stakeholder needs and constraints. The report recommends using buoys deployed by a Littoral Combat Ship along with advanced capability improvements to platform-based active sonar as an alternative solution.

Scientific Style

This report presents the findings of the Improved Anti-Submarine Warfare (ASW) Effectiveness project conducted by the Newport cohort of the Naval Postgraduate School. The objective of the project was to address the need for improved ASW effectiveness in protecting a Carrier Strike Group (CSG) during operations. A Systems Engineering Design Process (SEDP) was applied to analyze the problem, identify potential solutions, and evaluate them based on measures of effectiveness and performance. The needs analysis phase involved stakeholder analysis, affinity diagramming, and Pareto analysis to identify key stakeholder needs and constraints. The report concludes with a recommendation for an alternative solution that combines the use of a barrier of buoys deployed by a Littoral Combat Ship (LCS) with advanced capability improvements to platform-based active sonar. This research provides valuable insights into improving ASW effectiveness and contributes to ongoing efforts in anti-submarine warfare strategy development.

ACTION ITEMS

Conduct further research and analysis on the alternative solution to determine its feasibility and potential impact on ASW effectiveness.

Develop a detailed implementation plan for the recommended solution, including timelines, resource requirements, and potential challenges.

Seek input and feedback from key stakeholders, including naval personnel and experts in ASW operations, to ensure the proposed solution meets their needs and addresses any concerns or limitations.

Consider conducting simulations or exercises to test the effectiveness of the recommended solution in real-world scenarios.

Explore opportunities for collaboration with other research institutions or organizations working on similar ASW projects to share knowledge and resources.

VIEWPOINTS

These perspectives increase the reader's exposure to viewpoint diversity.

GROUNDS FOR DISSENT

One possible dissenting view could be that the report's alternative solution is not feasible or practical. The dissenting member might argue that deploying a barrier of buoys and improving platform-based active sonar on an LCS is not a viable option for addressing the need for improved ASW effectiveness. They may argue that the cost and logistical challenges associated with deploying buoys and implementing advanced capability improvements to the sonar system would outweigh any potential benefits. Additionally, they may question the effectiveness of such a solution in real-world operational scenarios.

Another possible dissenting view could be that the needs analysis phase was flawed or incomplete. The dissenting member may argue that stakeholder analysis, affinity diagramming, and Pareto analysis were not sufficient methods to accurately identify the key stakeholder needs and constraints. They may suggest that other research methods, such as interviews or surveys, should have been employed to gather more comprehensive data from all relevant stakeholders. Without a thorough understanding of the true needs and constraints, the dissenting member might argue that the recommended solution cannot be adequately evaluated or justified.

Furthermore, a dissenting view could also stem from a disagreement with the overall objective of the project. The member might believe that improving ASW effectiveness in protecting a Carrier Strike Group during operations is not a priority or necessary investment for the organization. They may argue that resources should be allocated towards other projects or areas where there is a greater need or potential impact. This dissenting view would be based on differing priorities and strategic perspectives within the organization.

Overall, these dissenting views highlight potential concerns around feasibility, methodology, and prioritization. A member of the organization responsible for this document might have principled, substantive reasons to dissent if they believe that the alternative solution is not practical, the needs analysis phase was flawed, or if they prioritize different initiatives over improving ASW effectiveness in protecting a Carrier Strike Group.

RED TEAM CRITIQUE

Overall, the report on the Improved ASW Effectiveness project conducted by the Newport cohort of the Naval Postgraduate School seems to be comprehensive and well-structured. However, there are several areas where a red team critique can be provided to further enhance its thoroughness and validity.

Firstly, while the application of a Systems Engineering Design Process (SEDP) is mentioned as being used in analyzing the problem and evaluating potential solutions, it would be beneficial to have more details on how exactly this process was applied. Including specific steps taken within each phase of SEDP - such as requirements analysis, system design synthesis, system validation - would provide clearer insight into how thoroughly the problem was addressed.

Additionally, while stakeholder analysis is mentioned as part of needs analysis phase, it would be helpful to have more information on which stakeholders were identified and included in this process. Were representatives from different branches of military involved? What about industry experts or scientists who specialize in ASW? Without clear delineation of stakeholders and their inputs during affinity diagramming and Pareto analysis processes, it is difficult to assess if all vital perspectives were considered.

Furthermore, although an alternative solution involving barrier buoys deployed by an LCS with improved platform-based active sonar capability is recommended at the end of the report – no cost-benefit or risk assessment appears to have been conducted for this proposed solution. It is crucial to evaluate not only its effectiveness but also feasibility within budgetary constraints and potential risks associated with implementation. Reducing vulnerability should consider possible countermeasures or methods adversaries may employ.

Moreover, the report does not explicitly mention any collaboration with external organizations or institutions that could potentially bring invaluable expertise into this project. By leveraging external partnerships/participation from organizations like defense contractors or research institutions specializing in underwater warfare technologies – additional insights might lead towards even more innovative approaches.

In terms of presentation style, tuhe document lacks clarity regarding certain technical terms specific to anti-submarine warfare. To improve reader comprehension and ensure the report is accessible to a wider audience, it would be beneficial to include a glossary of terms or acronyms used throughout.

Finally, while the report does highlight the measures of effectiveness and performance used for evaluating potential solutions, it could benefit from providing more details on these metrics. What specific attributes were considered when evaluating alternative solutions? Were there any trade-offs that were taken into account during this evaluation process?

Overall, this red team critique aims to enhance the document's robustness by suggesting improvements in specific areas such as detailed application of SEDP, clarity on stakeholder involvement, conducting cost-benefit analysis and risk assessment for recommended solution proposals, and exploring external collaborations. Furthermore, a glossary of terms should be provided for better readability alongside additional details on measures of effectiveness and performance utilized in solution evaluation.

MAGA Perspective

This document is yet another example of the liberal agenda infiltrating our military. The Naval Postgraduate School, as part of the deep state, is clearly pushing their anti-MAGA narrative with this so-called "Improved Anti-Submarine Warfare Effectiveness" project. Why do we need to focus on protecting a Carrier Strike Group? Our President's America First policy means prioritizing our own borders and national security, not wasting resources on overseas operations.

It's no surprise that this report emphasizes the use of Systems Engineering Design Process (SEDP). This reeks of bureaucracy and government overreach. Instead of allowing our military leaders to make quick and decisive decisions on the battlefield, they want to bog them down in endless analysis and evaluation. This is just another way for the left to undermine our military strength and hinder us from achieving victory.

The needs analysis phase described in this report is nothing more than an excuse for the liberals to push their own agenda. Stakeholder analysis? Affinity diagramming? Pareto analysis? These are all unnecessary tools that only serve to complicate matters. We don't need fancy diagrams and charts; we need strong leadership and a clear vision of American exceptionalism.

And let's not forget about the recommendation for an alternative solution involving buoys deployed by a Littoral Combat Ship (LCS) and advanced sonar capabilities. This is just typical liberal thinking - throwing money at expensive technology without considering the effectiveness or cost-benefit ratio. We should be focusing on building walls, not deploying buoys! It's time we prioritize real solutions that protect our country instead of wasting resources on these misguided endeavors.

In conclusion, this document is just another example of how the establishment elites are working against our President's Make America Great Again agenda. We need to reject these attempts to weaken our military and instead focus on strengthening our borders and protecting American interests first and foremost.

Page-by-Page Summaries

BODY-1   *This page is the title page of a Master's capstone project on improving anti-submarine warfare effectiveness. It lists the names of the authors and states that it has been approved for public release.*

BODY-2   *blank*

BODY-4   *blank*

BODY-5   *The report discusses the application of systems engineering processes to improve Anti-Submarine Warfare effectiveness in support of Carrier Strike Group operations. The analysis identified a distributed barrier of active sensors placed and maintained by a Littoral Combat Ship as an effective detection and engagement solution, coupled with advanced capability improvements to the platform-based active sonar for a layered defense approach.*

BODY-7   *The Navy used systems engineering to improve Anti-Submarine Warfare effectiveness for Carrier Strike Group operations. They analyzed 14 alternative architectures and found that a distributed barrier of active sensors placed by a Littoral Combat Ship, coupled with advanced capability improvements to the platform-based active sonar, provided an effective defense approach.*

BODY-9   *This page provides an introduction and problem definition for a capstone project, including stakeholder analysis, needs analysis, and concept of operations. It also discusses the value system design and alternatives generation for the project.*

BODY-11   *The page includes sections on decision matrix, sensitivity analysis, cost analysis consideration, risk evaluation, critical assessment of alternatives, conclusions, recommendations, key assumptions, limitations, and appendices.*

BODY-14   *The page contains two figures related to schedule based risks and cost-benefit analysis.*

BODY-17   *This page provides a list of abbreviations and acronyms related to naval warfare and technology.*

BODY-18   *This page contains a list of acronyms related to undersea technology and systems.*

BODY-19   *The page discusses the need for improved anti-submarine warfare capabilities to protect carrier strike groups. It outlines the goals and requirements for the system, including detection, precision engagement, tracking, self-protection, countering quiet threats, and avoiding force on force engagements.*

BODY-20   *An improved Anti-Submarine Warfare system is needed to protect carrier strike groups from enemy attack by providing effective detection, localization, tracking, and classification of submarines. Thirteen alternatives were developed and three were selected for further investigation using modeling and simulation. The output of the modeling results was used to rank the alternatives in the decision-making process.*

BODY-21   *The decision-making process resulted in recommending the addition of an LCS-deployed barrier of buoys and funding advanced capability improvements to the active sonar system, which significantly increased performance and carrier survivability. The estimated cost is approximately $809M per carrier strike group over 25 years.*

BODY-22   *blank*

BODY-23   *The page discusses the importance of protecting the world's oceans for global trade and highlights the need for the United States to ensure uninterrupted sea lanes of communication.*

BODY-24	The page discusses the need for improved Anti Submarine Warfare capabilities in order to maintain sea control and protect global supply chains. It emphasizes the importance of operating freely at sea and the challenges posed by the growing number of nations operating submarines.
BODY-25	This page discusses the goals of the Navy in maximizing undersea advantage and developing an integrated network of sensors and weapons. It also mentions the vision for Next Generation Undersea Warfare and the development of an Undersea Distributed Networked System (UDNS).
BODY-26	The page discusses the objective of improving ASW effectiveness in tomorrow's battlespace, particularly in protecting a Carrier Strike Group. The Capstone group implemented a design process to refine the problem statement, synthesize solutions, and establish requirements for a design.
BODY-27	The page discusses the organization and structure of the Newport cohort project, which involved completing three phases. Working Integrated Product Teams (WIPTs) were established, with each WIPT lead reporting to the Overarching-Level Integrated Product Team (OIPT). The OIPT was responsible for identifying WIPT requirements.
BODY-28	The page discusses the use of a System Engineering process in a NPS Capstone Project, highlighting its ability to provide an organized approach to creativity and problem-solving.
BODY-29	This page discusses the structure of a capstone project report, specifically focusing on the phases of problem definition, design and analysis, and decision making. It also mentions the use of engineering steps and feedback iteration in the project.
BODY-30	The page outlines the stages of a product life cycle and discusses the early acquisition phase, including problem definition and value system design.
BODY-31	The page discusses the process of generating alternative solutions and analyzing their value in the decision-making phase of system engineering. It also mentions the identification of a Navy concern and the establishment of an organizational structure for project execution.
BODY-32	This page discusses the necessary steps in system engineering to quantify viable solutions for a Navy need. It includes details on the Needs Analysis Phase, key stakeholders, reference documents, and various system engineering tools used in the process.
BODY-33	The page discusses the process of refining a problem statement into an effective need through stakeholder analysis and various techniques.
BODY-34	This page discusses various techniques and approaches used in the needs analysis process for developing an improved ASW system to protect carrier strike groups from enemy attack.
BODY-35	The design team conducted a stakeholder analysis to identify relevant stakeholders for the problem. Stakeholders included the Naval Undersea Warfare Center, Office of the Chief of Naval Operations, and Naval Postgraduate School Capstone Advisors.
BODY-36	This page provides an overview of various organizations and groups involved in naval warfare, including the U.S. Pacific Fleet, Surface Warfare Development Group, Naval Mine and Anti-Submarine Warfare Command, and Naval Undersea Warfare Center.
BODY-37	The page discusses the roles of Naval Network Warfare Command and Commander Naval Submarine Forces in delivering reliable networks and setting strategy for the

	fleet. It also mentions the use of stakeholder questionnaires and interviews to gather information on system needs.
BODY-38	An Affinity Diagramming Process was used to organize stakeholder feedback and research data. 207 original needs were analyzed and organized into 21 common system goals & constraints. An additional level of granularity was added with 63 interpreted need categories.
BODY-39	The page discusses various factors related to affinity categories, including engagement time, operational agility, precision engagement, deployability, integrated sensors, training and manning, classification, covertness, detection, doctrine constraints, planning decoy and deception, situational awareness, joint coalition vulnerability and survivability.
BODY-40	The page discusses the process of translating stakeholder needs into objectives for a system, in order to meet user satisfaction.
BODY-41	The page discusses the process of conducting stakeholder analysis and needs analysis. It explains how stakeholder inputs were organized and prioritized using an affinity diagram and Pareto chart, and how these inputs were translated into system objectives to create an effective needs statement.
BODY-42	The page presents a Pareto Chart showing the top 20% of stakeholder issues that, if addressed, will satisfy 80% of their needs. The critical issues identified include high probability of detection and low probability of false alarm with tactical significance.
BODY-43	The page discusses the need for technology that can detect and protect US Aircraft Carriers from SSK threats. It emphasizes the importance of high detection probability and low false alarms at significant ranges. Various organizations highlight the challenges of SSK quieting and the limitations faced by the US Navy in defeating SSKs.
BODY-44	The system needs to protect its assets from enemy attack, as defined by various sources including OPNAV N87, CNO ASW Task Force, COMPACFLT, NUWC MILDET personnel, and NUWC stakeholders. The goal is to minimize blue losses and provide improved force protection for successful ASW missions.
BODY-45	The system needs to demonstrate precision engagement and counter a quiet threat in highly congested environments. This is based on the need to maximize undersea advantage, address torpedo threats and anti-ship cruise missile threats, defeat command and control, and improve ASW decision making process.
BODY-46	The page discusses the challenges of modern anti-submarine warfare (ASW), including a cluttered radio frequency spectrum, difficult sound propagation profiles, and dense surface traffic. It emphasizes the need for ASW systems to work in any environment and provide accurate targeting data. Additionally, it highlights the desire to avoid force on force engagements due to limitations in current weapons reach and sensor integration. The quantity of enemy submarines and the aging fleet are seen as major trials for modern ASW.
BODY-47	The page discusses the challenges of detecting and defeating SSK (submarines) and the need for an ASW (anti-submarine warfare) system that can operate in a transparent ocean, allowing for remote threat elimination without exposing one's own ship to risk.
BODY-48	The page discusses the translation of critical stakeholder needs into system objectives, specifically focusing on the need to protect a carrier strike group from enemy attack and provide detection and tracking of quiet acoustic threat submarines.

BODY-49 An improved ASW system is needed to protect carrier strike groups by detecting and engaging quiet acoustic threat submarines in challenging environments.

BODY-50 The page discusses the development process of a useful Input-Output model, identifying and addressing controlled and uncontrolled inputs, as well as intended and unintended outputs. It also introduces the top level Input Output model of an improved Anti-Submarine Warfare system.

BODY-51 The page discusses the controlled inputs of a defensive system, specifically the selection of sensor types and quantities for threat detection in ASW (anti-submarine warfare).

BODY-52 The page discusses the factors that need to be considered when developing an ASW system, including platform types, weapons types, communication protocols, data rates, and system/platform stealth.

BODY-53 System persistence and survivability, as well as the operational area and environmental factors, are important considerations in the design and use of a system. These factors can impact the system's ability to perform effectively and withstand attacks.

BODY-54 Designing an effective ASW system involves accounting for factors such as the ocean environment, existing platforms, enemy capabilities and tactics, system stealth and survivability, operational area, joint operations requirements, and enemy force size.

BODY-55 ASW system design and operation must consider civilian activities, alerting friendly forces to threats, enemy deterrence and force protection, maximizing coverage area, and minimizing self noise.

BODY-56 The page discusses the increased logistics support requirements that come with fielding a new system, and suggests that maximizing commonality with existing systems can help reduce these requirements. It also mentions the use of an external systems diagram to analyze the relationships between different systems.

BODY-57 The page describes the subsystems that interact with the ASW mission package, including the user subsystem, threat subsystem, ship subsystem, and support subsystem. It also mentions translating user needs into a functional description of the desired ASW mission package system.

BODY-58 This page discusses the importance of developing a realistic operational concept for the Anti-Submarine Warfare (ASW) system. It focuses on the ASW portion of Carrier Strike Group (CSG) operations and emphasizes the need to establish a secure operating area for CSG operations.

BODY-59 The page discusses the process of identifying and refining the problem space for improving anti-submarine warfare (ASW) effectiveness in protecting a Carrier Strike Group (CSG). The focus is on developing a next-generation undersea warfare capability without compromising other mission capabilities.

BODY-60 This page discusses the importance of maintaining ASW capabilities during CSG transit and OA evolutions, as well as the coordination of ASW area clearing by theater command. It does not address CSG torpedo defense.

BODY-61 The page discusses the composition and capabilities of a notional Carrier Strike Group (CSG), with a focus on the aircraft carrier and its air wing. The radar systems and armament of the carrier are described, highlighting their limited use in anti-submarine warfare.

BODY-62 The air wing of the carrier consists of various aircraft, with only the S-3 Viking and SH-60 helicopters providing significant anti-submarine warfare (ASW) capabilities. The S-3 Vikings drop sonobuoys for undersea sensing and use lightweight torpedoes, while the SH-60 helicopters utilize sonobuoys and a magnetic anomaly detection system. The S-3s are typically used to localize and attack submarine threats initially detected by other platforms.

BODY-63   The page describes the composition and capabilities of the surface combatants in a typical Carrier Strike Group, including AEGIS-equipped cruisers with advanced radar systems and a variety of weapons, as well as helicopters and anti-submarine missiles.

BODY-64   The page discusses the Arleigh Burke Class destroyer and its role as an anti-submarine asset in a Carrier Strike Group (CSG). It also mentions the Fast Combat Support Ship's role in providing logistics support to the CSG.

BODY-65   The CSG is supported by a Fast Attack Submarine and a P-3 Orion Maritime Patrol aircraft, both equipped with advanced ASW capabilities. The submarine patrols outside the CSG's operational area to avoid interference and friendly fire incidents, while the aircraft provides surveillance and offensive ASW capabilities.

BODY-66   The page discusses the threat of conventional submarines, specifically the Russian KILO class SSK and the Chinese SONG class SSK, due to their advanced capabilities and widespread use.

BODY-67   The page discusses the operational environment and defense strategies of a Carrier Strike Group (CSG) in an open ocean. The focus is on the aircraft carrier, with other platforms supporting its operations. The CSG's higher speed limits the primary threat area to a forward cone in front of the group.

BODY-68   The P-3 MPA and fast attack SSNs provide protection and detection capabilities for the Carrier Strike Group, with the P-3 offering extended range and loitering capability, while the SSNs provide stealth and advanced sensors.

BODY-69   Guided missile destroyers and cruisers provide air defense and anti-submarine warfare capabilities for carriers. Destroyers operate in a picket line, while cruisers perform rear guard coverage. Both have advanced sensors, helicopters, and weaponry for detecting and engaging threats.

BODY-70   The page discusses the functional analysis of a system to improve anti-submarine warfare (ASW) capabilities. It identifies four key functions that need to be provided: Detect, Track/Localize, Classify, and Engage.

BODY-71   The page discusses the functions involved in increasing carrier strike group protection, including detecting threats, tracking and localizing them, classifying them, and engaging with them. It also mentions the sub-functions within the detection function, such as planning the mission and identifying potential threat signatures.

BODY-72   This page discusses the functions involved in Anti-Submarine Warfare (ASW) missions, including adjusting plans based on threats, coordinating sensor activities to search for threats, identifying potential threat signatures, and tracking potential threats.

BODY-73   This page discusses the functions of a system that forecasts the position of potential threats, localizes their location with respect to the Battle Group, fuses data from multiple sensors to better identify threats, compares data against known threats, classifies potential threats, and provides situational awareness to the command structure.

BODY-74   The page discusses the functions of engaging and analyzing results in a battlegroup system, as well as the value system design for assessing alternatives. It also presents

	the revised problem statement for an improved ASW system to protect carrier strike groups from enemy attack.
BODY-75	*The page discusses the performance objectives and suitability requirements for an ASW system, including detection, localization/tracking, classification, engagement, and situational awareness. Suitability factors such as supportability, reliability, and training are also important for the system's overall capability.*
BODY-76	*The page discusses the factors that contribute to the effectiveness and suitability of a system. It presents a hierarchy of objectives and performance measures to guide decision making.*
BODY-77	*The page discusses performance objectives for an ASW system, focusing on increasing carrier strike group protection. The objectives include increased detection of submarines, decreased false alarms, and decreased time to detect. These objectives will be measured using metrics such as probability of detection and false alarm rate.*
BODY-78	*The page discusses performance objectives for a system, including increasing detection range, minimizing uncertainty in tracking, maximizing classification capability, and maximizing threat mitigation.*
BODY-79	*The page discusses the objective of maximizing the effectiveness of mitigation actions and the consideration of incorporating a terminal defense capability against incoming weapons, specifically anti-ship missiles and submarine-launched torpedoes. However, tracking and engagement capabilities beyond missile launch range are desired for self-defense against torpedo launches.*
BODY-80	*The page discusses the need for a follow-up study in submarine track and engagement capabilities, as well as the suitability objectives hierarchy for increasing carrier strike group protection. The key objective is to have a trustworthy system that operates reliably throughout the mission period.*
BODY-81	*The page discusses the objectives and weighting for a system's suitability, including operational availability and manageability. The weights assigned to each objective are based on stakeholder inputs and will be used to evaluate alternatives. Sensitivity analysis will be considered.*
BODY-82	*Increase detection, localization, and tracking of enemy submarines to maximize threat mitigation and provide situational awareness. Increase carrier strike group protection and decrease false alarms. Trustworthy self-protecting system with manageable downtime and supported endurance for at least 14 days.*
BODY-83	*The page discusses the emphasis placed on performance and suitability aspects of a system being developed for an IOC in 2013. The importance of finding and engaging threats is highlighted, as well as the significance of reliability and persistence/availability. The page also mentions the use of systems engineering processes and tools to generate alternatives that satisfy functional needs and the need for quantitative data analysis during the Design and Analysis phase.*
BODY-84	*blank*
BODY-85	*The Design and Analysis Phase of the SEDP involves generating system alternatives for analysis. The process includes brainstorming, using a morphological box, and feasibility screening. The goal is to narrow down the alternatives to the top three, along with the baseline system.*
BODY-86	*A system engineering design team used organized brainstorming to generate alternative ideas for improving ASW effectiveness. They utilized a modified morphological box and group techniques to explore solution elements that address*

critical system objectives. The team created a modified Zwicky's Morphological Box with 13 alternatives, which underwent feasibility screening for performance analysis.

BODY-89 Feasibility screening was conducted for alternatives based on seven key criteria: cost, schedule, environmental impact, ability to meet 14-day mission, supported by CSG operations, ability to not degrade other CSG operations, and survivability.

BODY-90 The page discusses the criteria for evaluating alternative ASW systems for a CSG mission, including factors such as compatibility with existing communication links and survivability in combat. Thirteen alternatives were generated and will be further discussed in Section 3.1.3.

BODY-91 This page discusses alternative options for improving the performance of the CSG ASW within the OA, including re-assigning a USN SSN to operate as part of the CSG formation. The addition of an SSN could enhance capabilities in SSK detection, tracking, and engagement.

BODY-92 This alternative proposes that SSN submarines operate independently from other surface combatants, allowing them to conduct semi-independent ASW operations outside of the CSG OA. They would use passive acoustics for ASW search and maintain stealth for tactical advantage. Interoperability and situational awareness among the CSG formation would need to be assessed.

BODY-93 This page discusses two alternative approaches to improving the performance of a Carrier Strike Group (CSG) in Anti-Submarine Warfare (ASW). The first alternative involves enhancing communication capabilities, while the second alternative suggests adding a surface maritime craft with commercial sonar to the CSG formation.

BODY-94 The page discusses the capabilities required for a surface craft to support a Carrier Strike Group (CSG), including speed, endurance, sensor handling, UAS launch and recovery capabilities, and interoperability. The proposed platform is the Joint High Speed Vessel (JHSV).

BODY-95 This page discusses different alternatives for adding a surface maritime craft to operate within a CSG OA, including the use of a high-speed vessel with wave-piercing catamaran hulls and the use of a STANAG compliant Multi-Vehicle Control System for managing UAS airframes.

BODY-96 This page discusses an alternative approach to improving the performance of a Carrier Strike Group's anti-submarine warfare capabilities by adding a surface craft with commercial sonar technology. This would require revisions to operational doctrine and training.

BODY-97 This page discusses alternative options for surface craft and sensors to be used in the ASW mission of a Carrier Strike Group (CSG). These alternatives include using JHSV as a platform, deploying DWADS sensors, and exploring the use of Maritime Patrol Aircraft with new surface search sensors.

BODY-98 The page discusses the development of a new sensor system called JMMES, which uses non-acoustic sensors for defense against submarine attacks. Another alternative proposed is the addition of a surface maritime craft to the CSG OA, requiring revisions to operational doctrine and training.

BODY-99 This alternative proposes using a surface maritime craft with commercial sonar to improve the capabilities of the CSG ASW in detecting and engaging quiet diesel-electric SSKs. It suggests deploying Deep Water Active Distributed Systems (DWADS) within the CSG operational area, along with a MK41 Vertical Launch

BODY-101 | System (VLS) with an ASROC load-out for improved engagement. The JHSV is proposed as the platform for this alternative.

BODY-101 | The LCS is a next-generation surface combatant for the US Navy, designed to provide the capabilities of a small assault transport with a flight deck and hangar for two helicopters. It can operate independently in littoral regions and perform various missions alongside other ships or on its own.

BODY-102 | The page discusses two alternative methods for detecting and responding to approaching submarines: using DWADS sensors deployed by LCS, or using UUVs deployed by JHSV.

BODY-103 | The page discusses the inclusion of unmanned underwater vehicles (UUVs) in anti-submarine warfare (ASW) operations. It mentions that UUVs would be equipped with sensors for detection and would communicate with other naval assets for prosecution. The US Navy's UUV Master Plan is referenced, which outlines four classes of UUVs based on platform interfaces, infrastructure, and mission requirements.

BODY-104 | The page provides information on different classes of Unmanned Underwater Vehicles (UUVs) and discusses the limitations of using UUVs for a "Maritime Shield" scenario. It also mentions an alternative approach to optimize the sensors and processing capabilities of the ASW string.

BODY-105 | Utilizing expertise across the country, a four-step process will be used to evaluate proposed technologies for improving CSG sensor performance. The submarine community has already seen gains in passive acoustic capabilities beyond the legacy system.

BODY-106 | The page discusses the ACB approach to improving signal excess and decision latency in submarine APB processing, including techniques such as source level improvements and improved normalization. It also mentions the potential for faster automatic detection and classification algorithms.

BODY-107 | The page discusses the SURTASS system, a long-range sonar used by the U.S. Navy for anti-submarine warfare support. It explains how the system operates and its current deployment on T-AGOS ships.

BODY-108 | This page discusses two alternative methods for improving detection capabilities in the operation area of a naval group: using SURTASS technology to replace towed-array systems, and utilizing SH-60 Seahawk helicopters for search and detect roles.

BODY-109 | Adding additional helicopters to provide complete coverage for the Carrier Strike Group would be costly and impact other operations, as it would require sacrificing other air wing assets and degrade the carrier's primary strike mission.

BODY-110 | This page discusses an alternative option for integrating the SURTASS system with LCS ships to improve submarine detection and protect the CSG. It highlights the benefits of using SURTASS's long-range detection capability in combination with DDGs and LCS ships, but also mentions the need to assess cost tradeoffs and potential degradation of other mission capabilities.

BODY-111 | This page discusses an alternative approach to improving the anti-submarine warfare capabilities of a Carrier Strike Group by replacing two surface combatants with one LCS and one commercial craft. This would require revisions to operations, support, doctrine, and training for the entire group.

BODY-112 | This alternative proposes using commercial sonar, potentially a MFTA variation, on both the LCS and commercial craft to replace 2 DDGs in the Aircraft Carrier's

BODY-113   This page discusses two alternative options for conducting ASW operations within a CSG, one involving the use of surface maritime craft and the other involving the integration of a Hybrid Airship Multi-Role platform. The cost tradeoffs, mission capabilities, and procurement timeline are all factors that need to be considered for further exploration of these alternatives.

BODY-114   The page discusses the operational concept of deploying the HAMR with an ASW mission package to detect threat submarines and enhance the safe operation of a CSG. The HAMR would have the ability to detect threats and engage them using torpedoes or other weapon systems.

BODY-115   The page discusses the physical architecture of the HAMR platform and the feasibility screening results for potential alternatives.

BODY-116   The page presents a table showing the feasibility screening results for various alternatives to the CSG baseline. The baseline and three other alternatives passed all screening criteria, while several others failed due to factors such as cost, availability, and survivability. Detailed analysis will be conducted on the viable alternatives before selecting the best candidate for the 2013 CSG baseline.

BODY-117   Several alternatives for a new sensor suite on existing aircraft have been examined, but most have failed due to various factors such as cost, time frame, and impact on other operations. Three feasible alternatives, including the Maritime Patrol Aircraft, are being considered for release in 2013.

BODY-118   The page discusses two alternative options for supporting the Carrier Strike Group (CSG) in anti-submarine warfare operations. One option involves using P-3 aircraft with EPAS sensors, while the other option involves utilizing LCS craft with DWADS sensors. Both options are considered feasible and have low vulnerability to threats.

BODY-119   The page discusses different alternatives for upgrading sensor and communication technologies for the AN/BQQ-10(V) Submarine Sonar system. One alternative is to apply an advanced processing research and development process currently used for submarines to existing/emergent Surface ASW technologies. This alternative would improve detection performance and classification ranges, meet operational requirements, and have a lower cost compared to other alternatives. Modeling and analysis are used to evaluate the effectiveness of these alternatives.

BODY-120   The page discusses the importance of selecting accurate models for analyzing system alternatives in a systems engineering project. It emphasizes the need for models that provide credible results and are directly related to key performance measures. The page also mentions specific metrics related to threat submarine detection, engagement, and carrier survivability, as well as the evaluation of reliability, maintainability, and availability.

BODY-121   The page discusses the objectives and measures of operational effectiveness and suitability for an ASW system. It focuses on the survival of the carrier as the key measure of effectiveness and considers attacks by Red Submarines.

BODY-122   The page discusses the ASW alternatives for detecting submarines in a theater of conflict, using sensors and weapons. The largest region is called Theater, which is a rectangular area of 100 by 100 nm.

BODY-123   The page discusses the modeling of theater level anti-submarine warfare (ASW) operations, including the use of a Carrier Strike Group (CSG) Operating Area (OA). The probability of carrier survival is dependent on the success of detecting and engaging red submarines in different regions.

BODY-124	*The page discusses the use of a spreadsheet model to calculate the probability of a Red submarine successfully attacking a carrier. The model includes three sub-models representing different alternatives and combines their results to determine carrier survival probabilities.*
BODY-125	*The page discusses a spreadsheet model that calculates the position of different platforms using speed and course information. Equations are used to compute the positions at each time step.*
BODY-126	*The page discusses the calculation of range between opposing force submarine and CSG platforms, using coordinates and indicators.*
BODY-127	*The page discusses the calculation of sensor abilities to detect submarines and the implementation of the Figure of Merit (FOM) in determining detection. The model computes parameters of the sonar equation and utilizes target strengths from NPS SE 3122 course material.*
BODY-128	*The page provides graphs showing the noise signatures of different surface vessels and the active target strength of submarines. These values are used as inputs in a model for sensitivity analysis.*
BODY-129	*The page discusses the use of an iso-velocity condition in a spreadsheet model to estimate the transmission and reception of energy in the environment. It explains how spherical spreading loss approximations are used to calculate passive and active transmission losses.*
BODY-130	*The page discusses background noise levels and their impact on passive sonar signal detection. It mentions the Wentz curve as a tool to depict these parameters and sets the detection thresholds for active and passive sensors. Fluctuations in signal and noise are also introduced into the model.*
BODY-131	*The page discusses the use of an M of N method to simulate the classification/decision process in torpedo engagement analysis. It also mentions the implementation of an Excel Workbook for quantitative analysis and sensitivity testing.*
BODY-132	*The page discusses the parameters and inputs required for a discrete time event simulation, including starting point, motion, signature levels, target strength, and background noise. A spreadsheet is used to modify these simulation input parameters.*
BODY-133	*Opposing submarine executes maneuvers and detects CVN acoustic signature, then executes attack tactic. Spreadsheet model shows positive signal excess for active sonar sensors of Carrier Strike Group against submarine and passive submarine sensors against CVN, DDGs, and CG.*
BODY-135	*The page discusses the updating of course and speed based on signal excess calculation and bearing to the CVN. It also mentions the engagement model for torpedoes and missiles.*
BODY-136	*The page explains how to calculate the weapon course and distance traveled by a weapon in order to intercept a target based on their speeds across the line of sight. Equations are provided for these calculations.*
BODY-137	*The page discusses equations for determining weapon speed and distance traveled, as well as the criteria for launching a weapon. It also explains how the results of an engagement are determined. The alternative model being investigated is focused on the probability of detection of a threat submarine.*

BODY-138	The page discusses the use of a sensor on the P-3C Orion aircraft for submarine detection, with the assumption that it has adequate capabilities to neutralize threats and low false detections.
BODY-139	The page provides specifications for the P-3C aircraft, including crew composition, endurance, cruise speed, and armaments. It also discusses the replacement aircraft, the P-8 Poseidon, and its capabilities for maritime operations. The EPAS sensor is most effective against surfaced or near surface submarines that are unaware of opposing forces.
BODY-140	The page discusses the method of employment for the MPA/EPAS system in detecting a threat submarine outside the CSG OA. The concept of employment is believed to provide the highest probability of detection. The submarine's speed is assumed to be 10 knots when outside the CSG OA.
BODY-141	The page discusses the need for a system to detect submarines before they reach a certain range. It suggests establishing a barrier for the submarine to cross and considers factors such as detection opportunities, sweep width, and flight characteristics of the detection system.
BODY-142	The page provides estimated performance characteristics for an EPAS sensor, including operating altitude, aperture, and probability of detection. It also calculates the sweep width of the sensor and discusses the probability of detecting a submarine as it transits across a theater.
BODY-143	The page discusses the calculation of probabilities related to the detection of submarines by the EPAS sensor system. It includes equations for determining the probability of exposure and the number of circuits made by the MPA barrier.
BODY-144	The page discusses equations and calculations related to the average transit time and probability of detection for a submarine barrier alternative model.
BODY-145	The barrier alternative combines the CSG with a perimeter detection and engagement system to detect and engage threat submarines. Active SONAR buoys are used to create an acoustic detection barrier, and if criteria are met, a helicopter may be launched for torpedo engagement.
BODY-146	The page discusses a model that aims to determine the probability of successfully engaging a threat submarine using a barrier alternative perimeter. A Monte Carlo simulation is used to statistically calculate this probability.
BODY-147	A model is used to simulate the placement and movement of buoys and a threat submarine. The buoys are placed randomly around a desired location, and the submarine moves towards the x-axis while the buoys drift randomly.
BODY-148	The page discusses the calculation of signal excess at buoys and the parameters used in the equation. It also mentions the hold time, engagement time, and flight time for engaging a threat submarine.
BODY-149	The page discusses the criteria for a successful engagement in a trial, where the engagement time is less than the hold time. It also mentions that the results of the barrier perimeter model will be presented in Section 3.2.4.2 and discusses the need to combine models to calculate overall carrier survival probability.
BODY-150	The page discusses the calculation of the Advanced Capabilities Build result and the event tree used to determine the overall probability of carrier survival.
BODY-151	The page presents event trees for the Baseline and Barrier alternatives, showing the probabilities of killing a Red submarine and the overall probability of carrier survival.

BODY-152 The event tree shows the probability of a red submarine being killed by different alternatives, such as the baseline and the barrier. The total probability of the submarine being killed is equal to the probability of the carrier surviving.

BODY-153 This page provides event trees and probabilities for different scenarios involving the killing of a red submarine and the survival of a carrier.

BODY-154 The Naval Simulation System (NSS) is a modeling and simulation tool used for multi-warfare mission analyses. It was compared to spreadsheet models but had initial issues with accuracy. NSS simulates all aspects of naval warfare, while spreadsheet models focus on relative performance. The Baseline alternative was modeled in NSS as a formation with specific ships and positions.

BODY-155 The page discusses the modeling and simulation of a submarine's patrol area and the changes made to the database for more realistic results. A Monte Carlo simulation was run to determine the probability of a carrier being hit by a torpedo.

BODY-156 Table 6 shows the results of a modeling analysis for carrier survival. The NSS model predicts a higher probability of carrier survival compared to the Baseline spreadsheet model, despite adjustments made to match assumptions. Stakeholder analysis contradicts the NSS results, suggesting further research is needed. Operational suitability is defined by operational availability and reliability.

BODY-157 This page discusses the concept of engagement reliability in a mission and how it is calculated using an exponential distribution. It also mentions the use of a simulation model called Tiger to calculate operational availability and engagement reliability.

BODY-158 The page discusses the collection of information for each component in the RBD and its input into the Tiger model. It also explains the calculation of time to failure for each equipment using exponential distribution.

BODY-159 The page discusses the different states of equipment in a simulation model and how failures can impact system downtime. It also mentions the calculation of repair time and downtime for equipment failures.

BODY-160 The page discusses the repair process and tracking of system uptime and downtime in a simulated mission. It also mentions the use of onboard replacement parts for repairs.

BODY-161 The page discusses the simulation process used to calculate uptime, downtime, and system reliability for a baseline system in ASW operations. It also mentions the calculation of MTBOMF and provides information on the system's ability to provide operational mission functions and complete engagements without failure.

BODY-163 The page provides baseline data on the mean time between failures (MTBF) and mean time to repair (MTTR) for various components of a naval ship. It also mentions that some failure rates are classified and provides explanations for using substitute values in those cases.

BODY-164 The page discusses the failure rates and critical states of various components in the SONAR Inboard Processing and Missile Tube Systems. It also mentions the maintenance restrictions during a 14-day ASW mission.

BODY-166 The page provides data on the Mean Time Between Failures (MTBF) and Mean Time to Repair (MTTR) for various components of an MPA system. It also explains the operational states and maintenance restrictions during flight time.

BODY-167 Maintenance can be conducted on systems while they are off, and if maintenance is not completed before a system needs to return to operation, it is considered in a downstate. The torpedo is critical for one hour during the ASW mission. The

Baseline system is described in the report's Baseline System RMA Model section. The Barrier system alternative components critical for ASW Operations are listed in the table and shown in Figure 72.

BODY-168   The page provides data on the reliability and repairability of various components in a barrier system, including buoys, communications link, command and control system, and torpedoes. The actual MTBF value for the torpedo is classified. The page also discusses the assumptions made regarding the use of a satellite as a communication link and the failure rate of buoys due to transmission loss. A conservative approach was taken in representing the barrier system alternative.

BODY-169   The page discusses the operational states and maintenance requirements of buoys, the Command and Control system on an LCS, and a torpedo during a 14-day ASW mission. It also mentions the ACB system alternative and its components.

BODY-170   The page discusses the use of the Barrier System Alternative in redundancy with the Advanced Capabilities Build System Alternative, and the addition of three MFTAs to the Baseline System to create the Advanced Capabilities Build System.

BODY-171   The page discusses the results of modeling for the Barrier with Advanced Capabilities Build System, including carrier survival, operational availability, and reliability. The results show that the Barrier model has higher effectiveness and suitability compared to the Baseline model.

BODY-172   Figure 74 shows the results of engagement scenarios between a threat submarine and CSG surface ships. Figure 75 displays the results of 10 runs, indicating that the Carrier Strike Group was successful in defeating the enemy submarine in 66.5% of engagements.

BODY-173   Results and statistics for 10 sets of 25 ensemble engagements, including the percentage of blue wins.

BODY-174   The barrier perimeter model detects and engages threat submarines with a success rate of 57.2%. The average distance of first engagement is 5,437 yards. This information will be used in the decision-making process to determine the most effective solution for protecting the CSG from submarine threats.

BODY-175   This page discusses the process of decision making and alternative scoring in order to determine the best solution for improving Anti-Submarine Warfare effectiveness. The alternatives were compared using a Decision Matrix, sensitivity analysis, cost modeling, and risk comparison.

BODY-176   The page discusses the process of creating a Decision Matrix to evaluate the value and effectiveness of alternative systems compared to a baseline system. Raw data scores are used to determine the utility and value of each alternative.

BODY-177   The page discusses the required ranges of effectiveness for an ASW system in protecting an aircraft carrier. The system's effectiveness is measured by its ability to prevent enemy attacks and its suitability as a reliable system.

BODY-178   The decision matrix shows that the ACB + Barrier system provides the most total system value, despite having a lower availability value due to increased failure rates. The Total Value Scores are based on critical assumptions and may be incorrect if these assumptions are flawed.

BODY-179   Sensitivity analysis was conducted on the global weights of different evaluation measures to determine their impact on the total system value. The results are provided in tables 15 and 16.

BODY-180   The sensitivity analysis shows that the ACB + Barrier System Alternative provides the greatest value for carrier survival and increased persistence objectives. The

	Maritime Patrol Aircraft (MPA) is equally valuable as the ACB + Barrier System Alternative for decreased downtime at a global weight of 0.75.
BODY-181	The page contains two sensitivity analysis figures, one for carrier survival and one for availability.
BODY-182	The page discusses the results of a sensitivity analysis and cost analysis for four alternatives. The ACB + Barrier System Alternative is recommended as it provides the most satisfaction to stakeholders.
BODY-183	The page discusses the cost estimation methodology used to determine the lifecycle cost of alternative systems. It explains the use of researched references, analogous systems, and expert estimates. The concept of net present value (NPV) is also introduced as a way to calculate the total lifecycle cost adjusted to current year dollars. A common cost model and set of assumptions were used for each alternative system.
BODY-184	Table 18 shows the NPVs for different alternatives relative to the CSG baseline program. The ACB and MPA alternatives have similar NPVs, but the Barrier alternative has a significantly higher NPV due to operational costs.
BODY-186	The page discusses risk evaluation in the ASW Program and the MSSE Capstone Project. Risks were identified using various techniques and assessed based on their likelihood of occurring and potential adverse consequences.
BODY-187	This page discusses the process of risk management in a project, including the use of a risk matrix to prioritize risks and the implementation of mitigation plans. It also mentions that this process was continuously performed throughout the project.
BODY-188	The page discusses the risks associated with different system alternatives in the MSSE Capstone Project. Risks are categorized based on performance, cost, and schedule, and are evaluated for each alternative. The Barrier with Advanced Capabilities Build Alternative combines risks from the Barrier System Alternative and the Advanced Capabilities Build Alternative.
BODY-190	Table 19 outlines performance-based risks for the baseline system and the Maritime Patrol Aircraft (MPA) alternative. Risks include schedule delays, lack of training opportunities, and aging/failing transducers. Mitigation plans involve using the current towed array system, developing synthetic training equipment, and implementing a transducer monitoring program. The MPA alternative may experience performance degradation due to MPA availability issues.
BODY-191	Risk assessment for Maritime Patrol Aircraft (MPA) alternative, including risks related to distance from MPA base, weather impacts, detection ability of EPAS, acquisition delay, and system performance. Mitigation plans include allocating more aircraft, using other sensors, and utilizing P-3 aircraft.
BODY-192	Risk 1: Barrier may drift faster than expected, requiring more frequent repositioning of buoys.
	Risk 2: Buoys may not meet performance values, so using a greater number of buoys and robust communications is recommended.
	Risk 1: Schedule risk may decrease performance on the DDG, so using the current Towed Array system on all ships is suggested.
	Risk 2: System may not perform as expected, so using the current Towed Array on
BODY-193	There is a risk of no significant improvement in detection performance or latency reduction. However, there is potential for performance gains by 2013. If gains are not realized, the system will be as good as the baseline system. Use the baseline system to mitigate this risk.

BODY-194   The page discusses cost-based risks for the Baseline System, Maritime Patrol Aircraft (MPA) Alternative, and Barrier Alternative. Risks include development cost growth, potential delays in acquisition, and increased maintenance costs. Mitigation plans involve managing costs, using traditional sensor types if needed, increasing maintenance checks and funding, and making buoys stationary and more powerful for longer use.

BODY-195   Risk 1: Inadequate funding for the MFTA program is unlikely due to its successful process. Risk 2: Lack of continuous funding for R&D may hinder the development of required technologies, with a medium probability of occurrence.

BODY-197   The page discusses various schedule-based risks and their mitigation plans for different systems, including the Baseline System, Maritime Patrol Aircraft Alternative, Barrier Alternative, and Advanced Capabilities Build Alternative.

BODY-198   The page discusses the identification, analysis, and mitigation plan for various risks associated with different system alternatives. It also mentions the critical assessment of alternatives based on total value score and life cycle cost.

BODY-199   The page discusses a cost-benefit analysis plot comparing different alternatives for an ASW system. The Advanced Capabilities Build alternative shows the highest performance gain at a relatively low cost increase, making it the preferred choice over the MPA/EPAS alternative.

BODY-200   The ACB + Barrier system is recommended as the best option for reducing the risk of enemy engagement on carrier high value targets. Although it has some risks, it provides the most capability within budget constraints. Further investigation and limitations of the systems engineering process are discussed.

BODY-201   The Systems Engineering Team recommends pursuing the development and fielding of the LCS deployed Barrier capability to protect the CVN during aircraft launch and recovery operations. The Advanced Capabilities Build alternative suffers from inadequate reliability, while the LCS deployed Barrier alternative has similar operational effectiveness outcomes and lower cost. The production rate of active sonobuoys is a significant cost driver for this solution.

BODY-202   The page discusses potential mitigations for the cost of ocean current effects on buoys and recommends pursuing both a Barrier capability and an Advance Capabilities Build solution to improve operational effectiveness. Key assumptions were made in the analysis, including not investigating the potential performance contribution of a self-defense function.

BODY-203   The page discusses limitations in modeling torpedo performance, attack by enemy submarines on screening assets, and the behavior of enemy submarines. These limitations may affect the effectiveness and realism of the models used.

BODY-204   The page discusses the potential contribution of systems that support attrition of enemy submarines before they reach the operating area, as well as the need to consider false alarms and their ramifications. The limitations of the systems engineering process are also identified, including the classification level of the report and the lack of modeling and simulation tools.

BODY-205   The page discusses the need for a tool to analyze ASW operations and the challenges of accessing actual performance and cost data.

BODY-206   This page is an appendix to a project management plan for improving anti-submarine warfare effectiveness at the Naval Postgraduate School.

BODY-208   Approval sheet for the MSSE Capstone project on improving anti-submarine warfare effectiveness. Approved by advisors and reviewed by academic associates and program managers.

BODY-211   This page lists key personnel and stakeholders involved in a capstone project, including directors, engineers, advisors, and team leaders.

BODY-212   This page is a table of contents for a document that includes an introduction, objectives, program details, risk management plan, organization and policy information, standards, schedule, and a list of references.

BODY-214   This document outlines the Project Management Plan for the Newport Cohort of the Naval Postgraduate School's Master of Science in Systems Engineering Capstone Project. The project focuses on assessing and improving Anti-Submarine Warfare Effectiveness based on the Chief of Naval Operations' Concept of Operations for the 21st Century.

BODY-215   The Improved ASW Effectiveness program aims to enhance anti-submarine warfare effectiveness by implementing systems engineering techniques. The program will follow a phased approach, including problem definition, design and analysis, and decision making. A risk management plan will be implemented throughout the process.

BODY-216   The page discusses the Systems Engineering Design Process (SEDP) and its role in defining and analyzing problems to find the best-value solution. It emphasizes the importance of problem definition and conducting a needs analysis using various techniques.

BODY-217   The page discusses the needs and constraints analysis, concept of operations, and functional analysis in system design. It also mentions the value system design and the use of analytical methods for expanding potential solutions.

BODY-218   Alternatives Generation and Modeling & Analysis are used to explore and evaluate potential solutions for a system. Techniques such as brainstorming, morphological box, feasibility screening, and quality functional deployment are utilized to generate alternatives that meet system objectives and constraints. Modeling is used to approximate performance attributes of the alternatives, while optimization and sensitivity analysis help determine the best solution.

BODY-219   The page discusses the decision-making phase of the SEDP, including alternative scoring and presentation techniques. It also mentions the establishment and maintenance of a risk management plan throughout the program lifecycle.

BODY-220   The page discusses the risks associated with the completion of a capstone project, as well as the deliverables that will be provided to project advisors. The Newport cohort will be organized into teams, with a lead for each team.

BODY-221   The page discusses the structure and decision-making policy of Integrated Product Teams (IPT) within a program. WIPTs are established to meet program objectives, with the OIPT responsible for identifying WIPT requirements. Decision making is performed by IPTs at the overarching or working level, aiming for consensus as the first option.

BODY-222   This page outlines the roles and responsibilities of key individuals involved in project coordination, decision-making, system integration, and information management.

BODY-223   The page outlines the roles and responsibilities of various team members in information management, including the Information Manager and Deputy, WIPT Leads, and individual team members. It also includes operational policies for

BODY-224 *meetings and documentation, as well as information management policies regarding artifact maintenance.*

BODY-224 *This page provides definitions for three categories of items: deliverables, controlled SE products, and reference material.*

BODY-225 *This page lists the controlled items that are produced and approved by the appropriate teams. It also mentions the process for making changes to these items.*

BODY-226 *Individuals are expected to come prepared to team meetings, with prior research and planning. Those who cannot attend must review meeting discussions. Each WIPT will divide work within their group, and noncompliance is deemed unacceptable. Anonymous evaluations will be conducted to identify non-contributors.*

BODY-227 *The page provides a milestone schedule for various tasks related to stakeholder requirements, system design, and decision making.*

BODY-228 *This page lists references related to anti-submarine warfare, systems engineering, and project management.*

BODY-229 *The page provides the initial distribution list for a document at the Dudley Knox Library, Naval Postgraduate School in Monterey, California.*

BODY-230 *The page provides a list of the professional backgrounds of team members in the Newport MSSE Cohort, including their roles and experience at NUWC in various engineering fields.*

BODY-231 *This page provides brief biographies of several engineers with experience in submarine systems and combat control systems.*

BODY-232 *The stakeholder questionnaire aims to gather information on the limitations faced by the US Navy in defeating SSK, technologies needed for better SSK prevention, challenges in detecting and defeating SSK, important features of a system to protect aircraft carriers, effective systems or processes for detecting/deterring SSK, and characteristics of a successful ASW mission.*

BODY-233 *The page discusses the main areas of concern for defeating SSK, improvements in the decision-making process for ASW, the greatest challenge in modern ASW, and a vision for a "perfect" ASW system. Stakeholder feedback indicated a desire for ASW improvement.*

BODY-234 *The design team conducted research to better understand the problem and stakeholder needs. They consulted materials on undersea distributed networked systems, ASW operations, next-generation undersea warfare, and the cooperative strategy for 21st century sea power.*

BODY-235 *Secret document outlining a framework for Full Spectrum ASW and a publication on Fleet Antisubmarine Warfare.*

BODY-236 *The page provides documentation of needs analysis research conducted through stakeholder interviews and materials research. The information was recorded in an electronic worksheet format to ensure traceability. The page includes a sample of the questionnaire data captured in the worksheet format.*

BODY-237 *This page provides a summary of the efforts and requirements for developing undersea distributed networked systems (UDNS), including enhanced situational awareness, faster engagement chain timeline, increased engagement effectiveness, relieving platforms to conduct other tasks, reducing risk to forces, and making sensor data available to all warfighters.*

BODY-238 *Scorecard results for the Baseline System are provided on this page.*

BODY-242 *Scorecard results for advanced processor build option.*

BODY-246 The page discusses the risks associated with the MSSE Capstone Project, including the risk of including classified material in the report and the risk of selecting a scope that is too large. These risks have been mitigated and retired.

BODY-247 The page discusses three potential risks in a project: the influence of a single stakeholder, lack of experience with new modeling tools, and misinterpreting stakeholder requirements. Mitigation plans have been implemented for each risk and are ongoing.

BODY-248 There is a high risk of not completing all required tasks and deliverables on time. Additional time and effort are being implemented to address this issue.

BODY-249 This page provides detailed cost information for four categories (design, production, operation, and disposal) over a 25-year lifecycle period. It includes cost assumptions and elements for each category and presents the data in a matrix format. The numbers represent the single NPV for each alternative using a discount rate of six percent.

BODY-250 The page discusses the yearly operational costs and disposal costs of a barrier alternative, including logistics, maintenance, repair, personnel training, and the cost of buoys. The production costs are separate from the operational costs.

BODY-251 This page displays a cost matrix for the accelerated development alternative of CSG, showing the costs for design, production, operation, and disposal over a period of 25 years. The net present value is 112.2.

BODY-252 The page provides a cost matrix for the design, production, operation, and disposal of an MPA/EPAS alternative. The undiscounted sum is $89.3 million with a present value of $0.7-$2.3 million.

BODY-253 The page provides a cost matrix for different years and stages of a project, showing the design, production, operation, disposal costs, and their present values.

BODY-254 This page is a list of references related to seapower, anti-submarine warfare, systems engineering, and surveys on various topics.

BODY-258 This page contains a list of references and sources related to various military vessels and technologies, including next-generation vessels, Army transformation at sea, aircraft procurement costs, and unmanned undersea vehicles.

BODY-262 The page provides a list of recipients for initial distribution, including defense organizations and individuals at the Naval Postgraduate School and Naval Undersea Warfare Center.

Notable Passages

BODY-7   "The analysis demonstrated that a distributed barrier of active sensors placed and maintained by a Littoral Combat Ship provided an effective detection and engagement solution. The team further concluded that coupling the barrier with development of advanced capability improvements to the platform-based active sonar provided an effective layered defense approach."

BODY-19   "The need for this capability is documented in the Chief of Naval Operations document 'A Cooperative Strategy for 21st Century Seapower.' As a means to provide the capability, the Naval Undersea Warfare Center (NUWC) Technical Director announced the NUWC Grand Challenge, a working vision for NUWC analysis centered on Next Generation Undersea Warfare. This vision focused on the theater-level warfare-from-under-the-sea capabilities that effectively support and enable networked Joint forces to be expeditionary, adaptable, and responsive, allowing them to perform a broad set of missions and tasks in support of the nation's defense strategy."

BODY-20   "An improved Anti-Submarine Warfare system is needed to protect carrier strike groups from enemy attack through effective, timely, and precise engagement by providing tactically significant detection, localization, tracking, and classification of quiet acoustic threat submarines in challenging environments."

BODY-21   "Our group recommends an alternative that maximizes performance within the cost constraint identified. This alternative is the addition of an LCS-deployed barrier of buoys in concert with funding advanced capability improvements to the platform based active sonar, which provided a significant increase in performance over the baseline system. The barrier alternative combined with accelerated development alternative provides a carrier survivability improvement of ~38% as compared to the baseline."

BODY-23   "Because the maritime domain—the world's oceans, seas, bays, estuaries, islands, coastal areas, littorals, and the airspace above them—supports 90% of the world's trade, it carries the lifeblood of a global system that links every country on earth."

BODY-24   "The ability to operate freely at sea is one of the most important enablers of joint and interagency operations, and sea control requires capabilities in all aspects of the maritime domain, including space and cyberspace. There are many challenges to our ability to exercise sea control, perhaps none as significant as the growing number of nations operating submarines, both advanced diesel-electric and nuclear propelled. We will continue to hone the tactics, training and technologies needed to neutralize this threat. We will not permit conditions under which our maritime forces would be impeded from freedom of maneuver and freedom of access, nor will we permit an adversary to disrupt the global supply chain by attempting to block vital sea-lines of communication and commerce. We will be able to impose local sea

BODY-25   "In the long term the key goal is to, 'build on these advances to fully leverage an integrated network of sensors coupled to stand-off weapons, thereby maximizing our advantages in persistence, speed, and precision as the conceptual framework for our future'."

BODY-26   "The objective of the Improved ASW Effectiveness project is to address the overarching need to improve ASW effectiveness in tomorrow's battlespace including operations near-land, with the need to establish area control in a congested, chaotic environment, while facing adversaries with advancing levels of technological sophistication. One of the primary missions for a United States Navy ASW system is to protect a Carrier Strike Group (CSG). The combat range of the carrier air wing

	usually necessitates strike group operations well within the operating range of hostile submarine forces. The effectiveness of existing ASW systems makes this a high risk scenario."
BODY-28	"The basic activities of systems engineering are usually concentrated on the evolution of an appropriate process to enable the definition, development, and deployment of a system or the formulation, analysis and interpretation of issues associated with one of these phases."
BODY-29	"A key aspect of the engineering steps depicted in Figure 3 is the secondary information flow. This feedback iteration path is a significant engineering process applied in this project. As efforts progressed on subsequent SEDP phases, iterative adjustments and refinement were made to earlier phase artifacts."
BODY-31	"In Chapter 1 of this document the system engineering team has identified a key Navy concern and need to form the basis of their integrating project. The team applied knowledge and skills gained through the Masters of Science in System Engineering curriculum to analyze this problem area in a formal, disciplined manner in accordance with the SEDP."
BODY-33	"Create a next generation undersea warfare capability through the implementation of an Undersea Distributed Networked System"
BODY-34	"An improved ASW system is needed to protect carrier strike groups from enemy attack through effective, timely, and precise engagement by providing tactically significant detection, localization, tracking, and classification of quiet acoustic threat submarines in challenging environments."
BODY-38	"The Affinity Diagramming process helped identify twenty-one (21) common system goals & constraints shared among the stakeholders and research data."
BODY-40	"The system should minimize the Fog of War."
BODY-41	"The Pareto chart is designed to utilize the data, not perception, to separate the few critical problems or issues from a multitude of possible problems or issues by graphically arranging the data according to frequency of occurrence."
BODY-42	"These 20% of the issues, if addressed, will satisfy 80% of the stakeholders' needs."
BODY-43	"OPNAV N87 cited 'any technology that will support active or passive detection at tactically significant ranges' as a current need for 'more effectively keeping an SSK from impeding US Aircraft Carrier operations'. In terms of 'important features of a system devised to protect US Aircraft Carriers from SSK' threats, it was expressed 'high probability of detection (Pd) and low probability of false-alarm (Pfa) at tactically significant ranges' are necessary. It was articulated a 'vision of a 'perfect' ASW system' without any consideration of current limitations (technologies, political, cost, etc) would 'detect everything automatically with 100% Pd and 0% Pfa.'" [Ref 10,
BODY-44	"NUWC stakeholders expressed the ASW system 'needs to reduce risk to [friendly] forces' while acknowledging ASW force 'tactical utility is based on balance of combat power and survivability' (i.e. dominance of either trait can prove detrimental to the ASW force). It was conveyed effective ASW must identify 'force vulnerability and risk assessment' for 'determination of the level of risk (via analysis tools and decision aids) at a given point, considering mission, tasks, rules of engagement, objectives, and other appropriate factors.'"
BODY-45	"The ability to neutralize any and all threat submarines whenever necessary represents the 'perfect' vision for a successful ASW mission."

BODY-47   "A 'perfect ASW system' was articulated as one 'that would allow killing a threat remotely while not exposing ones own ship to risk'" [Ref 14, NUWC USW Combat System Department Survey Response, Nov 2007]

BODY-48   "Shall protect a carrier strike group from enemy attack through timely and precise engagement."

BODY-49   "An improved ASW system is needed to protect carrier strike groups from enemy attack through effective, timely, and precise engagement by providing tactically significant detection, tracking, and classification of quiet acoustic threat submarines in challenging environments."

BODY-50   "To develop a useful Input-Output model all of the system's inputs and outputs must be identified, properly defined and addressed within the context of the system. The inputs can be divided into two broad categories, controlled and uncontrolled. Controlled inputs are those things that are intended to be put into the system. These are inputs the system needs to accomplish its mission. Uncontrolled inputs are artifacts of the operational environment or other unintended inputs that are not desired. These are the inputs we must deal with even though we have little or no control of them and they are often a disadvantage, not an aid, to the system in accomplishing its mission."

BODY-52   "Covert operation provides a significant tactical advantage. It increases the likelihood that the system will detect a threat prior to being counter detected by the treat. It also creates more uncertainty into the threats assessment of the tactical situation. Sufficient uncertainty can in itself be a deterrent."

BODY-53   "System Survivability: The system's ability to survive in an operational environment is critical to effective use. A system that is easily damaged or destroyed during normal usage is of little value in a combat situation. System survivability is influenced by system stealth, ability to avoid detection, ruggedness and ability to survive attack if detected and fired upon. All of these factors are reasonably controlled by design decisions."

BODY-55   "Enemy Deterrence and Force Protection: Enemy deterrence and friendly force protection are the primary functions of any ASW system. Effective deterrence equals a successful mission. Deterrence can be accomplished by destroying the enemy with either the ASW system's own weapons or by calling in attacks from other friendly forces. The enemy can also be deterred by diversion, either deceiving him into thinking friendly forces are elsewhere, overwhelming his sensors with multiple false targets or by providing such a known effective system that he dares not operate where it is present."

BODY-57   "The operational concept is a vision for what the system is, a statement of mission requirements, and a description of how it will be used."

BODY-58   "Create a next generation undersea warfare capability through the implementation of an Undersea Distributed Networked System"

BODY-59   "It is vital that the improvement to the ASW capability not be made at the expense of other CSG mission capabilities. The strike mission is the whole purpose for the CSG presence in OA, so the ASW system cannot impact the CSG ability to conduct flight operations. In addition to the submarine torpedo threat there are numerous airborne threats that must be countered. No reduction in this critical CSG air defense capability."

BODY-60   "For all of our assessments it was deemed necessary to destroy the threat submarine before it is capable of launching a torpedo at the CSG."

BODY-61	"The primary purpose of the carrier is to forward deploy naval airpower in the form of its attached air wing."
BODY-62	"The S-3 Vikings drop sonobuoys for undersea sensing. The S-3 Viking is capable of carrying multiple weapons, but utilizes lightweight torpedoes in the ASW role. Given their limited sonobuoy inventory, the S-3 Vikings are typically called upon to localize and attack submarine threats initially detected by other platforms."
BODY-63	"The SPY-1 is a high powered radar capable of acquiring and tracking over 100 targets at extended ranges. The CG Class carries an extensive array of weapons including surface-to-air missiles, surface-to-surface missiles, anti-submarine missiles, Tomahawk missiles and guns."
BODY-64	"The Arleigh Burke Class destroyer, Figure 19 is a high speed multi-mission guided missile destroyer (DDG). Like the larger cruisers the DDG Class it is built around the AEGIS weapons system. While the DDG is a capable strike and anti-air warfare platform, the destroyer is one of the CSGs primary anti-submarine assets. At least one of the DDG destroyers assigned to the CSG will be equipped with the Multi-Function Towed Array. This upgrade to the DDG Class standard Towed Array sonar system offers improved ASW acoustics tracking and detection. These vessels use their embarked SH-60 helicopters and ASROC missiles as their primary ASW weapons."
BODY-65	"The Los Angeles Class submarine (SSN) [Ref 34, Jane's Fighting Ships, 2008], Figure 21, is the backbone of the fast attack submarine fleet, far more numerous than the Seawolf [Ref 35, Jane's Fighting Ships, 2008] or Virginia [Ref 36, Jane's Fighting Ships, 2008] Classes. All United States Navy fast attack submarines are advanced ASW platforms with sophisticated hull mounted and towed sonar systems and heavyweight torpedoes. While the specific capabilities are highly classified, it is well known these SSN are capable of detecting, prosecuting and destroying virtually any vessel above or below the sea."
BODY-66	"For the purposes of this study, a calendar year 2013 notional ASW Threat to the CSG is defined as a Conventional Submarine (SSK). The wide proliferation of these advanced, quiet, diesel-electric submarines highlights their role as the primary threat of concern. Two examples of threats of concern are the Russian KILO class SSK, due to its widespread use, and the Chinese SONG class SSK."
BODY-68	"With its extended range and loitering capability the P-3 MPA has the capacity to remain on station over the CSG OA for prolonged periods, providing wide area protection for the CSG while it is on station."
BODY-69	"The DDG normally provide broad area coverage with their onboard sensors and their embarked Light Airborne Multi-Purpose System (LAMPS) equipped SH-60 ASW helicopters to prosecute contacts of interest."
BODY-73	"This function is one of the most important for this system as the decision to engage or not engage the potential threat will be based upon the classification. If the wrong classification is made, the consequences can be disastrous as it would lead to either engaging a target that was not actually a threat or by allowing a hostile threat to get closer to the battlegroup by misidentifying it as a friendly."
BODY-74	"An improved ASW system is needed to protect carrier strike groups from enemy attack through effective, timely, and precise engagement by providing tactically significant detection, localization, tracking, and classification of quiet acoustic threat submarines in challenging environments"
BODY-75	"Probability that the ASW system prevents enemy launch of an effective weapon against the aircraft carrier."

BODY-76	"The factors that make up the suitability aspects will never be given as the reason that a system is good, however they are the factors most likely encountered by the operator and will be noticed if they are not satisfactory."
BODY-77	"Any interruption into the threat timeline that results in no shot taken against the carrier strike group results in a 'win' for the top-level metric described above."
BODY-78	"The lower the AOU for a contact, the better chance that the influencing system will be deployed appropriately to counter the threat."
BODY-79	"The ability to track opposing force submarines with a high degree of reliability at appropriate ranges could contribute to this defense by reducing the potential of a surprise missile launch. This capability, however, is considered outside the scope of this engineering analysis problem as the Measure of Effectiveness is to reduce the likelihood of an effective torpedo launch against the aircraft carrier."
BODY-80	"As shown in Figure 28, the key suitability performance measure for the overall 'Increase Carrier Strike Group Protection' objective is that the system is 'Trustworthy'. Trustworthy means that the system will operate when needed by trained Fleet operators throughout the length of the mission."
BODY-83	"We believe that the most important system objectives are first, to find the threat, and then to effectively engage the threat. Therefore these top level objectives are given the highest individual weights, 30% and 25% respectively."
BODY-85	"The goal of our alternative generation working group was to provide several potential solutions in addition to the baseline 'Do Nothing' alternative. The group consensus was to apply a screening process to reduce the candidate pool to the top three alternatives, along with the baseline system."
BODY-86	"Our goal was to think outside the box and not limit any ideas to preconceived notions or solutions consisting of solely existing systems."
BODY-89	"Cost in Fiscal Year 2008 dollars was chosen as an element based on the fact that the defense budget is not unlimited and an appropriate cap on the price of our system needed to be established. A total procurement cost of less than one billion dollars was utilized."
BODY-91	"Improvements would manifest by the addition of another capable ASW platform to the CSG, improving aggregate capabilities in SSK detection, tracking and engagement. Compared to the other CSG surface combatants, SSN flexibility in platform/sensor deployment in the water column could represent an optimal complement in effective search for SSK (e.g. sensor placement to overcome thermocline shadow zones)."
BODY-92	"SSN typically operate independent of other surface combatants, greatly exercising self-regulated underway authority as necessary to fulfill objectives established by Fleet theater-level tasking."
BODY-93	"Endeavors to improve SSN external 'communications at speed and depth' represents a technology-enabler that could facilitate the necessary interoperability for this alternative."
BODY-96	This alternative seeks to exploit a surface maritime craft with commercial sonar as a means for improving the overall performance of the CSG ASW within the OA, by improving the aggregate CSG capabilities in SSK detection, tracking and engagement. The surface craft would support deployment of Deep Water Active Distributed System (DWADS) for active detection of quiet diesel-electric SSK, and deployment/recovery of 'Jet-Ski' vehicles with acoustic sensing.

BODY-99   "The surface craft would support deployment of Deep Water Active Distributed System (DWADS) for active detection of quiet diesel-electric SSK, deploying them within the CSG OA, similar to alternative 3. A unique aspect of this option is the addition of a MK41 Vertical Launch System (VLS) with an ASROC load-out: the intent being improvement to the overall performance in CSG engagement of threat SSK within the OA."

BODY-101 "The LCS is the US Navy's next-generation surface combatant and is intended to provide the capabilities of a small assault transport with a flight deck and hangar large enough to base two SH-60 Seahawk helicopters, combined with sufficient cargo volume to deliver multi-mission payloads."

BODY-102 "The DWADS sensors act as a 'tripwire', informing the LCS and CSG via a RF communication link of an approaching SSK. The LCS in this alternative also performs the prosecution of the target through the use of the SH-60 helicopters."

BODY-104 "The concept of a 'Maritime Shield' involved clearing and maintaining a large Carrier or Expeditionary Strike Group operating area free of threat submarines. Based on the performance needed, only the Large Class of UUVs would be applicable to this scenario. However, while providing an extension of off-board sensors to the CSG, the UUVs limited mobility and endurance make UUVs a less ideal candidate in this case. In addition, based on the present acquisition strategy for UUVs it is unlikely that a usable system would be fielded by 2013."

BODY-105 "Sample gains realized by the submarine community in the passive acoustic realm beyond the legacy Mil-Spec system are shown in Figure 40."

BODY-106 "The ACB approach would focus on two main areas: Signal Excess and Decision Latency. The focus on Signal Excess would be an effort to increase the acoustic processing performance of the sensors such that the target can be detected at smaller Signal to Noise Ratios (SNR) than the baseline system. Techniques that would support this effort include: Source level Improvements, clutter reduction and rejection, and improved normalization techniques. It is expected that approximately 2 dB of signal excess can be gained Decision Latency can be improved in multiple areas within the detection-to-engage timeline. These include 'time to detect', 'time to classify given detection', and 'time to engage'. The improvement in automatic detection and classification algorithms allow the processing to find detections and

BODY-108 This alternative proposed utilizing the SH-60 Seahawk helicopters in a search and detect role in additional to their existing mission of prosecuting targets detected by other platforms. This would be a significant expansion of the SH-60's role and workload. The helicopters would patrol the OPAREA adding their detection capabilities to the existing baseline systems. The notional coverage areas for each helicopter are shown in red in Figure 42. They could provide search coverage by seeding a field with sonobuoys or by utilizing their Magnetic Anomaly Detection (MAD) systems. Their AN/AQS-22 dipping sonar could be used to classify and track potential targets once detected.

BODY-109 "The primary concern with this alternative is its impact to the CSGs other operations. The twelve additional helicopters would have to be based and supported by the existing platforms. The only platform with sufficient capacity to carry this many helicopters is the carrier. Since even the carrier has finite space, these additional helicopters would have to be in lieu of other air wing assets. This would degrade the carrier's primary strike mission as helicopters are not effective strike aircraft."

BODY-110	"The high sensitivity of SURTASS sensor could help improve the detection of threat submarine from long ranges and used in combination with the DDGs and LCS could form a robust multi-static active detection system to help protect the CSG."
BODY-112	"The intent is to improve the overall performance of the CSG ASW within the OA, by improving the aggregate CSG capabilities in SSK detection, tracking and engagement."
BODY-113	"Further exploration of this alternative would need to assess cost tradeoffs of supplanting the operations cost of 2 DDG with the procurement and operations cost of the replacement LCS & JHSV. There would also need to be an analysis to ensure the replacement of the DDG with these surface craft does not degrade other mission capabilities of the overall CSG. For example, the LCS and JHSV cannot likely match the AEGIS Anti-Air Warfare capabilities of the 2 DDG; thus, would the AEGIS defense capabilities of the remaining DDG/CG prove sufficient for the CSG formation. Finally, there also will need to be an analysis whether the JHSV can be procured, modified and equipped with the acoustics detection
BODY-114	"As currently envisioned, the HAMR with ASW package would not only add an independent ability to detect submerged threats, but also add an engagement capability through employment of MK54 light weight torpedoes and possibly the HAAWC weapon system originally discussed as part of alternative 4."
BODY-116	"The CSG baseline (Do Nothing Alternative) passed all feasibility screening by default. It's measured ASW performance in the chosen environment is the baseline that other alternatives were compared against by the modeling and analysis team. Three other alternatives also passed all screening criteria. They are Alternative 4, Alternative 6 and Alternative 8. One of these alternatives could possibly replace the baseline in 2013."
BODY-118	"The P-3s are land based, requiring no support from the CSG and have the range and endurance to support anticipated CSG operations by rotating on station aircraft. The MPA squadron has ample aircraft quantities to maintain the required coverage, non-stop, for indefinite periods. The EPAS sensor is considered to be benign to the environment and the existing P-3 impacts are well documented and within acceptable standards. The MPA/EPAS concept will operate outside the CSG OPAREA so will not likely interfere with CSG operations."
BODY-119	"By applying this approach to the Surface Sonar baseline system, gains can be made that will, at a minimum increase detection performance and improve the 'detect to classification' timeline. Improvements in both of these areas will lead to a higher detection probability and support longer classification ranges."
BODY-120	"In the case of this systems engineering project, key measures of operational effectiveness performance include metrics associated with threat submarine detection, threat submarine engagement and carrier survivability. These measures require the selection or development of a model set which can estimate the detection capability of solutions under consideration, the ability of the solution to engage or attack the enemy submarine, and determine the output metric, (survival of the aircraft carrier) of each engagement. These metrics imply the need for a discrete event time domain model that will model the kinematics of all platforms, acoustics detection capability of sensors at discrete time steps, ability of the sensor to hold and localize the contact and weapon employment."
BODY-121	"The key measure of effectiveness for the ASW system is survival of the carrier at the center of the CSG. Since we are developing an ASW system to protect the carrier, we only consider attacks on the carrier, and other CSG members, by Red Submarines.

               We also consider the Red Submarine to behave in a 'kill or be killed' manner; that is the Red Submarine will pursue the carrier until either it sinks the carrier or is killed itself. The carrier and CSG are assumed to only address the Red submarine threat by attacking Red Submarines. The CSG will not alter operations to avoid a detected submarine."

BODY-124   *"The spreadsheet model will consist of three sub-models, a formation model representing the Baseline alternative, barrier search model outside the CSG OA representing the MPA alternative, and a barrier search model on the perimeter of the CSG OA representing the LCS alternative. The results of these sub-models will be combined in a top level spreadsheet that calculates the probability of a Red submarine successfully attacking the carrier."*

BODY-127   *"Following the calculation of the position of each platform in the scenario, the spread sheet model then computes the ability of the sensors on each platform to detect the opposing force submarine and also the ability of the opposing force submarine to detect each Carrier Strike Group platform. This component of the model requires the implementation of the Figure of Merit (FOM) [Ref 59, Hall, 2006: 207] and the calculation of Signal Excess above the FOM to determine if detection was made during that time step."*

BODY-130   *"The detection thresholds selected for the modeling analysis were 20 for active sensors and 10dB for passive sensors. These nominal values were chosen to illustrate the effect of detection threshold on detection range, and are set up parameters within the spread sheet model and to recognize the difficulty associated with detection of active targets in the presence of clutter."*

BODY-136   *"The distance the weapon travels before it hits the target is calculated by multiplying the Target range at Time Of Fire by fraction of total closing speed (weapon's speed in the line of sight plus the target's speed in the line of sight) generated by the weapon. Equations 8 and 9 are used to calculate the target's and weapon's speed in the line of sight. Equation 10 calculates the distance traveled by the weapon. Inspection of Equation 10 will show that if the target is opening (i.e. VTx is negative) the distance traveled by the weapon will be greater than the range at Time of Fire."*

BODY-137   *"The decision to launch a weapon is based on the target being in range, and accumulating sufficient data to accurately place the weapon. Determining if the target is in range is simply a matter of checking whether the distance traveled by the weapon is less than the maximum range of the weapon. The determination of whether sufficient data has been accumulated is based on the time that the target is tracked. The criterion is defined as the target being detected for X of the last Y glimpse intervals. The X portion of the criterion provides a minimum time that the target must be tracked before launching a weapon, while the Y portion allows intermittent contact to contribute to the firing solution."*

BODY-139   *"The technology incorporated by the EPAS sensor will be most effective against surfaced or near surface submarine targets. Operationally, this will correspond to submarines that are transiting on or near the surface either to snorkel (recharging batteries) or to perform communications functions. This condition is most likely to occur when the submarine that has not yet detected the presence of the opposing force, i.e. the CSG. Consequently, it makes the most sense to use this sensor at a significant distance from the CSG, with the MPA operating in a largely autonomous mode."*

BODY-140   *"The general case for analysis is that the MPA will be assigned an Area of Responsibility (AOR) that is outside the CSG OA and within the larger theater and*

	that the submarine can attack from any direction. It would be reasonable to consider other situations that include apriori knowledge of threat activities, but for the purposes of this analysis the more general case will be considered."
BODY-141	*"The limiting factor is that the barrier must be maintained outside the range at which the submarine is likely to be alerted to the CSG and submerge. This range is taken to be 5 NMI."*
BODY-142	*"The calculation of the probability that a submarine is detected as it transits across the theater to the CSG OA, which is our metric P(d), is given by the following relationship:*
BODY-148	*"The model considers the decision time and ready time to be constants of ten minutes and five minutes, respectively. The flight time is modeled as a random time due to the random LCS location at any given time. The worst-case distance the LCS can be from a buoy is considered to be the case when a buoy is at one corner of the OA and the LCS is located at the opposite corner of the 30 nm by 30 nm OA square. This distance is ~85,000 yards, and assuming a helicopter speed of 125 knots, the maximum flight time of the helicopter is ~20 minutes. Therefore, the flight time is modeled as a uniform random variable between one and 20 minutes."*
BODY-149	*"For any given trial, an engagement is considered to be successful if the engagement time is less than the hold time. In other words, if a buoy is still detecting the threat submarine at the time the helicopter arrives on station to engage by dropping a torpedo, the engagement is modeled as being successful."*
BODY-152	*"Adding the probability of the Red submarine being killed by the Barrier and the probability of the Red submarine being killed by the baseline gives the total probability of the Red submarine being killed, which is equal to the probability of the carrier surviving."*
BODY-154	*"An important concept to note is that NSS simulates all aspects of naval warfare, and is aimed at producing information on the overall operations and results of a particular warfare scenario. In contrast, the spreadsheet models are aimed only at determining the relative performance of the alternatives under analysis. Therefore only the aspects that impact the differences in alternative performance are modeled, and the models are of the lowest fidelity that allows successful prediction of each alternative's relative performance. This low fidelity results in spreadsheet models that appear quite unrealistic compared to NSS, but in fact the spreadsheet models produce a more accurate prediction of relative system performance."*
BODY-156	*"The NSS model produced a much higher probability of carrier survival than the Baseline spreadsheet model (96.7% vs. 66.5%). This disparity occurred even though the NSS model was adjusted to match, as much as the NSS's architecture would allow, the assumptions and performance parameters of the spreadsheet model."*
BODY-157	*"The ASW Operational Availability (Ao) and Engagement Reliability (Re) Model is a simulation model utilizing the Naval Sea Systems Command (NAVSEA) Tiger Version 8.21.42 Availability and Reliability Computer Program within the Naval Supply Systems Command (NAVSUP) Readiness Based Sparing (RBS) Workstation Version 5.1."*
BODY-158	*"Each Tiger simulation follows this sequence. 1. Time to fail "t" is calculated for each equipment (block in the reliability bock diagram) using the following equations. The equipment time to failure values are assumed to have an exponential distribution about the equipment mean time between failure (MTBF)."*
BODY-159	*"There is no effect on Re and Ao when equipment is turned off. When equipment is turned off in a phase TIGER assumes a 0% failure rate. This disallows a failure*

BODY-172   occurrence by this equipment and does not contribute toward system downtime for Ao."

BODY-172   "After verifying that the spreadsheet model performed as expected through numerous validation runs, conducted while varying controlled parameters (fluctuation standard deviation, source level, detection threshold, target strength, acoustic signature level, initial range and bearing of opposing submarine), the analysis team executed ten series of 25 engagement ensembles and evaluated the results."

BODY-174   This section of the report has documented the process and tools the system engineering team utilized to produce results needed to support the decision phase of the SEDP. The report describes the current baseline system the Navy operates to satisfy the Effective Need, and identifies 13 alternative candidates that are evaluated to determine if any of them can contribute to more effectively satisfying this need. Using key feasibility measures the team identified three distinct alternatives having potential to contribute to a more effective solution to the protection of the CSG from submarine threats. The team has used models and historic data to generate measures of performance for operational effectiveness and operational suitability. The Decision Making phase of the systems engineering process will seek to apply utility scoring functions to this information and combine it with estimates of cost and risk for

BODY-175   "Through Alternative Scoring (including the formation of a Decision Matrix, conduct of a Sensitivity Analysis, comparison of System Life Cycle Costs, and comparison of associated Risks), the four alternatives were compared, resulting in identification of the best solution when compared to the remaining alternatives."

BODY-177   "Protection of the high value aircraft carrier was considered to be the most important objective of the system and if this was not realized on a consistent basis, then the system would prove to be less than useful. Contributing to the overall effectiveness of the system were the key metrics of detecting the enemy submarine outside the range of his offensive weapons, localization and tracking of the enemy submarine target to allow for follow on actions, and classification which would ensure that the target being tracked is in fact an enemy vessel thereby avoiding a friendly fire situation."

BODY-178   "Based on the importance, or weight of each system objective and the degree of value to which each alternative system would provide toward accomplishing that objective, the decision matrix indicates which system will provide the highest degree of Total Value. The ACB + Barrier system received the highest Total Value Score. This indicates that the ACB + Barrier system provides the most total system value."

BODY-180   "The results of sensitivity analysis conclude, that for all global weights, the ACB + Barrier System Alternative provides the greatest value toward accomplishing the carrier survival and the increased persistence system objectives."

BODY-182   "Sensitivity Analysis reveals that no global weights are considered sensitive and reaffirms the results of the decision matrix; the ACB + Barrier System Alternative is recommended as the system to provide the most satisfaction to the stakeholders."

BODY-183   "The concept behind NPV is that it represents the total lifecycle cost of a given alternative adjusted to current year dollars. To calculate the NPV for an alternative, Equation 24 is used: 1 (1) N n FV NPV k = $//=//+//\sum$ Where, FV is the future dollar value for year n, k is the discount rate, and N is the total number of years. The NPV is the sum of the yearly discounted cash flows over the timeframe of interest."

BODY-184 "The NPVs for the ACB and MPA alternatives are of a similar magnitude, however the Barrier alternative is shown to have a significantly higher NPV. The primary driver for this separation is attributed to the operational costs of the buoy replenishment segment of the Barrier alternative."

BODY-186 "A risk is defined as the measure of the inability to achieve program objectives within cost and schedule constraints. Risk management is as an organized, systematic decision-making process that effectively identifies, assesses, monitors, controls and documents risks that are associated with a program."

BODY-187 "High priority risks may cause major program disruption. Mitigation plans are required and must be executed."

BODY-191 Risk of the detection ability of EPAS. This risk was assessed at a E5. EPAS cannot detect a target that is below a certain depth. If the opposing force submarine does not enter the required depth threshold they will not be detected. This is a limitation of system. Cannot Mitigate

BODY-194 "Risk that the EPAS System may have development cost growth. This risk was assessed at a C5. A new system will most likely see increased cost. This may lead to program cancellation if development cost exceeds the Nunn-McCurdy threshold. Early mitigation is to rigorously manage cost. If risk is realized traditional sensor types could be used but would result in reduced performance."

BODY-198 "In order to provide a recommendation to the decision maker of the alternative that will provide the most satisfaction to the stakeholders, the design team considered for each alternative the Total Value Score and the Life Cycle Cost. This created a cost-value comparison for each alternative in which the system that 'cost less and did more' could be identified, as well as alternatives that would be clearly dominated by other alternatives."

BODY-199 "The Advanced Capabilities Build alternative shows a performance gain of nearly 162% over the MPA/EPAS alternative for a relatively low cost increase of 26%. This represents a 'good trade' in which a major performance increase is gained through a relatively low cost increase."

BODY-200 "Because the ACB + Barrier system Life Cycle Cost is under the 1 billion dollar threshold as established during the feasibility screening phase, this alternative was seen as providing the most capability to the fleet within reasonable budget constraints. Although ultimately left to the decision maker, the design team does not advocate cutting costs at the expense of capability."

BODY-201 "The systems engineering team recommends that the customer pursue the development and fielding of the LCS deployed Barrier capability."

BODY-202 "The Potential Performance Contribution of a Self Defense Function Was Not Investigated. As discussed in Chapter 3 of this report, the Self Defense function represents the ability to defeat a submarine launched torpedo. If it is possible to successfully design and build this capability it has the potential to contribute significantly to the overall probability of CVN survival during torpedo attack."

BODY-204 "The scoping of scenario and CONOPS that was necessary for our problem domain analysis precluded consideration of the contribution that might be made by systems that support attrition of enemy submarines before they arrive at the designated operating area. Further consideration should be given to such system solutions in the future, as they have the potential to significantly reduce the expected number of enemy submarine engagements incurred by the CVN strike group."

BODY-214 "maximize our undersea advantage anywhere in the world by leveraging advances in acoustic processing, data collection and sharing, communications, collaborative real-time planning, reachback support, rapid maneuver, and precision engagement".

BODY-215 "The objectives of the Improved ASW Effectiveness program is to implement the techniques in a systems engineering methodology to address the overarching need to improve ASW effectiveness in tomorrow's battlespace including operations near-land, with the need to establish area control in a congested, chaotic environment, and facing adversaries with every advancing levels of technological sophistication."

BODY-216 During Problem Definition the SEDP will focus upon interdisciplinary methods for defining a vision of what constitutes a trustworthy system, in terms of meeting the stakeholder needs through value system design. Issue formulation, analysis and interpretation will be applied to define the problem space, employing various analytical methods to broaden creativity and reduce predisposition and bias. Problem definition is crucial as it greatly establishes the basis for all subsequent SEDP analysis and evaluation: the 'foundation' of the project. Iteration and periodic Stakeholder reviews will be used to ensure an effective problem definition.

BODY-218 "Modeling and Analysis will be performed to approximate performance attributes of alternatives under consideration. Modeling will be used to represent or describe an important property of a system to be brought into being, or to analyze a system already in existence. The purpose for Modeling is to provide insight relative to the specified alternatives, better understand system relationships and required data, and ultimately assist in making informed decisions."

BODY-219 "Value Modeling is a decision theory approach that can accommodate a Stakeholder's preferences in terms of value and risk. An Additive Value Model applies Stakeholder value preferences to convert 'raw' performance results into a weighted evaluation."

BODY-221 All decision making will be performed by Integrated Product Teams (IPT) either at the Overarching-Level (OIPT) or the Working-Level (WIPT). Therefore, issues will be discussed in a small group environment, and final decisions will be made and promulgated by the appropriate IPT. This policy will circumvent the inefficiency related to large group dynamics. The general decision making procedure will be as follows: 1. Strive for consensus as the first option. The PM or IPT Lead will determine whether or not consensus can be reached. While the WIPT focus upon issues

BODY-247 "There is a fairly high likelihood that all stakeholder requirements have not been incorporated. The consequence of this is that the system would not perform as required by users/stakeholders and this would be a high severity issue."

BODY-248 "There is a high risk that the amount of work remaining will result in a shortfall of deliverables by the provided need dates."

NPS-SE-08-002

NAVAL POSTGRADUATE SCHOOL

MONTEREY, CALIFORNIA

Improved Anti-Submarine Warfare (ASW) Effectiveness
MSSE Capstone Project

James Broadmeadow	Nguyen Nguyen
Francis Dziekan	Patrick Roach
Francis Frantz	Jeffrey Sammis
Rodney Gudz	Scott Santos
Patrick Kelley	Kenneth Silveria
Shawn Kennedy	Cullen Smith
Christine Moreira	Kirk Volk
	Steven Wright

Approved for public release; distribution is unlimited

Prepared for: Chairman of the Systems Engineering Department in partial fulfillment of the requirements for the degree of Master of Science in Systems Engineering

THIS PAGE INTENTIONALLY LEFT BLANK

NAVAL POSTGRADUATE SCHOOL
Monterey, California 93943-5000

Daniel T. Oliver
President

Leonard A. Ferrari
Executive Vice President and
Provost

This report was prepared for the Chairman of the Systems Engineering Department in partial fulfillment of the requirements for the degree of Master of Science in Systems Engineering.

Reproduction of all or part of this report is authorized.

This report was prepared by the Masters of Science in Systems Engineering (MSSE) Cohort # 311-062 from the Naval Undersea Warfare Center Division, Newport (NUWCDIVNPT):

James Broadmeadow	Frank Dziekan	Francis Frantz
Rodney Gudz	Patrick Kelley	Shawn Kennedy
Christine Moreira	Nguyen Nguyen	Patrick Roach
Jeffrey Sammis	Scott Santos	Kenneth Silveria
Cullen Smith	Kirk Volk	Steven Wright

Reviewed by:

E. P. Paulo, Ph. D.

M. M. Rhoades

Project Advisor

Project Advisor

Released by:

David H. Olwell, Ph.D.

Dan C. Boger, Ph.D.

Department of Systems Engineering

Interim Vice President and
Dean of Research

THIS PAGE INTENTIONALLY LEFT BLANK

REPORT DOCUMENTATION PAGE			Form Approved OMB No. 0704-0188
	Public reporting burden for this collection of information is estimated to average 1 hour per response, including the time for reviewing instruction, searching existing data sources, gathering and maintaining the data needed, and completing and reviewing the collection of information. Send comments regarding this burden estimate or any other aspect of this collection of information, including suggestions for reducing this burden, to Washington headquarters Services, Directorate for Information Operations and Reports, 1215 Jefferson Davis Highway, Suite 1204, Arlington, VA 22202-4302, and to the Office of Management and Budget, Paperwork Reduction Project (0704-0188) Washington DC 20503.		
1. AGENCY USE ONLY *(Leave blank)*	**2. REPORT DATE** June 2008	**3. REPORT TYPE AND DATES COVERED** Technical Report	
4. TITLE AND SUBTITLE: Improved Anti-Submarine Warfare (ASW) Effectiveness		**5. FUNDING NUMBERS**	
6. AUTHOR(S) James Broadmeadow, Frank Dziekan, Francis Frantz, Rodney Gudz, Patrick Kelley, Shawn Kennedy, Christine Moreira, Nguyen Nguyen, Patrick Roach, Jeffrey Sammis, Scott Santos, Kenneth Silveria, Cullen Smith, Kirk Volk, Steven Wright			
7. PERFORMING ORGANIZATION NAME(S) AND ADDRESS(ES) Naval Postgraduate School Monterey, CA 93943-5000		**8. PERFORMING ORGANIZATION REPORT NUMBER**	
9. SPONSORING /MONITORING AGENCY NAME(S) AND ADDRESS(ES) N/A		**10. SPONSORING/MONITORING AGENCY REPORT NUMBER** NPS-SE-08-002	
11. SUPPLEMENTARY NOTES The views expressed in this report are those of the author and do not reflect the official policy or position of the Department of Defense or the U.S. Government.			
12a. DISTRIBUTION / AVAILABILITY STATEMENT Distribution Statement A		**12b. DISTRIBUTION CODE**	
13. ABSTRACT (maximum 200 words) The protection of our nation's ability to operate military forces freely and safely across the world's oceans remains a paramount goal of the United States Navy. The NUWC Division Newport cohort applied the disciplined practice of systems engineering processes to analyze and improve upon Anti-Submarine Warfare effectiveness in support of Carrier Strike Group operations. The cohort sought customer feedback to understand and formalize the perceived needs and formulate and rank candidate solutions to meet these needs. The systems engineering team, seeking solutions that provide improved Carrier Strike Group defense from undersea threats, generated 14 alternative architectures for analysis. The alternatives that passed feasibility screening underwent performance and cost modeling, reliability screening, and risk analysis to help provide a basis for comparison. The analysis demonstrated that a distributed barrier of active sensors placed and maintained by a Littoral Combat Ship provided an effective detection and engagement solution. The team further concluded that coupling the barrier with development of advanced capability improvements to the platform-based active sonar provided an effective layered defense approach. This rigorous process demonstrated the value of the systems engineering process and identified key areas for continued investigation to support continued United States Navy dominance of the undersea domain.			
14. SUBJECT TERMS Anti-Submarine Warfare, Carrier Strike Group, Undersea Distributed Networked Systems, Advanced Capability Builds; Littoral Combat Ship		**15. NUMBER OF PAGES** 262	
		16. PRICE CODE	
17. SECURITY CLASSIFICATION OF REPORT Unclassified	**18. SECURITY CLASSIFICATION OF THIS PAGE** Unclassified	**19. SECURITY CLASSIFICATION OF ABSTRACT** Unclassified	**20. LIMITATION OF ABSTRACT** UL

NSN 7540-01-280-5500

Standard Form 298 (Rev. 2-89)
Prescribed by ANSI Std. 239-18

THIS PAGE INTENTIONALLY LEFT BLANK

ABSTRACT

The protection of our nation's ability to operate military forces freely and safely across the world's oceans remains a paramount goal of the United States Navy. The NUWC Division Newport cohort applied the disciplined practice of systems engineering processes to analyze and improve upon Anti-Submarine Warfare effectiveness in support of Carrier Strike Group operations. The cohort sought customer feedback to understand and formalize the perceived needs and formulate and rank candidate solutions to meet these needs. The systems engineering team, seeking solutions that provide improved Carrier Strike Group defense from undersea threats, generated 14 alternative architectures for analysis. The alternatives that passed feasibility screening underwent performance and cost modeling, reliability screening, and risk analysis to help provide a basis for comparison. The analysis demonstrated that a distributed barrier of active sensors placed and maintained by a Littoral Combat Ship provided an effective detection and engagement solution. The team further concluded that coupling the barrier with development of advanced capability improvements to the platform-based active sonar provided an effective layered defense approach. This rigorous process demonstrated the value of the systems engineering process and identified key areas for continued investigation to support continued United States Navy dominance of the undersea domain.

THIS PAGE INTENTIONALLY LEFT BLANK

TABLE OF CONTENTS

1 INTRODUCTION 1
   1.1 BACKGROUND 1
   1.2 OBJECTIVE 4
   1.3 CAPSTONE PROJECT 4
      1.3.1 Project Organization 5
      1.3.2 System Engineering Process 6

2 PROBLEM DEFINITION 11
   2.1 NEEDS ANALYSIS 11
      2.1.1 Stakeholder Analysis 13
      2.1.2 Needs and Constraints Analysis 18
         2.1.2.1 Pareto Analysis 19
         2.1.2.2 Critical Needs to System Objectives Translation 26
         2.1.2.3 Effective Needs Statement Formulation 27
      2.1.3 Input-Output Model Analysis 27
         2.1.3.1 Model Development Process 28
         2.1.3.2 Anti-Submarine Warfare System Model 28
      2.1.4 External Systems Diagram 34
      2.1.5 Concept of Operations 35
         2.1.5.1 Carrier Strike Group CONOPS 36
         2.1.5.2 CSG ASW System CONOPS (circa 2013) 39
      2.1.6 Functional Analysis 48
         2.1.6.1 Detect 49
         2.1.6.2 Track/ Localize 50
         2.1.6.3 Classify 51
         2.1.6.4 Engage 52
   2.2 VALUE SYSTEM DESIGN 52
      2.2.1 Performance Objectives Hierarchy 55
         2.2.1.1 Detection Performance Objectives 55
         2.2.1.2 Localization/Tracking Performance Objectives 56
         2.2.1.3 Classification Performance Objectives 56
         2.2.1.4 Engagement Performance Objectives 56
         2.2.1.5 Self Protect 57
      2.2.2 Suitability Objectives Hierarchy 58
         2.2.2.1 Increase Persistence 58
         2.2.2.2 Decrease Downtime 58
         2.2.2.3 Manageable System 59
      2.2.3 Weighting 59

3 DESIGN AND ANALYSIS 63
   3.1 ALTERNATIVES GENERATION 63
      3.1.1 Alternatives Generation Process 63

     3.1.1.1 Organized Brainstorming 64
     3.1.1.2 Zwicky's Morphological Box 64
     3.1.1.3 Feasibility Screening 67
   3.1.2 **Individual Alternatives 68**
     3.1.2.1 Alternative 1: Re-assign SSN to the CGS Formation 69
     3.1.2.2 Alternative 2: Maritime Ship in CSG 71
     3.1.2.3 Alternative 3: Maritime Ship in Op Area 73
     3.1.2.4 Alternative 4: Maritime Patrol Aircraft ASW Sensor 75
     3.1.2.5 Alternative 5: Commercial Barrier 76
     3.1.2.6 Alternative 6: LCS Barrier 78
     3.1.2.7 Alternative 7: Commercial Craft UUV Barrier 80
     3.1.2.8 Alternative 8: Advanced Capabilities Build (ACB) 82
     3.1.2.9 Alternative 9: Surveillance Towed-Array Sensor System (SURTASS) 85
     3.1.2.10 Alternative 10: Helicopter Searching 86
     3.1.2.11 Alternative 11: SURTASS and LCS Integration 88
     3.1.2.12 Alternative 12: LCS and Commercial Craft 89
     3.1.2.13 Alternative 13: HAMR Integration 91
   3.1.3 **Feasibility Screening Results 93**
   3.1.4 **Feasible Alternatives 95**
     3.1.4.1 Maritime Patrol Aircraft (MPA) Alternative 95
     3.1.4.2 Barrier Alternative 96
     3.1.4.3 Advanced Capabilities Build Alternative 97
 3.2 **MODELING AND ANALYSIS 97**
  3.2.1 Modeling and Analysis Approach 98
  3.2.2 Operational Effectiveness 99
     3.2.2.1 Baseline 102
     3.2.2.2 MPA Alternative Model 115
     3.2.2.3 LCS Barrier Alternative Model 122
     3.2.2.4 Model integration 127
     3.2.2.5 NSS Model Comparison 132
  3.2.3 Operational Suitability 134
     3.2.3.1 Process 135
     3.2.3.2 Baseline System RMA Model 139
     3.2.3.3 Maritime Patrol Aircraft (MPA) System Alternative RMA Model 142
     3.2.3.4 Barrier System Alternative RMA Model 145
     3.2.3.5 ACB System Alternative RMA Model 147
     3.2.3.6 Barrier with Advanced Capabilities Build Alternative RMA Model 148
  3.2.4 Modeling Results 149
     3.2.4.1 Baseline Modeling Results 149
     3.2.4.2 Barrier Perimeter Modeling Results 152
4 DECISION MAKING 153
 4.1 **ALTERNATIVE SCORING 153**

		4.1.1	Decision Matrix	153
		4.1.2	Sensitivity Analysis	156
	4.2	COST ANALYSIS CONSIDERATION		160
	4.3	RISK EVALUATION		164
	4.4	CRITICAL ASSESSMENT OF ALTERNATIVES		176
5	CONCLUSIONS			179
	5.1	RECOMMENDATION		179
	5.2	KEY ASSUMPTIONS		180
	5.3	LIMITATIONS		182

APPENDIX A 184

APPENDIX B 207

APPENDIX C 209

APPENDIX D 211

APPENDIX E 213

APPENDIX F 215

APPENDIX H 226

LIST OF REFERENCES 231

INITIAL DISTRIBUTION LIST 239

LIST OF FIGURES

Figure 1 - World Wide Shipping Lanes [Ref 79, National Geographic, 2008] 1
Figure 2 - Modern Carrier Strike Group Underway [Ref 84, Strategypage.com, 2008] 2
Figure 3 - Systems Engineering Design Process [Ref 5, Paulo, 2006] 4
Figure 4 - WIPT Structure 6
Figure 5 – Systems Engineering Steps [Ref 6, Sage and Armstrong, 2000] 7
Figure 6 - Product Life Cycle [Ref 7, Blanchard and Fabrycky 2006: 27] 8
Figure 7 - Problem Definition 9
Figure 8 - Affinity Results - Top Tier Stakeholder Goals & Constraints 17
Figure 9 - Mapping Needs Elements into Affinity Categories 18
Figure 10 - Needs Analysis Process 19
Figure 11 - Pareto Chart 20
Figure 12 - Top Level Input Output Model 29
Figure 13 - ASW External Systems Diagram 34
Figure 14 - ASW Problem Focus Process 37
Figure 15 - Nimitz Class Carrier (CVN) [Ref 23, Jane's Fighting Ships, 2008] 39
Figure 16 - S-3 Viking [Ref 25, USN Fact File, 2008] 40
Figure 17 - SH-60 [Ref 26, Jane's Fighting Ships, 2008] 41
Figure 18 - Ticonderoga Class Cruiser (CG) [Ref 30, Jane's Fighting Ships, 2008] 41
Figure 19 - Arleigh Burke Class Destroyer (DDG) [Ref 32, Jane's Fighting Ships, 2008] 42
Figure 20 - Sacramento Class AOE [Ref 33, USNR, 2007] 42
Figure 21 - Los Angeles Class Submarine (SSN) [Ref 34, Jane's Fighting Ships, 2008] 43
Figure 22 - P-3 Orion [Ref 38, Jane's Fighting Ships, 2008] 44
Figure 23 - Carrier Strike Group Notional Configuration 46
Figure 24 - ASW Functional Hierarchy 49
Figure 25 - Performance Objectives Hierarchy 53
Figure 26 - Suitability Objectives Hierarchy 54
Figure 27 - Performance Objectives Weighting 60
Figure 28 - Suitability Objectives Weighting 60
Figure 29 - Modified Zwicky's Morphological Box 66
Figure 30 – Alternative 1 Notional Operational Context 70
Figure 31 – Alternative 2 Notional Operational Context 72
Figure 32 – High Speed Vessel / Theater Support Vessel Pictorial [Ref 43,Sample, 2004] ...73
Figure 33 – Alternative 3 Notional Operational Context 74
Figure 34 - MPA/EPAS Employment [Ref 81, Personal Computer Interactive Multi-Sensor Trainer (PCIMAT), 2006] 75
Figure 35 – Alternative 5 Notional Operational Context 77
Figure 36 – Alternative 6 Notional Operational Context 79
Figure 37 - Conceptual LCS Depictions [Ref 50, Pike, 2007] 80
Figure 38 – Alternative 7 Notional Operational Context 81
Figure 39 - ARCI/APB Process 83
Figure 40 - Sample Processing Gains from Submarine APB Process 84
Figure 41 - SURTASS Employment [Ref 53, Gentry, 2007] 86
Figure 42 - Helicopter Coverage Areas 87

Figure 43 - Alternative 12 Notional Operational Context 90
Figure 44 - Picture of Prototype HAMR [Ref 56, Airliners.net, 2008] 92
Figure 45 - Physical Architecture for HAMR Alternative 93
Figure 46 - Modeling Universe 100
Figure 47 - Baseline Engagement Model Block Diagram 103
Figure 48 - Active Sonar Equation Depiction [Ref 82, NUWC Director Undersea Warfare] 104
Figure 49 - Surface Vessel Radiated Noise Levels [Ref 58, Green, 2007] 106
Figure 50 - Submarine Active Target Strength [Ref 80, Urick, 1983: 310] 107
Figure 51 - Spherical Spreading Loss Depiction [Ref 83, Fleet Forces Command, 2006] ... 107
Figure 52 - Wentz Curve [Ref 59, Hall, 2006: 195] 108
Figure 53 - Illustration of Detection Threshold and Noise Fluctuations [Ref 58, Green, 2007] 109
Figure 54 - Spread Sheet Control 110
Figure 55 - Environmental and Target Strength Control Sheet 111
Figure 56 – Single Engagement Analysis Run 112
Figure 57 - Geographic Plot Example 113
Figure 58 - P-3C Maritime Patrol Aircraft [Ref 38, Jane'sfighting ships, 2008] 116
Figure 59 - MPA/EPAS Employment 118
Figure 60 – Conceptualization of the Barrier Alternative OA Geometry 123
Figure 61 – Single-line Barrier Alternative Model 124
Figure 62 – Barrier Alternative Perimeter Model Trial Geometry at Time = 0 125
Figure 63 - Timeline Displaying Hold Time and Engagement Time 127
Figure 64 - Carrier Survival Event Tree 128
Figure 65 - Baseline Event tree 129
Figure 66 - Barrier Event Tree 129
Figure 67 - MPA Event Tree 130
Figure 68 - Advanced Capabilities Build Event Tree 131
Figure 69 - Barrier Plus MPA Event Tree 131
Figure 70 Baseline System RBDs 140
Figure 71 - MPA System RBDs 143
Figure 72 Barrier System RBDs 145
Figure 73 - ACB System RBDs 148
Figure 74 - ScoreCard worksheet example 150
Figure 75 - Results of 10 sets of 25 Ensemble Engagements 151
Figure 76 - Results and Descriptive Statistics for Baseline 151
Figure 77 - Carrier Survival Sensitivity Analysis 159
Figure 78 - Availability Sensitivity Analysis 159
Figure 79 - Reliability Sensitivity Analysis 160
Figure 80 – CSG Advanced Capabilities Build Alternative LCCP 163
Figure 81 – MPA/EPAS Alternative LCCP 163
Figure 82 - Barrier Alternative LCCP 164
Figure 83 - Representative Risk Matrix 165
Figure 84 - Performance Based Program Risks 167
Figure 85 - Cost Based Risks 171

Figure 86 - Schedule Based Risks 174
Figure 87 - Cost-Benefit Analysis Plot 177

LIST OF TABLES

Table 1 - UUV Classes 82
Table 2 - ASW System Feasibility Screening 94
Table 3 - P-3C Specifications 117
Table 4 - EPAS Estimated Performance Characteristics 120
Table 5 - Barrier Signal Excess Equation Parameters 126
Table 6 - NSS Modeling results 134
Table 7 - Baseline RMA Data 141
Table 8 - MPA System RMA Data 144
Table 9 - Barrier System RMA Data 146
Table 10 - Integrated Modeling Results 149
Table 11 – Barrier Perimeter Model Results 152
Table 12 - Raw Data Matrix 154
Table 13 - Required Ranges of Effectiveness 155
Table 14 - Decision Matrix 156
Table 15 - Sensitivity Matrix Global Weight 1, Carrier Survival 157
Table 16 - Sensitivity Matrix Global Weight 1, Ao 157
Table 17 - Sensitivity Matrix Global Weight 1, Re 158
Table 18 – NPVs for Alternatives Relative to CSG Baseline 162
Table 19 - Performance Based Risks 168
Table 20 - Cost Based Risks 172
Table 21 - Schedule Based Risks 175
Table 22 - Summary of Risks by System Alternative 176

ACRONYM LIST

ACB – Advanced Capabilities Build

APB – Advanced Processing Build

AOU – Area of Uncertainty

ARCI – Acoustic Rapid COTS Insertion

ASROC – Anti-Submarine Rocket

ASW – Anti Submarine Warfare

BG – Battle Group

CG – Cruiser

CFB – Cross Functional Board

CSG – Carrier Strike Group

CNO – Chief of Naval Operations

COMPACFLT – Commander Pacific Fleet

CONOPS – Concept of Operations

COTS – Commercial Off The Shelf

CSF-USE – Commander Naval Submarine Forces, head of Undersea Enterprise

CVW – Carrier Air Wing

DDG – Destroyer

DSA – Deployable SONAR Array

DWADS – Deep Water Active Deployable System

HAMR – Hybrid Aircraft Multi Role

HS – Helicopter Squadron

IOC – Initial Operation Capability

LAMPS – Light Airborne Multi-Purpose System

LCCP – Life Cycle Cost Profile

LCS – Littoral Combat Ship

LFA – Low Frequency Active

LSE – Lead System Engineer

MAP – Maritime Air Patrol

MFA – Mid-Frequency Active

MFTA – Multi Function Towed Array

MILDET – Military Detachment

MIW – Mine Warfare

MPA – Maritime Patrol Aircraft

M&S – Modeling and Simulation

MOE – Measure of Effectiveness

MSSE – Master of Science System Engineering

NETWARCOM – Naval Network Warfare Command

NMAWC – Naval Mine and Anti-Submarine Warfare

NPS – Naval Postgraduate School

NUWC – Naval Undersea Warfare Center

PACOM – Pacific Commander

Pd – Probability of Detection

Pfa – Probability of False Alarm

PMP – Project Management Plan

PM – Program Manager

OA – Operational Area

OIPT – Overarching-Level Integrated Product Team

OPNAV – Office of the Chief of Naval Operations

RDT&E – Research Development Test and Evaluation

RMA – Reliability Maintainability Availability

ROE – Rules of Engagement

SEDP – System Engineering Design Process

SNR – Signal to Noise Ratio

SWDG – Surface Warfare Development Group

SURTASS – Surveillance Towed Array Sensor System

TR – Technical Report

TRL – Technology Readiness Level

UAV – Unmanned Air Vehicle

UDNS – Undersea Distributed Networked System
UUV – Unmanned Undersea Vehicle
UNREP – Underway Replenishment
VLS – Vertical Launch System
WIPT – Working Integrated Product Team
ZMB - Zwicky's Morphological Box

EXECUTIVE SUMMARY

With the proliferation of advanced submarine technology, the preservation of the capability for our naval forces to operate freely across the globe remains paramount. The need for this capability is documented in the Chief of Naval Operations document "A Cooperative Strategy for 21st Century Seapower." As a means to provide the capability, the Naval Undersea Warfare Center (NUWC) Technical Director announced the NUWC Grand Challenge, a working vision for NUWC analysis centered on Next Generation Undersea Warfare. This vision focused on the theater-level warfare-from-under-the-sea capabilities that effectively support and enable networked Joint forces to be expeditionary, adaptable, and responsive, allowing them to perform a broad set of missions and tasks in support of the nation's defense strategy. This Capstone project assesses what potential improvements can be provided in the near–term (by 2013) to increase the protection given to a carrier strike group during operations.

Using an initial problem statement of "Improved Anti-Submarine Warfare Effectiveness", the project team worked with key stakeholders to establish the operational needs required by the Carrier Strike Group for successful completion of the assigned operations. Following receipt of the requirements from the stakeholders, a needs analysis was performed to pull out the salient characteristics required of the system. Techniques, such as Affinity diagramming, were utilized to identify 21 goals with 63 derived requirements for the system development. Based on a Pareto Analysis across the goals and requirements, six critical needs were identified as the key stakeholder Anti-Submarine Warfare system objectives in the areas of Detection, Precision Engagement, Tracking, Self Protect, Counter Quiet Threat, and Avoiding Force on Force Engagements.

Using these six critical needs as the basis for the systems requirements, functional and objective hierarchies were developed to define the system capabilities and the measures of performance that would be utilized to assess the overall effectiveness of the yet to be formulated system alternatives. These hierarchies in concert with the analysis results from concept of operations, system input-output diagrams and external systems diagrams were used to set the boundaries of the system to be developed. The results of this effort when combined with the stakeholder's analysis resulted in the following effective need statement:

"An improved Anti-Submarine Warfare system is needed to protect carrier strike groups from enemy attack through effective, timely, and precise engagement by providing tactically significant detection, localization, tracking, and classification of quiet acoustic threat submarines in challenging environments."

Following the identification of the effective need, the project team commenced an alternatives generation process to explore solutions capable of satisfying the effective need. Using a Zwicky's Morphological Box analysis, a total of 13 alternatives were developed as potential systems to meet the effective need. These alternatives considered both materiel and non-materiel solutions, in addition to assessing the use of both commercial and military platforms and sensors to meet the desired needs. The alternatives analysis also included a 'do-nothing' baseline alternative based upon the current legacy systems projected to the 2013 timeframe. Applying feasibility criteria developed through a combination of the stakeholder requirements and the team's experience, three alternatives in addition to the do-nothing baseline alternative were selected for further investigation utilizing modeling and simulation.

Excel-based modeling was developed to assess the effectiveness of each of the alternatives based on the top-level objective of "Increasing the Carrier Strike Group Probability of Survival." This modeling was developed to accurately model the physics-based SONAR aspects of the system while providing transparent insight into the underlying model detection and classification performance needed to fully characterize each alternative's performance. Additional modeling was done to support Reliability, Maintainability, and Availability analysis of each alternative in addition to a Life Cycle Cost Analysis to facilitate comparison among the system alternatives.

The output of the modeling results was used in the Decision Making process to provide a ranking across the alternatives. Sensitivity analysis was conducted to measure the impact on value scoring results based on changes in global weighting. Parameter weighting was generated from stakeholder inputs relative to the objectives hierarchies. Additionally, another inferred alternative was generated by combining two of the alternatives that passed feasibility screening. This alternative was also evaluated and included in the decision making process. A risk analysis was also conducted for each system alternative that passed feasibility screening.

As a result of the decision making process, our group recommends an alternative that maximizes performance within the cost constraint identified. This alternative is the addition of an LCS-deployed barrier of buoys in concert with funding advanced capability improvements to the platform based active sonar, which provided a significant increase in performance over the baseline system. The barrier alternative combined with accelerated development alternative provides a carrier survivability improvement of ~38% as compared to the baseline. The estimated cost in today's dollars is ~$809M per carrier strike group over a 25-year lifecycle timeframe.

THIS PAGE INTENTIONALLY LEFT BLANK

1 INTRODUCTION

1.1 BACKGROUND

The protection of our nation's ability to operate military forces freely and safely across the world's oceans remains a paramount goal of our nation's Navy. The need for this capability is summarized in the Chief of Naval Operations document "A Cooperative Strategy for 21st Century Seapower" [Ref 1, ADM Roughhead, Gen Conway, ADM Allen, 2007]. This combined Navy, Marine Corp and Coast Guard policy statement highlights the importance of the world's oceans through the following statement:

> *"Because the maritime domain—the world's oceans, seas, bays, estuaries, islands, coastal areas, littorals, and the airspace above them—supports 90% of the world's trade, it carries the lifeblood of a global system that links every country on earth."*

Figure 1 graphically illustrates the importance of the ocean environment to world wide commerce. The vital nature of these Sea Lanes of Communication (SLOC) requires that the United States possess the capability to ensure that these routes will not be interrupted by the actions of another nation or group.

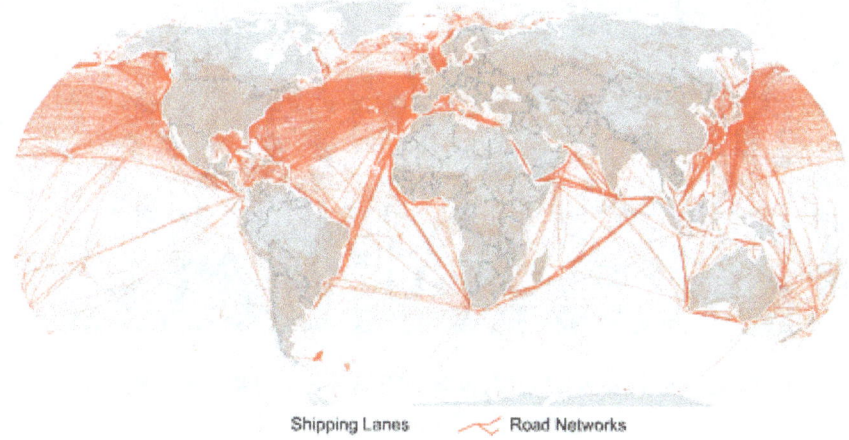

Figure 1 - World Wide Shipping Lanes [Ref 79, National Geographic, 2008]

The reference document *"A Cooperative Strategy for 21st Century Seapower"* provides the initial statement of need for our problem definition and further identifies a military capability need related to control of the seas. The following paragraph exemplifies the urgency of providing an improved capability to execute Anti Submarine Warfare operations in support of overarching military strategies.

> *"The ability to operate freely at sea is one of the most important enablers of joint and interagency operations, and sea control requires capabilities in all aspects of the maritime domain, including space and cyberspace. There are many challenges to our ability to exercise sea control, perhaps none as significant as the growing number of nations operating submarines, both advanced diesel-electric and nuclear propelled. We will continue to hone the tactics, training and technologies needed to neutralize this threat. We will not permit conditions under which our maritime forces would be impeded from freedom of maneuver and freedom of access, nor will we permit an adversary to disrupt the global supply chain by attempting to block vital sea-lines of communication and commerce. We will be able to impose local sea control wherever necessary, ideally in concert with friends and allies, but by ourselves if we must."* [Ref 1, ADM Roughhead, Gen Conway, ADM Allen, 2007]

Figure 2 - Modern Carrier Strike Group Underway [Ref 84, Strategypage.com, 2008]

Additional details regarding high level goals, challenges and the future environment for 21st Century Anti-Submarine Warfare (ASW) operations were documented in the *"Chief of Naval Operations' Task Force ASW "Anti-Submarine Warfare Concept of Operations for the 21st Century."* [Ref 2, Task Force ASW, 2007]. Here it was stated that the near term goal for the Navy is to, *"maximize our undersea advantage anywhere in the world by leveraging advances in acoustic processing, data collection and sharing, communications, collaborative real-time planning, reach-back support, rapid maneuver, and precision engagement"*. In the long term the key goal is to, *"build on these advances to fully leverage an integrated network of sensors coupled to stand-off weapons, thereby maximizing our advantages in persistence, speed, and precision as the conceptual framework for our future"*.

In response to the shifting strategic environment brought about by this concept, the Technical Director of the Naval Undersea Warfare Center (NUWC) announced a working vision for NUWC centered on Next Generation Undersea Warfare. This vision focused on the theater-level warfare-from-under-the-sea capabilities that effectively support and enable networked Joint forces to be expeditionary, adaptable, and responsive, allowing them to perform a broad set of missions and tasks in support of the nation's defense strategy. [Ref 3, McCormack, 2007] Central to this vision was a call for the development of an Undersea Distributed Networked System (UDNS) to meet the ASW demands of the vast ocean environment.

This document details the culmination of an assessment of Improved Anti-Submarine Warfare (ASW) Effectiveness by the Newport Cohort of the Naval Postgraduate School (NPS) Master of Science in Systems Engineering (MSSE) Capstone Project. The team has applied a formal Systems Engineering Design Process (SEDP), depicted in Figure 3 to evaluate the current needs, identify potential capability gaps, develop requirements and assess alternatives in accordance with an approved Project Management Plan (PMP) in Appendix A.

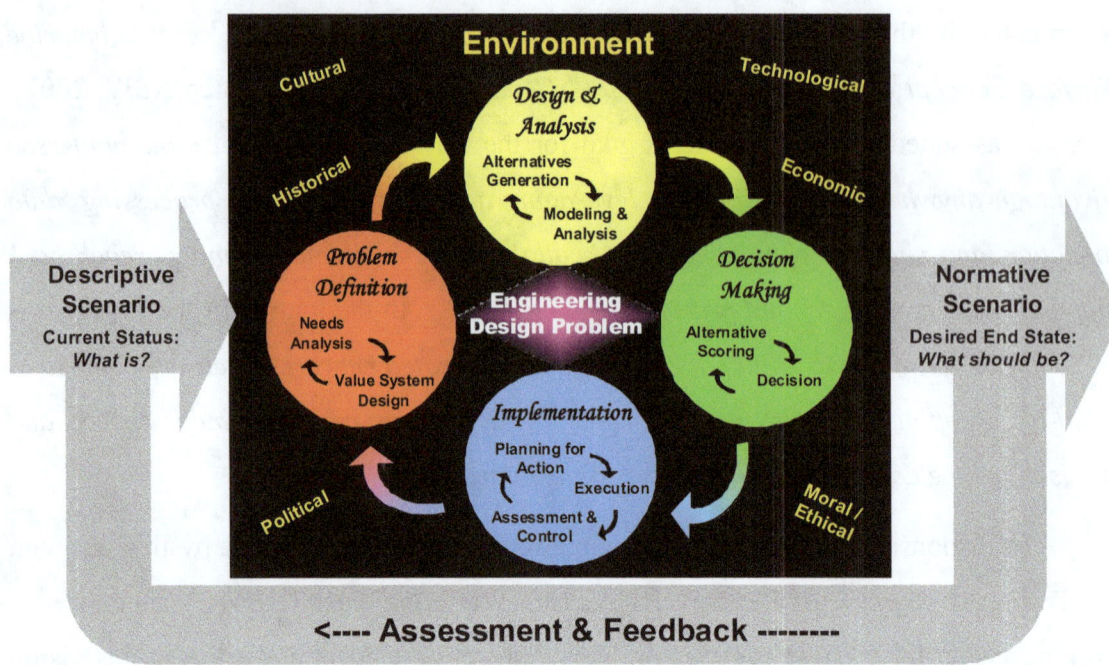

Figure 3 - Systems Engineering Design Process [Ref 5, Paulo, 2006]

1.2 OBJECTIVE

The objective of the Improved ASW Effectiveness project is to address the overarching need to improve ASW effectiveness in tomorrow's battlespace including operations near-land, with the need to establish area control in a congested, chaotic environment, while facing adversaries with advancing levels of technological sophistication. One of the primary missions for a United States Navy ASW system is to protect a Carrier Strike Group (CSG). The combat range of the carrier air wing usually necessitates strike group operations well within the operating range of hostile submarine forces. The effectiveness of existing ASW systems makes this a high risk scenario. [Ref 4, Grace Jean, 2008]

1.3 CAPSTONE PROJECT

The Capstone group, starting in June of 2007, implemented the SEDP and the associated principles to refine the problem statement, to synthesize potential solutions, to evaluate them based on Measures of Effectiveness and Performance using analytic and simulation based tools, and to establish the requirements necessary to produce a design baseline. The scope of the project involved completion of the first three phases identified in the SEDP, to include needs analysis, analysis of alternatives, and provision of a feasible solution.

1.3.1 Project Organization

The Newport cohort was organized into Working Integrated Product Teams (WIPTs), headed by a WIPT lead. Each WIPT lead was a member of the Overarching-Level Integrated Product Team (OIPT) headed by the Project Manager (PM). This philosophy is expressed pictorially in Figure 4. The team-members who make up the capstone team with their biographical information are identified in Appendix B.

WIPTs were established as necessary to meet project objectives within each project phase. As a WIPT completed their assigned tasking the WIPT lead reported out to the OIPT and members were reassigned as necessary to support other tasking. The OIPT was responsible for identifying the WIPT requirements throughout each project phase. The breakdown of the WIPTs and their assigned team members along with the teams operating policies are detailed in Appendix A.

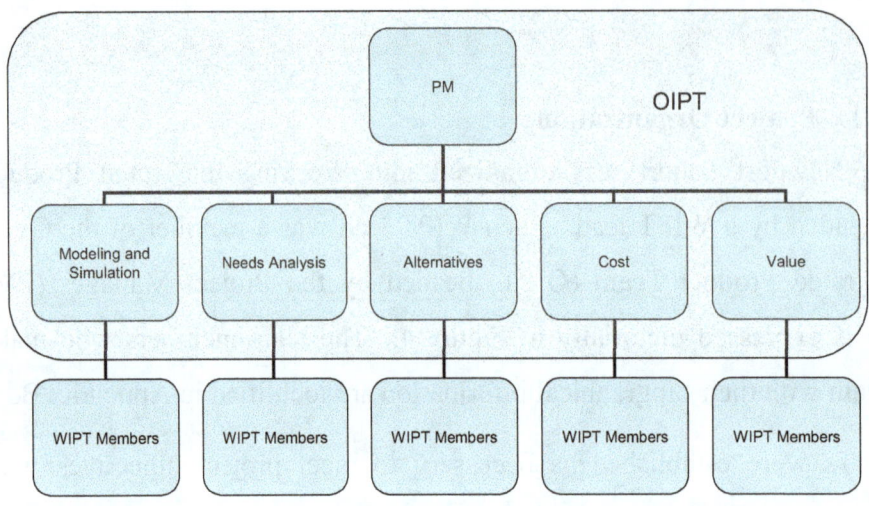

Figure 4 - WIPT Structure

1.3.2 System Engineering Process

A tailored SEDP was utilized in the performance of this NPS Capstone Project. The process used was founded on the SEDP frame work outlined in the NPS System Engineering Curriculum as pictured in Figure 3. [Ref 5, Paulo, 2006] At a fundamental level, the rationale for using a System Engineering process is founded on the idea that it can provide an organized approach to creativity. According to the Sage and Armstrong text, *Introduction to System Engineering*: [Ref 6, Sage and Armstrong, 2000: 14]

> *"The basic activities of systems engineering are usually concentrated on the evolution of an appropriate process to enable the definition, development, and deployment of a system or the formulation, analysis and interpretation of issues associated with one of these phases."*

This concept of the Formulation, Analysis, and Interpretation engineering steps, served as the underlying outline of the project analysis within the SEDP and closely relates to the overall structure of this capstone project report. The focus of this project addressed the first three phases of the SEDP; Problem Definition, Design and Analysis, and Decision Making. These SEDP phases are well supported by the Sage and Armstrong basic system engineering steps, depicted in Figure 5. Formulation of the problem maps to the SEDP Problem Definition phase, Analysis relates to the SEDP Design and Analysis phase, and finally the Interpretation step supports the Decision Making phase. A key aspect of the engineering steps depicted in Figure 3 is the secondary information flow. This feedback iteration path is a significant engineering process applied in this project. As efforts progressed on subsequent SEDP phases, iterative adjustments and refinement were made to earlier phase artifacts.

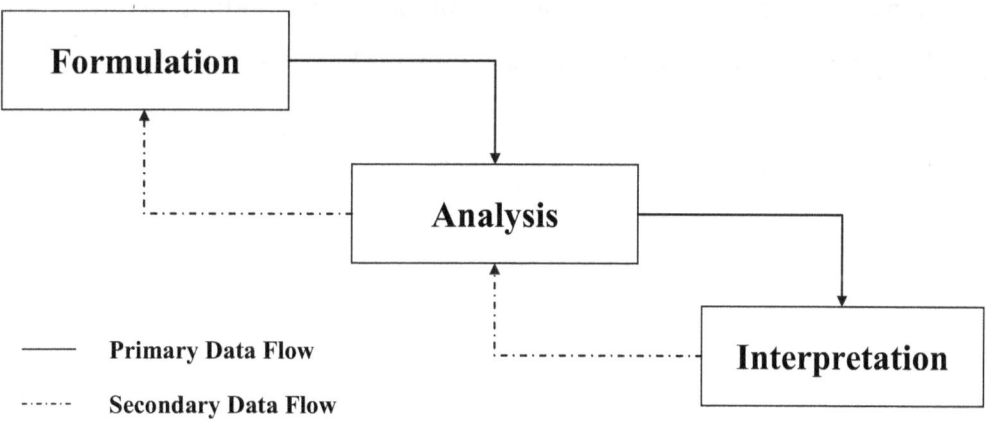

Figure 5 – Systems Engineering Steps [Ref 6, Sage and Armstrong, 2000]

From the perspective of product life cycles as described by *Blanchard and Fabrycky*, Figure 6, [Ref 7, Blanchard and Fabrycky 2006: 27] the SEDP was appropriate for our use since the project focused on performing early acquisition phase conceptual definition and the supporting functional analysis of an improved ASW system. The SEDP Problem Definition, Design and Analysis, and Decision Making phases provided an excellent framework suitable for the project engineering efforts.

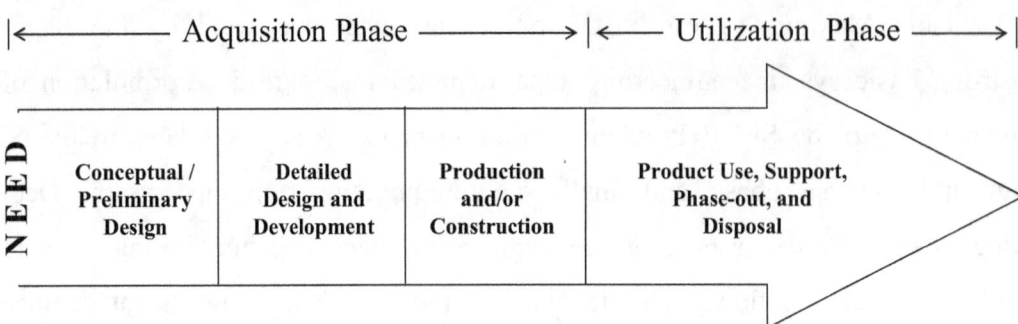

Figure 6 - Product Life Cycle [Ref 7, Blanchard and Fabrycky 2006: 27]

In performing the SEDP, as applied to the early acquisition lifecycle phase, the team started with a primitive need statement and conducted research, stakeholder questionnaires, and various techniques for defining the problem and creating a value system design. A depiction of the relationships of the problem definition efforts is shown in Figure 7. Details of this phase will be addressed in Chapter 2.

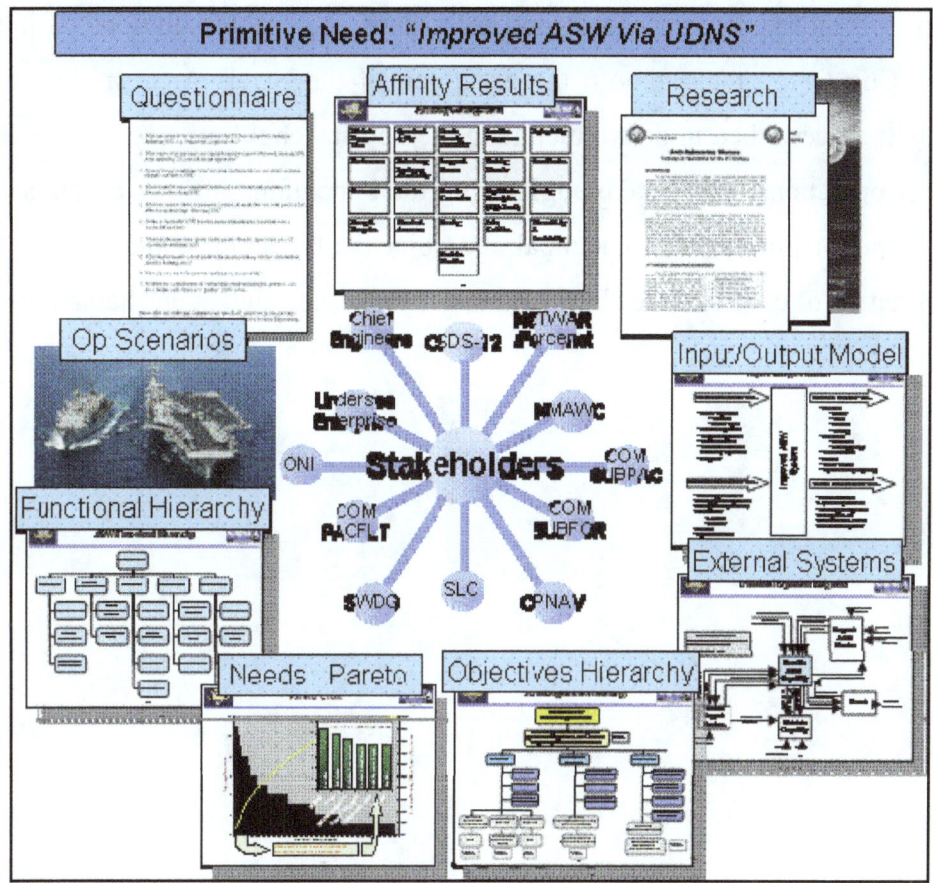

Figure 7 - Problem Definition

In the Design and Analysis phase, possible alternative solutions to the defined problem were generated and screened, resulting in a set of feasible alternatives suitable for modeling analysis. The final SEDP phase is Decision Making, where each alternative's modeled MOE's, RMA, Cost, and Risk were compiled and analyzed for the purposes of weighing and comparing the relative value scores.

In Chapter 1 of this document the system engineering team has identified a key Navy concern and need to form the basis of their integrating project. The team applied knowledge and skills gained through the Masters of Science in System Engineering curriculum to analyze this problem area in a formal, disciplined manner in accordance with the SEDP. Further, the team established an organizational structure and process which is documented in the Project Management Plan to embark on and execute the necessary system engineering steps towards quantifying viable solutions to this Navy need. In Chapter 2 of this report, the execution of the Needs Analysis Phase of this process will be described in detail, including the key stakeholders, reference documents, concept of operations, and system engineering tools including affinity diagrams, Pareto analysis, input/output models, functional and objective hierarchies, and results that lead to the formation of the Effective Needs Statement and associated quantifiable objectives.

2 PROBLEM DEFINITION

2.1 NEEDS ANALYSIS

In June 2007 the Newport cohort considered application of the SEDP process to a **Primitive Need Statement** expressed by the NUWC Technical Director's grand challenge: [Ref 3, McCormack, 2007]

"Create a next generation undersea warfare capability through the implementation of an Undersea Distributed Networked System"

This initial problem statement was socialized with key stakeholders from the ASW community (refer to Section 2.1.1) during project inception, after which the team reached consensus that this was a worthy topic. The team performed a Needs Analysis as a means to refine this initial problem statement into an effective need that would most effectively capture the group stakeholder needs. This Analysis was conducted to establish an Effective Needs Statement for the project, utilizing many of the following SEDP techniques:

Stakeholder Analysis – This approach is used to identify the relevant stakeholders, develop a list of questions and/or desired information sought from the stakeholders, conduct interviews and research, and consolidate the information that is gained. Our design team collated a significant amount of interview data and applied an Affinity Diagramming Process to organize this language information and identify system goals & constraints (refer to Section 2.1.1).

Needs and Constraints Analysis – This analysis is used to ascertain those goals and constraints of greatest concern/desire by key stakeholders. Pareto Analysis was applied to the Affinity Diagramming results to capture the relative significance, from a stakeholder perspective, among the various stakeholder needs. This analysis provided a traceable method for translation of stakeholder feedback into a succinct statement of effective needs.

Input-Output Model Analysis – This graphical technique is used to scope and bound the problem by defining the boundaries of the system and boundary conditions (e.g., analyze inputs and focus outputs). Our design team generated an Input-Output Model diagram addressing the stakeholder primitive need and conducted an iterative review and refinement with key clients. Our analysis established various elements necessary to accomplish undersea warfare, acknowledging a System-of-Systems aggregation for effective ASW. Section 2.1.3 discusses these elements in further detail.

External Systems Diagram – This graphical model defines the interactions among external systems and shows the interdependencies between those systems and the system under development.

Concept of Operations – The Concept of Operations defines a stakeholder vision for what the system is, a statement of mission requirements, and a description of how the system will be used. Our focus was placed upon operational use requirements related to ASW conduct.

Functional Analysis – This analysis approach is used to determine 'what' the system must do, not 'how' the system will function. The analysis provides a basis for developing innovative alternatives in follow-on phases. This analysis not only looked at system functional composition, but also flows among system functional components.

All of these approaches and techniques were conducted in an iterative manner, resulting in concurrent activities being coordinated by the team to ensure a cohesive process. Details of the Needs Analysis techniques are provided in the following sections, and these techniques bound the problem space with results that support the agreed-to Effective Needs Statement reached with the stakeholders at the second In-Process Review held 7 March 2008:

Effective Needs Statement

"An improved ASW system is needed to protect carrier strike groups from enemy attack through effective, timely, and precise engagement by providing tactically significant detection, localization, tracking, and classification of quiet acoustic threat submarines in challenging environments"

2.1.1 Stakeholder Analysis

Our design team began the problem definition process by conducting a Stakeholder Analysis to identify the relevant stakeholders for the problem. Typical stakeholders can be owners, users, customers, clients, managers, maintainers, administrators, and regulators of the system [Ref 6, Sage and Armstrong, 2000: 90] to be brought into being, where each stakeholder may have a significantly different perspective of the system and the system's requirements. [Ref 8, Buede, 2000: 122] Of the various stakeholders engaged as part of system problem definition, the following is a representative sample of the relevant stakeholder organizations that participated in the needs analysis, where specific inputs are denoted in Section 2.1.2:

Sponsors, Clients, Decision-Makers:

- Naval Undersea Warfare Center (NUWC) – This naval laboratory provides full spectrum research, development, test and evaluation, engineering and fleet support for submarines, autonomous underwater systems, and offensive and defensive weapons systems associated with undersea warfare. NUWC is also the home of the directors for Naval Undersea Warfare and Undersea Distributed Networked Systems (i.e., commissioned USW Grand Challenge, established as the project Primitive Need).

- Office of the Chief of Naval Operations (OPNAV), Submarine Warfare Division, N87 – This office is the warfare resource sponsor responsible for Submarine program assessment and budgetary process controls on behalf of the Deputy-CNO for Resources, Warfare Requirements and Assessments (N8). The CNO ASW Cross Functional Board (CFB) includes a team of ASW professionals, led by OPNAV N874, establishing requirements for coordinated ASW across air, surface and subsurface elements.

- Naval Postgraduate School (NPS) Capstone Advisors – These individuals provide guidance regarding SEDP execution and alignment with NPS Masters of Science in Systems Engineering (MSSE) integrating project compliance.

System Users:

- U.S. Pacific Fleet (COMPACFLT) – This organization supports the U.S. Pacific Command's theater strategy, providing interoperable, trained and combat-ready naval forces to U.S. Pacific Command (PACOM) and other U.S. Unified Commanders. As such, the U.S. Pacific Fleet is a "force provider" to unified commanders in various regions around the world. On any given day, ships and squadrons from the U.S. Pacific Fleet are on deployment, which can include an aircraft carrier strike group configuration incorporating ASW assets.

- Surface Warfare Development Group (SWDG) – This group acts as the center for the development and improvement of Fleet tactics and doctrine in surface, air, undersea, electronic, and amphibious warfare.

- Naval Mine and Anti-Submarine Warfare Command (NMAWC) – This organization is the primary command through which issues related to Mine Warfare (MIW) and Anti-Submarine Warfare (ASW) are coordinated with tactical development agencies and commands. NMAWC focuses efforts across numerous resource sponsors, systems commands, research laboratories, training organizations, and operational commands to ensure Navy-wide competency in the MIW and ASW mission areas.

- Military Detachment (MILDET) Naval Undersea Warfare Center (NUWC) – These personnel act as fleet representatives who provide systems operation and maintenance perspective during NUWC conduct of systems engineering, inclusive of all Program Stages or Lifecycles (i.e. Planning, RDT&E and Acquisition).

Analysts:

- Naval Undersea Warfare Center – This group of representatives provide full-spectrum Planning, RDT&E and Acquisition systems engineering and management for submarines, autonomous systems, and offensive and defensive weapons systems associated with undersea warfare, inclusive of Chief Warfare-Discipline Engineers and Navy Technical Warrant Holders.

- Naval Network Warfare Command (NETWARCOM) – Delivers and operates a reliable, secure and battle-ready global network for the Fleet, inclusive of FORCEnet enterprise alignment and integration initiatives. NETWARCOM leads the development, integration and execution of Information Operations effect for the Fleet.

- Commander Naval Submarine Forces, head of Undersea Enterprise (CSF-USE) – Sets the strategy, priorities, requirements, and overarching direction for suppliers, resource sponsors, and producers to ensure a quality product for the enterprise customers (stakeholders and resources supporting or operating SSNs, SSGNs, SSBNs, fixed surveillance, or mobile surveillance forces).

Our design team developed a stakeholder questionnaire in order to establish a standard set of interview elements for each stakeholder. The questionnaire was composed of questions that characterize the stakeholder needs, while encouraging stakeholder creativity. Appendix C identifies the resulting stakeholder questionnaire that was employed.

Interviews with relevant stakeholders were conducted to collect their expressed system needs, wants and desires. Interviews conducted with stakeholders were most often done on a one-to-one basis, with no observed opportunities for conduct of group interviews en-mass. The latter would have afforded an opportunity for various stakeholders to engage in group brain-storming techniques; however, stakeholder commitments did not permit this to occur.

In addition to stakeholder interviews, the design team also conducted significant research to better characterize the problem space and facilitate stakeholder needs concurrence. Various source materials were consulted as part of this research, including those references suggested by stakeholders as germane subject-matter.

All of the resulting Needs Analysis language information from both stakeholder interviews and materials research was captured in an electronic worksheet format to ensure the information was suitably recorded and documented for traceability. Appendix

D denotes the worksheet format that was utilized to record both stakeholder feedback and research data.

An Affinity Diagramming Process was used to organize the varied language information collated from the stakeholder interviews and materials research. A total of 207 original needs were analyzed by the team and organized into groups perceived to be of common goals or constraints. The Affinity Diagramming process helped identify twenty-one (21) common system goals & constraints shared among the stakeholders and research data. The aggregate results of this analysis are depicted in Figure 8; however, the 21 categories did not provide sufficient granularity in terms of needs characteristics. Therefore the analysis team revisited the original needs and derived an intermediary level of 63 interpreted needs. Figure 9 provides an example of Affinity Categories derived for ASW system "Detection" and "Doctrine" that were translated into more granular interpreted need categories. The additional granularity of 63 interpreted need categories was deemed necessary to illuminate needs/constraints not revealed by the original 21 categories (detailed results are provided in Appendix E)

Affinity Categories

Minimize Engagement Time	Operational Agility	Tactics, Planning, DOTMLPF	Precision Engagement	Deployability
Environment	Redundancy, Persistence, Affordability	Integrated Sensors	Training, Manning	Classification
Covertness	Detection	Doctrine, Constraints	Key Mission Description (High Level)	Planning
Decoy & Deception	Situational Awareness	Sensing	Joint, Coalition	Vulnerability & Survivability
		Decision Timeline		

Figure 8 - Affinity Results - Top Tier Stakeholder Goals & Constraints

Affinity Results (sample)

Affinity Category		Original Needs Elements	
Goal/Constraint	Count	Interpreted Need	Count
Detection	15	The system should provide high Pd and Low Pfa with tactical significance	11
		The system should maximize search rate	3
		The system should maximize kill rate	1
Doctrine-Constraints	19	The system should avoid force-on-force engagements	8
		The system must secure friendly maneuver area: Sea Shield/Base/Strike	4
		The system should minimize the Fog of War	1
		The system should optimize command structure to support Joint ASW execution	1
		The system needs to accommodate non-ASW tasking of assets	1
		The system should be offensive vice defensive	4

Figure 9 - Mapping Needs Elements into Affinity Categories

2.1.2 Needs and Constraints Analysis

Once the stakeholder inputs were gathered and organized as part of the stakeholder analysis the next task was to garner stakeholder perspective of the 'needs' in the context of current conditions, future environment, resources to bring to bear, etc. The end state of the needs analysis is the effective need or the revised problem statement. [Ref 5, Paulo 2006] The effective need is formulated by translating the stakeholder needs into a statement of the system's objectives which, if met, will bring the greatest degree of satisfaction to the user and critical stakeholders. [Ref 5, Paulo 2006] The process of translating stakeholder needs into the objectives that comprise the effective need is shown in Figure 10.

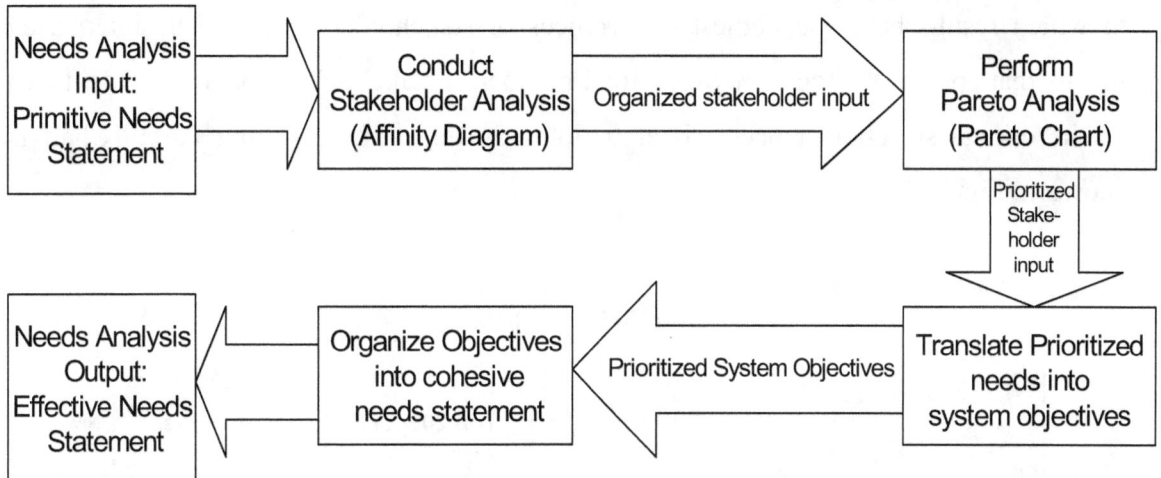

Figure 10 - Needs Analysis Process

As a product of the stakeholder analysis as described in Section 2.1.1 the stakeholder inputs were categorically organized in the affinity diagram shown in Figure 8. The next step in the process was to prioritize the stakeholder inputs. The tool chosen to perform the prioritization was a Pareto chart. Once the most critical stakeholder needs were identified in the Pareto Chart the task of translating the needs into system objectives was applied. The resulting prioritized list of system objectives was manipulated to organize the objectives into a cohesive and comprehensive effective needs statement. Each step of this process, its output, and product of the overall process, the effective needs statement, will be described in detail in the following sections.

2.1.2.1 *Pareto Analysis*

Utilizing the Pareto chart to prioritize the stakeholder inputs was a natural fit. The Pareto chart is designed to utilize the data, not perception, to separate the few critical problems or issues from a multitude of possible problems or issues by graphically arranging the data according to frequency of occurrence. [Ref 5, Paulo 2006] The stakeholder analysis generated 207 individual stakeholder inputs – clearly a multitude of data elements. The individual inputs were subsequently categorized into 67 interpreted results and the occurrences of stakeholder inputs assigned to each interpreted result were tallied. The interpreted need results shown in Figure 9 were sorted and plotted according to which results have the highest occurrences of stakeholder inputs. The interpreted results that contain the top 20% of the total number of stakeholder inputs were identified as the critical stakeholder needs. [Ref 9, John F. Reh] The resulting Pareto Chart is shown in Figure 11.

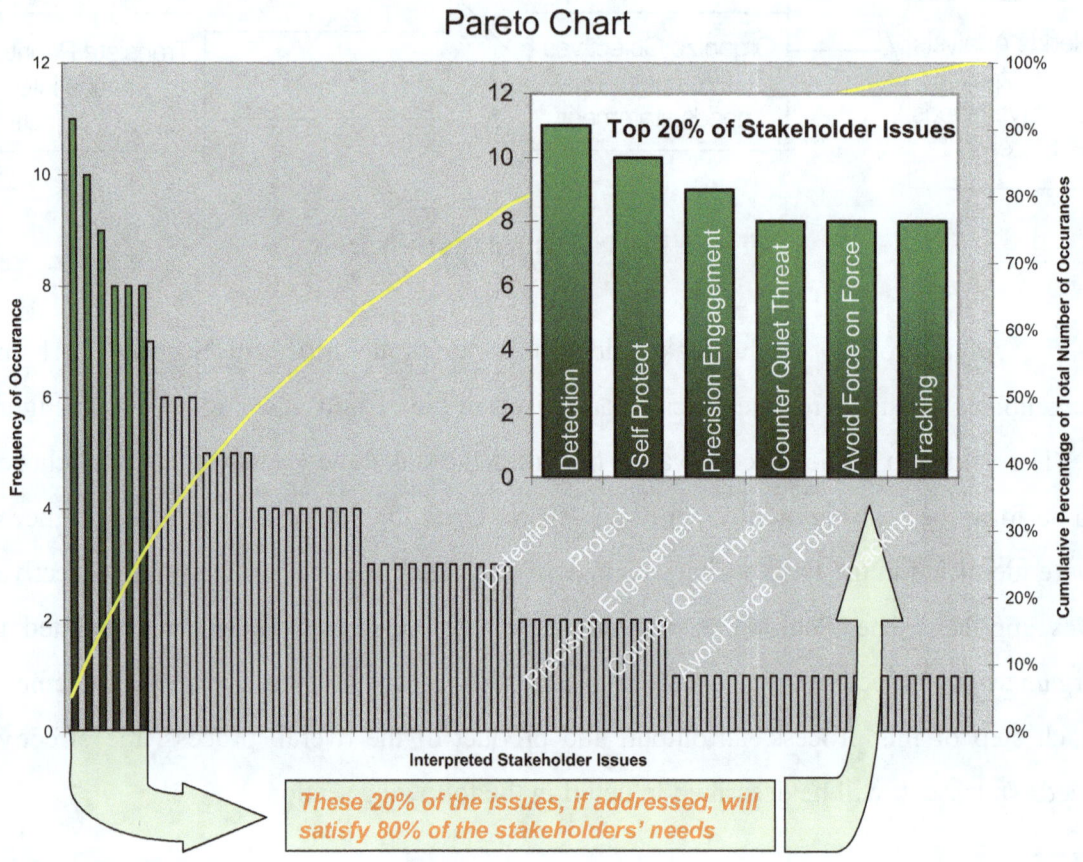

Figure 11 - Pareto Chart

The critical issues that were identified are prioritized below where the text is the verbatim description from the affinity diagram and the parenthetical is the Pareto chart reference:

1. **The system should provide high probability of detection (Pd) and low probability of false alarm (Pfa) with tactical significance (Detection)**. This interpreted need was based upon the following original needs:

1. OPNAV N87 cited "any technology that will support active or passive detection at tactically significant ranges" as a current need for "more effectively keeping an SSK from impeding US Aircraft Carrier operations". In terms of "important features of a system devised to protect US Aircraft Carriers from SSK" threats, it was expressed "high probability of detection (Pd) and low probability of false-alarm (Pfa) at tactically significant ranges" are necessary. It was articulated a "vision of a 'perfect' ASW system" without any consideration of current limitations (technologies, political, cost, etc) would "detect everything automatically with 100% Pd and 0% Pfa." [Ref 10, ASW Cross Functional Board Survey Response Oct 2007]

2. CNO ASW Task Force cited the "need to maximize enemy detections, tracking, and engagement opportunities" as the key underpinnings to enable the 'persistent detection & cueing' deemed necessary to bring 21st century ASW to fruition. [Ref 2, CNO ASW CONOPS, 2007: 5]

3. COMPACFLT cited the "challenges of SSK quieting" as a key challenge to an ASW ability to "detect, identify and defeat SSK." It was clarified "automated detection and localization" would be "important features of a system devised to protect US Aircraft Carriers from SSK". It was further stated "automation for acoustic operator detection and localization" could bring improvements to the ASW "decision making process". [Ref 11, COMPACFLT Survey Response, Oct 2007]

4. NUWC stakeholders expressed the ASW system must exhibit "zero false alarms" in order to meet observed Fleet needs [Ref 12, Monti, 2007: 14], whereby the "prosecution of false targets" is one of the "major limitations the US Navy is currently facing in defeating SSK." [Ref 13, NUWC Chief Technology Officer Survey Response, Oct 2007] The advent of "threat advances in quieting and endurance" was cited as a fundamental "challenge to ASW abilities to detect, identify and defeat SSK". [Ref 14, NUWC USW Combat System Department Survey Response, Nov 2007]

2. **The system needs to protect its assets from enemy attack (Self Protect).** This interpreted need was based upon the following original needs:
    1. OPNAV N87 defined the advent of "no or minimum blue losses" as one of the major characteristics associated with a successful ASW mission. [Ref 10, ASW Cross Functional Board Survey Response Oct 2007]
    2. CNO ASW Task Force cited the "need to provide improved levels of force protection" as the key goal of ASW defense-in-depth. [Ref 2, CNO ASW Task Force: 5]
    3. COMPACFLT cited "no loss of blue CVN [Aircraft Carrier]" as the principle definition of a successful ASW mission. [Ref 11, COMPACFLT Survey Response, Oct 2007] The Fleet Forces Command identified "establishment of [threat] submarine warning and exclusion zones as an important enabler of success" for Aircraft Carrier ASW. [Ref 15, Commander U.S. Fleet Forces Command, 2006: 25]
    4. NUWC MILDET personnel defined a successful ASW mission where "ship and crew safety was never compromised" and "the ship was never detected." It was expressed "acoustic masking or noise attenuation designed for [Aircraft] Carrier use" would be an important feature for protecting US Aircraft Carriers from SSK threats. [Ref 16, NUWC MILDET Survey Response, Nov 2007]
    5. NUWC stakeholders expressed the ASW system "needs to reduce risk to [friendly] forces" [Ref 12, Monti, 2007: 3] while acknowledging ASW force "tactical utility is based on balance of combat power and survivability" (i.e. dominance of either trait can prove detrimental to the ASW force). [Ref 17, Christian, 2007: 5] and [Ref 18, Huges, 2000] It was conveyed effective ASW must identify "force vulnerability and risk assessment" for "determination of the level of risk (via analysis tools and decision aids) at a given point, considering mission, tasks, rules of engagement, objectives, and other appropriate factors."

3. **The system must demonstrate precision engagement with on demand responsiveness (Precision Engagement).** This interpreted need was based upon the following original needs:
    1. CNO ASW Task Force expressed the "need to maximize our undersea advantage anywhere in the world by leveraging advances in collaborative real-time planning, reach-back support, rapid maneuver, and precision engagement." [Ref 2, CNO Task Force ASW, 2007: 1]
    2. COMPACFLT stated the ability to "address torpedo threats and anti-ship cruise missile threats" are important features for protecting U.S. Aircraft Carriers from threat SSK, where "the ability to neutralize any and all threat submarines whenever necessary" represents the 'perfect' vision for a successful ASW mission. [Ref 11, COMPACFLT Survey Response, Oct 2007]
    3. NUWC stakeholders expressed the "ability to defeat [threat] command and control" remains a formidable challenge in confronting SSK, and "tools to assess risk and exploit situational awareness" are necessary to improve the ASW decision making process. [Ref 19, NUWC Chief Engineer Survey Response, Oct 2007] It was also clarified the strategy for shaping adversary behavior may likely "include a family of lethal and non-lethal weapons" while broadening the ways and means in which the weapons are brought to bear. [Ref 17, Christian, 2007: 24] The ASW solution should optimally combine sensors, command and control, and influencer components to "increase engagement effectiveness (probability)" against threat SSK. [Ref 12, Monti, 2007: 3]
4. **The System needs to counter a quiet threat in highly congested environment where acoustic performance is affected by excessive noise density and poor propagation (Counter Quiet Threat).** This interpreted need was based upon the following original needs:
    1. COMPACFLT stated a "diversity in acoustic environment" combined with a "quiet threat, with many in quantity" as the greatest challenges in

modern ASW. [Ref 11, COMPACFLT Survey Response, Oct 2007] The Fleet Forces Command further acknowledged the ASW environment often poses "a cluttered Radio Frequency spectrum from surface vessel traffic and land sources." [Ref 15, Commander U.S. Fleet Forces Command, 2006: 22]

2. CNO ASW Task Force foresees a maritime environment of increasing challenges, earmarked by "difficult sound propagation profiles and dense surface traffic" resulting in a "cluttered and chaotic operating environment" where "defeating stealthy enemies will be an exceptional challenge." [Ref 2, Task Force ASW, 2007: 1]

3. NUWC stakeholders articulated the ASW system should "work in any environment to accurately provide time sensitive targeting data directly to a firing platform." [Ref 12 Monti, 2007: 14] The ASW system must provide the "capability to conduct operations in highly contested areas, in the presence of [threat] forces" [Ref 17, Christian, 2007: 7] and under challenging "ambient noise levels and reverberation" for potential mission areas. [Ref 11, COMPACFLT Survey Response, Oct 2007]

5. **The system should avoid force on force engagements (Avoid Force On Force).** This interpreted need was based upon the following original needs:

1. CNO ASW Task Force foresees "limitations in current weapons reach and sensor integration drives many of today's ASW operations toward 'force on force' engagements that place our forces at risk." [Ref 2, Task Force ASW, 2007: 4]

2. NUWC MILDET personnel expressed SSK are relatively "cheap to make, and there are already quite a few of them," whereby their quantity poses a major limitation upon ASW. Combined with a "continuous challenge in upgrading an aging fleet", and the "challenge in maintaining ASW superiority with a reduction in [U.S. Navy] submarines," these force ratios were seen as the greatest trial for modern ASW. [Ref 16, NUWC MILDET Survey Response, Nov 2007]

3. NUWC stakeholders likewise perceived "threat numbers as a key challenge facing our ability to detect, identify and defeat SSK." [Ref 14, NUWC USW Combat System Department Survey Response, Nov 2007] The theme to "replace force-on-force engagement with distributed force and massed effects" was reconfirmed as a key precept for theater ASW risk management. [Ref 17, Christian, 2007: 7] A "perfect ASW system" was articulated as one "that would allow killing a threat remotely while not exposing ones own ship to risk" [Ref 14, NUWC USW Combat System Department Survey Response, Nov 2007]

6. **The System needs to detect and hold targets with low acoustic target strength (Tracking).** This interpreted need was based upon the following original needs:
    1. OPNAV N87 perceived "the low source level or quiet condition of the SSK" as the principle challenge upon the ability to detect, identify and defeat SSK. It was expressed "an acoustic advantage over the threat systems" is an important feature for any system devised to protect U.S. Aircraft carriers from SSK. In this context, it was articulated the greatest challenge in modern ASW is "to the greatest extent possible, make the ocean transparent" as necessary to detect, track and hold an adversary SSK. [Ref 10, ASW Cross Functional Board Survey Response Oct 2007]
    2. NUWC stakeholders likewise expressed "full undersea transparency" as a vision for a perfect ASW system. [Ref 20, NUWC Engineering, and Analysis Department Survey Response 11/5/2007] A perceived challenge in modern ASW is establishment of threat SSK information that enables an "ability to exploit at a distance in a timely manner." [Ref 19, NUWC Chief Engineer Survey Response, Oct 2007] It was regarded the types of technologies currently needed to more effectively keep an SSK from impeding U.S. Aircraft Carrier operations must enable a "capability to operate in a transparent ocean – optically, magnetically, electrically and acoustically" [Ref 13, NUWC Chief Technology Officer Survey Response, Oct 2007] which may require "longer range sensors" [[Ref 14,

NUWC USW Combat System Department Survey Response, Nov 2007] or distributed sensors to improve detection and tracking while avoiding force-on-force engagements. It was further conceded the "hold time in tracking systems" is another challenge facing the detect and hold of quiet SSK at any significant distance. [Ref 13, NUWC Chief Technology Officer Survey Response, Oct 2007]

These six interpreted needs represent the most critical stakeholder needs, per Pareto prioritization, and represent the candidates for translation into system objectives.

2.1.2.2 *Critical Needs to System Objectives Translation*

The next step required to arrive at the effective needs statement was to translate the critical stakeholder needs into system objectives. The translation process included grouping similar needs and rearranging the need statement into concise objective statements. The critical needs identified above became the system objectives listed below:

- **Shall protect a carrier strike group from enemy attack through timely and precise engagement.**

  This objective was derived from the following stakeholder needs:
    – The system needs to protect its assets from enemy attack
    – The system must demonstrate precision engagement with on demand responsiveness

- **Shall provide tactically significant detection, tracking, and classification of quiet acoustic threat submarines in a challenging environment**

  This objective was derived from the following stakeholder needs:
    – The system should provide high Pd and low Pfa with tactical significance

- Needs to counter a quiet threat in highly congested environment where acoustic performance is affected by excessive noise density and poor propagation
- Need to detect and hold targets with low acoustic target strength

- **Shall avoid force on force engagements**

    This objective was derived from the following stakeholder need:
    - The system should avoid force on force engagements

    The three system objectives listed above formed the basis for formulating the effective needs statement.

2.1.2.3 *Effective Needs Statement Formulation*

The system objectives derived from the critical needs were utilized to formulate the effective needs statement. The system objective statements in original format did not create a cohesive effective needs statement. Therefore, the objectives were edited and manipulated to form the cohesive effective needs statement. Great care was taken to ensure that no changes were made to the intent of any individual objective statement. The resultant effective needs statement is in quotations.

> *"An improved ASW system is needed to protect carrier strike groups from enemy attack through effective, timely, and precise engagement by providing tactically significant detection, tracking, and classification of quiet acoustic threat submarines in challenging environments."*

2.1.3 Input-Output Model Analysis

The Input-Output model is a tool that enables the design team to bound and define the expected inputs and outputs of the system being designed. It characterizes both the boundaries and boundary conditions of the system.

2.1.3.1 Model Development Process

To develop a useful Input-Output model all of the system's inputs and outputs must be identified, properly defined and addressed within the context of the system. The inputs can be divided into two broad categories, controlled and uncontrolled. Controlled inputs are those things that are intended to be put into the system. These are inputs the system needs to accomplish its mission. Uncontrolled inputs are artifacts of the operational environment or other unintended inputs that are not desired. These are the inputs we must deal with even though we have little or no control of them and they are often a disadvantage, not an aid, to the system in accomplishing its mission.

The outputs can likewise be separated into two major categories, intended and unintended. Intended outputs are the results we want the system to achieve in the environment in which it is operating in. Unintended outputs are the byproducts of the system that have no added value in the system's operation and are often detrimental to its effectiveness. Occasionally unintended outputs have a positive effect on the system, but often times more than not, they have a negative affect.

Delineating and assessing each of these inputs and outputs ensures that most of the affects the outside world has on the system (inputs) are addressed and attention is focused on the system outputs. By doing this we can assure that all of the requirements are met (desired outputs) and minimize undesired byproducts.

2.1.3.2 Anti-Submarine Warfare System Model

The top level Input Output model of the improved ASW system is shown in Figure 12. This figure shows the high level inputs and outputs of the system. These inputs and outputs are broken down into further detail and discussed in the following paragraphs.

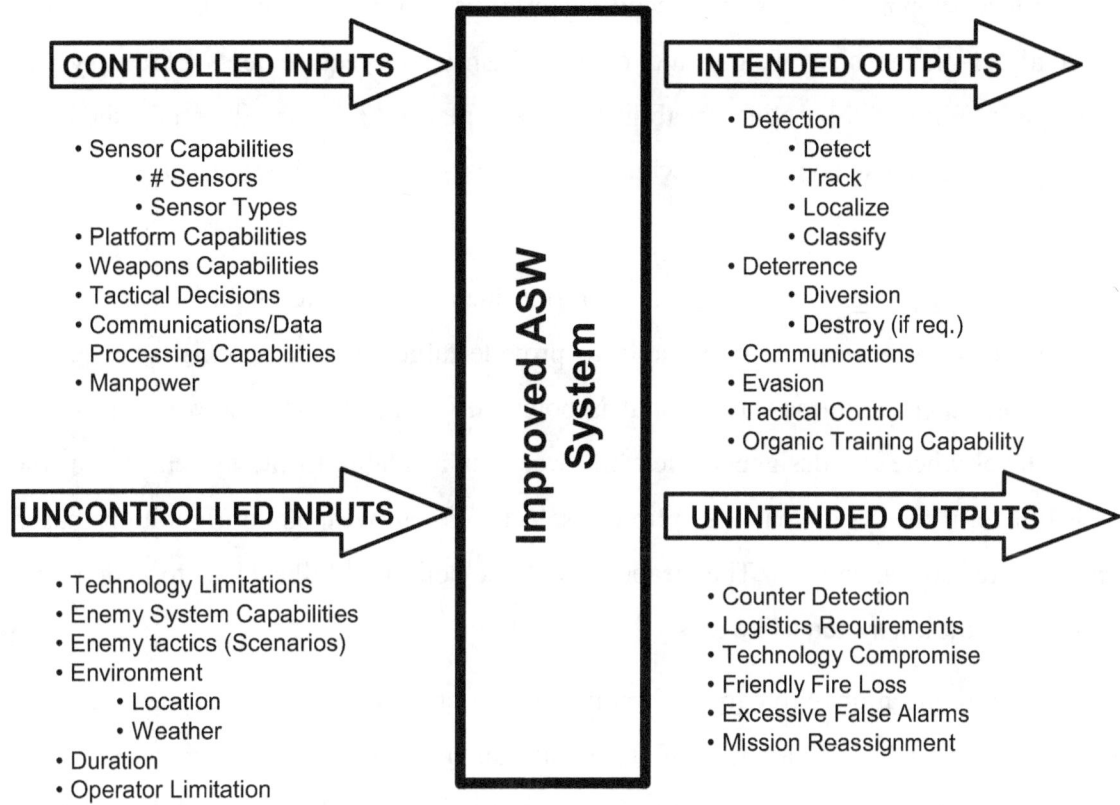

Figure 12 - Top Level Input Output Model

2.1.3.2.1   Controlled Inputs

<u>Sensor Types/Quantities:</u>   One of the primary functional requirements of any defensive system is the ability to detect threats. This function is provided by the systems sensors in conjunction with inboard processing and operator interaction. The primary detection mechanisms in the ASW arena are the acoustic sensors. This is a controllable input since selection of the sensor types and quantities are a conscious decision made during the design process.

Platform Types/Quantities: Any ASW system developed will need to interact with and be supported by existing capitol platforms. Platform selection will have a direct affect on the size, weight and other infrastructure requirements of the system developed. While the baseline capability of these platforms is already established, the development team has control over which platforms the system will be designed to work with.

Weapons Types/Quantities: In order to influence the threat the ASW system must either have its own weapons or be able to provide targeting data to existing weapons systems on other platforms. This input is potentially controllable at two levels; at the design level where the designers select the weapons available to the system and at the tactical level if the system has the option to select different weapon configurations based on the operational situations. The weapons could be both hard-kill such as torpedoes and missiles or soft kill systems like decoys and countermeasures.

Communications Protocols: Communication protocols, along with the data rates, will dictate the type and amount of data that can be transferred among the system's components and with external systems. They will be controlled by system design choices and the interface requirements of the external systems.

Data Rates: The data rates, along with the communications protocols, will dictate the type and amount of data that can be transferred among the system's components and with external systems. They will be controlled by system design choices and the interface requirements of the external systems.

System/Platform Stealth: Covert operation provides a significant tactical advantage. It increases the likelihood that the system will detect a threat prior to being counter detected by the treat. It also creates more uncertainty into the threats assessment of the tactical situation. Sufficient uncertainty can in itself be a deterrent. Alternative design selections and operational employment guidelines, such as use of active sensor modes vice passive, and propulsion choices, will be some controlling factors in system stealth. Other factors, such as noise monitoring systems and shock/vibration isolation mounts will also influence platform stealth.

System Persistence: System Persistence, the ability to maintain consistent tactical information for a significant period of time, will factor strongly in the operational use of the system. Highly persistent systems can be placed into the operational mission much earlier and require less support, e.g. replacement or refueling, during use. The systems power use and power source decisions will control its ability to persist in the field for extended periods of time.

System Survivability: The system's ability to survive in an operational environment is critical to effective use. A system that is easily damaged or destroyed during normal usage is of little value in a combat situation. System survivability is influenced by system stealth, ability to avoid detection, ruggedness and ability to survive attack if detected and fired upon. All of these factors are reasonably controlled by design decisions.

Operational Area: The Operational Area (OA) where the system will be employed is both a controlled and an uncontrolled input. Part of determination of where the system will be used is by friendly force tactical decisions and part is influenced by the enemy's operational decisions. We initially determine in what situations we wish to deploy the system but cannot always influence where the enemy chooses to operate.

Performance Prediction: The system's predicted performance significantly influences the user's operation employment and the tactical decisions made during the mission. The system's inherent performance characteristics as well as the accuracy of the models used to predict its performance are determined during the design and manufacturing processes.

2.1.3.2.2 Uncontrolled Inputs

Environment: Many factors influencing key performance parameters such as: background noise both natural and man-made; sea state (can system be deployed in bad weather) and friendly fire concerns are directly influenced by environmental factors we have no control over. Weather, other naval and civilian traffic and the physics of the ocean environment are factors we must live with and try to account for in the design process.

Existing Capitol Platforms: The system must interact with and/or be deployed from or with existing capitol platforms and it is impractical to affect significant tactical deployment modifications to existing submarines, carriers etc.

Enemy Capabilities: The capability of the enemy platforms and advanced weapons are critical design considerations in the development of the ASW system that we have no control over and in many cases limited knowledge of.

Enemy Tactics: Enemy tactical decisions will significantly affect the performance of the ASW system and predictions of anticipated tactics will be critical in developing accurate measures of performance. Although enemy tactics are not directly controllable, proper design and employment of our ASW system may have an impact on how enemy platforms react in certain situations

System Stealth, Persistence and Survivability: Ultimately system stealth, persistence and survivability will all be limited by the state of the available technology and the resources available for system development and production

Operational Area (Enemy tactical decisions): The Operational Area (OA) of the system is both a controlled and an uncontrolled input. Part of determination of where the system will be used is by friendly force operational decisions and part is in the enemy's control. We decide in what situations we wish to deploy the system but cannot always influence where the enemy chooses to operate.

Joint Operations Requirements: Joint operations are a fact of modern naval combat and the interoperability requirements are controlled at a higher level and must be complied with by the ASW system.

Enemy Force Size: Like their tactical decisions, the enemy force size will significantly affect the performance of the ASW system and predictions of anticipated force composition will be critical in developing accurate measures of performance.

Civilian Activities (i.e. Merchant traffic): Like joint operations, civilian activities occurring in close proximity to the operation area are a part of modern naval combat operations and must be taken into account during the ASW system design and operation employment.

2.1.3.2.3 Intended Outputs

Friendly Alertment: Alerting friendly forces to the presence of a threat is a key capability of the ASW system. This will be a factor of both the system's detection capability and its ability to communicate efficiently with other battlegroup assets. Effective Alertment allows friendly forces to flee from or engage the threat.

Enemy Deterrence and Force Protection: Enemy deterrence and friendly force protection are the primary functions of any ASW system. Effective deterrence equals a successful mission. Deterrence can be accomplished by destroying the enemy with either the ASW system's own weapons or by calling in attacks from other friendly forces. The enemy can also be deterred by diversion, either deceiving him into thinking friendly forces are elsewhere, overwhelming his sensors with multiple false targets or by providing such a known effective system that he dares not operate where it is present.

Coverage Area: Maximizing coverage area considerably increases the effectiveness of the system. System capabilities, such as search rate, detection range and operational employment guidelines help influence the amount of area a system can cover in a given timeframe.

2.1.3.2.4 Unintended Outputs

Self Noise: A byproduct of any operational system is self noise. Noise radiated out into the environment will adversely affect system stealth. Internalized self noise will negatively impact the effectiveness of the systems own sensors. Efficient designs minimize but cannot eliminate self noise.

Increased logistics support requirements: Fielding of any new system brings with it increased logistics requirements such as spares, consumables and maintainers/operators to support its operation. Maximizing commonality with existing systems and minimizing maintenance requirements can help reduce this byproduct.

2.1.4 External Systems Diagram

In working to develop the boundaries of the system, an external systems diagram, or "Super System" diagram was developed, as shown in Figure 13, to analyze the input/output relationships between our system, the ASW suite, and the relevant systems it would interact with. This method describes the system being designed as a subsystem of a larger group of systems. The systems are described in the diagram by their functional need.

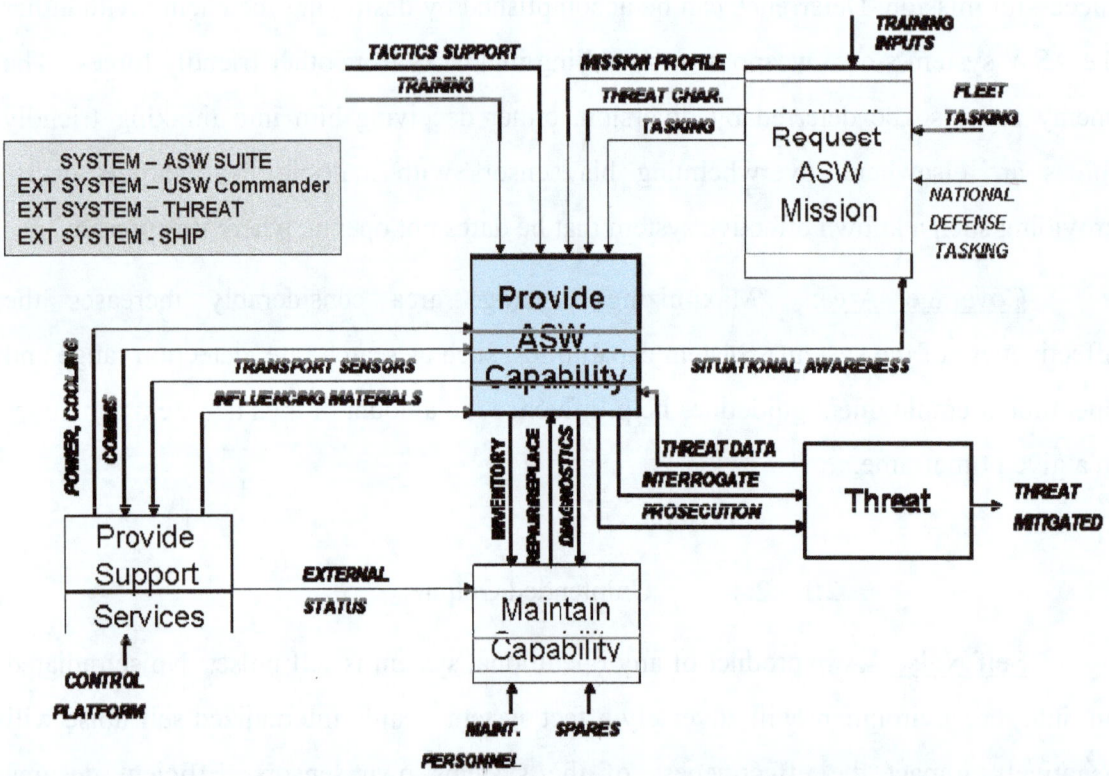

Figure 13 - ASW External Systems Diagram

Below is a description of each of the subsystems that have an interaction with the ASW mission package:

- User Subsystem – Request ASW Services
    o Inputs to this subsystem include: National Defense tasking, Fleet tasking, training inputs, and situational awareness data from the ASW subsystem.
    o Outputs from this subsystem include: Mission profiles, threat characteristics, and tasking inputs to the system.
- Threat Subsystem – Threat
    o Inputs to this subsystem include: interrogation data (sensor data), and prosecution from the ASW suite.
    o Outputs from this subsystem include: Sensor data back to the ASW suite, and mitigation of the threat.
- Ship – Provide Support Services
    o Inputs to this subsystem include: Sensor transportation requests, data to be sent off-board.
    o Outputs from this subsystem include: power, cooling, and other support services to the ASW suite, incoming data communications, status of the ship, and material to be used in threat mitigation.
- Support – Maintain Capability
    o Inputs to this subsystem include: Maintenance personnel, spares, configuration requests and diagnostics from the ASW suite, and external status of the host platform systems.
    o Outputs from this subsystem include: System control and repair/replace recommendations.

As a result of this analysis our user needs were translated into a functional description of the desired ASW mission package system.

2.1.5 Concept of Operations

The operational concept is a vision for what the system is, a statement of mission requirements, and a description of how it will be used. [Ref 8, Buede, 2000: 42, 139]

Development of a realistic operational concept is vital to put the problem into context. The Systems Engineering Design Team must understand how the user interacts with the system to bound the problem and define the solution spaces. In the case of the Anti-Submarine Warfare (ASW) system this project team is investigating, a multi-layered Concept of Operations (CONOPS) must be assessed to consider both the full spectrum of Carrier Strike Group (CSG) operations and the specific focus of ASW missions in support of the CSG.

This CONOPS addresses the operational use lifecycle for CSG operations in the 2013 timeframe, with an emphasis upon ASW conduct: this CONOPS does not specifically address other lifecycles for CSG/ASW systems (e.g. lifecycle periods for system development, pre-initial operational capability, retirement, etc) although the design team considered contributions and influences from these lifecycles during Alternatives Generation. Carrier Strike Group ASW represents a complex system of systems approach leveraging capabilities of all Carrier Strike Group components and their support elements: this CONOPS attempts to frame the CSG/ASW environment in a descriptive context, inclusive of relevant operational use requirements.

2.1.5.1   *Carrier Strike Group CONOPS*

A comprehensive CSG CONOPS is very complex and multifaceted. It would take into account various CSG operations and options, many of which are not necessarily relevant to the improved ASW efforts of this project. In order to maintain focus, a limited CONOPS was developed to concentrate upon the CSG ASW perspective. Virtually all of the CSG's varied missions require it to establish itself in an Operating Area (OA) that is reasonably secured from assault by a threat. Safe CSG operation within an OA represents the principle concern chosen for the ASW analysis.

This focus on the ASW portion of the overall CSG operations is the result of the needs analysis conducted by the project team. This needs analysis is described in detail in section 2 of this report. Starting from the NUWC Technical Director's grand challenge to "Create a next generation undersea warfare capability through the implementation of an Undersea Distributed Networked System", [Ref 3, McCormack,

2007] and the Chief of Naval Operations' Anti-Submarine Warfare Concept of Operations for the 21st Century, the team worked with input from numerous stakeholders to identify their needs and bound the problem space. The salient concern common to all of these sources was the need to improve protection of the CSG from advanced submarine threats. This refinement process is illustrated in Figure 14, which proved complementary with the other applied needs analysis techniques, particularly the Section 2.1.2 Needs and Constraints Pareto analysis results.

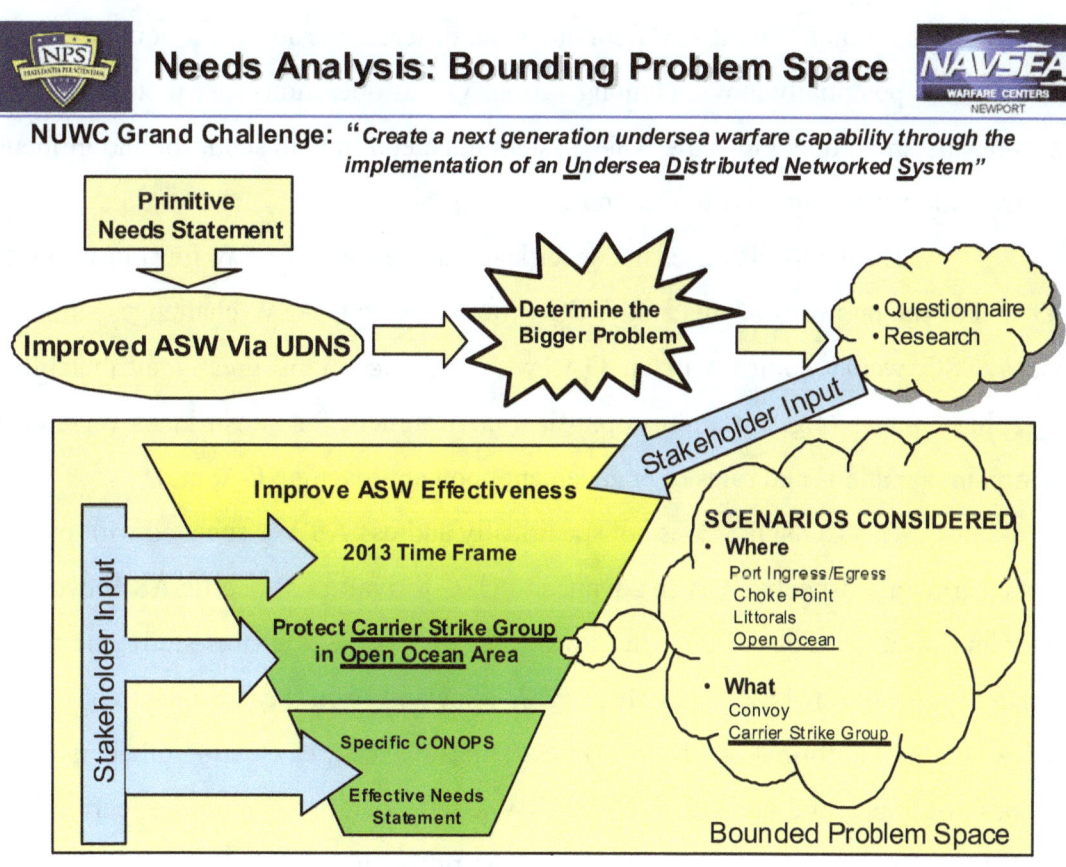

Figure 14 - ASW Problem Focus Process

It is vital that the improvement to the ASW capability not be made at the expense of other CSG mission capabilities. The strike mission is the whole purpose for the CSG presence in OA, so the ASW system cannot impact the CSG ability to conduct flight operations. In addition to the submarine torpedo threat there are numerous airborne threats that must be countered. No reduction in this critical CSG air defense capability can be justified to improve ASW operations. In order to maintain on station endurance, underway replenishment must also continue regardless of the ASW threat. As support vessels have no significant contribution to the ASW mission there is little chance that improved ASW capability will adversely impact this operational requirement.

For any tactically significant operation of a CSG, an appropriate OA is selected and a CSG transit route to the OA is established. The CSG transits to the OA and establishes itself on station. Both the CSG transit route and OA must be scouted to determine the threat level and cleared of unacceptable threats by the ASW system. Once on station in the initial OA the CSG conducts the ordered mission for a nominal 14-day period of time, potentially moving among various OA as operations may dictate. In order to ensure safe strike operations the ASW system must continue to scout for and influence submarine threats during CSG transit and OA evolutions.

This CONOPS does not specifically address CSG ASW for transit to/from an OA. For the purposes of this study, CSG transit presents ASW challenges similar to those a CSG would confront in an OA, with the exceptions greatly attributable to geographic features (e.g. variation in physical environment for transit lanes versus OA; variation in operations and rules of engagement upon approaching OA; etc).

This CONOPS does not specifically address ASW associated with friendly assets clearing a prospective OA in advance to CSG arrival: this specific ASW evolution is coordinated at the theater command level. For the purposes of this study, the theater command direction of ASW 'area clearing' is allocated to in-theater assets not directly attached to the CSG formation. In this context, the advance area clearing of a perspective OA does not impact the immediate CSG ASW assets operating within the 'current' OA (e.g. CSG surface combatants; maritime patrol aircraft assigned to the CSG; etc).

Operational requirements for CSG Torpedo Defense are not specifically addressed, as early stakeholder feedback indicated CSG ASW must forestall/deny any threat of a 'launch first' opportunity of significant CSG susceptibility (i.e. CSG torpedo defense was deemed beyond the scope of this project, and to be treated as invariable). For all of our assessments it was deemed necessary to destroy the threat submarine before it is capable of launching a torpedo at the CSG. Any successful torpedo launch by the hostile SSK is deemed a mission failure. Finally, all CSG operational discussions are documented herein in a manner so as to remain unclassified.

2.1.5.2 CSG ASW System CONOPS (circa 2013)

It is important to note there really is no single definition of a CSG, as strike groups are formed and disestablished on an as-needed basis, and the composition of one CSG may be different from another. [Ref 21, USN, 2007] A "standard" CSG composition is defined in terms of the capabilities required to accomplish all tasks in a notional threat environment against a notional threat, thereby the means to provide an initial crisis response mission from a rotationally deployed forward posture. [Ref 22, Pike, 2007] For the purposes of this study, a calendar year 2013 notional CSG composition is defined as follows:

The centerpiece of the CSG is the Aircraft Carrier (CV/CVN) and its associated Carrier Air Wing (CAW). The primary purpose of the carrier is to forward deploy naval airpower in the form of its attached air wing. The Nimitz Class carrier [Figure 15] has multiple advanced search and fire control radar systems as well as hull mounted sonar. The focus of the radar capability is supporting air wing flight operations and ownship air defense and is of limited use in the ASW role. The carrier's self defense armament consists of Sea Sparrow missiles and Phalanx close in weapon system. The Sea Sparrow theater defense missile provides anti-aircraft defense out to 24 nautical miles. The Phalanx system, with its self-contained radar system, provides defense against anti-ship missiles and hostile aircraft out to approximately 3 nautical miles. [Ref 23, Jane's Fighting Ships, 2008]

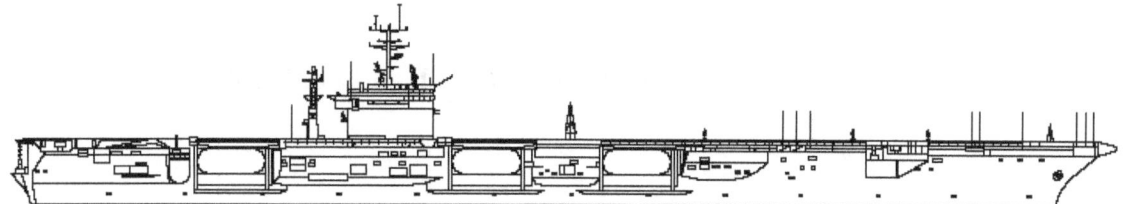

Figure 15 - Nimitz Class Carrier (CVN) [Ref 23, Jane's Fighting Ships, 2008]

The air wing is comprised of up to 85 aircraft, including F-14s; F/A-18s; EA-6Bs; E-2Cs; S-3A/Bs; SH-60Fs, HH-60Hs. [Ref 24, USN Fact File, 2008] Most of these assets support the carriers primary strike role or provide air defense. Only the S-3 Viking aircraft, Figure 16, and SH-60 helicopters, Figure 17, provide any significant ASW capability. The S-3 Vikings drop sonobuoys for undersea sensing. The S-3 Viking is capable of carrying multiple weapons, but utilizes lightweight torpedoes in the ASW role. [Ref 25, USN Fact File, 2008] Given their limited sonobuoy inventory, the S-3 Vikings are typically called upon to localize and attack submarine threats initially detected by other platforms.

The SH-60B helicopters utilize sonobuoys and the AN/ASQ-81 Magnetic Anomaly Detection (MAD) System. [Ref 26, Jane's Fighting Ships, 2008] [Ref 27, Jane's Fighting Ships, 2008] The SH-60F variant replaces the sonobuoys with the AN/AQS-13 dipping sonar with ranges up to 20 nm. Both SH-60 aircraft use lightweight torpedoes and depth bombs as ASW weapons. The S-3's have been by and large phased out of the ASW role, whereby the SH-60 helicopters dominate the CSG ASW role of aircraft engagement of an SSK.

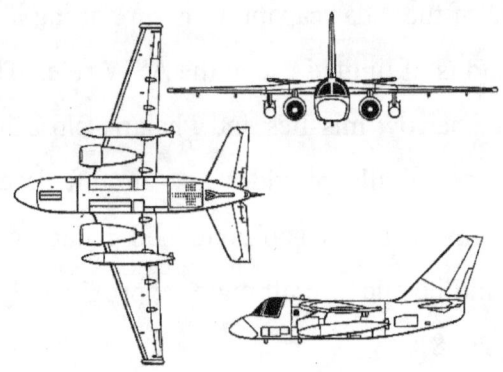

Figure 16 - S-3 Viking [Ref 25, USN Fact File, 2008]

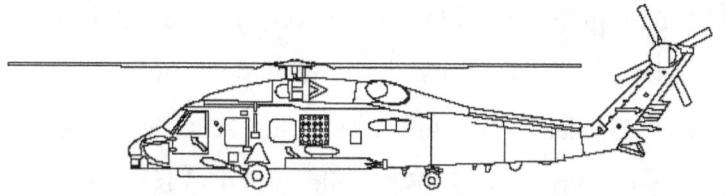

Figure 17 - SH-60 [Ref 26, Jane's Fighting Ships, 2008]

The CSG will typically include four surface combatants. These combatants will include, at a minimum, three Cruiser/Destroyers (CG/DDG) with AEGIS air warfare capability and one CG/DDG with the Multi-Function Towed Array (MFTA) sonar upgrade to its existing AN/SQS-53 active-passive sonar system. [Ref 28, Jane's Fighting Ships, 2008]

The Ticonderoga (AEGIS) Class (CG) Cruisers, Figure 18, are designed to provide a highly capable air warfare platform. [Ref 29, USN Reserve Intelligence Program, 2007] The CG Class is equipped with the state-of-the-art SPY-1 phased array radar system that forms the backbone of the AEGIS Anti-Air Warfare (AW) weapon system. The SPY-1 is a high powered radar capable of acquiring and tracking over 100 targets at extended ranges. The CG Class carries an extensive array of weapons including surface-to-air missiles, surface-to-surface missiles, anti-submarine missiles, Tomahawk missiles and guns. [Ref 30, Jane's Fighting Ships, 2008] These Cruisers also carry SH-60 helicopters. The helicopters and Anti-Submarine Rocket (ASROC) missiles are their primary ASW offensive tools. [Ref 31, Jane's Fighting Ships, 2008]

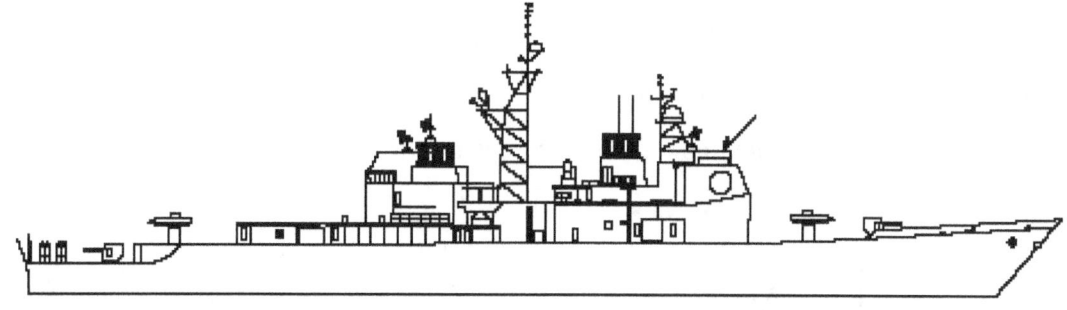

Figure 18 - Ticonderoga Class Cruiser (CG) [Ref 30, Jane's Fighting Ships, 2008]

The Arleigh Burke Class destroyer, Figure 19 is a high speed multi-mission guided missile destroyer (DDG). [Ref 32, Jane's Fighting Ships, 2008] Like the larger cruisers the DDG Class it is built around the AEGIS weapons system. [Ref 34, USN Reserve Intelligence Program, 2007] While the DDG is a capable strike and anti-air warfare platform, the destroyer is one of the CSGs primary anti-submarine assets. At least one of the DDG destroyers assigned to the CSG will be equipped with the Multi-Function Towed Array. This upgrade to the DDG Class standard Towed Array sonar system offers improved ASW acoustics tracking and detection. These vessels use their embarked SH-60 helicopters and ASROC missiles as their primary ASW weapons.

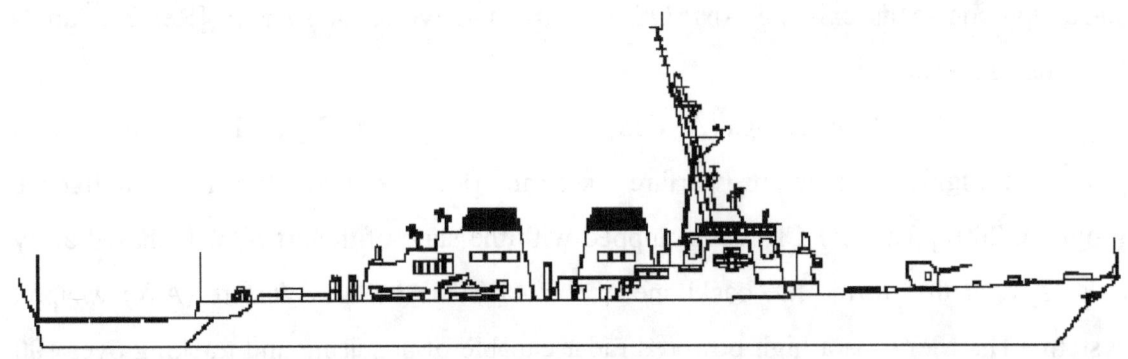

Figure 19 - Arleigh Burke Class Destroyer (DDG) [Ref 32, Jane's Fighting Ships, 2008]

The CSG will also include one Fast Combat Support Ship (AOE), Figure 20. [Ref 33, USNR, 2007] These vessels carry the vast amounts of fuel and ammunition stores needed to resupply the forward deployed CSG. The presence of these ships provides key logistics capability for the forward endurance of the CSG. These AEO vessels have limited sensor capabilities and only defensive weapons. From an ASW perspective the AEO are potential targets that pose no threat to the hostile submarine.

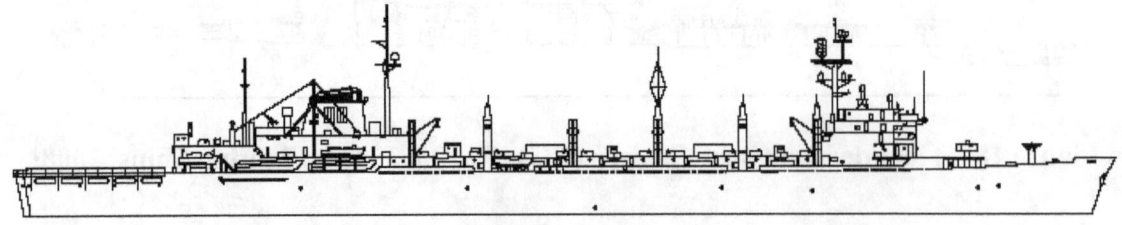

Figure 20 - Sacramento Class AOE [Ref 33, USNR, 2007]

The CSG will be supported by at least one Fast Attack Submarine. The submarine will typically patrol just outside of the CSG's OA to prevent interfering with the group's ASW efforts and minimizing the potential for friendly fire incidents. The Los Angeles Class submarine (SSN) [Ref 34, Jane's Fighting Ships, 2008], Figure 21, is the backbone of the fast attack submarine fleet, far more numerous than the Seawolf [Ref 35, Jane's Fighting Ships, 2008] or Virginia [Ref 36, Jane's Fighting Ships, 2008] Classes. All United States Navy fast attack submarines are advanced ASW platforms with sophisticated hull mounted and towed sonar systems and heavyweight torpedoes. While the specific capabilities are highly classified, it is well known these SSN are capable of detecting, prosecuting and destroying virtually any vessel above or below the sea.

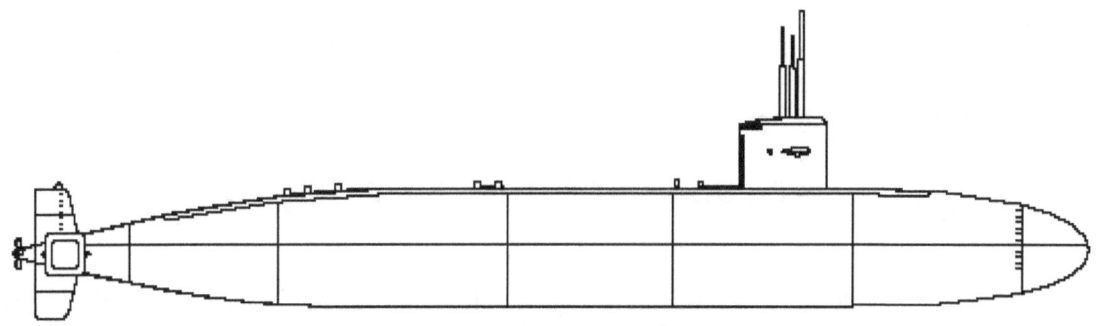

Figure 21 - Los Angeles Class Submarine (SSN) [Ref 34, Jane's Fighting Ships, 2008]

The CSG will have the support of one P-3 Orion Maritime Patrol aircraft, Figure 22. These shore based aircraft will be rotationally deployed in-theater to provide ASW support. Originally developed as a long range ASW platform the P-3's role has expanded to include surveillance of the battlespace over land as well as at sea. The Orion's sensors include a large array of sonobuoys, radar and a Magnetic Anomaly Detector. Offensive ASW capabilities are afforded by depth bombs, lightweight torpedoes and mines. [Ref 37, Jane's Fighting Ships, 2008] [Ref 38, Jane's Fighting Ships, 2008]

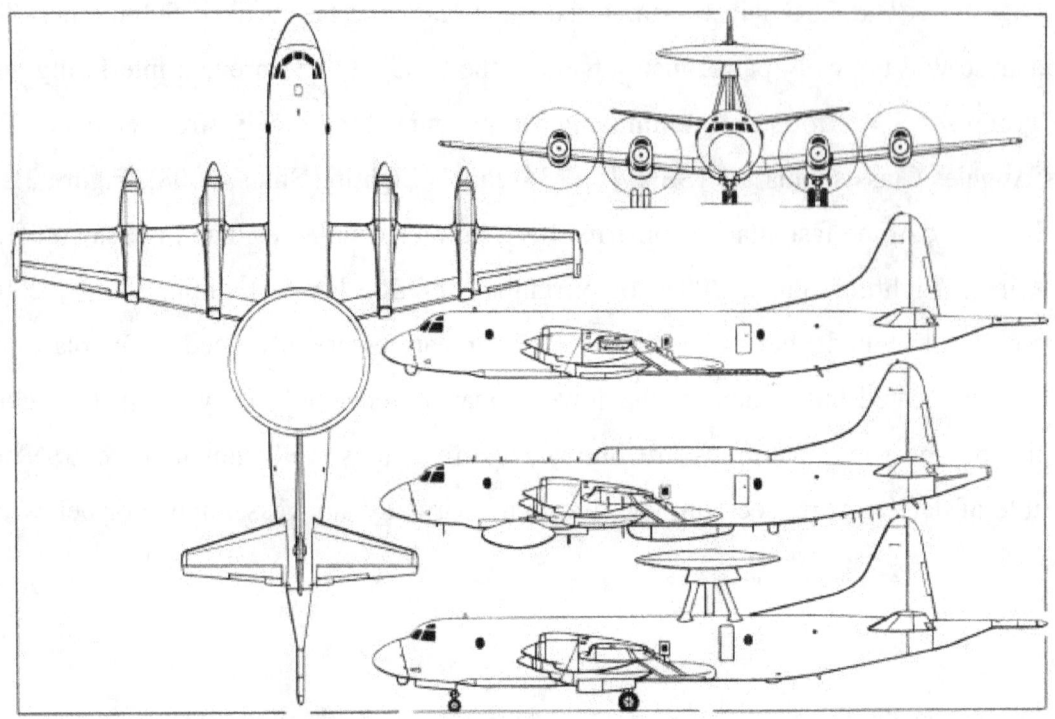

Figure 22 - P-3 Orion [Ref 38, Jane's Fighting Ships, 2008]

For the purposes of this study, a calendar year 2013 notional ASW Threat to the CSG is defined as a Conventional Submarine (SSK). The wide proliferation of these advanced, quiet, diesel-electric submarines highlights their role as the primary threat of concern. Two examples of threats of concern are the Russian KILO class SSK, due to its widespread use, and the Chinese SONG class SSK.

The Russian Kilo class SSK is currently in use by the Russian, Indian, Chinese, Iranian, Polish and Romanian navies. [Ref 39, Jane's Underwater Warfare Systems, 2008] Its advanced MGK-400EM Sonar is capable of detecting surface ships at ranges greater than 40 miles and submarines at ranges beyond 10 miles. Their TEST-71 torpedoes carry a 205 kg warhead and have a 20 nautical mile range.

The Chinese SONG class SSK is an indigenously produced submarine incorporating German diesel and French sonar technology. [Ref 40, Jane's Underwater Warfare Systems, 2008] The French TSM 2225 Sonar provides advanced search and targeting capabilities. Its Russian design Yu-3/4 torpedoes are capable of running to 8 nautical miles and carry a 100kg warhead. [Ref 41, Jane's Underwater Warfare Systems, 2008]

The focus of the CSG is the Aircraft Carrier; all other platforms are included to support its operation. The typical CSG OA is defined by a 30 x 30 nautical mile area that offers the most advantageous operational environment: assumed in this report to be an open ocean environment having acoustically isotropic bathymetry characteristics. The Aircraft Carrier maintains a constant forward motion of roughly 15 knots, changing heading to remain within the OA, while launching and recovering aircraft. When compared to the SSK, the CSGs higher speed will limit the primary threat area to a forward cone projected in front of the CSG, bounded by limiting lines of approach. Few threat submarines can close on the strike group from a chasing approach; thus, ASW defense in close proximity to the CSG formation is greatly characterized by the forward area projected between the limiting lines of approach. Figure 23 provides a plan view geographic depiction of the CSG formation, friendly SSN, and a threat SSK (note the MPA is not explicitly shown, although MPA support for the CSG OA is assumed).

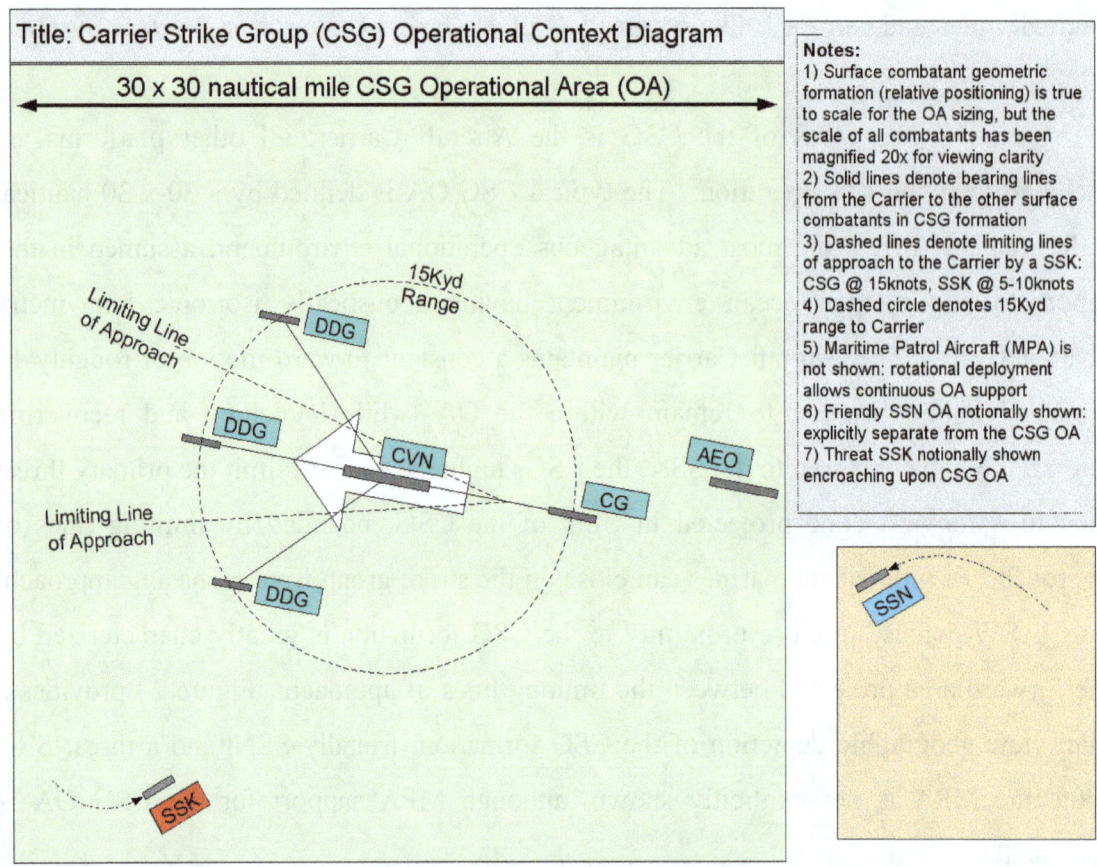

Figure 23 - Carrier Strike Group Notional Configuration

With its extended range and loitering capability the P-3 MPA has the capacity to remain on station over the CSG OA for prolonged periods, providing wide area protection for the CSG while it is on station. Longer term coverage will require rotating in-theater MPA assets so as to support the CSG over the nominal 14-day period. The P-3 provides significant ASW sensor capabilities with its large sonar buoy inventory, radar and magnetic anomaly detector. It can also deter or destroy submarine threats with its lightweight torpedoes and mines.

The fast attack SSNs primary advantage is stealth. Its advanced sensors and heavyweight torpedoes are capable of detecting and destroying all known submarine threats. It provides forward scouting and clearing capability, including advance clearing of a prospective OA in advance to CSG arrival, as well as maintaining a defensive posture once on station outside of the current CSG OA.

The guided missile destroyers (DDG) will normally spread out in a picket line covering the forward arc between the limiting lines of approach, at a range of 15Kyd away from the Carrier. The DDG normally provide broad area coverage with their onboard sensors and their embarked Light Airborne Multi-Purpose System (LAMPS) equipped SH-60 ASW helicopters to prosecute contacts of interest. In the 2013 timeframe approximately 1 DDG will have the Multi-Function Towed Array (MFTA) upgrade, offering improved ASW acoustics detection and tracking: this MFTA-equipped DDG will typically take the picket position directly forward of the Carrier. The DDG can directly influence threats with their onboard lightweight torpedoes, but these are primarily utilized for self defense or when the pursuit duration exceeds the helicopters capabilities. The embarked ASW helicopters are very effective influencers with their high closing speed, accurate dipping sonar (i.e. for SSK re-acquire) and onboard weaponry. The primary ASW helicopter limitations are their relatively short loitering capability and wide variety of non-ASW demands on their time: thus, the ASW helicopters are primarily employed in an ASW 'pounce/engage' role, vice an ASW 'search & detect' role. The DDG have Vertical Launch System (VLS) capability with Anti-Submarine Rockets (ASROC) for engaging SSK. The DDG are fast, maneuverable vessels that will break formation and directly pursue a threat if required.

In the CSG context, the guided missile cruiser (CG) is primarily an air defense platform and as such operates in relatively close proximity to the carrier, at a range of 15Kyd directly behind the Carrier. This platform possesses a significant ASW capability. It has advanced onboard sensors and ASW weaponry including VLS ASROC strike capability, as well as embarked LAMPS equipped SH-60 helicopters. The CG will typically perform rear guard ASW coverage and will prosecute targets that penetrate the destroyer's picket line.

Of the 4 DDG/CG surface combatants, at least 3 will have AEGIS air warfare capability with SPY phased array radar fire control systems, enabling effective surface-to-air missile defense.

As a final line of defense the carrier itself has sensors, LAMPS equipped SH-60 helicopters and lightweight torpedoes. As a practical matter, a threat submarine's effective attack range is outside the carrier's defensive radius given the greater range, speed and lethality of the threat SSK launched torpedoes.

2.1.6 Functional Analysis

The purpose of the functional analysis was to decompose the top-level effective need into a series of functions that describe what functions/capabilities must be performed by the system to meet the overall stakeholder need. It is necessary when developing the functional hierarchy, that it shows the "what to do" of the system and not the "how to do it" which would lead to constraining the actual development of the system.

The functional hierarchy and functional flow analysis were conducted using the CSG ASW CONOPS to establish an operational context while seeking the functional definition necessary to meet the "Improve ASW to protect the CSG" effective need. This capability, reflected by the results of our stake holder analysis, requires that four key supporting functions be provided if we are to realize this goal. As shown in Figure 24, these key functions are Detect, Track/Localize, Classify, and Engage. The following paragraphs will describe each of these functions and their associated sub-functions in more detail.

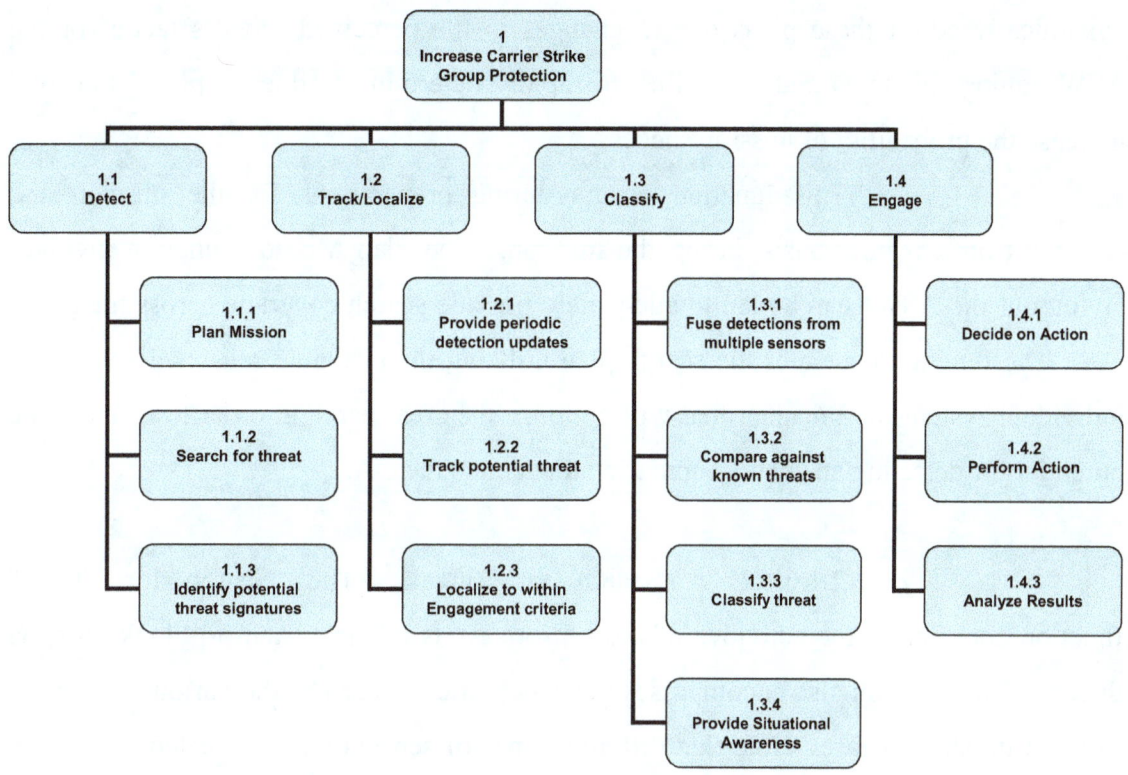

Figure 24 - ASW Functional Hierarchy

2.1.6.1 Detect

The Detect function covers all aspects of the system required to find the threat. As shown in Figure 24, the detection function can be further decomposed into three sub-functions: Planning the mission; Searching for the threat; and identifying potential threat signatures. Descriptions of these sub-functions are shown in the paragraphs below.

2.1.6.1.1 Plan Mission. The ASW operational capability package that this Systems Engineering Development process is defining is likely to be a complex system that incorporates both sensing and influence capability that will be implemented in a squadron of vessels. Based on stakeholder interviews, a mission planning capability will be needed to improve the quality of employment plans developed by the crew in response to higher level tasking. These plans will likely include optimal sensor placement and settings to improve the likelihood of contact detection, the ability to dynamically adjust these plans due to changes in the perceived threat's tactics or the ASW equipment status and the ability to rapidly determine 'influence plans' that will increase the probability of mission success.

This function occurs during preparations for the mission and continues on a regular basis during the mission. The Plan Mission function involves laying out the ASW search plan to adequately provide search coverage across the entire OA. The function generates the search plan utilizing the available sensors/assets in the individual systems in a manner that will optimize the area search in order to increase the potential for detecting an enemy submarine that enters the OA.

2.1.6.1.2 Search for Threat. The "Search for Threat" function coordinates the activities of the sensors/assets of the system to "look" for the threat. This function also encompasses the capabilities of each of the various sensors to find the threat signature. Note that different types of sensors will be treated differently and that multiple methods may be utilized to support this function.

2.1.6.1.3 Identify Potential Threat Signatures. This "Identify Potential Threat Signatures" function covers that actual detection of the submarine. In this function, the data provided by the system sensors/assets is processed to distinguish the actual "signature" of the platform from the clutter and other background noise captured by the sensor

2.1.6.2 Track/ Localize

2.1.6.2.1 Provide Periodic Detection Updates. Once the potential threat has been identified, this function provides periodic updates on the threat characteristics. These characteristics can include speed, bearing from battle group, and threat bands identified.

2.1.6.2.2 Track Potential Threat. This function takes information provided by the periodic updates and begins to track the potential threat.

This function allows the system to "forecast" the position of the system for a given timeframe.

2.1.6.2.3 Localize to Within Engagement Criteria. The "Localize to Within Engagement Criteria" function takes the potential threat track updates and identifies the treat location with respect to the Battle Group. The location of the threat must be known within an Area of Uncertainty (AOU) that supports the selected engagement action.

2.1.6.3 Classify

2.1.6.3.1 Fuse Detection from Multiple Sensors. This function takes the detections and track updates from the various sensors and system assets and fuses them together to better identify the potential threat.

2.1.6.3.2 Compare against Known Threats. Following the fusion of the data from multiple sensors/assets, it is necessary to compare that data against known data collected about specific threats. The known data can be based on previous encounters with the threat or by specific intelligence collection efforts.

2.1.6.3.3 Classify Threat. Once the comparison is finished it is necessary to classify the potential threat. This classification of the threat can take one of three values; hostile threat, unknown, friendly forces. This function is one of the most important for this system as the decision to engage or not engage the potential threat will be based upon the classification. If the wrong classification is made, the consequences can be disastrous as it would lead to either engaging a target that was not actually a threat or by allowing a hostile threat to get closer to the battlegroup by misidentifying it as a friendly.

2.1.6.3.4 Provide Situational Awareness. This function provides an overall accurate picture of the battlespace, allowing the command structure to have an overall awareness of the tactical picture. The function would, at a minimum, provide a description of the battlegroup, its performance, and the location of all contacts being tracked by the system.

2.1.6.4 Engage

2.1.6.4.1 Decide on Action. This function analyzes all of the potential engagement options that can be applied against a specific threat. The function would assess the potential for destroying the threat and/or rendering it incapable of completing its mission, either result increasing the survivability of the carrier strike group.

2.1.6.4.2 Perform Action. This function performs the selected engagement action, coordinating the operation of the various assets in the battlegroup to complete the action.

2.1.6.4.3 Analyze Results. These functions assess the outcome of the engagement and determine whether the target needs to be re-engaged in which a new engagement action must be undertaken, or whether the target can be determined to no longer be a threat to the battle group.

2.2 VALUE SYSTEM DESIGN

Value System Design forms the foundation of criterion through which alternatives are assessed and ultimately modeled for suitability and compliance with user needs. In entering this phase of the analysis, the outcome of the needs analysis was the revised problem statement (i.e. effective need), which was stated as follows:

> *"An improved ASW system is needed to protect carrier strike groups from enemy attack through effective, timely, and precise engagement by providing tactically significant detection, localization, tracking, and classification of quiet acoustic threat submarines in challenging environments"*

The newly defined effective need now serves as the starting point for the value hierarchy. Research supporting the stakeholder analysis, discussed in section 2.1.2, identified the capabilities the customer wanted in the system. A top level objective for the system was defined to capture the effectiveness of the system. The hierarchy for the performance objectives is shown in Figure 25.

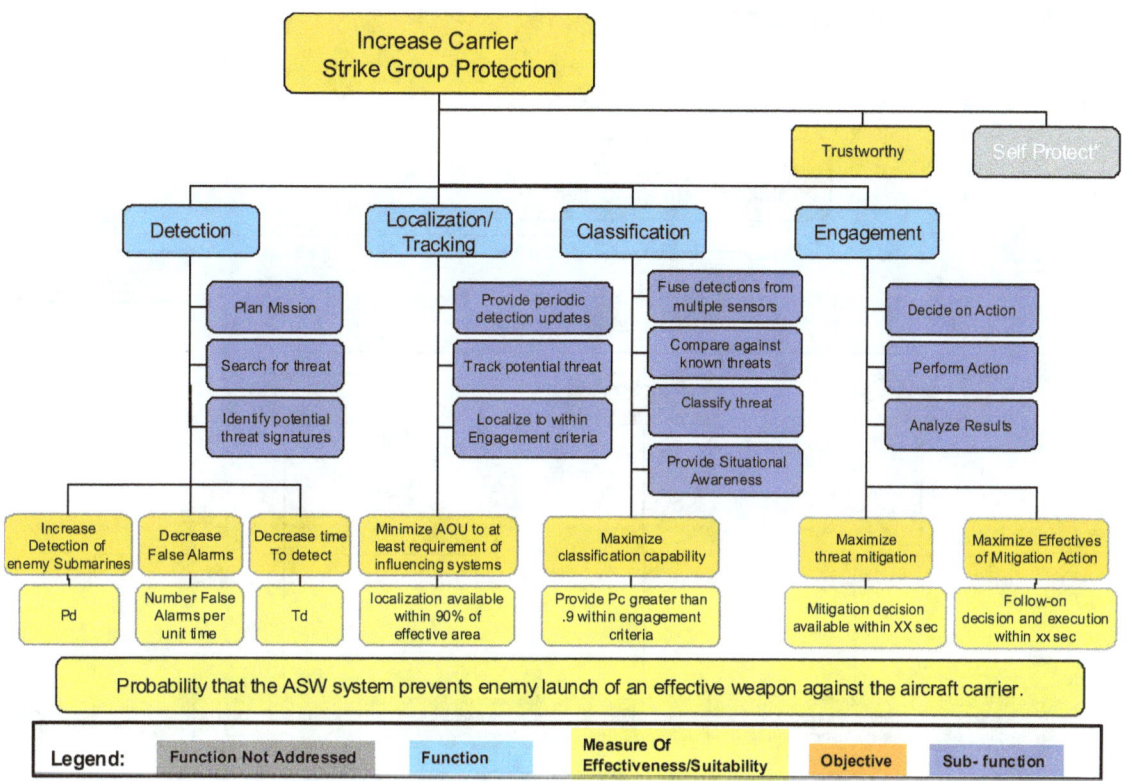

Figure 25 - Performance Objectives Hierarchy

Additionally, it was noted that based on stakeholder input, and common sense, that a suitability aspect was needed to help fully define the overall capability of the system. In addition to achieving an effective operating performance, the system needs to be capable of being operated by the Fleet in the environment it was made for, and reliably throughout the mission. The Objectives Hierarchy for Suitability is shown in Figure 26.

As can be seen in Figure 26, Suitability covers the underlying features that can make or break a system, including supportability, reliability, and training. No matter how well this system will be able to detect submarines, if it is not available when the threat enters detection range or the operator cannot properly utilize the system to identify the threat, the overall effect would be the same as if the system was not there. The factors that make up the suitability aspects will never be given as the reason that a system is good, however they are the factors most likely encountered by the operator and will be noticed if they are not satisfactory.

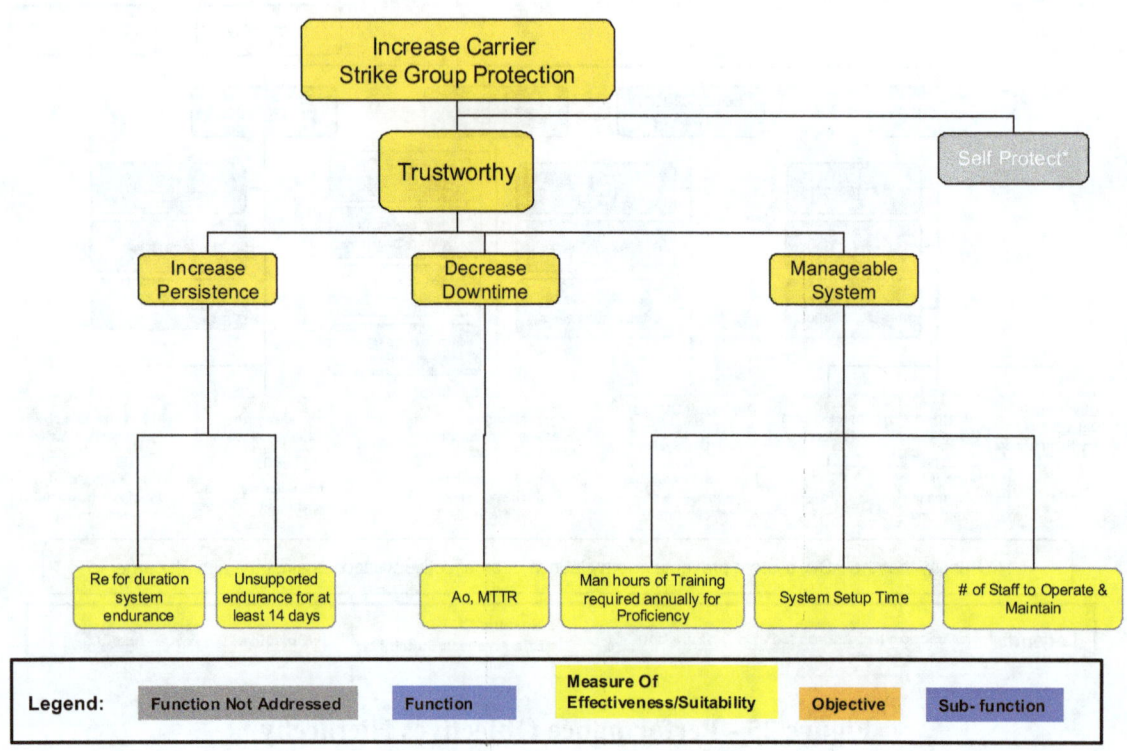

Figure 26 - Suitability Objectives Hierarchy

The main items to be modeled for determining the recommended alternative will be the top-level objectives for both performance and suitability. The objectives were further decomposed to next level to provide the components that make up the top-level objective and to be able to give insight into the individual pieces should the need arise during decision making The individual objectives and associated performance measures will be discussed in the following paragraphs. Following discussion of the individual measures, there is a discussion on the weighting of each of the measures during the decision making process.

2.2.1 Performance Objectives Hierarchy

As shown in Figure 25, the overall effectiveness objective was to "*Increase Carrier Strike Group Protection*". The effectiveness portion of each system will be evaluated using the measure "***Probability that the ASW system prevents enemy launch of an effective weapon against the aircraft carrier.***" This means that the success of the system will be directly related to the capability of the system to disrupt the threat sensor to shooter timeline. It should be stated that preventing an enemy launch of a weapon against the carrier does not necessarily require destruction of the threat submarine. Any interruption into the threat timeline that results in no shot taken against the carrier strike group results in a "win" for the top-level metric described above.

The system will be assessed on its performance against the top-level metric shown above. In cases where the overall performance against that metric is close, assessments against the lower level metrics will be undertaken as to be able to provide distinguishing characteristics among the alternatives. These lower-level metrics were decomposed from the top-level metric and are discussed in the following paragraphs.

2.2.1.1 *Detection Performance Objectives*

Three performance objectives were defined for the Detection Function: Increased Detection of Submarines, Decrease False Alarms, and Decrease Time to Detect. A description of these objectives and the associated metrics are listed below:

- Increased Detection of Submarines – By increasing detection performance, there are more opportunities for the threat to be found and countered. This objective will be measured by the metric, Probability of Detection.
- Decreased False Alarms – Reducing the number of false alarms from the detection processing allows for the operator and ship decision making team to concentrate on resolving the status of known threats only. This will be measured by the number of False alarms per unit time or False Alarm Rate.

- Increased Range at Detection – Increasing the range at which the initial opportunity to detect occurs allows for either more time for the remaining steps in the detect-to-engage sequence or for a longer range at which to intercept the threat. This will be evaluated using detection range Rd.

2.2.1.2 Localization/Tracking Performance Objectives

A single performance objective was identified for this function. The objective, minimize the Area of Uncertainty (AOU) to the requirement of the influencing systems, was defined to have the localization of the contact being tracked to be within the requirements of an individuals influencing systems. The lower the AOU for a contact, the better chance that the influencing system will be deployed appropriately to counter the threat. This objective will be measured by having the localization within 90% of the effective area of the influencing system.

2.2.1.3 Classification Performance Objectives

A single performance objective, Maximize Classification Capability, was identified for this function. Maximizing the classification capability allows for a higher percentage of all contacts to be correctly identified as friendly or threat. The criteria for this objective are for the Probability of Classification greater than 0.9 within the recommended engagement criteria. Based on the results of the affinity diagramming portion of the needs analysis and utilizing the ASW-related expertise resident within the CAPSTONE project group, the 0.9 Probability of correct classification was deemed to be a reasonable measure of performance to support the overall objective of the system.

2.2.1.4 Engagement Performance Objectives

Two performance objectives, Maximize Threat Mitigation and Maximize Effectiveness of Mitigation Action, were identified for this function. The first objective, Maximize Threat Mitigation, is a time based criteria limiting the time needed to make a mitigation decision from the options presented by each alternative. It will be measured by the time required to make the mitigation decision.

The second objective, Maximize Effectiveness of Mitigation Action, is another time-based criterion. Increasing the mitigation effectiveness reduces the number of attempts needed to eliminate the threat. This will be measured by the amount of time needed to decide and execute the next course of action.

2.2.1.5 *Self Protect*

During our functional analysis review, members of the system engineering team discussed the possible incorporation of a terminal defense capability against incoming weapons. This function is a natural element of the layered defense concept and is included in our objectives hierarchy in acknowledgement of the potential contribution to the overall Measure of Effectiveness. For our problem domain, the most likely attacks from submarines are those conducted utilizing an anti-ship missile or those conducted using submarine launched torpedoes.

The submarine launched anti-ship missile defense system is considered a part of the larger air defense system by our engineering team. The ability to track opposing force submarines with a high degree of reliability at appropriate ranges could contribute to this defense by reducing the potential of a surprise missile launch. This capability, however, is considered outside the scope of this engineering analysis problem as the Measure of Effectiveness is to reduce the likelihood of an effective torpedo launch against the aircraft carrier. A solution that provides tracking and engagement capability at ranges beyond the effective missile launch range would be desirable to support this mode of self defense.

Defense against a torpedo launch was considered but deemed outside the scope of our engineering analysis due to the lack of adequate tools for modeling this rapid time sequence of events and possible classification issues. Analysis of the performance of a torpedo defense system would require the ability to perform time domain analysis of the following parameters:

- Enemy submarine CVN localization accuracy capability
- Enemy submarine torpedo launch reliability
- Enemy torpedo target acquisition and homing capability

- Enemy torpedo detonation reliability
- CVN Maneuver Tactics
- Torpedo Detection and Tracking System capability
- Torpedo influence, either counter measure or anti-torpedo torpedo performance

Based on the limitation of available modeling and analysis tools, the system engineering team recommends that a follow on study be conducted in this functional area should the results of the submarine track and engagement capabilities not provide sufficient performance to meet customer needs.

2.2.2 Suitability Objectives Hierarchy

As shown in Figure 28, the key suitability performance measure for the overall *"Increase Carrier Strike Group Protection"* objective is that the system is *"Trustworthy"*. Trustworthy means that the system will operate when needed by trained Fleet operators throughout the length of the mission. It will be assessed through the evaluation of lower-level objectives. These objectives will be described in the next paragraph.

2.2.2.1 Increase Persistence

The first suitability objective is to increase persistence, resulting in reliable performance throughout the mission period. It is necessary for the system to be operational across a 14 day mission described in the CONOPs. For the system to have maximum effectiveness, it needs to be operational with no system failures during the mission. The criterion to be evaluated for this objective is the Reliability (Re) for system and unsupported endurance across a nominal 14 day mission.

2.2.2.2 Decrease Downtime

The second suitability objective is to decrease downtime, or to maximize system availability. This metric applies when maintenance and recovery actions need to be taken. The criterion used for this objective is Operational Availability (Ao) defined as the uptime over total mission time.

2.2.2.3 Manageable System

The final Suitability objective is to have a manageable system. This objective is centered on training, system set-up, manning requirements. If the system cannot be utilized by the Fleet operators or the operator training lacks the necessary instruction, the system will not perform up to the required needs. The criteria for this objective include number of operators needed to operate the system, number of hours of training need by those operators, and the amount of system setup time needed.

2.2.3 Weighting

After finalizing the objectives hierarchy for the system, the next step was to assign weights to each of the objectives. The weights are used to show the relative importance of the objectives with respect to the others. These weights will be utilized when comparing the alternatives to fairly evaluate the attributes of each of the alternatives. The weights are based on the stakeholders' inputs that were discussed earlier in this report. Figure 27 and Figure 28 show the relative weighting of each of the top-level objectives and the total weighting of all the objectives.

The values of the weights were based on the subjective assessment by the team of the stakeholder preferences. It is understood that the values of the individual weights can have an affect on the overall outcome of the alternative assessment. As such, sensitivity analysis of the metrics will be considered.

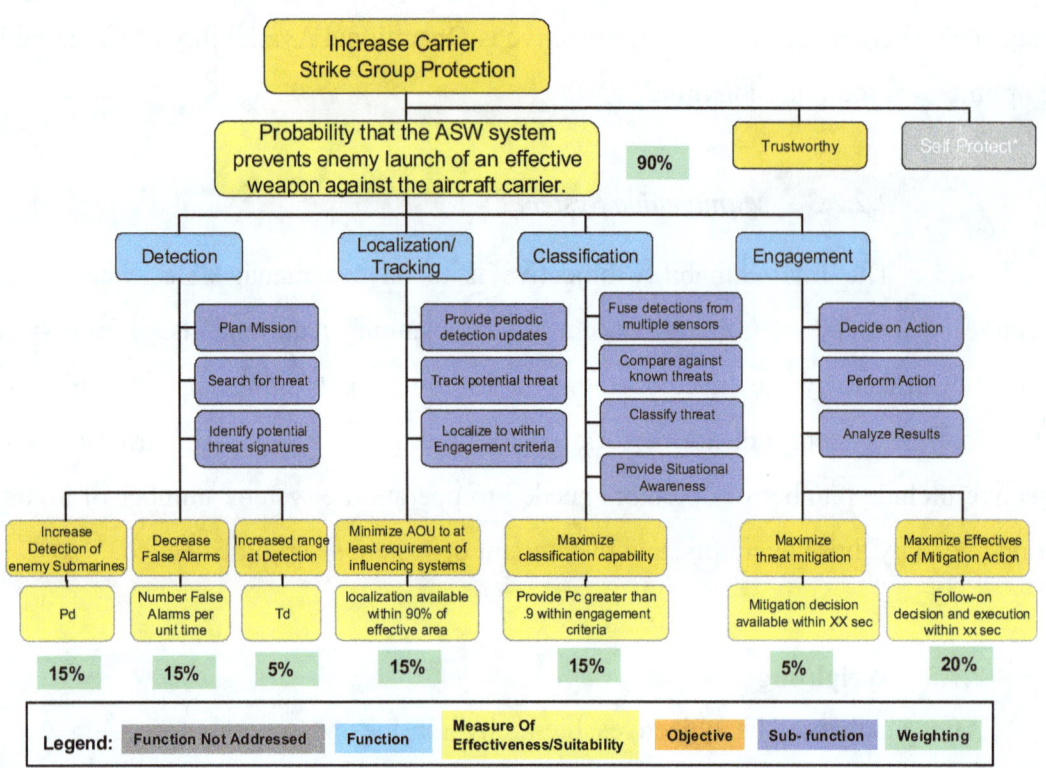

Figure 27 - Performance Objectives Weighting

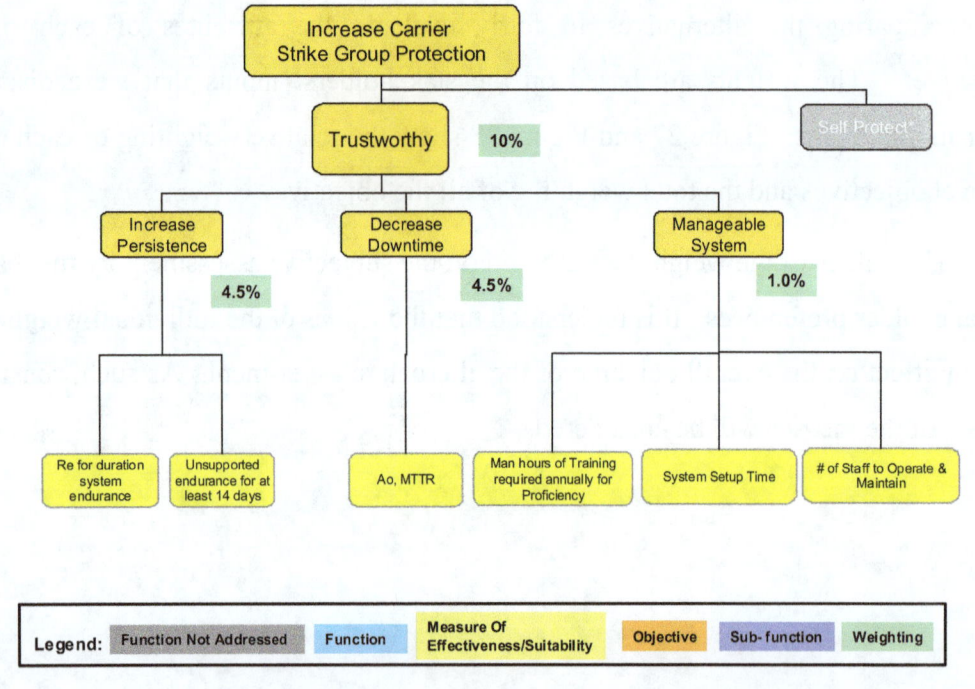

Figure 28 - Suitability Objectives Weighting

As can be seen in the figures, a higher emphasis was placed upon performance of the system with respect to the suitability aspects. As we are developing this system for an IOC in 2013, it is expected that the suitability of the system will meet the requirements needed or can be worked during the production phase. The weighting of the lower level objectives are also shown. This was done as stated above as a discriminator in the case where two systems exhibit similar performance. We believe that the most important system objectives are first, to find the threat, and then to effectively engage the threat. Therefore these top level objectives are given the highest individual weights, 30% and 25% respectively.

For the suitability objectives, it was deemed that the reliability and persistence/availability of the system were more important objectives for the system at this juncture of the project than the training aspects provided by the alternatives.

Through the application of systems engineering processes and tools, the team has produced those products associated with the Needs Analysis phase of the SEDP that are necessary to proceed to the Design and Analysis Phase. The creation of the Effective Needs Statement and the formulation of the Objectives Hierarchy mark critical steps in the systems engineering process and require review and approval by decision makers. These products form the basis for the generation of alternatives under the Design and Analysis Phase. Alternatives that satisfy the key functional needs of the system are synthesized and evaluated in accordance with the performance measures identified in the objectives hierarchy. Systems engineering tools creative process are key to the generation of a range of alternatives that may show promise in the satisfaction of customer needs. Screening of these candidates for feasibility and generations of metrics for alternatives deemed feasible during the Design and Analysis phase requires the generation, gathering and analysis of quantitative data during this phase. These steps will be described in detail in Chapter 3 of this report.

THIS PAGE INTENTIONALLY LEFT BLANK

3 DESIGN AND ANALYSIS

3.1 ALTERNATIVES GENERATION

An important step in the Design and Analysis Phase of the SEDP is the generation of viable system alternatives that are screened for feasibility and passed on to the modeling team for analysis and comparison. Several alternatives were generated based on their ability to meet the effective need of the system as described in Section 2.1.2.3. Our team did not place any design constraints while generating alternatives. The following sections describe the alternatives generation process, feasibility screening, results, and also provide a brief description of each alternative. The baseline and three alternatives were selected for modeling and analysis and are described with additional details.

3.1.1 Alternatives Generation Process

Alternatives Generation was conducted to arrive at candidate solutions that address the system objectives developed during the Problem Definition Phase. Alternatives Generation utilized several popular SEDP techniques to explore solution alternatives for the system under consideration. The alternatives generation consisted of three phases. The first phase was a group brainstorming session. The next phase used a modified morphological box to derive alternatives. The final phase was a feasibility screening used to narrow down the number of systems that would be modeled and analyzed against each other.

The goal of our alternative generation working group was to provide several potential solutions in addition to the baseline 'Do Nothing' alternative. The group consensus was to apply a screening process to reduce the candidate pool to the top three alternatives, along with the baseline system. The following sections describe the process utilized to define and screen the alternatives.

3.1.1.1 Organized Brainstorming

Our system engineering design team formed an alternatives generation working group tasked to get together and brainstorm various alternatives for the improved ASW effectiveness system. Our goal was to think outside the box and not limit any ideas to preconceived notions or solutions consisting of solely existing systems. We utilized our objectives hierarchy and our functional descriptions as the basis for coming up with several ideas. We utilized information found on the internet, inputs from stakeholders and other systems currently employed in ASW as inputs to a modified morphological box (matrix of functional components utilized to organize logical alternatives). Our team applied group techniques for open exploration of solution elements that address each critical system objective.

3.1.1.2 Zwicky's Morphological Box

Our group decided to utilize a Zwicky's Morphological Box (ZMB) to gather brainstorming results for objective-elements, and group these into 'alternatives' that address all system objective categories. [Ref 6, Sage and Armstrong, 2000] Since our alternatives consisted of several grouped objects in each row that formed a system of systems, we were not able to employ a traditional ZMB. The rows we created in the morphological box consisted of system components (various platforms, each with a possible combination of functional components) that could be logically grouped together to form our various system alternatives.

The columns in our ZMB were chosen to represent the platforms, quantity and the four major functions of our ASW System (Detection, Track, Localization and Engagement). The result of several brainstorming sessions was the creation of the modified Zwicky's Morphological Box shown in Figure 29 below. A detailed description of each of these 13 alternatives is found in Section 3.1.2. Each of the alternatives went through a feasibility screening process to determine which ones would be provided to the modeling team for performance analysis.

Alt	Type	Platform	Quantity	Detect Capability	Localize/Track	Classify	Engage Capability
BL	Materiel (Baseline)	DDG/CG	4	Hull Active and Passive Arrays	Legacy Processing	Legacy Processing	Countermeasures
				Towed Passive Array	Complete Data Fusion	Complete Data Fusion	ATT/CVLWT
				MFTA (MF Bi-Statics) Upgrade (on 1 combatants)			Mk-46 Torpedo
				RADAR (AEGIS/SPY on 3 combatants)			Mk-54 Torpedo
				ESM (Electronic Surveillance Measures)			Verticle Launch ASROC (VLA)
				Visual			Gun
				OTS Buoys			Evade
							Decoy
		CVN	1	RADAR	Legacy Processing	Legacy Processing	Evade
				ESM	Complete Data Fusion	Complete Data Fusion	Decoy
		MPA (Pouncer)	14-Day In-Theater Support	DIFAR/DICASS Buoys	Legacy Processing	Legacy Processing	ATT/CVLWT
				APS 137 PDR	Complete Data Fusion	Complete Data Fusion	Mk-46
				Distant Thunder (Bi-Statics)			Mk-54
				EER Buoy Concept			Decoy
				Digital Magnetic Anomaly Detection (MAD)			
		Helo (Pouncer)	10 (collectively)	DIFAR/DICASS Buoys	Legacy Processing	Legacy Processing	ATT/CVLWT
				Dipping SONAR	LAMPS	LAMPS	Mk-46
				ESM			Mk-54
				RADAR			Decoy
1	Non-Materiel (added to baseline)	Sub	Re-assign SSN to the CSG formation	ESM	Legacy Processing	Legacy Processing	MK48 ADCAP
				Sphere Passive and Active	Improved Processing	Improved Processing	ATT/CVLWT
				LAB Array	Complete Data Fusion	Complete Data Fusion	Evade
				Hull Passive (PNB/PBB)			Countermeasures
				HF Passive and Active			
				TB-16/TB-23/TB-29			
				AI&R or (WLR-9)			
				WAA			
2	Materiel (added to Baseline)	Commercial Craft	Add one Commercial Craft to CSG formation	DWADS	COTS/NDI	Leverage Surrogate	Mk-46 Torpedo
				Commercial Sonar			Mk-54 Torpedo
		UAV	Add to CSG inventory	MVCS			Countermeasures
				EPAS (Electro Optical)	COTS/NDI	Leverage Surrogate	
3	Materiel (added to Baseline)	Commercial Craft	Commercial Craft in CSG Op Area (not in formation)	DWADS	COTS/NDI	Leverage Surrogate	Mk-46 Torpedo
				Commercial Sonar			Mk-54 Torpedo
							Countermeasures
		Jet Ski	Commercial	Towed Sonar	COTS/NDI	Leverage Surrogate	
4	Materiel (revision to Baseline)	MPA	14-Day In-Theater Support	DIFAR/DICASS Buoys	Legacy Processing	Legacy Processing	ATT/CVLWT
				APS 137 PDR	Improved Processing	Improved Processing	HAAWC
				Distant Thunder (Bi-Statics)	Complete Data Fusion	Complete Data Fusion	Mk-46
				EER Buoy Concept			Mk-54
				Network Enabled ASW System (NEASW)			Mk-48 ADCAP
				Digital Magnetic Anomaly Detection (MAD)			Nuclear Weapon
							Decoy
				EPAS (Electro Optical)	COTS/NDI	Leverage Surrogate	HAAWC (High Altitude ASW Weapon - MK54)
5	Materiel (added to Baseline)	Commercial Craft	Commercial Craft in CSG Op Area (not in formation)	DWADS	COTS/NDI	Leverage Surrogate	Verticle Launch ASROC (VLA)
				Commercial Sonar			
		LCS	LCS in Op-Area (not in formation)	NDI Sonar	COTS/NDI	Leverage Surrogate	Evade
6	Materiel (added to Baseline)	Deployed Array	Based on LCS & AEO	Deployed / Moored Sonar Arrays (perimeter screen)			
		Deployed USV w TA	Based on LCS & AEO	Deployed USV (or UUV) with Forward-Look & Towed Sonar			

65

Alt	Type	Platform	Quantity	Detect Capability	Localize/Track	Classify	Engage Capability
7	Materiel (added to Baseline)	Commercial Craft	Add Craft in 30x30 Op Area	Commercial Sonar	COTS/NDI	Leverage Surrogate	
		Deployed USV w TA	Commercial Craft deploy	USV with Forward-Look & Towed Sonar	COTS/NDI	Leverage Surrogate	
8	Materiel (acquisition)	Accelerate ASW Program of Record (POR) capabilities to fulfill anticipated CY2013 shortfalls (e.g. accelerate acquisition/production to meet 2013 fielding). An example is acceleration of Advanced Processing Build (APB) updates to DDG Sonar. Also see Alt					
9	Materiel (added to Baseline)	SURTASS integration with CSG	Existing In-Theater SURTASS	SURTASS LFA (i.e. improve sharing of SURTASS 'results' from existing Shore/Surrogate to CSG)	Legacy Processing	Legacy Processing	
					Complete Data Fusion	Complete Data Fusion	
10	Materiel (acquisition)	Revise doctrine for POR (2013) 'pouncer' helicopter to not only engage, but also detect SSK. Increase helicopter procurement to accommodate mission/role expansion, plus materiel update for helicopter detection/re-acquire capabilities (i.e. sonar buoys an					
11	Materiel (deleted from Baseline)	2 DDGs		Hull Active and Passive Arrays. UTAS. MSOBS. UDS. DWADS	LCS and Legacy capability plus data fusion	LCS and Legacy capability plus data fusion	ATT/CVWLT, Mk-46, Mk-54, Mk-48, Depth Charge
		2 LCS	LCS with USV				
		SURTASS integration with CSG	Existing In-Theater SURTASS	SURTASS LFA (i.e. improve sharing of SURTASS 'results' from existing Shore/Surrogate to CSG)	Legacy Processing plus Complete Data Fusion	Legacy Processing plus Complete Data Fusion	
12	Materiel (deleted from Baseline)	2 DDGs		Hull Active and Passive Arrays. UTAS. MSOBS. UDS. DWADS	LCS and Legacy capability plus data fusion	LCS and Legacy capability plus data fusion	ATT/CVWLT, Mk-46, Mk-54, Mk-48, Depth Charge
		2 LCS	LCS with USV				
	Materiel (Added to Baseline)	Commercial Craft	Add one Commercial Craft to CSG formation	Commercial Sonar and DWADS	COTS/NDI	Leverage Surrogate	
		Jet Ski	Commercial Craft deploy	Towed Sonar	COTS/NDI	Leverage Surrogate	
13	Materiel (added to Baseline)	HAMR (Hybrid lighter than-air platform)	14-Day In-Theater Support	DIFAR/DICASS Buoys	Legacy Processing	Legacy Processing	Mk-46
				APS 137 PDR	Improved Processing	Improved Processing	Mk-54
				Distant Thunder (Bi-Statics)	Complete Data Fusion	Complete Data Fusion	Mk-48 ADCAP
				EER Buoy Concept			HAAWC
				Network Enabled ASW System (NEASW)			
				Digital Magnetic Anomaly Detection (MAD)			
				EPAS (Electro Optical)			
				Dipping Sonar			

Figure 29 - Modified Zwicky's Morphological Box

3.1.1.3 Feasibility Screening

The next step in the process was to perform a feasibility screening of the alternatives described in Figure 29 above. To do this seven key criteria which included cost, schedule, environmental impact, ability to meet 14-day mission, supported by CSG operations, ability to not degrade other CSG operations, and survivability. These criteria were chosen based on feedback from key stakeholders and their relevance to the alternatives ability to meet the objective of the system. A brief description of each feasibility criteria element and why they were chosen is provided below.

Cost: Cost in Fiscal Year 2008 dollars was chosen as an element based on the fact that the defense budget is not unlimited and an appropriate cap on the price of our system needed to be established. A total procurement cost of less than one billion dollars was utilized. [Ref 72, U.S. DoD, 2004]

Schedule: Our stakeholders indicated that the improved ASW System was required by 2013. This was important since many technologies are not mature enough to be fielded as part of an integrated system within this timeframe.

Environmental Impact: The Navy has become increasingly aware of the potential impacts on the ocean environment of our systems and their components. Since environmental awareness is likely to increase and the Navy's desire to be compliant with current policy, our team felt this was an important element in the screening process. Of primary concern were increases in active signal transmission levels and/or frequencies of occurrence and the potential for disposal of environmentally hazardous materials.

Ability to meet 14-Day Mission: Based on current Concept of Operations, the improved ASW System is expected to have reliability and availability to meet a minimum mission length of 14 days.

Supported by CSG Operations: The ability of the improved ASW System to support CSG Operations is important. If the system does not have the communication links or underway replenishment capabilities currently utilized by the CSG, it will not be considered as viable to this mission.

<u>Does not Degrade other CSG Operations</u>: The primary mission of the CSG is to support aircraft flight operations in a designated open-ocean area. The ability of the CSG to support aircraft takeoffs, landings, logistics, maintenance, and communications must not be diminished by the addition of an improved ASW System. Examples of unacceptable ASW system attributes would be reducing the available runway space, aircraft communication interference, and additional airspace restrictions.

<u>Survivability</u>: The system's ability to survive in the combat environment during the mission is essential. The main aspect considered by this criterion is whether the material making up the alternative has the potential to be easily defeated in a combat situation. To the extreme perspective, an alternative would fail to provide improved CSG ASW capability if oriented around a single immobile platform operating outside the CSG operation area, without its own credible self-defense capability. An alternative containing such architecture would itself require protection services from the CSG or require its own additional defensive capability. If the prospective system could easily be detected and defeated by the enemy threat it would be deemed infeasible for the purposes of the alternative feasibility screening.

We applied a simple Go/No-Go test to each element of the matrix for all the alternatives under consideration. This test was based on all information currently available for each system. In the case where clear evidence did not exist, the team used its best judgment to estimate the likelihood of meeting the particular metric. The results of the feasibility screening are discussed in Section 3.1.3 below.

3.1.2 Individual Alternatives

The alternative generation process detailed in section 3.1.1 resulted in thirteen alternatives to the baseline. A description of each alternative concept is contained in sections 3.1.2.1 through 3.1.2.13. All but two of the proposed alternatives were additive to the existing baseline. Alternatives 11 and 12 replaced two of the existing CSG platforms with alternative vessels. All thirteen of these alternatives were subjected to the feasibility screening process described in section 3.1.3

3.1.2.1 Alternative 1: Re-assign SSN to the CGS Formation

This alternative proposes re-assignment of a USN SSN to operate as part of the CSG formation within the OA. The SSN assignment to the CSG formation would be drawn from the currently planned allocation of in-theater assets: an SSN normally operating outside of the CSG OA. This re-tasking of an existing SSN represents a non-materiel alternative by its reuse of planned/allocated in-theater assets, albeit operational doctrine and training for the entire CSG, SSN included, would require notable revision to facilitate effectiveness.

This alternative seeks to exploit unique capabilities of the SSN platform as a means for improving the overall performance of the CSG ASW within the OA. Improvements would manifest by the addition of another capable ASW platform to the CSG, improving aggregate capabilities in SSK detection, tracking and engagement. Compared to the other CSG surface combatants, SSN flexibility in platform/sensor deployment in the water column could represent an optimal complement in effective search for SSK (e.g. sensor placement to overcome thermocline shadow zones). Figure 30 provides a notional operational context for SSN addition to the CSG formation, whereby the 'forward picket' of 3 surface combatants defined by the CSG baseline (Section 2.1.5) has been augmented with the SSN addition (i.e. a 'forward picket' of 4 platforms).

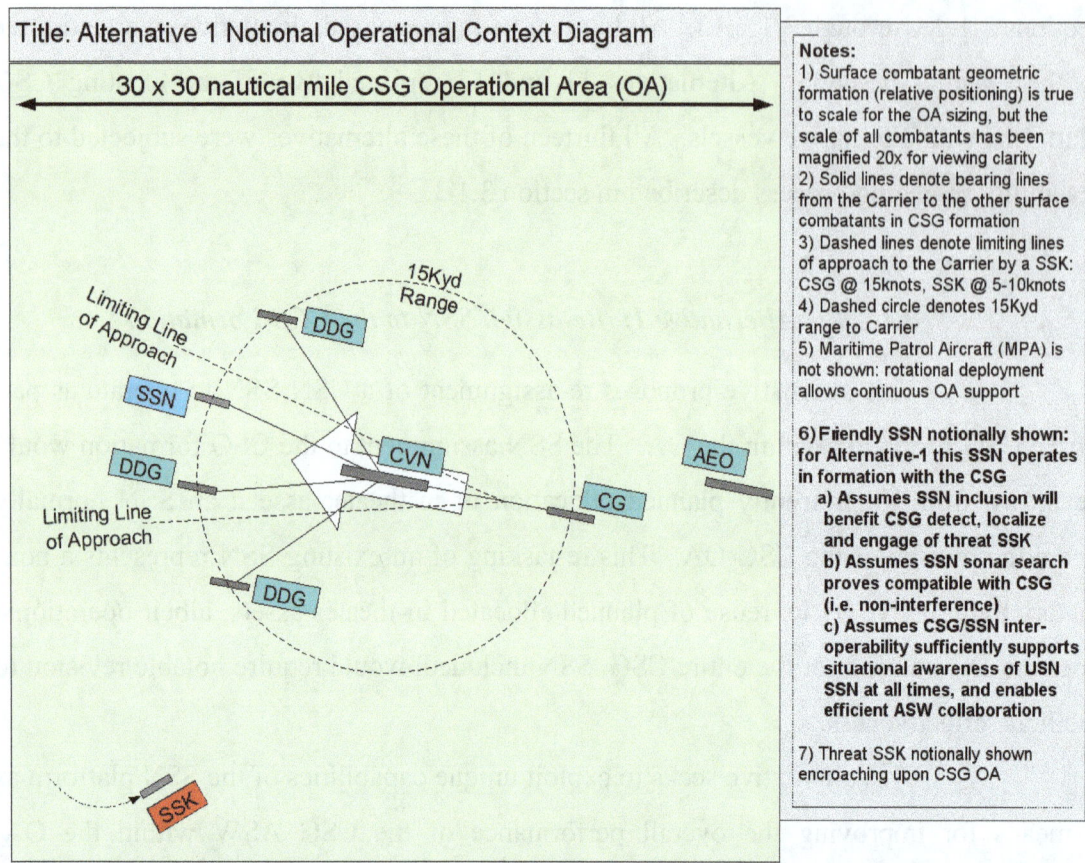

Figure 30 – Alternative 1 Notional Operational Context

    This alternative represents a major departure from existing doctrine by virtue SSN typically operate independent of other surface combatants, greatly exercising self-regulated underway authority as necessary to fulfill objectives established by Fleet theater-level tasking. SSN ASW tasking routinely manifests in assignment to an area outside of the CSG OA, using water-space management as necessary to avert platform interference, freeing the SSN to conduct semi-independent ASW operations to detect/influence threat SSK. In contrast to ASW in a CSG formation where surface combatants rely heavily upon active acoustic search, the SSN would typically conduct ASW search using passive acoustics while maintaining stealth for tactical advantage.

    Further exploration of this alternative would need to assess the overall interoperability among the CSG formation given SSN addition to the group. Key areas to evaluate would be acoustic search modes of operation and performance, and overall CSG situational awareness necessary to ensure safe and efficient ASW collaboration among all assets. The latter facet is particularly crucial in terms of establishing safe operations where absolute geo-spatial knowledge of all friendly assets is paramount to diminishing the probability of fratricide.

Endeavors to improve SSN external 'communications at speed and depth' represents a technology-enabler that could facilitate the necessary interoperability for this alternative. Analysis of current and projected Technical Readiness Level (TRL) for associated capabilities would need to be further explored to establish the overall feasibility and suitability of this alternative.

3.1.2.2 *Alternative 2: Maritime Ship in CSG*

This alternative proposes addition of a surface maritime craft to operate as part of the CSG formation within the OA. Addition of a surface craft to the CSG represents a materiel approach supplementing the existing CSG baseline; thus, an increase in CSG Operations & Support will be necessary to accommodate this alternative. The operational doctrine and training for the entire CSG, inclusive of this surface craft, would require notable revision to facilitate effectiveness.

This alternative seeks to exploit a surface maritime craft with commercial sonar as a means for improving the overall performance of the CSG ASW within the OA, by improving the aggregate CSG capabilities in SSK detection, tracking and engagement. The surface craft would support Unmanned Aerial System (UAS) launch and recovery, organically deploying UAS to provide a remote over-the-horizon ASW detection capability for the CSG. Figure 31 provides a notional operational context for the surface craft in addition to the CSG formation, whereby the 'forward picket' of 3 surface combatants defined by the CSG baseline has been augmented with the surface craft (i.e. a 'forward picket' of 4 platforms).

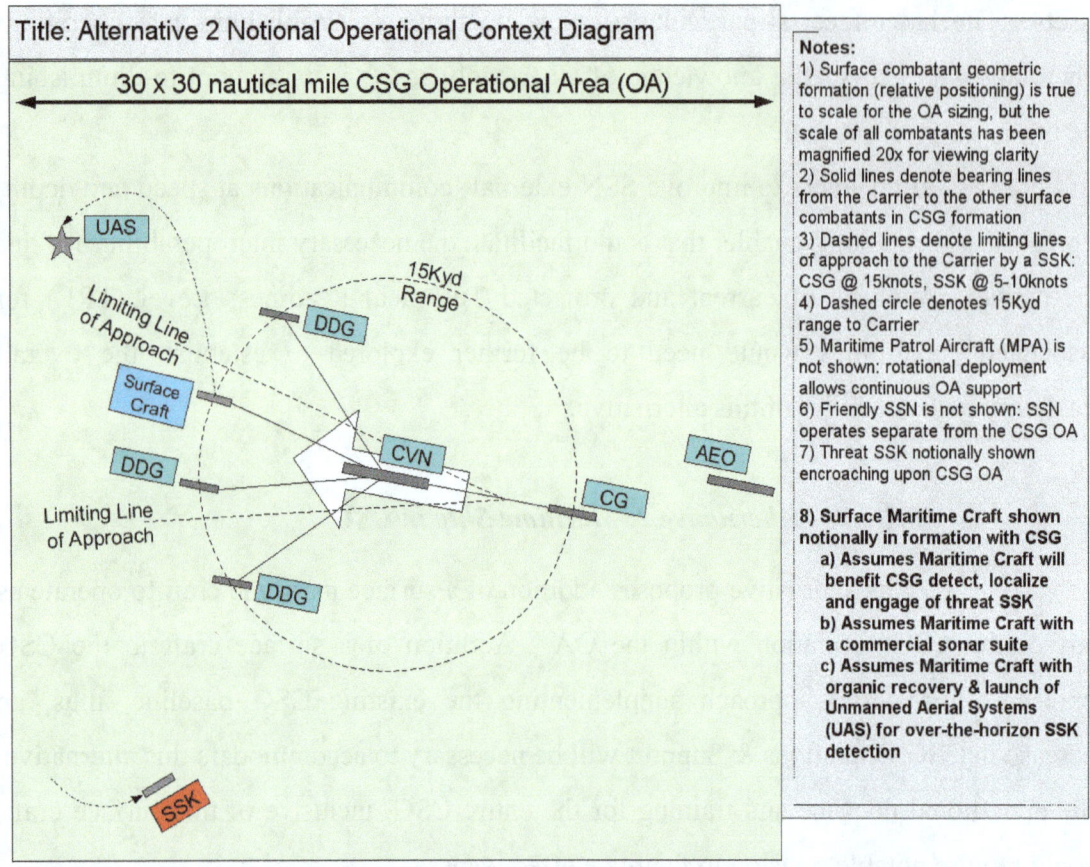

Figure 31 – Alternative 2 Notional Operational Context

The surface craft would need to meet or exceed the following capabilities:

- Sufficient speed to remain with the CSG formation
- Endurance commensurate with CSG, with underway replenishment (UNREP) compatibility in rapport with CSG;
- Support for unique acoustics sensor handling/placement;
- Support for unique UAS launch, control and recovery capabilities;
- Interoperability with CSG components for collaborative ASW.

Further exploration of this alternative would need to assess availability of surface maritime craft capable of reliably supporting the above deep-water performance with tenable life-cycle cost. The proposed platform is the Joint High Speed Vessel (JHSV) greatly based upon the U.S. Services leased 'Spearhead' Theater Support Vessel – 1st Experimental (TSV-1X) [Ref 42, Orme, 2003] and 'Swift' High Speed Vessel Two

(HSV-2) [Ref 43,Sample, 2004] shown in Figure 32. Both platforms possess wave-piercing catamaran hulls of modest length (e.g. ~320 feet) for deep-water high speed (over 40 knots), the basis for the JHSV. A Fiscal Year 2003 RDT&E contract award permitted TSV-1X deployment in support of Operation Enduring Freedom/Operation Iraqi Freedom which demonstrated invaluable capabilities relative to TSV/HSV; [Ref 44, Fiscal Year 2006 President's Budget, 2005:65-82] however, this was in the context of intra-theater sealift support, [Ref 45, Trauth, et all, 2005:51-56] vice a platform augmented for ASW (e.g. towed array handling) with sustained operation in a CSG formation.

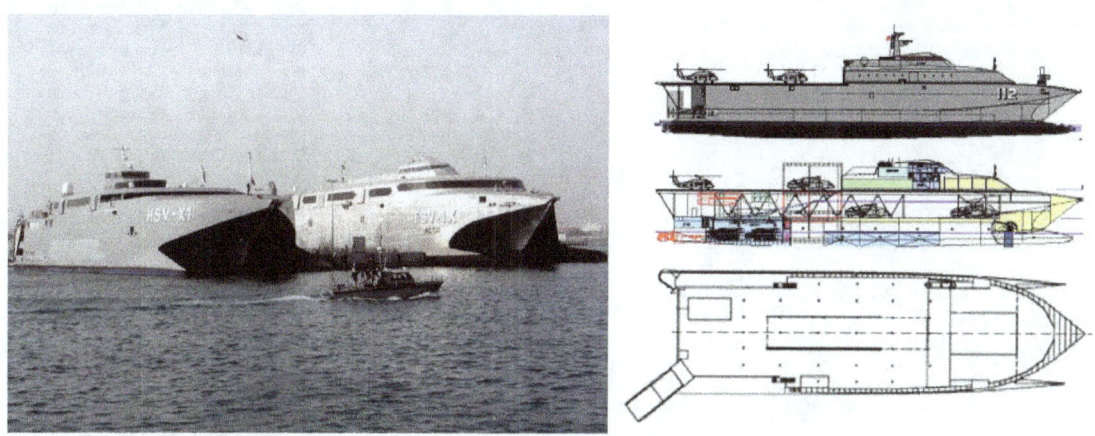

Figure 32 – High Speed Vessel / Theater Support Vessel Pictorial [Ref 43,Sample, 2004]

This alternative proposes use of the STANAG compliant Multi-Vehicle Control System (MVCS) for control and management of Tier 1 through Tier 3 UAS airframes. The NAVAIR PMA-263 sponsored MVCS system provides high Technical Readiness Level (TRL) given its demonstration on various USN platforms and military ground stations. Compliant UAS are currently used in maritime interdiction and over-the-horizon detection and tracking.

3.1.2.3 Alternative 3: Maritime Ship in Op Area

This alternative is similar to the preceding one, in that it proposes addition of a surface maritime craft to operate within the CSG OA; however, this surface craft is not part of the CSG formation. Addition of a surface craft to the CSG OA represents a materiel approach supplementing the existing CSG baseline; thus, an increase in CSG Operations & Support will be necessary to accommodate this alternative. The operational doctrine and training for the entire CSG, inclusive of this surface craft, would require notable revision to facilitate effectiveness.

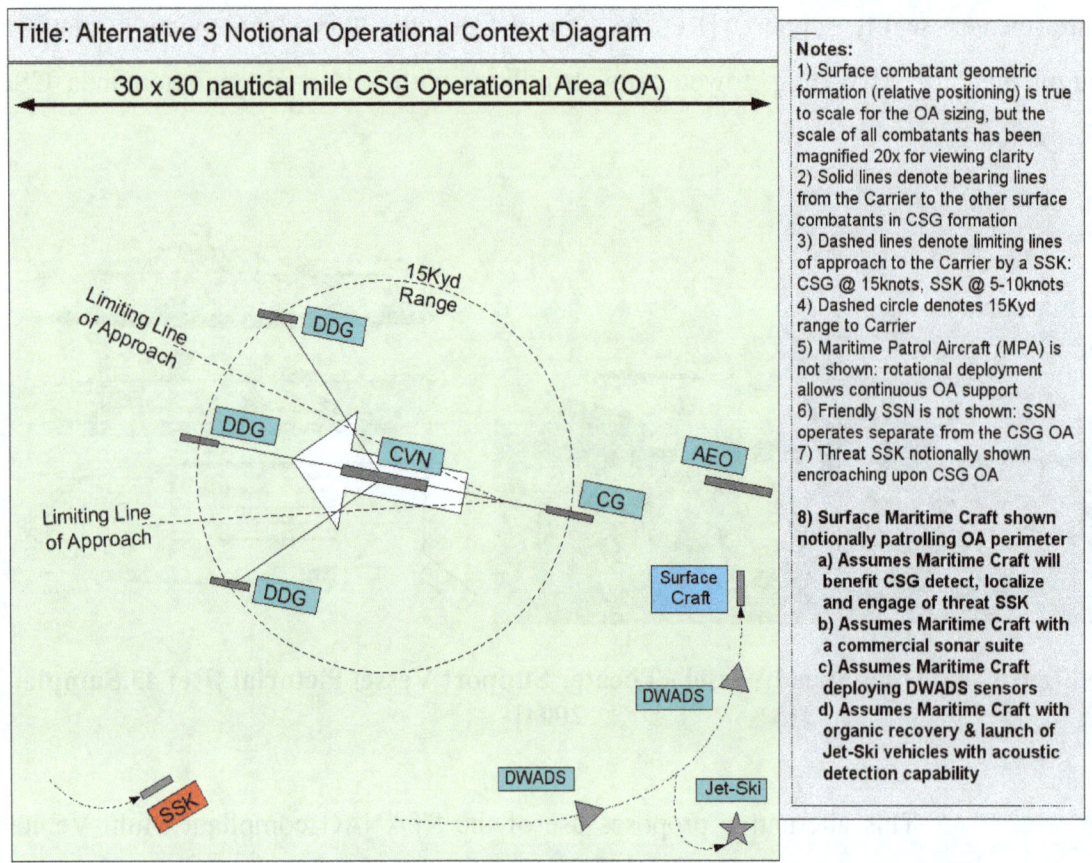

Figure 33 – Alternative 3 Notional Operational Context

This alternative seeks to exploit a surface maritime craft with commercial sonar as a means for improving the overall performance of the CSG ASW within the OA, by improving the aggregate CSG capabilities in SSK detection, tracking and engagement. The surface craft would support deployment of Deep Water Active Distributed System (DWADS) for active detection of quiet diesel-electric SSK, and deployment/recovery of 'Jet-Ski' vehicles with acoustic sensing. Figure 33 provides a notional operational context for the surface craft patrolling the 'perimeter' of the CSG OA, deploying the DWADS and Jet-Ski sensors.

Similar to the preceding alternative, the surface maritime craft proposed for this alternative is the JHSV (see Figure 32), as this platform shows promise for accommodating the unique acoustic sensor handling/placement, the planned deployment of DWADS sensors, and the Jet-Ski launch and recovery. Further exploration of this alternative would need to assess availability of the DWADS sensors (Office of Naval Research FY07 advanced technology program) and feasibility of Jet-Ski autonomy (currently of unknown TRL).

3.1.2.4 Alternative 4: Maritime Patrol Aircraft ASW Sensor

This alternative is based on the availability of a new type of surface search sensor to be mounted on Maritime Patrol Aircraft (MPA) and supporting the ASW mission of the CSG. It is anticipated that this sensor will be able to detect near or on-surface submarine targets at significant altitude and range, thus providing wide area ASW search capability. The system concept is illustrated in Figure 34.

Figure 34 - MPA/EPAS Employment [Ref 81, Personal Computer Interactive Multi-Sensor Trainer (PCIMAT), 2006]

This new sensor has been called LASH (Littoral Airborne Sensor – Hyperspectral) and EPAS (Electro-Optic Passive ASW System)) and now goes by the acronym JMMES (Joint Multi-Mission-Electro-Optic System) and is currently being developed under the Office of the Secretary of Defense (OSD) Joint Capability Technology Demonstration Program. The system uses 4 non acoustic sensors – a visible, multi-spectral imager, a low-light spectral detector, a low-light zoomed camera, and a mid-wave infrared detector. [Ref 46, Military & Aerospace Electronics, Dec. 2006] [Ref 47, Defense Technical Information Center, 2006]

For the purposes of this study, this alternative is employed as a layer of defense that will provide added security from hostile submarine attack to the "Baseline" alternative, i.e. the program of record CSG. As originally conceived, this alternative also employed the High Altitude ASW Weapon (HAAWC). Further consideration of the concept revealed that because of the limited range of the EPAS sensor, there was no need to develop or employ a standoff weapon to support this concept. [Ref 48, Federation of American Scientists, 1999] [Ref 49, Pike, 2007]

3.1.2.5 Alternative 5: Commercial Barrier

This alternative is similar to alternative 3, in that it proposes addition of a surface maritime craft to operate within the CSG OA; however, this surface craft is not part of the CSG formation. Addition of a surface craft to the CSG OA represents a materiel approach supplementing the existing CSG baseline; thus, an increase in CSG Operations & Support will be necessary to accommodate this alternative. The operational doctrine and training for the entire CSG, inclusive of this surface craft, would require notable revision to facilitate effectiveness.

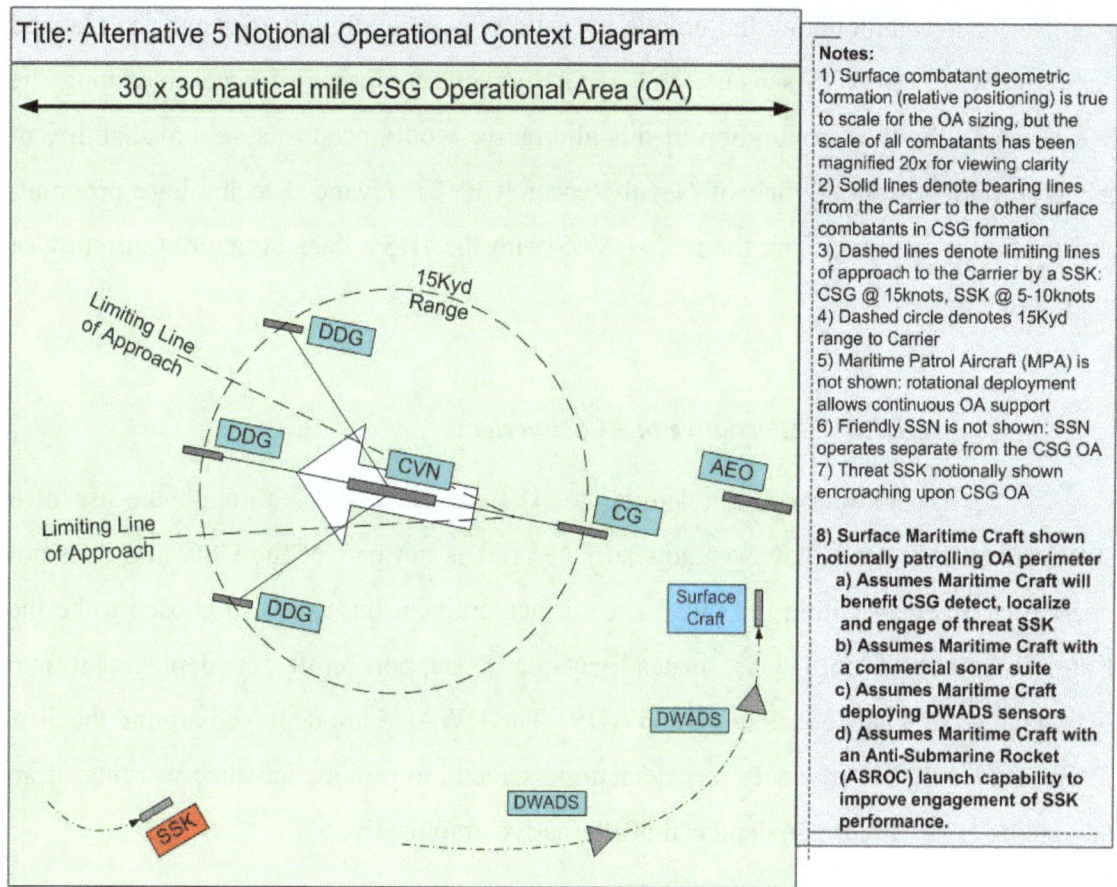

Figure 35 – Alternative 5 Notional Operational Context

This alternative seeks to exploit a surface maritime craft with commercial sonar as a means for improving the overall performance of the CSG ASW within the OA, by improving the aggregate CSG capabilities in SSK detection, tracking and engagement. The surface craft would support deployment of Deep Water Active Distributed System (DWADS) for active detection of quiet diesel-electric SSK, deploying them within the CSG OA, similar to alternative 3. A unique aspect of this option is the addition of a MK41 Vertical Launch System (VLS) with an ASROC load-out: the intent being improvement to the overall performance in CSG engagement of threat SSK within the OA. Figure 35 provides a notional operational context for the surface craft patrolling the 'perimeter' of the CSG OA, deploying the DWADS.

Similar to the preceding alternatives 2 and 3, the surface maritime craft proposed for this alternative is the JHSV (see Section 3.1.2.3), as this platform shows promise for accommodating the unique acoustic sensor handling/placement, the planned deployment of DWADS sensors, and a deck structure capable of accommodating the MK41 VLS. Further exploration of this alternative would need to assess availability of the DWADS sensors (Office of Naval Research FY07 advanced technology program) and feasibility of integrating the MK41 VLS with the JHSV deck structure (currently of unknown TRL).

3.1.2.6 *Alternative 6: LCS Barrier*

This alternative is similar to Alternatives 2 and 3 through the use of a surrogate surface craft; however, this surface craft is not part of the CSG and does not operate exclusively within the OA. The surface craft, in this scenario chosen to be the Littoral Combat Ship (LCS), instead acts as a support craft for deployment and maintenance of a barrier screen of DWADS. The DWADS are deployed around the 30 x 30 nautical mile OA and acts as a detection "screen" to provide advance warning of an advancing SSK. Figure 36 depicts this alternative graphically.

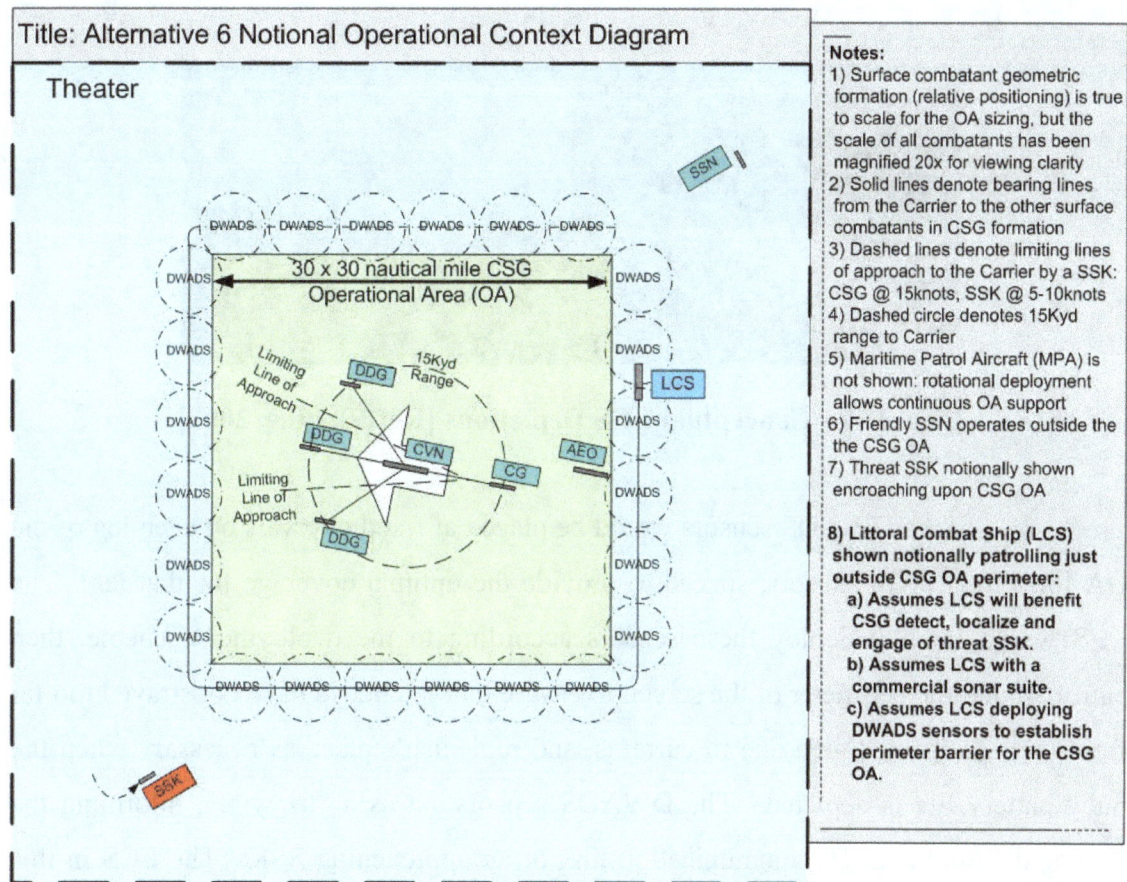

Figure 36 – Alternative 6 Notional Operational Context

The LCS is the US Navy's next-generation surface combatant and is intended to provide the capabilities of a small assault transport with a flight deck and hangar large enough to base two SH-60 Seahawk helicopters, combined with sufficient cargo volume to deliver multi-mission payloads. The concept behind the LCS is that it provides a high-speed complement to existing DD(X) and CG(X) by operating in environments where it is less desirable to employ larger, multi-mission ships. It will have the capability to deploy independently to overseas littoral regions, remain on station for extended periods of time either with a battle group or through a forward-basing arrangement and will be capable of underway replenishment. It will operate with Carrier Strike Groups, Surface Action Groups, in groups of other similar ships, or independently for diplomatic and presence missions. [Ref 50, Pike, 2007] Figure 37 shows proposed conceptual sketches for the LCS.

Figure 37 - Conceptual LCS Depictions [Ref 50, Pike, 2007]

Six DWADS sensors would be placed at fixed intervals on each leg of the OA for a total of 24 sensors; spaced to provide the optimal coverage for that leg. The LCS would initially deploy these sensors according to the deployment scheme, then patrol around the perimeter of the screen to ensure that the buoys have not strayed too far from their designated area due to currents, and replenish/replace as necessary when the buoy battery life is depleted. The DWADS sensors act as a "tripwire", informing the LCS and CSG via a RF communication link of an approaching SSK. The LCS in this alternative also performs the prosecution of the target through the use of the SH-60 helicopters. Alternatively if the placement of the LCS along the boundary does not allow for immediate attack, the LCS can work with the CSG to place more immediate resources on the target.

As with earlier alternatives, an assessment of the availability of the DWADS sensors (Office of Naval Research FY07 advanced technology program) and the production/availability of the LCS would be required.

3.1.2.7 Alternative 7: Commercial Craft UUV Barrier

The idea of a "tripwire" barrier to detect an encroaching SSK was again leveraged for Alternative 7, this time pairing the JHSV as the surrogate, with Unmanned Undersea Vehicles (UUVs) to act as the detection method. The approach has the JHSV deploying a number of UUVs along the perimeter of the CSG OA which would then assume a set search pattern. Detection of the SSK would be via a combination of onboard sensors including passive and non-acoustic ASW sensors. Once detection has been made the UUV would surface and communicate via RF link with the JHSV and/or CSG for prosecution.

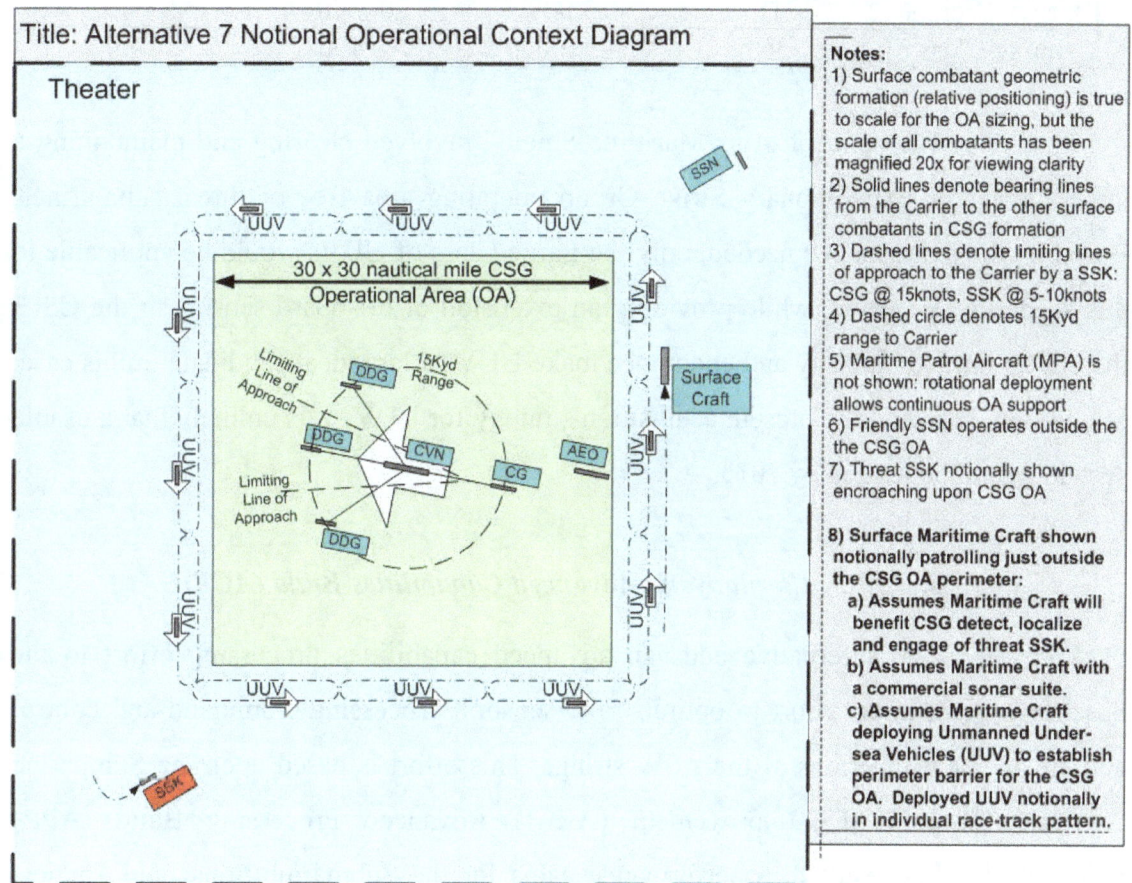

Figure 38 – Alternative 7 Notional Operational Context

The inclusion of UUVs into ASW operations was emphasized as part of the US Navy's UUV Master Plan for littoral and support operations. [Ref 51, ASNRD&A, Nov 2004] Four classes of vehicles are being considered for development based on platform interfaces, existing infrastructure, and mission requirements. The nominal performance characteristics for each class are shown in Table 1.

Table 1 - UUV Classes

Class	Diameter (inches)	Displacement (lbs.)	Endurance (hours)	Payload (ft3)
Man-Portable	3-9	< 100	10 – 20	<0.25
Light Weight	12.75	~ 500	10 – 40	1 – 3
Heavy Weight	21	< 3,000	20 – 80	4 – 6
Large Class	>36	~ 20,000	>> 400	15 – 30

The concept of a "Maritime Shield" involved clearing and maintaining a large Carrier or Expeditionary Strike Group operating area free of threat submarines. Based on the performance needed, only the Large Class of UUVs would be applicable to this scenario. However, while providing an extension of off-board sensors to the CSG, the UUVs limited mobility and endurance make UUVs a less ideal candidate in this case. In addition, based on the present acquisition strategy for UUVs it is unlikely that a usable system would be fielded by 2013.

3.1.2.8 *Alternative 8: Advanced Capabilities Build (ACB)*

This alternative adds an advanced capabilities processing effort to the baseline system in an effort to optimize the sensors, processing, command and control and engagement functions of the ASW string. This effort is based upon the Submarine Acoustic Rapid COTS Improvement (ARCI) Advanced Processing Build (APB) approach that has resulted in performance gains for the Submarine Sonar and Tactical Control applications.

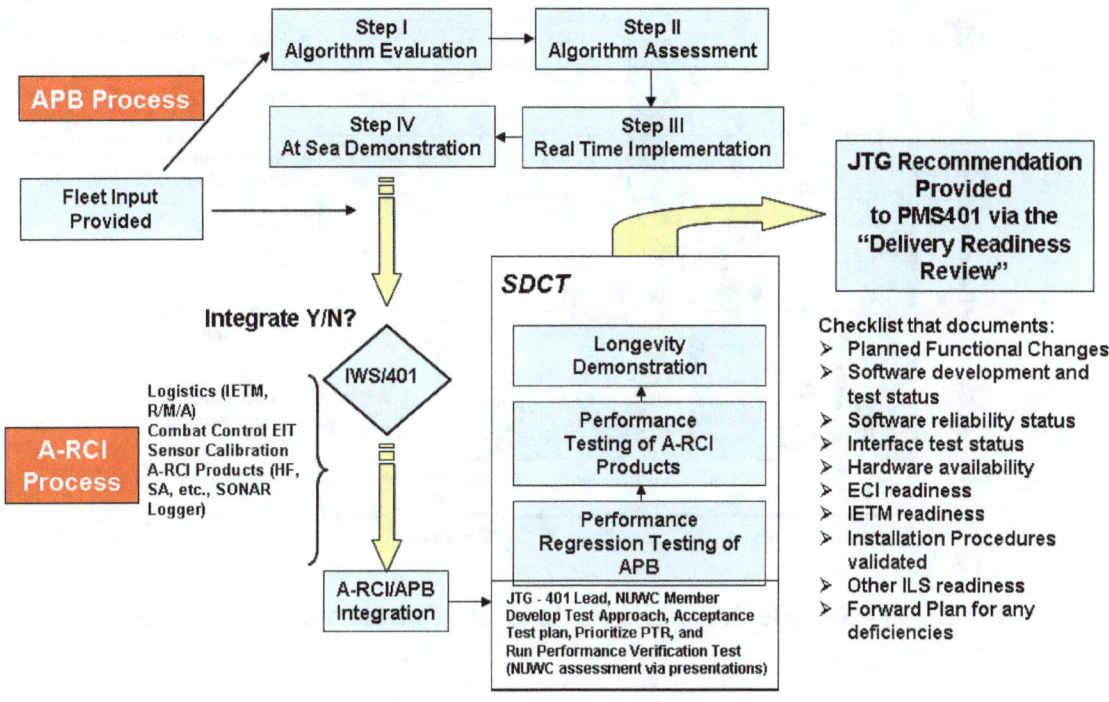

Figure 39 - ARCI/APB Process

The approach is to utilize the pockets of expertise scattered across the country to provide potential solutions for increasing the performance of the CSG sensors. A four step process leading to system integration and checkout as shown above in Figure 39 will be utilized to independently evaluate the proposed technologies for feasibility and improved performance. Sample gains realized by the submarine community in the passive acoustic realm beyond the legacy Mil-Spec system are shown in Figure 40.

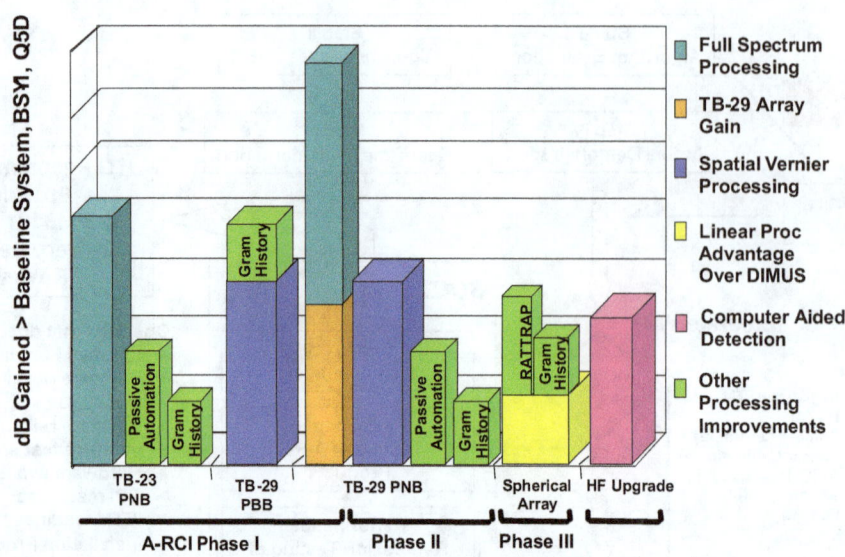

Figure 40 - Sample Processing Gains from Submarine APB Process

The ACB approach would focus on two main areas: Signal Excess and Decision Latency. The focus on Signal Excess would be an effort to increase the acoustic processing performance of the sensors such that the target can be detected at smaller Signal to Noise Ratios (SNR) than the baseline system. Techniques that would support this effort include: Source level Improvements, clutter reduction and rejection, and improved normalization techniques. It is expected that approximately 2 dB of signal excess can be gained

Decision Latency can be improved in multiple areas within the detection-to-engage timeline. These include "time to detect', "time to classify given detection", and "time to engage". The improvement in automatic detection and classification algorithms allow the processing to find detections and classify threat quicker than the operators. It is expected that this can be done approximately 3-6 ping cycles sooner than the baseline system, thereby gaining back valuable time.

This alternative also encompasses the 'acquisition acceleration' of ASW sensor, processing, command and control and engagement functions emergent in the 2013 timeframe. For example, the MFTA capability is an expected ASW acoustic sensor component for the CSG baseline; however, production will curtail its deployment to only one surface combatant of the CSG in this timeframe. This alternative proposes acquisition increase for such emergent ASW capabilities so as to accelerate the technology production for CSG deployment in 2013 (e.g. equip all four CSG DDG/CG surface combatants with MFTA, if optimal).

3.1.2.9 Alternative 9: Surveillance Towed-Array Sensor System (SURTASS)

The U.S. Navy developed the SURTASS in 1980, and the Fleet started to use it in 1984. The SURTASS has played a major role in ASW support to Navy's tactical forces. The SURTASS operates in both passive and active mode. The passive sensors that have improved sensitivity and signal processing can detect targets at long range against the quiet submarine. The detection capability is increased, and the higher resolution spectrum analysis helps improve the target bearing. The SURTASS Low Frequency Active (LFA) is long-range low frequency sonar designed to detect the quieter submarine. The LFA system consists of a large source array for active transmission and a separated array of receivers. The SURTASS is mounted in the T-AGOS ships as a single line or as twin line.

The Navy currently has eight SURTASS ships (four LANT and four PAC). The SURTASS program is operated by civilians contracted to SPAWAR. The operations are based in Norfolk, Virginia, with operation ports in Glasgow Scotland, Rota Spain, Yokohama Japan, Pearl Harbor Hawaii, Port Huneme California. [Ref 52, Pike, 2008]

The following figure shows how the SURTASS is employed under the sea. [Ref 53, Gentry, 2007]

Figure 41 - SURTASS Employment [Ref 53, Gentry, 2007]

This alternative applies the technology of SURTASS to replace the towed-array of the DDG in the baseline that will help improve the capability of detection. The LFA is modified to the mid-frequency active (MFA) will provide an effective detection of the quiet threats within the operation area of the BG without harming to the sea mammals.

3.1.2.10 Alternative 10: Helicopter Searching

This alternative proposed utilizing the SH-60 Seahawk helicopters in a search and detect role in additional to their existing mission of prosecuting targets detected by other platforms. This would be a significant expansion of the SH-60's role and workload. The helicopters would patrol the OPAREA adding their detection capabilities to the existing baseline systems. The notional coverage areas for each helicopter are shown in red in Figure 42. They could provide search coverage by seeding a field with sonobuoys or by utilizing their Magnetic Anomaly Detection (MAD) systems. Their AN/AQS-22 dipping sonar could be used to classify and track potential targets once detected.

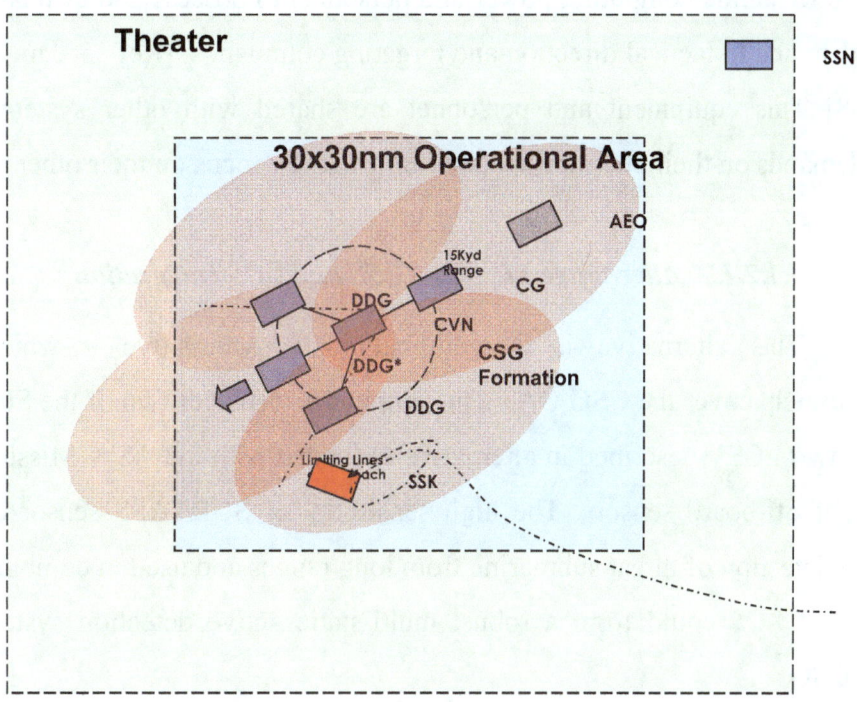

Figure 42 - Helicopter Coverage Areas

In order to provide complete CSG coverage a minimum of four SH-60s would have to be airborne in the search and detect role at any given time. Providing 24 hour ASW coverage with an aircraft with a four hour airborne endurance would stress their capabilities. As the existing helicopters are normally fully engaged, this would necessitate equipping the strike group with additional helicopters. Assuming that each aircraft can conduct two missions per day this would require adding twelve SH-60s to the CSGs complement. Each additional SH-60 costs $20.25 million [Ref 54, Jane's Information Group, 2008], resulting in a $243 million procurement cost. Additional sonobuoys and torpedoes would have to be procured to outfit these helicopters.

The primary concern with this alternative is its impact to the CSGs other operations. The twelve additional helicopters would have to be based and supported by the existing platforms. The only platform with sufficient capacity to carry this many helicopters is the carrier. Since even the carrier has finite space, these additional helicopters would have to be in lieu of other air wing assets. This would degrade the carrier's primary strike mission as helicopters are not effective strike aircraft. The SH-60's LAMPS MK III ASW system is not fully self-contained. It relies on the host platform to provide the computing power and personnel to process and evaluate SONAR and MAD data and to tactical direction and targeting commands. [Ref 55, Jane's Fighting Ships, 2008] This equipment and personnel are shared with other systems and the increased demands on their attention would diminish their focus on their other tasks.

3.1.2.11 Alternative 11: SURTASS and LCS Integration

This alternative is a modification to Alternative 9 which utilizes SURTASS to help cover the CSG OA. This option also replaces two of the Surface Ship DDGs with two LCS' (described in alternative 6) loaded with the ASW Mission Module and a host of off-board sensors. The high sensitivity of SURTASS sensor could help improve the detection of threat submarine from long ranges and used in combination with the DDGs and LCS could form a robust multi-static active detection system to help protect the CSG.

The SURTASS operates in both passive and active modes. The passive sensors have improved sensitivity and improved signal processing that can detect quiet submarines at long ranges. The detection capability is increased due to long range transmission of low frequencies, and the high resolution spectrum analysis helps improve the target bearing. The SURTASS Low Frequency Active (LFA) is long-range low frequency sonar designed to detect the quieter submarine. The LFA system consists of a large source array for active transmission and a separate array of receivers. The SURTASS is mounted in the T-AGOS ships as a single line or as twin line.

By taking advantage of the SURTASS long range detection capability and utilizing the versatile LCS in combination with current DDGs, the CSG would have more time to prepare for engagement and a greater chance of survivability.

Further exploration of this alternative would need to assess cost tradeoffs of supplanting the operations cost of 2 DDG with the procurement and operations cost of the replacement LCS and operational costs of SURTASS. There would also need to be an analysis to ensure the replacement of the DDG with these surface craft does not degrade other mission capabilities of the overall CSG. For example, the LCS cannot likely match the AEGIS Anti-Air Warfare capabilities of the 2 DDG; thus, would the

AEGIS defense capabilities of the remaining DDG/CG prove sufficient for the CSG formation. Additionally the SURTASS platform operating outside the CSG would be very vulnerable to offensive enemy attack with little or no self defense mechanism.

3.1.2.12 Alternative 12: LCS and Commercial Craft

This alternative is a materiel approach that is similar to the prior alternative in that it explores 'replacement' of surface combatants that comprise the baseline CSG formation, as opposed to merely adding new components. The intention is to render an alternative that improves the overall CSG ASW performance, while offsetting costs by supplanting existing surface combatants with less expensive platforms. This alternative proposes replacement of 2 DDG in the baseline CSG formation with 1 LCS plus 1 commercial craft. The CSG Operations & Support will require revisions as necessary to accommodate this alternative. The operational doctrine and training for the entire CSG, inclusive of these substitute surface craft, would require notable revision to facilitate effectiveness.

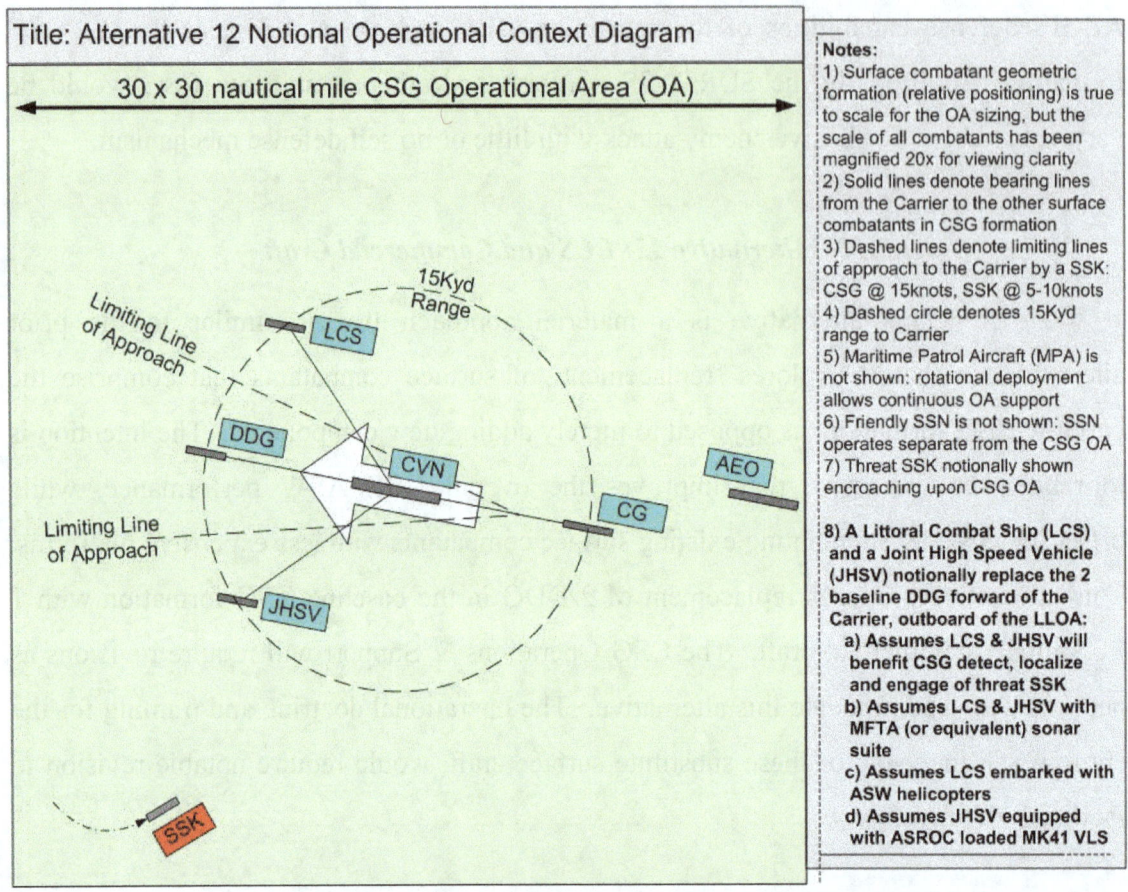

Figure 43 - Alternative 12 Notional Operational Context

This alternative seeks to employ commercial sonar, potentially a MFTA variation, for both the LCS and the commercial craft that would supplant 2 DDG forward of the Aircraft Carrier. The intent is to improve the overall performance of the CSG ASW within the OA, by improving the aggregate CSG capabilities in SSK detection, tracking and engagement.

Similar to the preceding alternative 6, the LCS (see Figure 37) was chosen as a capable platform for the ASW role; however, this alternative proposed the LCS will supplant an existing DDG in the CSG formation. In this context, the proposal calls for an LCS embarked with SH-60 Seahawk helicopters, and a multi-mission payload offering an ASW acoustics package (e.g. MFTA or equivalent). These capabilities will meet the need for a platform that can keep pace with the CSG, while offering the ASW detection and engagement capabilities commensurate with the DDG in the CSG.

Similar to the preceding alternatives 2 and 3, the surface maritime craft proposed for this alternative is the JHSV (Figure 32), as this platform shows promise for accommodating the desired ASW acoustic package (e.g. MFTA or equivalent), with a deck structure capable of accommodating the MK41 VLS (e.g. ASROC capability). These capabilities will meet the need for a platform that can keep pace with the CSG, while offering the ASW detection and engagement capabilities commensurate with the DDG in the CSG.

Further exploration of this alternative would need to assess cost tradeoffs of supplanting the operations cost of 2 DDG with the procurement and operations cost of the replacement LCS & JHSV. There would also need to be an analysis to ensure the replacement of the DDG with these surface craft does not degrade other mission capabilities of the overall CSG. For example, the LCS and JHSV cannot likely match the AEGIS Anti-Air Warfare capabilities of the 2 DDG; thus, would the AEGIS defense capabilities of the remaining DDG/CG prove sufficient for the CSG formation. Finally, there also will need to be an analysis whether the JHSV can be procured, modified and equipped with the acoustics detection upgrades within the 2013 timeframe.

3.1.2.13 Alternative 13: HAMR Integration

This alternative adds a Hybrid Airship Multi-Role (HAMR) lighter-than-air platform to conduct ASW operations within CSG Op Area. A picture of a prototype airship is shown in Figure 44. [Ref 56, Airliners.net, 2008] The alternative adds the HAMR platform to the baseline. In doing so it seeks to improve CSG ASW performance through the employment of embarked detection and engagement capabilities. The HAMR operates independent of the CSG but within the CSG Operations area.

Figure 44 - Picture of Prototype HAMR [Ref 56, Airliners.net, 2008]

The operational concept for this alternative entails the deployment of the HAMR to the CSG area of operation with an ASW mission package. Once on station, the HAMR conducts deployment of sonobuoy fields to detect threat submarines to aide in establishment of the safe CSG operation. A notional physical architecture is depicted in Figure 45.

As currently envisioned, the HAMR with ASW package would not only add an independent ability to detect submerged threats, but also add an engagement capability through employment of MK54 light weight torpedoes and possibly the HAAWC weapon system originally discussed as part of alternative 4. [Ref 57, NUWC Keyport MSSE Cohort, 2008] With this capability the HAMR could independently prosecute detected threats or the engagement functions in the baseline CSG could pounce on detected threats.

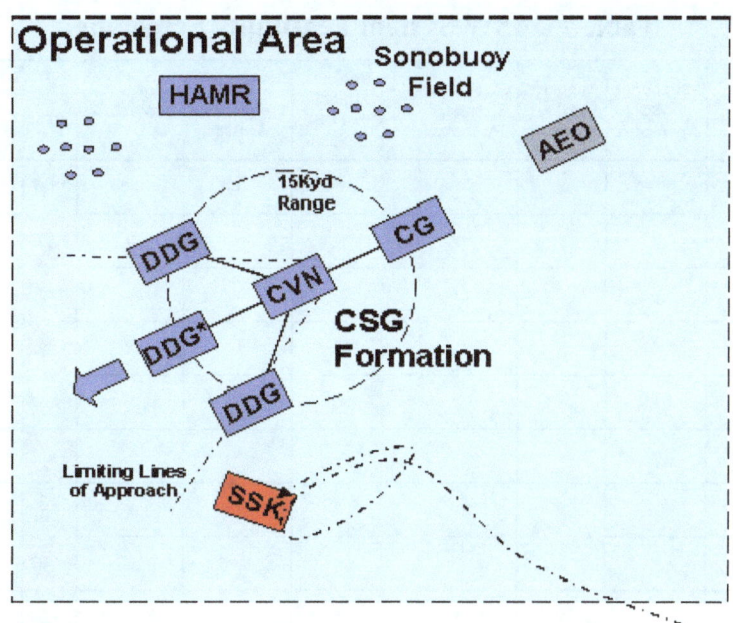

Figure 45 - Physical Architecture for HAMR Alternative

The unit depicted in Figure 44 is a Lockheed Martin N791LM. This aircraft is a prototype of the envisioned HAMR platform. As currently planned, the HAMR project expects to produce two prototype HAMR airframes for evaluation testing. Testing is planned though 2013 with transition to production and ultimate introduction to the fleet following those evolutions. [Ref 57, NUWC Keyport MSSE Cohort, 2008]

3.1.3 Feasibility Screening Results

The project team applied a feasibility study to screen the number of viable alternatives to be passed on for modeling and analysis based on the feasibility criteria described in the section 3.1.1.3 above. Criteria were selected based upon interpretation of feedback received from key stakeholders.

Each alternative, including the baseline was thoroughly investigated and evaluated against the above set of criteria. An alternative was deemed not feasible if it failed any of the customer constraints. Only those alternatives that pass all criteria were chosen for modeling and analysis. The results of the feasibility screening are shown in Table 2 below:

Table 2 - ASW System Feasibility Screening

Customer Constraint	Available by 2013	Supports CSG Operations	Supports 14 Day Operation	Environmental Impact Acceptable	Doesn't Degrade Other CSG Operations	Total Procurement < $1 Billion	Survivability	Pass or Fail	Comments
Baseline	Y	Y	Y	Y	Y	Y	Y	PASS	This is the CSG Baseline
Alternative 1	Y	Y	Y	Y	Y	Y	N	FAIL	Risk of Shooting at our own Sub
Alternative 2	N	Y	Y	Y	Y	N	Y	FAIL	Not available in time, and exceeds cost
Alternative 3	N	Y	Y	Y	Y	N	Y	FAIL	Not available in time, and exceeds cost
Alternative 4	Y	Y	Y	Y	Y	Y	Y	PASS	Could be feasible
Alternative 5	N	Y	Y	Y	Y	N	Y	FAIL	Not available in time, and exceeds cost
Alternative 6	Y	Y	Y	Y	Y	Y	Y	PASS	Could be feasible
Alternative 7	N	Y	Y	Y	Y	N	Y	FAIL	Not available in time, and exceeds cost
Alternative 8	Y	Y	Y	Y	Y	Y	Y	PASS	Could be feasible
Alternative 9	Y	Y	Y	Y	Y	Y	N	FAIL	SURTASS lack of self defense
Alternative 10	Y	Y	N	Y	N	Y	Y	FAIL	Require additional Helos at other mission expense
Alternative 11	Y	N	Y	Y	N	N	N	FAIL	SURTASS and LCS Availability
Alternative 12	N	Y	Y	Y	N	N	Y	FAIL	Not available in time, exceeds cost, expense of AEGIS AW
Alternative 13	N	Y	Y	Y	Y	Y	Y	FAIL	Not available in time

The CSG baseline (Do Nothing Alternative) passed all feasibility screening by default. It's measured ASW performance in the chosen environment is the baseline that other alternatives were compared against by the modeling and analysis team. Three other alternatives also passed all screening criteria. They are Alternative 4, Alternative 6 and Alternative 8. Details of these alternatives are provided in Section 3.1.2. One of these alternatives could possibly replace the baseline in 2013. Detailed modeling and analysis of these three alternatives was performed with results documented in Section 3.2. These alternatives will also have to go through a final test for sensitivity, detailed cost analysis and risk evaluation prior to being chosen the best candidate for 2013 CSG baseline.

The feasibility screening eliminated several alternatives based on their inability to pass all customer constraints. A brief summary of the results follows:

- Alternative 1 failed survivability due to the potential to attack our own submarine if situational awareness is not fully maintained.

- Alternatives 2, 3, 5, 7 and 12 all failed due to two factors. These alternatives are not anticipated to be achievable in the 2013 timeframe and they all exceed the $1 Billion dollar procurement cap. Alternative 12 further failed due to an anticipated impact to the CSG AEGIS air warfare capability.

- Alternative 9 failed survivability due to the fact that the SURTASS platform operates outside the protection of the other CSG assets and does not have sufficient self defense capabilities in the event it is attacked by enemy forces.

- Alternative 10 failed both the 14 day availability and impact on other CSG operations. It will be difficult to maintain constant helicopter presence for prolonged periods for several reasons and sacrificing other aircraft for helicopter support will adversely impact other CSG missions.

- Alternative 11 failed several categories, including: Supported by CSG, does not degrade other CSG operations, cost and survivability (primarily SURTASS related).

- Alternative 13 is not anticipated to be available in the 2013 time frame and therefore failed screening based on this.

3.1.4 Feasible Alternatives

The three alternatives, Maritime Patrol Aircraft, Barrier, and Advanced Capabilities Build were examined in terms of performance, cost, and risk. The highest score will be recommended for release to the CSG baseline in 2013. A discussion on the feasibility of these alternatives is provided below.

3.1.4.1 Maritime Patrol Aircraft (MPA) Alternative

The Maritime Patrol Aircraft ASW sensor, as discussed in section 3.1.2.4, is the addition of a new sensor suite on existing P-3C Orion. The system is also slated for inclusion on the P-3's planned replacement the P-8 Poseidon, scheduled for LRIP production beginning in 2010. While the exact technology readiness level of this system is not established, the program is planning to complete multi-mission, multi-aircraft trials and complete the development of a concept of operations during DoD Fiscal year 2009. Given its current state of development, it is expected that, assuming successful demonstration of the technology, that this system would be available, at least in limited quantities, for operational use in the 2013 timeframe.

The P-3s are land based, requiring no support from the CSG and have the range and endurance to support anticipated CSG operations by rotating on station aircraft. The MPA squadron has ample aircraft quantities to maintain the required coverage, non-stop, for indefinite periods. The EPAS sensor is considered to be benign to the environment and the existing P-3 impacts are well documented and within acceptable standards. The MPA/EPAS concept will operate outside the CSG OPAREA so will not likely interfere with CSG operations.

The anticipated $84.5 million procurement cost is well below the $1 billion dollar threshold. The survivability of the MPA/EPAS system is considered to be high as it has a low vulnerability to the threat submarine and is likely to be operating at considerable distances from other threat forces.

3.1.4.2 Barrier Alternative

The Barrier alternative as discussed in Section 3.1.2.6 is the inclusion of an LCS craft supporting the CSG by operating as a surrogate craft for deployment of DWADS sensors. This is an additional capability being placed into the OPAREA that does not utilize existing CSG resources and will not impact the CSG's other operations. The LCS is a purpose built, high speed, multi-mission naval platform. As such it has sufficient capability to keep up with the CSG and support extended operations. The advanced systems onboard make this a highly survivable platform. The lead ship has already been christened and fully operational vessels will be readily available to support the CSG by the goal date of 2013. The Navy intends to procure these multi-mission vessels, regardless of the CSG ASW applications. Therefore the LCS procurement is a sunk cost and was not considered against the feasibility screening criteria.

The DWADS sensors are the subject of an ongoing Office of Naval Research FY07 advanced technology program. DWADS is a combination of and upgrade to existing sensor and communication technologies and it is anticipated that they will be in full rate production by 2013. This uncertain TRL is a source of cost and schedule risk for this alternative.

3.1.4.3 Advanced Capabilities Build Alternative

The Advanced Capabilities Build alternative as discussed in Section 3.1.2.8 is the application of an advanced processing research and development process currently in use as a technology feeder for the AN/BQQ-10(V) Submarine Sonar system, applying it to existing/emergent Surface ASW technologies for the 2013 CSG (e.g. MFTA). This advanced processing work in concert with planned COTS technology upgrades (hardware and software) have been providing performance improvements into the submarine fleet on an annual basis. By applying this approach to the Surface Sonar baseline system, gains can be made that will, at a minimum increase detection performance and improve the "detect to classification" timeline. Improvements in both of these areas will lead to a higher detection probability and support longer classification ranges.

As this process is currently in use for the submarine force, having an improved performance baseline to support operations in the 2013 timeframe is achievable. As the end result of this alternative is improved hardware and software that is built upon the system utilized in the baseline scenario, it meets the CSG operation, survivability, and 14 day duration feasibility requirements by default. Current Submarine force funding for this effort across a similar timeframe is in the $300M - $500M range, including all research efforts, transition to production and installation with life-cycle support, well under the cost requirement. Lastly, as it is an upgrade to the baseline system focused solely on the improving the ASW performance, it will not degrade other CSG operations and will have an acceptable environmental impact.

3.2 MODELING AND ANALYSIS

The purpose of modeling within the systems engineering development process is to provide a consistent, quantitative method to evaluate key measures of effectiveness and measures of performance for system alternatives under consideration. The modeling and analysis efforts are conducted as an integral part of the Design and Analysis phase of the SEDP. The systems engineering team must use caution when selecting models to support this phase of analysis. Models must be selected and/or developed which have sufficient fidelity that they provide credible results while proving outputs that are directly related to the key performance measures that have been identified through the Needs Analysis process. In addition, any known shortfalls or deficiencies within the selected models should be identified and presented to the decision maker. This leads to transparency in the alternative scoring process and will result in a more satisfied customer and removes any bias or prejudice on the part of the system designers related to specific solutions.

In the case of this systems engineering project, key measures of operational effectiveness performance include metrics associated with threat submarine detection, threat submarine engagement and carrier survivability. These measures require the selection or development of a model set which can estimate the detection capability of solutions under consideration, the ability of the solution to engage or attack the enemy submarine, and determine the output metric, (survival of the aircraft carrier) of each engagement. These metrics imply the need for a discrete event time domain model that will model the kinematics of all platforms, acoustics detection capability of sensors at discrete time steps, ability of the sensor to hold and localize the contact and weapon employment.

In addition to these key measures of operational effectiveness, the systems engineering team also evaluated the Reliability, Maintainability and Availability of feasible solutions to provide measures of operational suitability.

3.2.1 Modeling and Analysis Approach

The modeling and analysis effort has two parts, operational effectiveness and operational suitability. Operational effectiveness corresponds to the Objectives Hierarchy performance measure "Probability that the ASW system prevents enemy launch of an effective weapon against the aircraft carrier" (see Figure 25). The

Objectives Hierarchy decomposes this measure into other lower level measures supporting the Detection, Localization/Tracking, Classification, and Engagement. Analyzing operational effectiveness at the carrier survival level simplifies the modeling effort because results only have to be collected for one measure instead of the seven measures that would need to be individually modeled if the analysis were done at the lower level. The probability of carrier survival implicitly includes the lower level measures since the lower level measures are tied to the functions required for carrier survival.

Operational Suitability corresponds to the Trustworthy block of Figure 26. Of the performance measures that contribute to Trustworthiness, Operational Availability (Ao) and Reliability (Re) are modeled. The Number of Staff to operate and maintain the system was approximated by best engineering/logistics judgment, and was accommodated as part of the cost modeling and analysis. The other Measures of Suitability were not modeled for several reasons. One, the requirement for fourteen day endurance, is covered by the feasibility screening. Man-hours of Required Training, and System Setup Time require more detailed alternative definition than is possible at the level of this project, and should be assessed at the next level of development.

3.2.2 Operational Effectiveness

The key measure of effectiveness for the ASW system is survival of the carrier at the center of the CSG. Since we are developing an ASW system to protect the carrier, we only consider attacks on the carrier, and other CSG members, by Red Submarines. We also consider the Red Submarine to behave in a "kill or be killed" manner; that is the Red Submarine will pursue the carrier until either it sinks the carrier or is killed itself. The carrier and CSG are assumed to only address the Red submarine threat by attacking Red Submarines. The CSG will not alter operations to avoid a detected submarine.

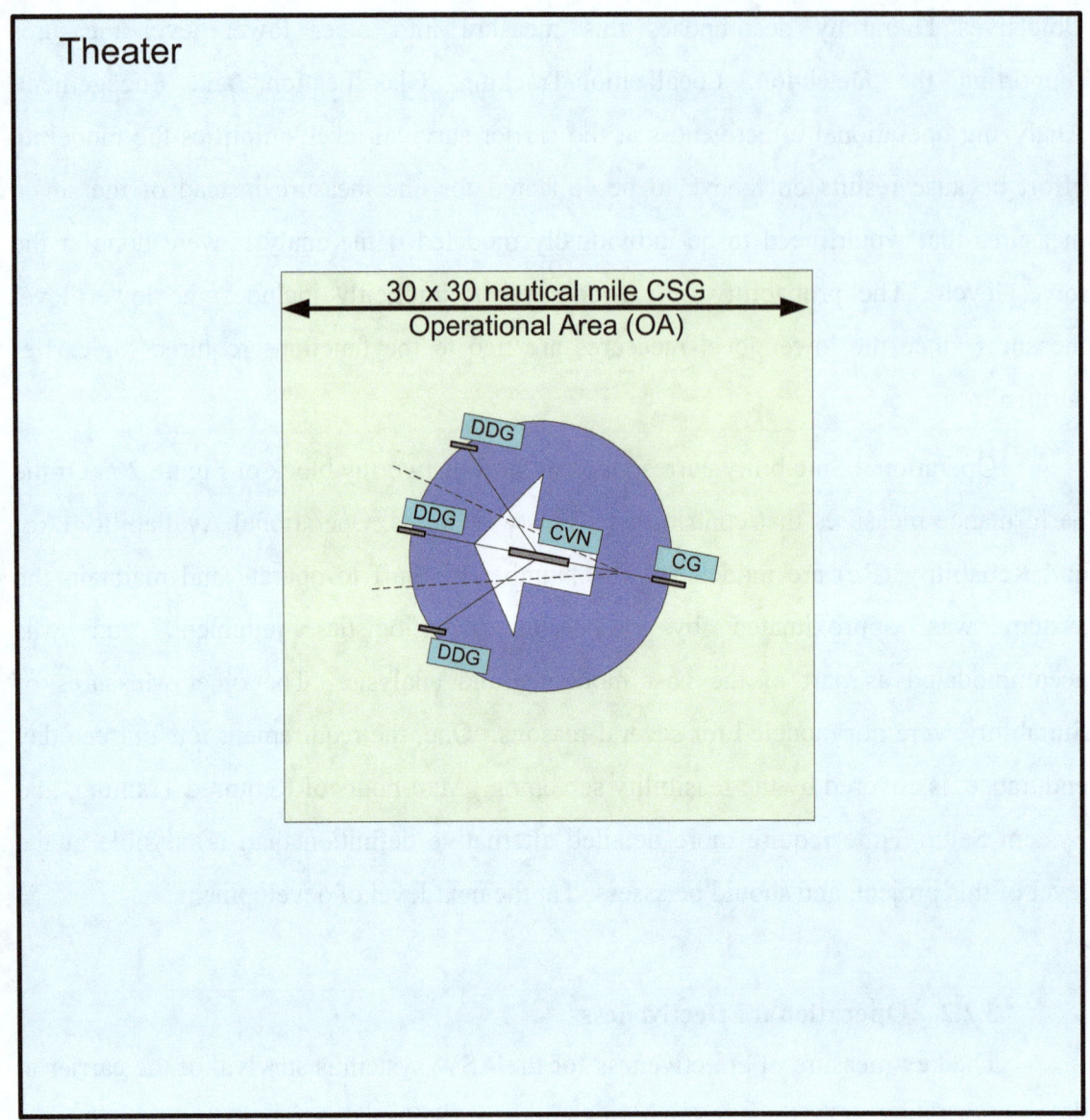

Figure 46 - Modeling Universe

The ASW alternatives consist of combinations of sensors and weapons operating in the three regions depicted in Figure 46. These regions are more important to modeling the detection element of the proposed solutions than the engagement. The largest region, Theater, is a notional area representing and the entire area of conflict. For the modeling effort, Theater is considered to be a rectangle 100 by 100 nm. This size is based on making the Theater significantly larger than the CSG OA so that Red submarines will be exposed to theater level ASW forces that may be part of a proposed solution. Theater level operations are modeled as an area search.

The CSG OA is a 30 by 30 nm box that the CSG is assigned to operate within. From a modeling stand point the CSG OA provides three elements that may be part of a proposed solution. The boundary between the OA and the Theater provides an opportunity for a barrier search solution. The OA region, outside of the portion occupied by the CSG formation, is modeled as an area search, similar to the Theater (light-blue) region. The portion of the OA occupied by the CSG formation has unique modeling aspects that will be discussed in the Baseline section below.

Modeling the various ASW alternatives involves analysis of detection and engagement probabilities in the regions shown in Figure 46, as well as the Red submarine migration across the boundaries between those regions. At the highest level Red submarines will be randomly distributed throughout the Theater (light-blue) region in Figure 46, including the portion of the theater region occupied by the CSG OA and the CSG formation.

The probability of carrier survival can be thought of as one minus the probability of the attacking red submarine's survival. This assumes a kill or be killed scenario; the red submarine will continue its attack on the carrier until either it launches a torpedo attack on the carrier or is destroyed by Blue forces.

For modeling purposes we assume that the Red submarine is initially located at the outer boundary of the "Theater" region of Figure 46. The Red submarine will traverse the theater region moving toward the CSG OA. As the Red submarine traverses the theater region it provides an opportunity for Blue forces to detect and engage it. If the Blue forces are successful the Red submarine is destroyed in the theater region and the carrier survives.

If the Blue forces do not destroy the red submarine in the theater region it has an opportunity to penetrate the boundary between the theater region and CSG OA. Once again this presents Blue forces an opportunity to detect and engage the red submarine. If the Red submarine enters the CSG OA, it will maneuver to intercept the CSG. The formations screening ships will have an opportunity to kill the Red submarine as it penetrates the formation.

The spreadsheet model will consist of three sub-models, a formation model representing the Baseline alternative, barrier search model outside the CSG OA representing the MPA alternative, and a barrier search model on the perimeter of the CSG OA representing the LCS alternative. The results of these sub-models will be combined in a top level spreadsheet that calculates the probability of a Red submarine successfully attacking the carrier.

Each sub-model calculates the probability of the Red submarine being killed by the associated alternative. In addition the Baseline models determine whether the Red submarine was killed before it was able to launch a successful attack on the carrier. The probability of Red submarine kill is a function of detection probability, reaction/decision time, and weapon effectiveness. Since all the alternatives use similar weapons, the probability of a single weapon killing the target is 1.0. Detection probability and reaction/decision time are represented as discussed in the sub-model sections.

Each model will produce a probability of the Red submarine being killed by a specific alternative. These probabilities will be combined, using an event tree approach, to produce the overall probability of carrier survival for the Baseline alone, the Baseline plus the LCS, the Baseline plus the MPA, and the Advanced Capabilities Build.

3.2.2.1 *Baseline*

The systems engineering team's Modeling and Simulation IPT elected to utilize a readily available tool to support analysis of key operational effectiveness parameters related to the baseline system performance. The M&S IPT was responsible for estimating expected performance measures, as identified in the objectives hierarchy of section 2.2, for the baseline system and for feasible alternatives.

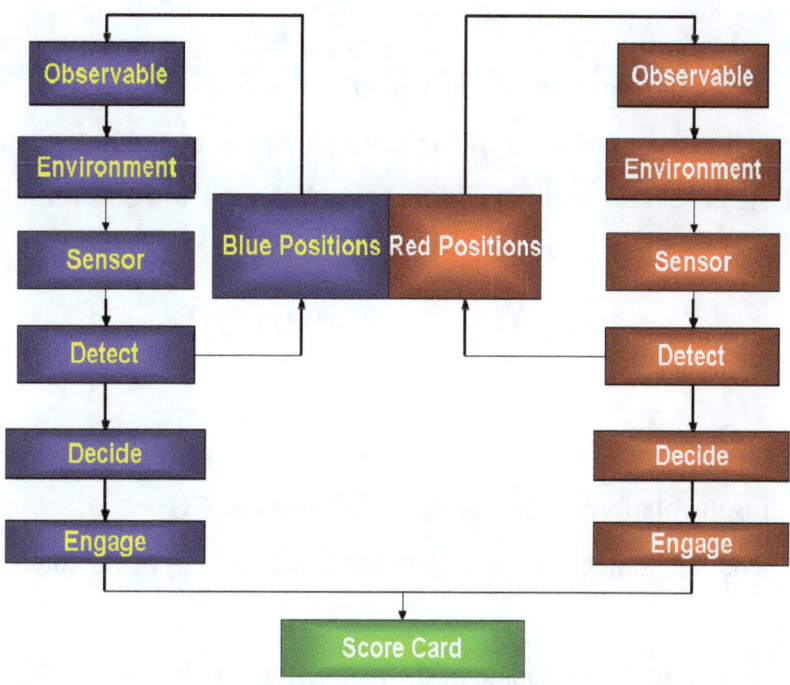

Figure 47 - Baseline Engagement Model Block Diagram

The basic block diagram of the spread sheet model is shown in Figure 47. The central element of this model is the computation of the position information for the CSG ships and the opposing force submarine. Using time steps that are set up in the geometry sheet, the model calculates the position of each platform using the speed and course for that time step. These equations are implemented in the spreadsheet model to compute the positions for each platform at each time step.

$$X(I) = X(I) + V(I) * COS(\varphi(I)) * \Delta T \qquad \textbf{Equation 1}$$

$$Y(I) = Y(I) + V(I) * SIN(\varphi(I)) * \Delta T \qquad \textbf{Equation 2}$$

where

X is the X position of the platform in yards

Y is the Y position of the platform in yards

I is the platform index (submarine, CVN, DDG, CG)

V is the velocity of the platform in yards per second

ΔT is the time step in seconds

When the position of each platform is updated, the range between the opposing force submarine and each of the CSG platforms is computed and used in the calculation of signal excess and also in the calculation of torpedo run. The range is calculated as:

$$R(I) = \sqrt{(X(I)-X_s)^2 - (Y(I)-Y_s)^2}$$ **Equation 3**

Where,

I is the platform indicator for CVN, DDG or CG

R is the Range between platform I and the opposing force submarine in yards

X(I) is the X coordinate of the platform in yards

Xs is the X coordinate of the submarine in yards

Y(I) is the Y coordinate of the platform in yards

Ys is the Y coordinate of the submarine in yards

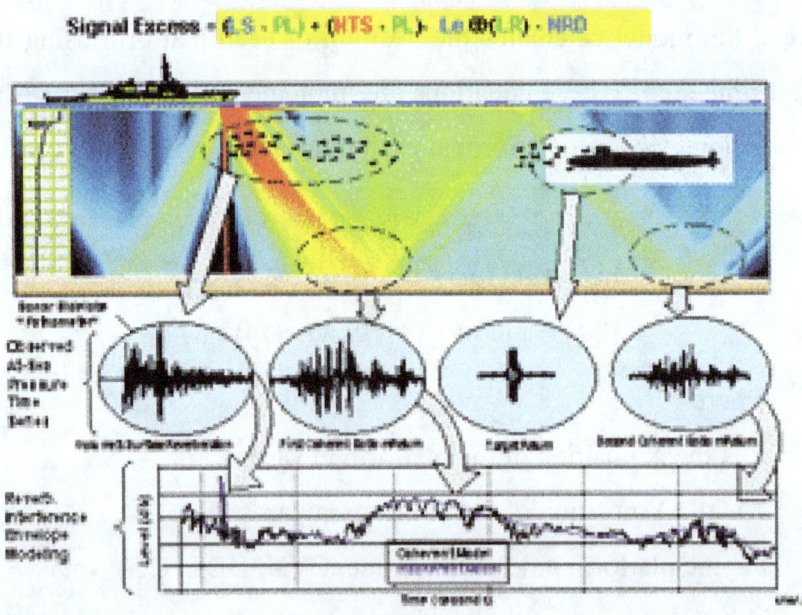

Figure 48 - Active Sonar Equation Depiction [Ref 82, NUWC Director Undersea Warfare]

Following the calculation of the position of each platform in the scenario, the spread sheet model then computes the ability of the sensors on each platform to detect the opposing force submarine and also the ability of the opposing force submarine to detect each Carrier Strike Group platform. As described in Section 2.1.5, the Cruiser and Destroyers of the CSG utilize active bow sonar to detect and track the opposing submarine, while the opposing submarine uses passive hull sonar to detect and track the Carrier Strike Group platforms. This component of the model requires the implementation of the Figure of Merit (FOM) [Ref 59, Hall, 2006: 207] and the calculation of Signal Excess above the FOM to determine if detection was made during that time step. This concept is graphically depicted in Figure 48.

$$FOM active\ (reverberation-limited) = SL + TS - RL - DT \quad \textbf{Equation 4}$$

$$SE = SL - 2PL - RL - DT \quad \textbf{Equation 5}$$

Where

SE is the signal excess in dB

SL is the active sonar source level in dB

PL is the propagation loss in dB

TS is the target strength in dB

RL is the reverberation level in dB

DT is the detection threshold in dB

Computing the signal excess for each time step in the simulation requires that the model compute each of the parameters of the sonar equation, including the observable, the energy propagation through the environment and the ability of the sensor to detect the received signal. The passive and active sonar equations were implemented in this spreadsheet, assuming a constant, range independent, iso-velocity sound velocity profile.

The passive and active target strengths utilized by the spread sheet model were derived from NPS SE 3122 course material. Figure 49 [Ref 58, Green, 2007] shows the range of passive acoustic noise signatures for various classes/sizes of surface vessels. Utilizing this graph values were selected for the aircraft carrier (CVN) from the Battleship operating curve at 15 knots and the CG/DDG values were selected for the Destroyer operating at 15 knots. These parameters are inputs to the model via the scenario control sheet and may be modified to support sensitivity analysis.

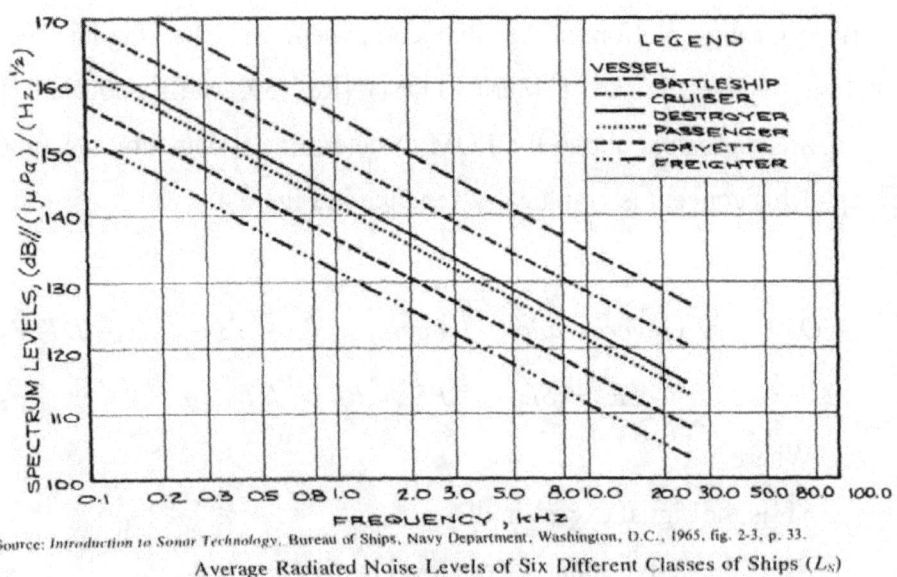

Figure 49 - Surface Vessel Radiated Noise Levels [Ref 58, Green, 2007]

The active target strength of the submarine was also required to support the spread sheet model. Figure 50 [Ref 58, Green, 2007] shows an azimuthal estimate of submarine active target strength. From these figures a value of 10dB was selected based on the smoothed azimuthal estimate. This appears to be a good average value, but does not account for the peaks and nulls associated with the beam, bow and stern aspects.

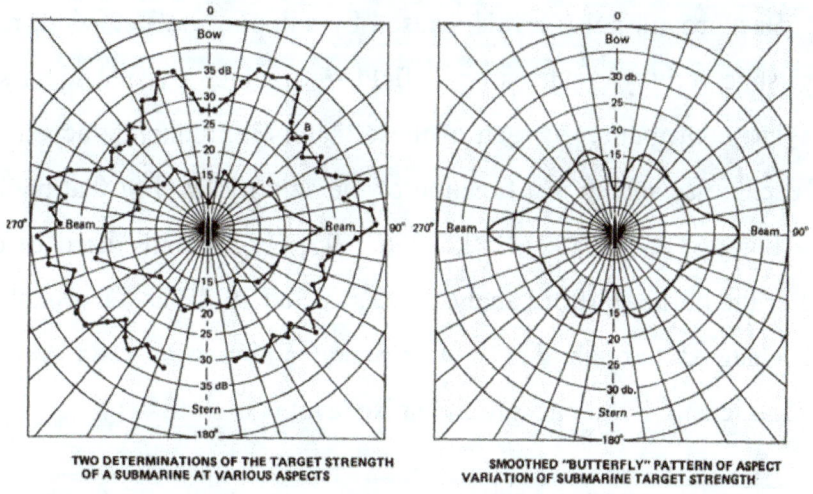

Figure 50 - Submarine Active Target Strength [Ref 80, Urick, 1983: 310]

The selection of an iso-velocity condition allows the spread sheet model to utilize spherical spreading loss approximations to estimate the effect of the environment on the transmission and reception of energy. Using this method the one-way passive transmission loss is computed as 20Log(Range) and the two way active transmission loss is computed as 2*20Log(Range) or 40Log(Range) (Figure 51).

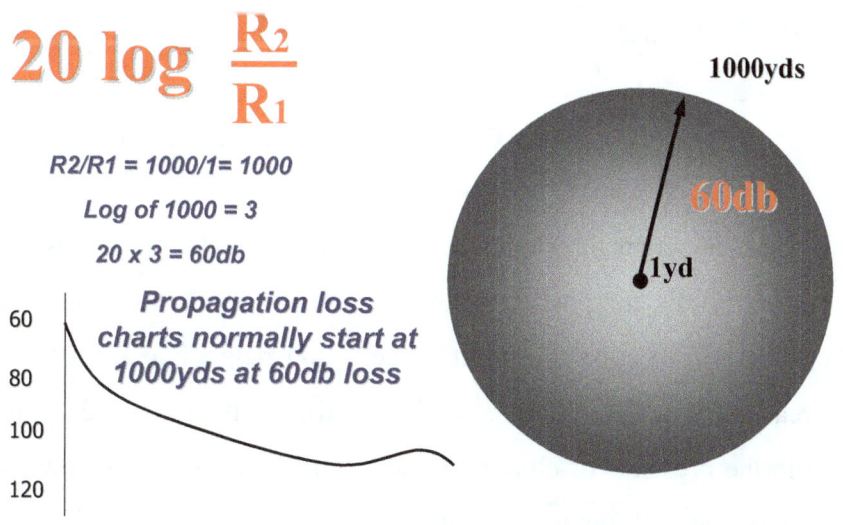

Figure 51 - Spherical Spreading Loss Depiction [Ref 83, Fleet Forces Command, 2006]

Background noise levels, caused by shipping traffic, wind, rain, biologic activity and seismic activity creates a noise field from which passive sonar signals must be detected. The contribution of each of these factors is frequency dependent, and the amplitude of each noise source is a function of the activity level of that parameter. The Wentz curve (Figure 52, [Ref 59, Hall, 2006: 195]) is normally used to depict these parameters. For the purpose of our analysis we selected 70 dB as a nominal value. This value can be changed through the Environmental and Sensor Data worksheet if an assessment of the sensitivity to background noise level is desired.

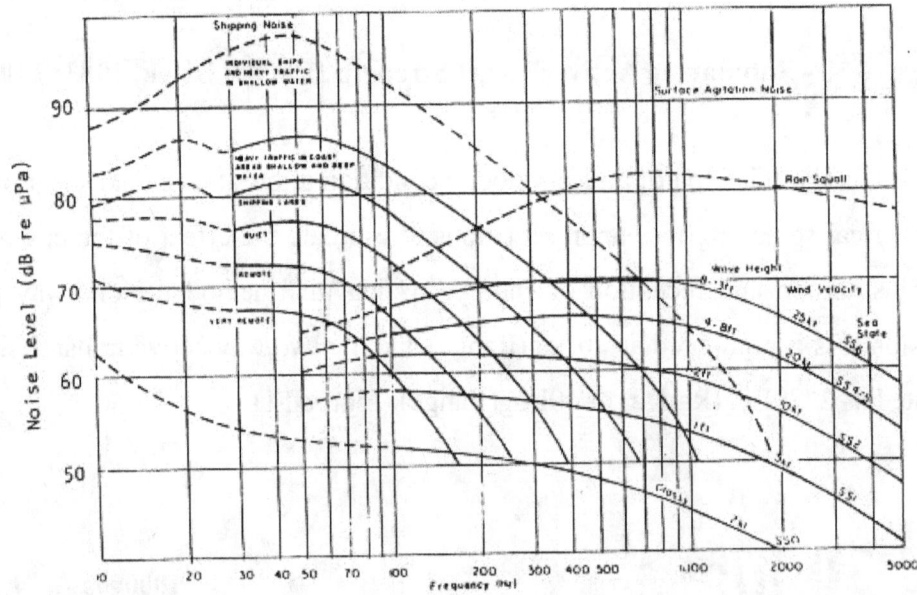

Figure 52 - Wentz Curve [Ref 59, Hall, 2006: 195]

The detection thresholds selected for the modeling analysis were 20 for active sensors and 10dB for passive sensors. These nominal values were chosen to illustrate the effect of detection threshold on detection range, and are set up parameters within the spread sheet model and to recognize the difficulty associated with detection of active targets in the presence of clutter. In addition, signal and noise fluctuations were introduced into the model using a Gaussian distribution with a mean of 0dB and a sigma of 9dB for passive and 12dB for active. Figure 53 [Ref 58, Green, 2007] illustrates the effects of these fluctuations on the detection process. The introduction of the random signal fluctuations allows the team to utilize an M of N method [ditto] to simulate the classification/decision process during the torpedo engagement analysis.

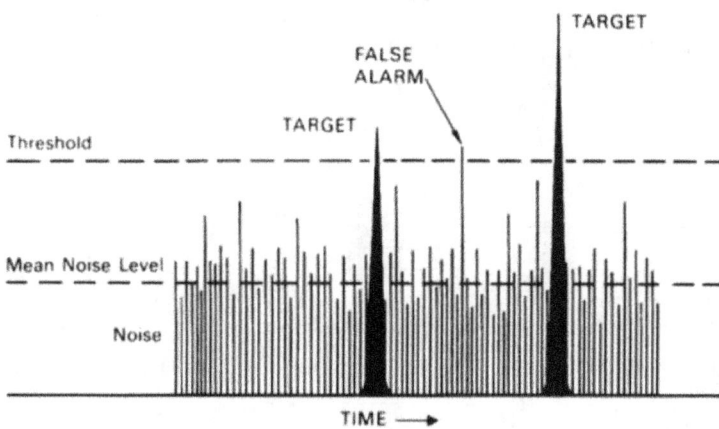

The higher the threshold is above the mean level of the noise, the lower the probability of a spike of noise crossing it and producing a false alarm.

Figure 53 - Illustration of Detection Threshold and Noise Fluctuations [Ref 58, Green, 2007]

Satisfying the need for quantitative value of key performance measures was accomplished through the implementation of an Excel WorkBook with Worksheets organized to support scenario setup parameters, environmental parameters, geometric position data and resultant sensor detection estimates, tracking and engagement analysis and finally a scorecard to allow for Monte Carlo replication of the results. Figure 54 shows the top level control for this WorkBook. This page allows the initial scenario parameters, including the range and bearing of the submarine at the start of the problem which is randomly set for each run using the RandBetween() function for both Range and Bearing from the aircraft carrier at problem start. In addition, to support sensitivity analysis, the user may elect to modify the CSG surface combatant screen formation parameters to investigate the impact of a longer range to the screen from the aircraft carrier or a wider search angle which the 3 DDG platforms will be distributed about as discussed in the CONOPS for this problem.

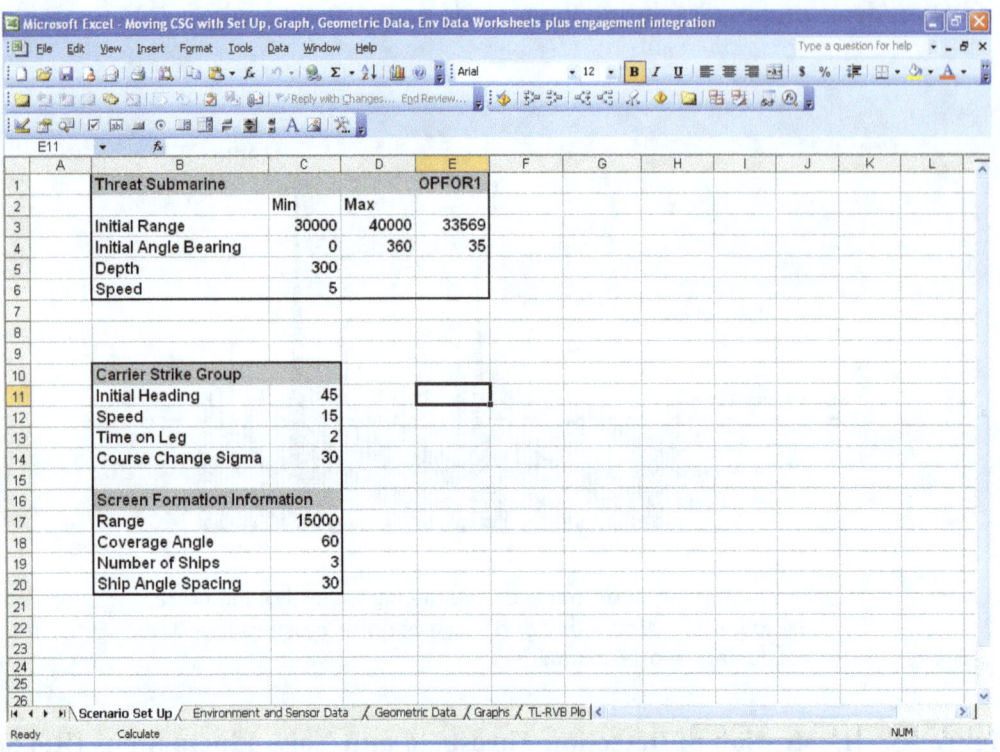

Figure 54 - Spread Sheet Control

In addition to these scenario set-up parameters which control the initial starting point and motion of the carrier strike group and submarine platforms, the discrete time event simulation requires inputs for passive signature levels for the surface vessels, active target strength for the submarine and also the background noise level that interferes with passive detection. Also, the fluctuation in signals and noise as seen by the detection process is modeled via this spread sheet. Figure 55 provides a depiction of the Sensor and Environment Control Worksheet which allows the system engineering team to modify these simulation input parameters.

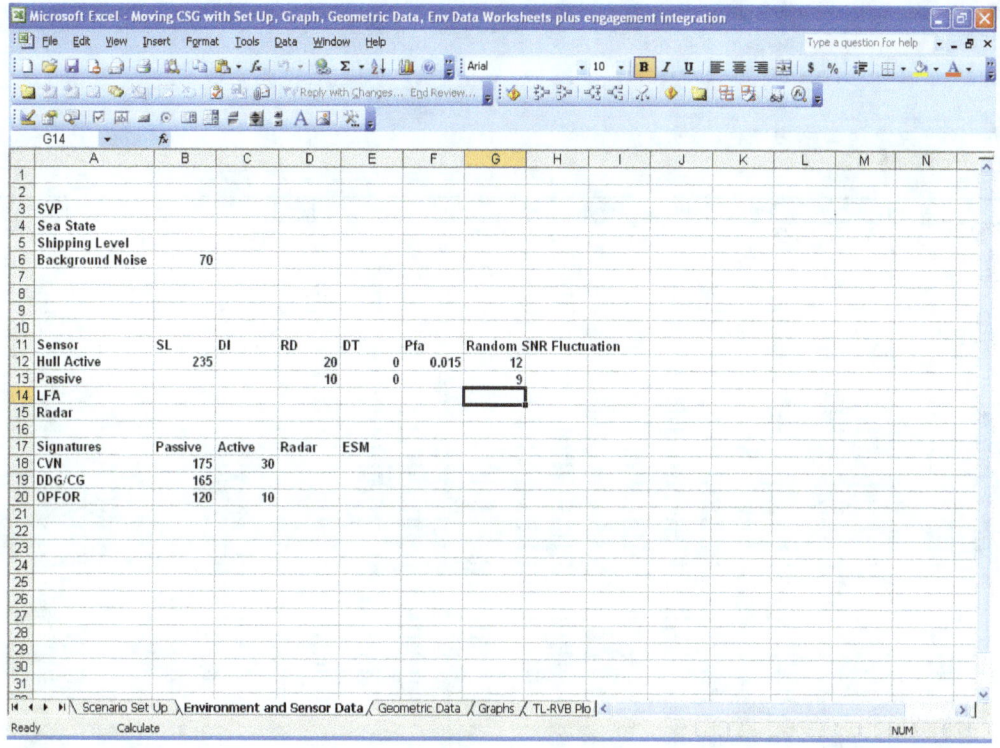

Figure 55 - Environmental and Target Strength Control Sheet

At problem start the opposing submarine will execute maneuvers every two hours, changing course between 45 and 225 degrees. The submarine maintains this race track pattern until its sensors can detect the CVN acoustic signature. Upon detection the submarine will execute an attack tactic by assuming an intercept course with the CVN. Figure 56 below is a screen capture of a single engagement analysis run using the spread sheet model. Although too small for legibility, the green highlights indicate positive signal excess for the active sonar sensors of the Carrier Strike Group (DDG 1, DDG 2, DDG 3 and CG 1) against the submarine and of the passive submarine sensors against the CVN, DDGs and CG.

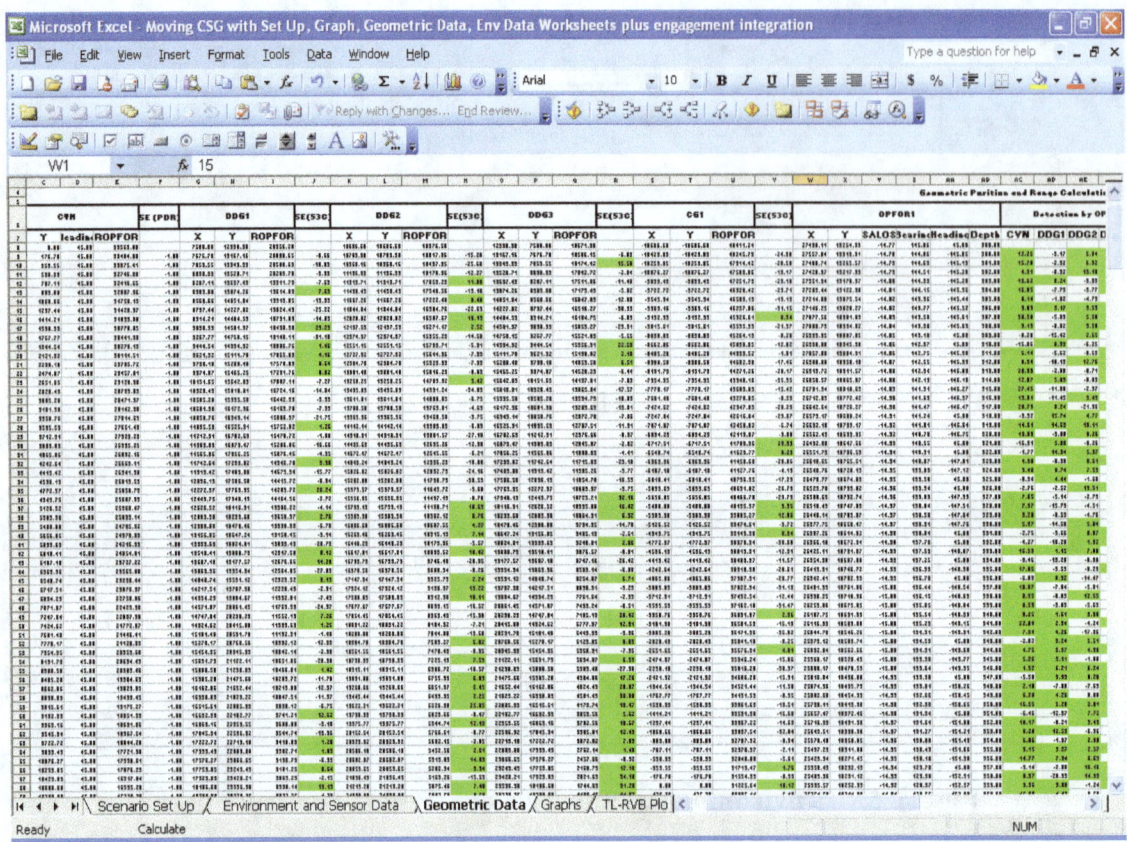

Figure 56 – Single Engagement Analysis Run

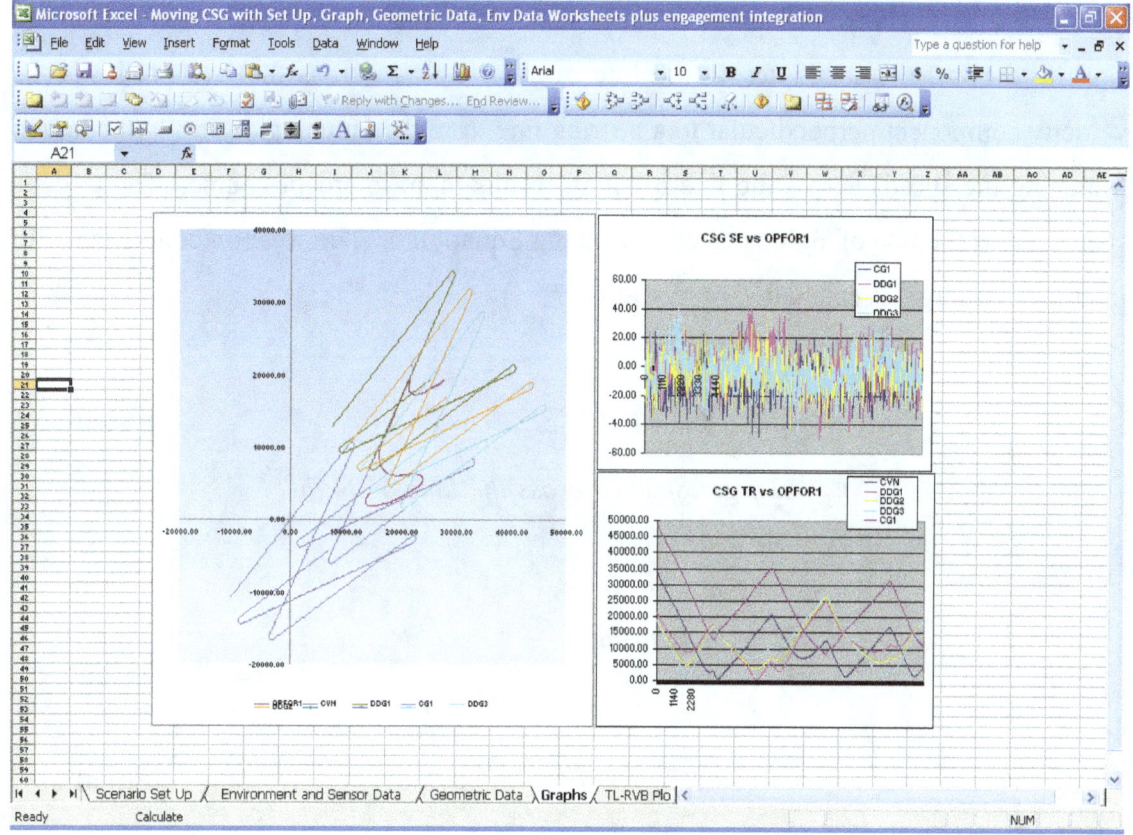

Figure 57 - Geographic Plot Example

The course is updated each time step based on the signal excess calculation and calculation of the bearing to the CVN. CSG course, speed and screen formation parameters may also be modified by the user to support sensitivity analysis. The base course and speed utilized for our analysis was 45 degrees and 15 knots, with course maneuvers every 2 hours. This approach allowed the CSG to remain within the 30x30 nautical mile operating area without the need for computing the proximity of the CSG to the edge of the operating area. Figure 57 depicts the geometry resulting from one of our analysis runs as well as the signal excess versus time for the CSG against the submarine and the time versus range plots for each platform in the CSG to the submarine.

The engagement model, used for both torpedoes and missiles, consists of three parts; the calculation of weapon course and run to the target, the decision to launch, and the determination of the result.

The weapon course is set to match the weapon's speed across the line of sight to the target's speed across the line of site. Speed across the line of site is the velocity component perpendicular to a bearing line from the launch platform to the target. Matching the speeds across the line of sight, results in an intercept course. The target's speed across the line of sight is calculated using Equation 6. The weapon course that will intercept the target is calculated by Equation 7.

$$V_{Ty} = V_T * (CSE_T - B_T) \qquad \textbf{Equation 6}$$

V_{Ty} = Target Speed Across the Line of Sight
V_T = Target Speed
CSE_T = Target Course
B_T = Target Bearing

$$CSE_W = \sin^{-1}\left(\frac{V_{Ty}}{V_W}\right) + B_T \qquad \textbf{Equation 7}$$

CSE_W = Weapon Course
V_W = Weapon Speed

The distance the weapon travels before it hits the target is calculated by multiplying the Target range at Time Of Fire by fraction of total closing speed (weapon's speed in the line of sight plus the target's speed in the line of sight) generated by the weapon. Equations 8 and 9 are used to calculate the target's and weapon's speed in the line of sight. Equation 10 calculates the distance traveled by the weapon. Inspection of Equation 10 will show that if the target is opening (i.e. V_{Tx} is negative) the distance traveled by the weapon will be greater than the range at Time of Fire.

$$V_{Tx} = V_T \cdot \cos(B_T - CSE_T) \qquad \textbf{Equation 8}$$

V_{Tx} = Target Speed in the Line of Sight
V_T = Target Speed

$$V_{Wx} = V_W \cdot \cos(CSE_W - B_T) \qquad \textbf{Equation 9}$$

V_{Wx} = Weapon Speed in the Line of Sight

$$D_W = R_T \cdot \left(\frac{V_{Wx}}{(V_{Wx} + V_{Tx})} \right) \qquad \textbf{Equation 10}$$

D_W = Distance Traveled by Weapon
R_T = Target Range

The decision to launch a weapon is based on the target being in range, and accumulating sufficient data to accurately place the weapon. Determining if the target is in range is simply a matter of checking weather the distance traveled by the weapon is less than the maximum range of the weapon. The determination of whether sufficient data has been accumulated is based on the time that the target is tracked. The criterion is defined as the target being detected for X of the last Y glimpse intervals. The X portion of the criterion provides a minimum time that the target must be tracked before launching a weapon, while the Y portion allows intermittent contact to contribute to the firing solution.

The results of an engagement are determined by comparing the time the Red submarine is hit by a Blue weapon with the time the Red submarine launches a weapon against the Blue carrier. If the Red submarine is hit before launching a weapon against the carrier, the carrier is scored as surviving. If the Red submarine launches a weapon against the carrier before being hit by a blue weapon, then the carrier is considered killed.

3.2.2.2 MPA Alternative Model

Because this alternative is employed as a layer of defense, the performance metric investigated must be one that is readily applied to the results of the modeling efforts of the other alternatives. The metric selected is the probability of detection (*Pd*) of a threat submarine attempting to reach the CSG OA. It is considered reasonable to assume that if detected by the MPA/EPAS system, that the MPA aircraft has adequate organic prosecution capability to neutralize the threat, thus increasing the probability of survival of the Aircraft Carrier. Another underlying assumption is that the rate of false detections will be low and not significantly impact the ability of the system to perform an effective search.

The expected platform for deployment and use of this sensor is the P-3C Orion. The P-3C is a land-based, long range, ASW patrol aircraft (Figure 58 and Table 3, [Ref 38, Jane'sfighting ships, 2008]). It is typically configured with submarine detection sensors such as sonobuoys (active, passive and multi-static systems) and magnetic anomaly detection (MAD) equipment. The avionics system is integrated by a general purpose digital computer that supports all of the tactical displays, monitors and automatically launches ordnance and provides flight information to the pilots. Each MPA squadron has nine aircraft and is deployed to sites outside the United States for approximately six months at a time.

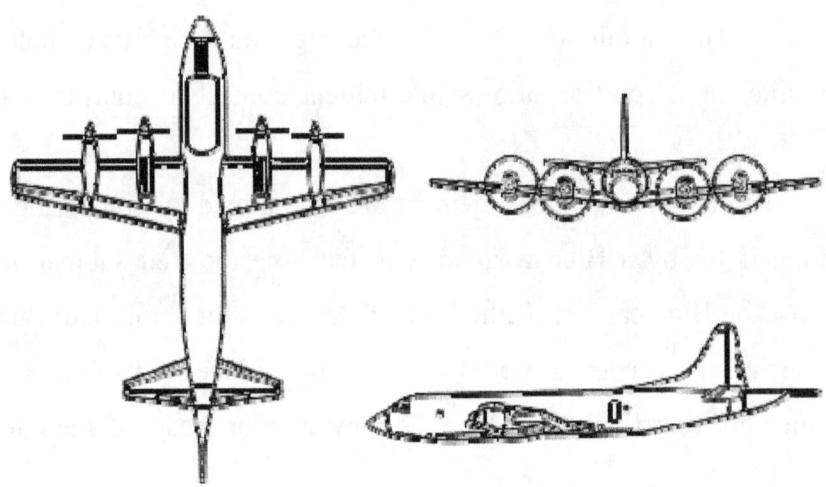

Figure 58 - P-3C Maritime Patrol Aircraft [Ref 38, Jane'sfighting ships, 2008]

Table 3 - P-3C Specifications

Crew Composition	11 (Normal)
Endurance	10-13 Hours
Cruise Speed	330 Knots
Armaments	20000 lb max of:
(varies by mission)	2000 lb mines
	LWT torpedoes
	MK101 Depth Bombs
	Sonobuoys

A program of record replacement aircraft for the P-3C is the P-8 Poseidon Multi-mission Maritime Aircraft (MMA). The P-8 is a modified Boeing 737 that will be equipped with modern ASW; anti-surface warfare (ASuW); and Intelligence, Surveillance and Reconnaissance (ISR) sensors for broad-area, maritime and littoral operations. The Navy expects to buy 34 low-rate initial production (LRIP) aircraft in the years '10, '11 and '12, and then transition beyond that in the year '13, to hit full-rate production. [Ref 49, Pike, 2007]

The technology incorporated by the EPAS sensor will be most effective against surfaced or near surface submarine targets. Operationally, this will correspond to submarines that are transiting on or near the surface either to snorkel (recharging batteries) or to perform communications functions. This condition is most likely to occur when the submarine that has not yet detected the presence of the opposing force, i.e. the CSG. Consequently, it makes the most sense to use this sensor at a significant distance from the CSG, with the MPA operating in a largely autonomous mode. The MPA's response to threat detection will be to attack with torpedoes. In the event that the threat eludes the initial attack, reacquisition and re-attack can be performed using conventional sensors including MAD and sonobuoys.

As previously discussed, this sensor is only effective against a surfaced or near surface target. It will be best employed when the submarine has not yet detected the presence of the opposing forces. Consequently, the MPA/EPAS system will execute its search in those areas where the threat submarine is unlikely to be alerted to the presence of opposing forces.

The general case for analysis is that the MPA will be assigned an Area of Responsibility (AOR) that is outside the CSG OA and within the larger theater and that the submarine can attack from any direction. It would be reasonable to consider other situations that include *apriori* knowledge of threat activities, but for the purposes of this analysis the more general case will be considered.

Figure 59 describes the method of employment of the MPA/EPAS system for this analysis. It is believed that this concept of employment (COE) will provide the greatest probability of detection of the submarine for the general case.

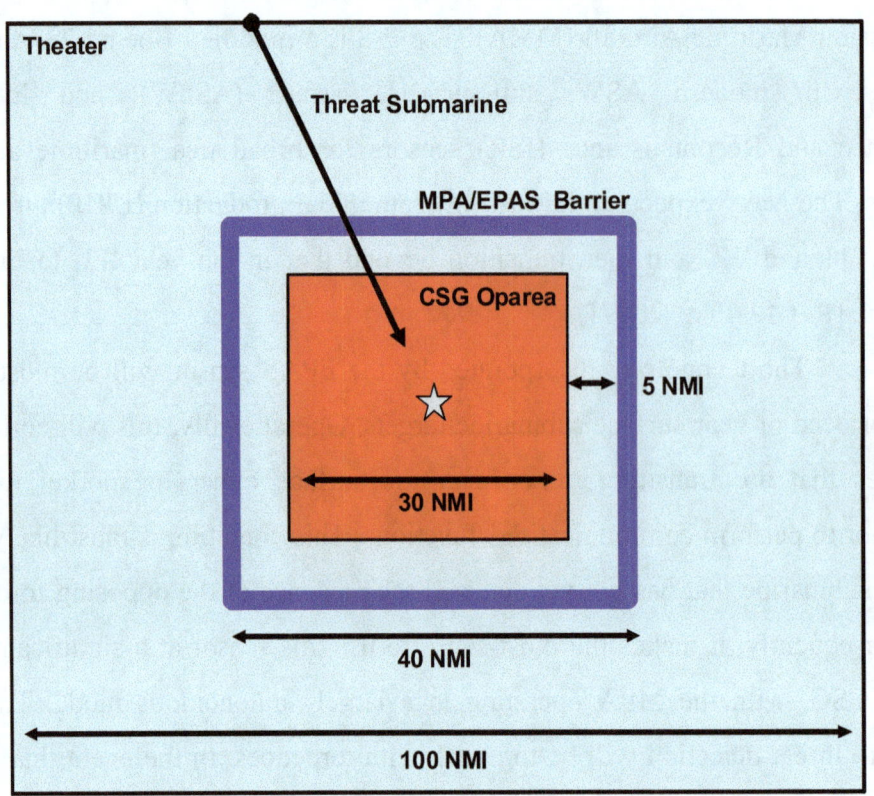

Figure 59 - MPA/EPAS Employment

Because the threat submarine is attempting to get within the CSG OA, it will have to transit across the operational theater, which is defined as a 100 x 100 nm area. In the modeling of other alternatives, the submarine speed is taken to be 5 knots. In this case its speed is taken as 10 knots, under the assumption that it will be less concerned with stealth when outside the CSG OA. It can be reasonably assumed that the transiting submarine prior to entering the CSG OA will change its behavior to a stealthier, continually submerged mode. Consequently, the MPA/EPAS system must detect the threat before the submarine reaches this range. The range from the CSG OA where the submarine makes this transition is taken to be within 5 miles of the OA perimeter.

The submarine is modeled as transiting a straight course, beginning at a randomly determined position on the perimeter of the theater and heading for the center of the CSG OA. Because the threat submarine is in motion, and its initial position in time and space is unknown, there is no benefit to performing a methodical search of the entire AOR. It can be demonstrated that a more effective technique is to establish a notional barrier that the submarine must cross in order to achieve its purpose.

Because speed, sweep width and endurance of the search platform are fixed, it is desirable to maximize the number of opportunities for detection. This corresponds to making the Circuit length of the barrier as short as possible. The limiting factor is that the barrier must be maintained outside the range at which the submarine is likely to be alerted to the CSG and submerge. This range is taken to be 5 NMI.

In determining the probability of detecting a submarine that is attempting to transit the theater, several factors are taken into consideration.

- The opportunities for detection presented by the threat submarine
- The instantaneous area coverage by EPAS (sweep width)
- The flight characteristics of the MPA

The threat submarine is characterized as transiting towards the center of the CSG OA, beginning at a random point on the periphery of the defined theater. It is advancing at 10 knots and coming to the surface or near surface for 1 hour out of 6 (16.7% of the time): the time near the surface provides the submarine the opportunity to run diesel engines to charge its batteries or to perform communications functions. It is during this period that it is vulnerable to detection by the MPA/EPAS system. This is considered to be a reasonable characterization of behavior for a diesel electric submarine transiting to an area where it expects to find opposition forces.

The EPAS sensor is currently under development. Consequently its performance characteristics and concept of operation have not yet been fully established. For the purposes of this analysis the following values for this sensor type have been determined, by best engineering judgment, as reasonable estimates of the future sensors performance.

Table 4 - EPAS Estimated Performance Characteristics

Nominal Operating Altitude	10000 Ft.
Downward Looking Aperture	60°
Probability of Detection	0.90

Given the parameters for operating altitude and aperture, the sweep width of the sensor can be readily calculated:

$$Sweep\ width\ =\ Altitude\ x\ SIN\left(\frac{60}{2}\right)\ x\ 2\ =\ 10000\ ft\ \sim\ 1.5 NMI \quad \textbf{Equation 11}$$

The typical mission duration for the MPA is 10-13 hours. If a 12 hour mission duration is assumed and a transit time of 2 hours from the MPA base to its AOR, a total on station time per aircraft mission is 8 hours. The typical cruise speed for the MPA is 330 knots, giving the aircraft 2640 nautical miles of search per mission. The previously described search track is square, 40 NMI on a side, or 160 NMI for a single circuit.

The calculation of the probability that a submarine is detected as it transits across the theater to the CSG OA, which is our metric P(d), is given by the following relationship:

$$P(d)\ =\ P(exposure)\ x\ P(d_{EPAS})\ x\ \#Looks \quad \textbf{Equation 12}$$

P(exposure) is defined as the probability that the submarine will be both within the width of the barrier, defined by the sweep width of the EPAS sensor, and at a detectable depth at any given time.

$P(d_{EPAS})$ is defined as the probability of detection by the EPAS sensor system. The value of $P(d_{EPAS})$ is 0.90 as this was shown in an earlier table.

Looks is defined as the number of circuits of the barrier the MPA will make during the time required by the submarine to transit the width of the MPA barrier.

P(exposure) is determined by taking the product of two other probabilities: the probability that the submarine is within the MPA barrier/EPAS sweep width and the probability that the submarine is susceptible to detection at or near the surface. Determining what percentage of time the submarine is within the "barrier" is simply the ratio of the width of the theater to the sweep width of the sensor (1.5 NMI/15 NMI = 0.10). The probability that the sub is susceptible to detection is determined from the ratio of submerged time to surfaced time during its transit (6:1 or 0.167). Consequently:

$$P(exposure) = 0.10 \times 0.167 = .0167 \qquad \textbf{Equation 13}$$

Looks is determined by determining the number of times the MPA will complete a circuit of the barrier during the period that the submarine will transit across the theater.

$$\# \ Looks = \frac{time \ of \ transit}{time \ per \ circuit} \qquad \textbf{Equation 14}$$

The submarine speed of transit is known and is 10 knots. The distance of the transit varies with the heading angle of the submarine relative to the geometry of the theater. That is, the distance is shorter for a transit perpendicular to the boundaries than the distance for a transit that is at an angle to the boundaries. Since the range of angles that can be realized is from 0 to 45 degrees, and the submarine's initial position on the theater boundary is random, the mean heading is taken as 22.5 degrees from perpendicular. This corresponds to an average transit time of

$$\textit{Average Transit Time} = \frac{15\ NMI}{\left(\cos(22.5)\ x\ 10\ knots\right)} = 1.623\ Hrs \quad \textbf{Equation 15}$$

The time per circuit of the barrier is determined from the airspeed of the MPA (330 knots) and the circumference of the barrier (40 NMI x 4 = 160 NMI).

$$\textit{Circuit time} = \frac{\textit{Circuit Distance}}{\textit{Airspeed}} \sim .5\ hours \quad \textbf{Equation 16}$$

The approximating of this value is legitimate as the aircraft will not likely fly a perfectly straight course nor will it execute perfectly square turns at the corners of the barrier.

Average number of circuits per submarine transit follows:

$$\#\ Looks_{avg} = \frac{1.623\ hours}{0.5\ hours} = 3.246 \quad \textbf{Equation 17}$$

Calculation of *P(d)*. The Probability of Detection for a single submarine transit (average) is now given;

$$P(d) = P(exposure)\ x\ P(d_{EPAS})\ x\ \#looks \quad \textbf{Equation 18}$$
$$P(d) = .0167\ x\ .9\ x\ 3.246 = .0488 \sim 0.05$$

3.2.2.3 *LCS Barrier Alternative Model*

The modeling of the perimeter portion of the barrier alternative is discussed in this section. The barrier perimeter acts in parallel with the CSG to complete the barrier alternative in the form of a layered defensive and offensive system. Both components of the barrier alternative (CSG and barrier perimeter) are modeled separately and the effective performance of the entire alternative is shown in section 3.2.4.2.

As described in Section 3.1.2.6, the barrier alternative is the combination of the CSG with the addition of a barrier perimeter detection and engagement system. The perimeter portion of the barrier alternative is designed to provide both detection and engagement of incoming threat submarines along the CSG OA boundary. An LCS surface ship continuously places, replenishes, and monitors free-floating active SONAR buoys along the OA perimeter, creating an active acoustic submarine detection barrier. When detection criteria are met within a given buoy, information is communicated to the LCS via the communication link. Based on engagement doctrine and information provided by the buoys, LCS personnel will decide whether or not to launch a helicopter from the LCS to the area of interest for torpedo engagement of the threat submarine. Figure 60 shows a conceptualization of the barrier alternative OA geometry including buoy locations.

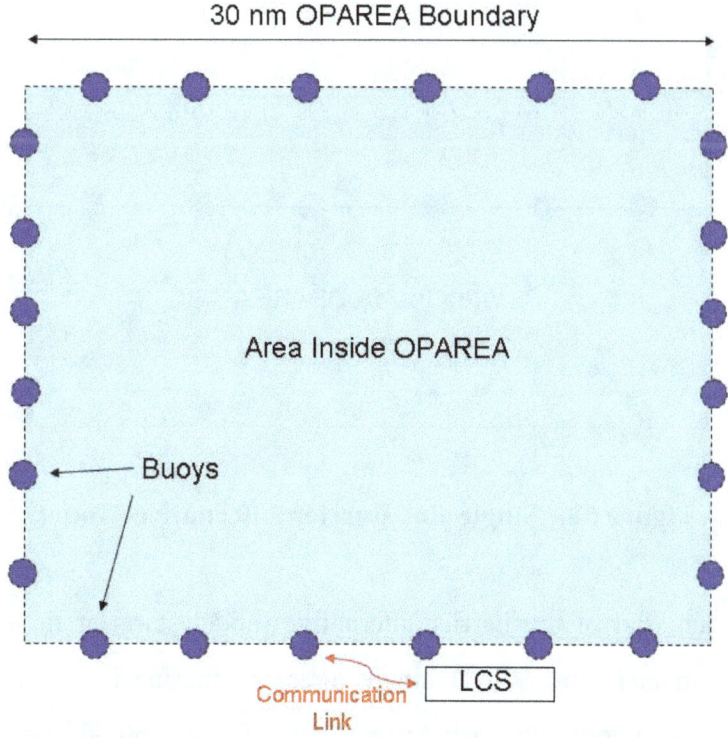

Figure 60 – Conceptualization of the Barrier Alternative OA Geometry

Based on the previously stated modeling goal, the primary model objective is to determine the probability that the barrier alternative perimeter successfully engages an incoming threat submarine as it approaches the OA boundary. Due to the symmetry of the square OA, the barrier alternative perimeter model may be simplified to the examination of the probability of defeating the threat submarine crossing one side of the 30 nm OA. A Monte Carlo spreadsheet simulation of a red submarine perpendicularly approaching a 30 nm line of buoys was developed to statistically determine this probability. This single-line model concept is shown in Figure 61.

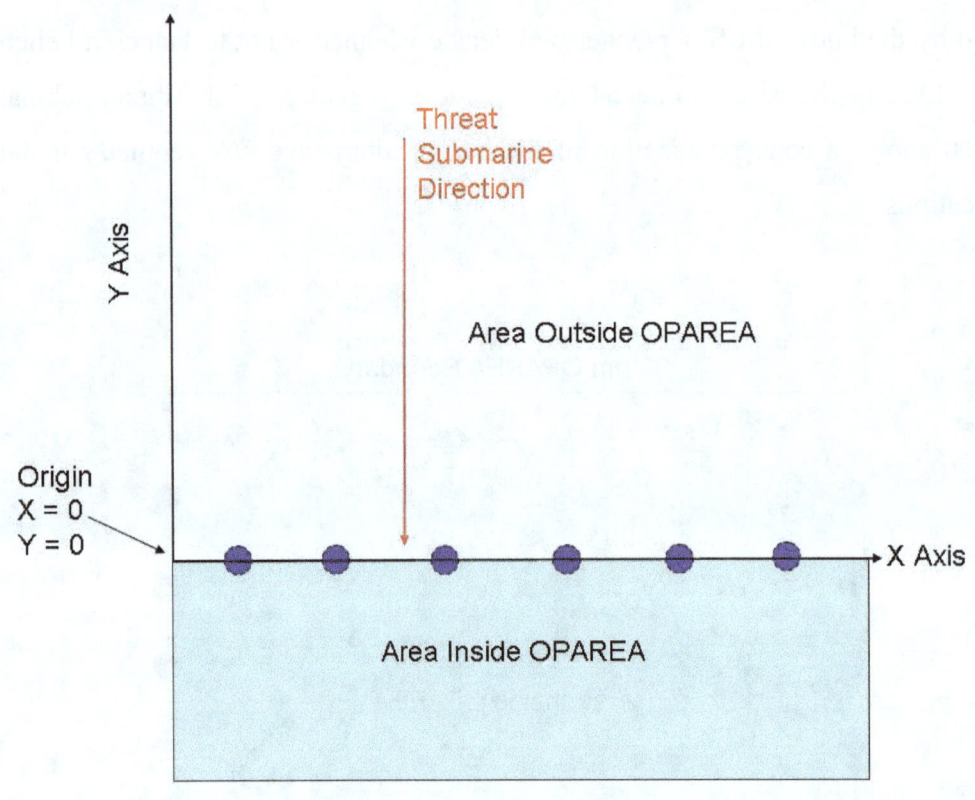

Figure 61 – Single-line Barrier Alternative Model

Each trial of the barrier alternative model starts at time $t = 0$ with the geometry as shown in Figure 62. A single threat submarine is positioned at location (x, y) where x is a random number between 0 and 30 nm (~60,000 yards) and y is set equal to 20,000 yards. Ideally, the buoys are uniformly spaced along the x-axis between $x = 0$ and $x = 60,000$ yards. However, due to buoy drift and varying buoy placement times, the model alters these ideal uniform buoy locations by adding a uniform random variable between +/- 3000 yards to both the x and y position of each buoy.

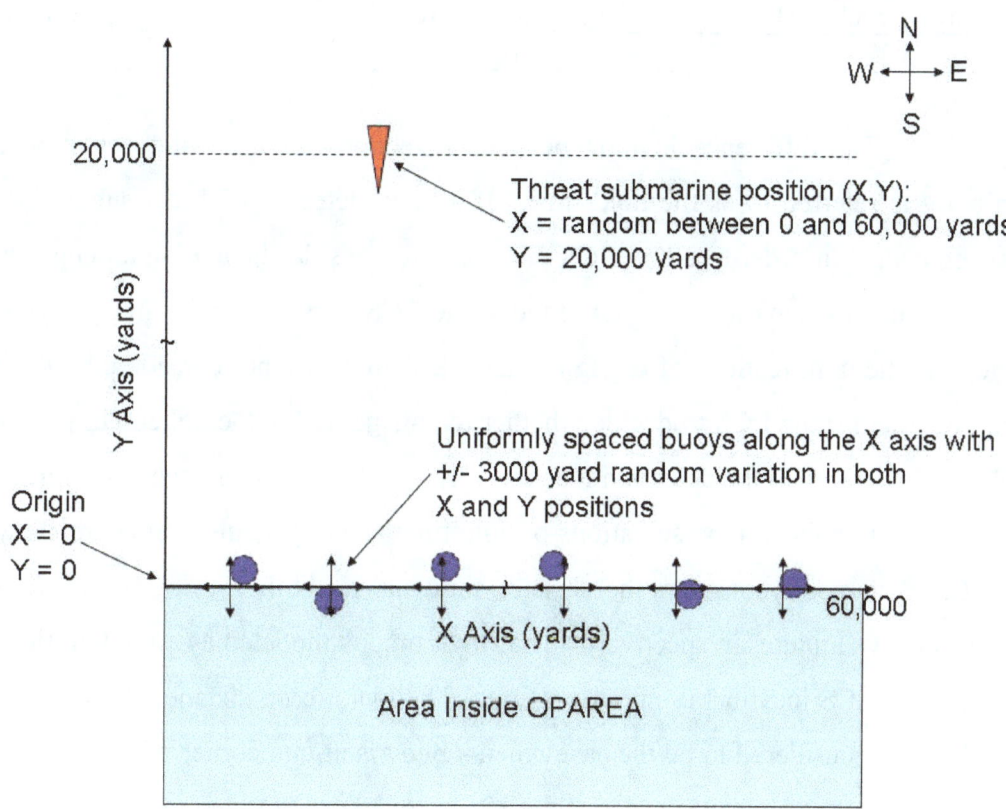

Figure 62 – Barrier Alternative Perimeter Model Trial Geometry at Time = 0

After the threat submarine and buoys are placed as described above at time $t = 0$, the model increments time in one minute intervals. As time increments, the threat submarine moves perpendicularly towards the x-axis (South) at a constant speed of five knots and the buoys each drift with independent random motion at an average speed of one knot.

At each step in time, the signal excess at each buoy is calculated using Equation 5. The model parameters used in this equation are shown in Table 5. A detection is defined to be whenever the signal excess calculation exceeds 0 dB.

Table 5 - Barrier Signal Excess Equation Parameters

Source Level (dB)	Target Strength (dB)	Recognition Threshold (dB)
195	10	20

The difference in time between detection initiation and cessation on a given buoy is referred to as the hold time. If a buoy detects the threat submarine, the LCS is contacted in order to allow LCS personnel to consider launching an engagement against the threat submarine. For this model, the LCS personnel will always decide to engage, and the ramifications of engaging false detections are not considered. The total amount of time for the LCS to decide whether to engage, ready the helicopter personnel, and fly the helicopter to the detection location is referred to as the engagement time.

Graphical representations of hold time and engagement time are shown in Figure 63. The model considers the decision time and ready time to be constants of ten minutes and five minutes, respectively. The flight time is modeled as a random time due to the random LCS location at any given time. The worst-case distance the LCS can be from a buoy is considered to be the case when a buoy is at one corner of the OA and the LCS is located at the opposite corner of the 30 nm by 30 nm OA square. This distance is ~85,000 yards, and assuming a helicopter speed of 125 knots, the maximum flight time of the helicopter is ~20 minutes. Therefore, the flight time is modeled as a uniform random variable between one and 20 minutes.

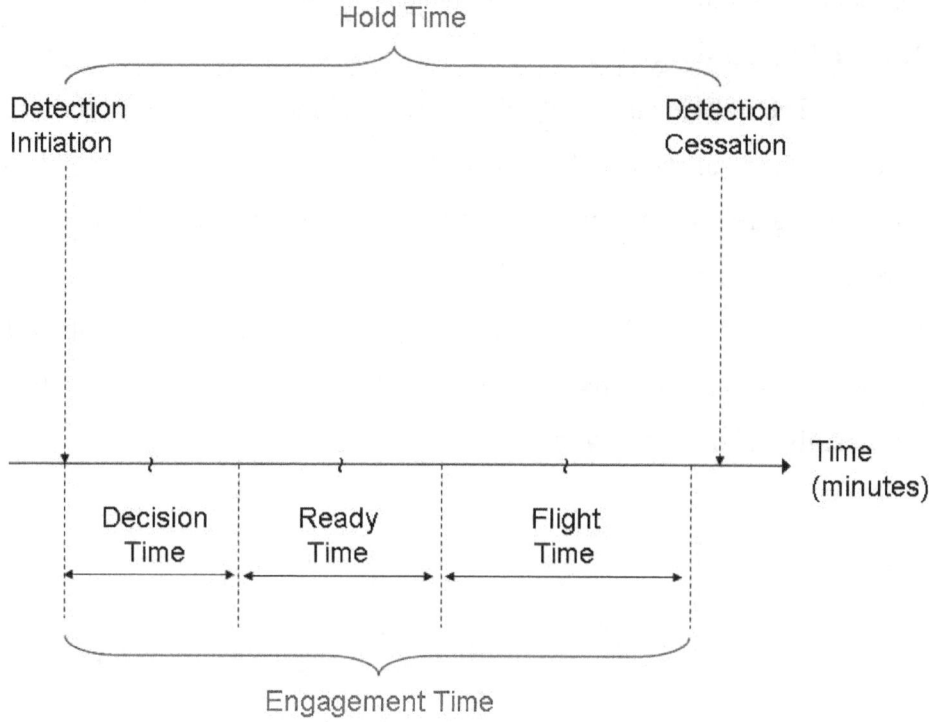

Figure 63 - Timeline Displaying Hold Time and Engagement Time

For any given trial, an engagement is considered to be successful if the engagement time is less than the hold time. In other words, if a buoy is still detecting the threat submarine at the time the helicopter arrives on station to engage by dropping a torpedo, the engagement is modeled as being successful. For each trial, the threat submarine may or may not be detected, and if it is detected, the engagement is either successful or it is not. If an engagement is successful, the model calculates how far away from the OA boundary the threat submarine was at the time of the initial detection.

The results of the barrier perimeter model are presented in Section 3.2.4.2.

3.2.2.4 *Model integration*

Since the alternatives consist of one or more alternatives added to the Baseline, the results of the Barrier and MPA models need to be combined with the Baseline model results to calculate the overall probability of carrier survival as discussed in Section 3.2.2. The Advanced Capabilities Build result is calculated by running the Baseline model with the input parameters changed to reflect the improved performance of the Advanced Capabilities Build.

The individual model results are combined using the event tree shown in Figure 64. The logic of the event tree is implemented in a Microsoft Excel spreadsheet. Each circle in Figure 64 represents one of the alternative models discussed above. The "Yes" branches represent the probability of the associated alternative stopping the red submarine. The "No" branches represent the probability of the Red submarine getting through the associated alternative. The sum of the "Yes" branch probabilities is the overall probability of carrier survival.

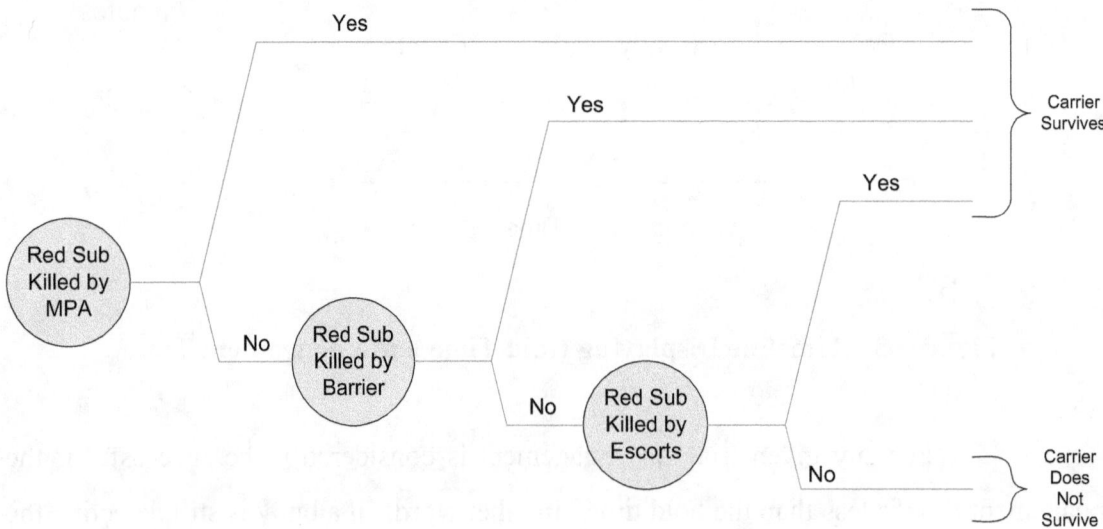

Figure 64 - Carrier Survival Event Tree

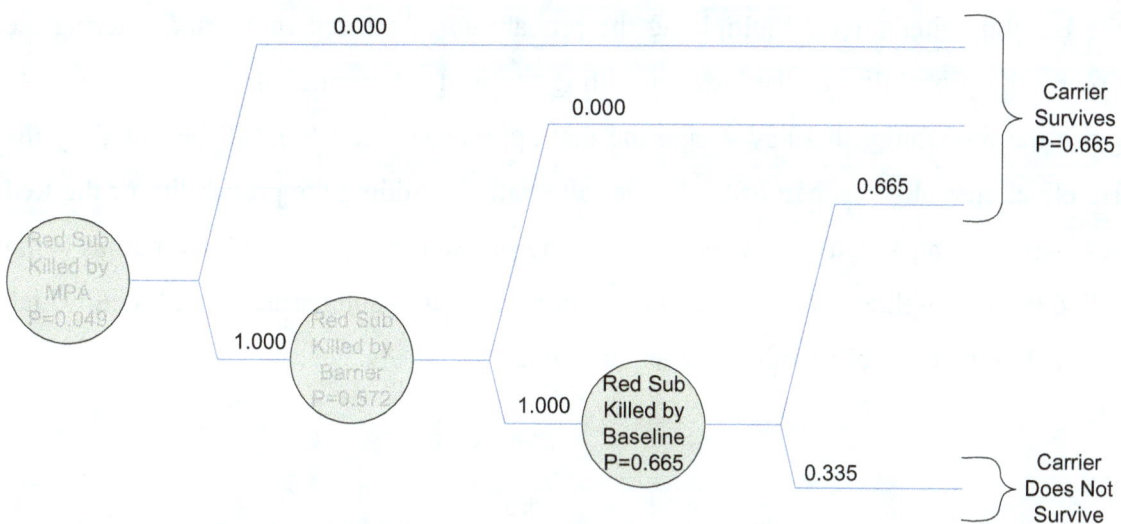

Figure 65 - Baseline Event tree

Figure 65 is the event tree for the Baseline alternative. Only the baseline node is active, with a Probability of kill against the Red submarine of 0.665, which was calculated by the baseline model. The overall probability of carrier survival is 0.665.

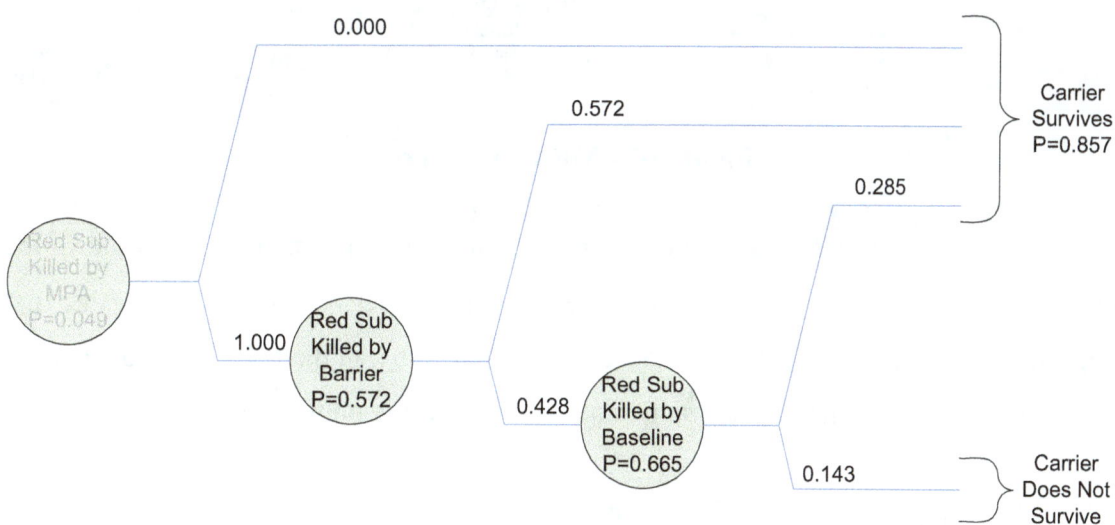

Figure 66 - Barrier Event Tree

Figure 66 is the event tree for the Barrier alternative. It has two active nodes, the Baseline and the Barrier. As the tree shows, the first opportunity to kill the Red submarine is at the barrier. The barrier model calculated the probability that a submarine would be killed passing through the barrier to be 0.572. This leaves a probability of 0.428 (Pk-1) that the red submarine will enter the OA and be engaged by the Baseline alternative. Multiplying the probability of the red submarine entering the OA by the probability of the baseline killing the Red submarine after it enters the OA, gives the probability that any submarine that approaches the CSG will be killed by the Baseline alternative, as part of the barrier alternative. Adding the probability of the Red submarine being killed by the Barrier and the probability of the Red submarine being killed by the baseline gives the total probability of the Red submarine being killed, which is equal to the probability of the carrier surviving.

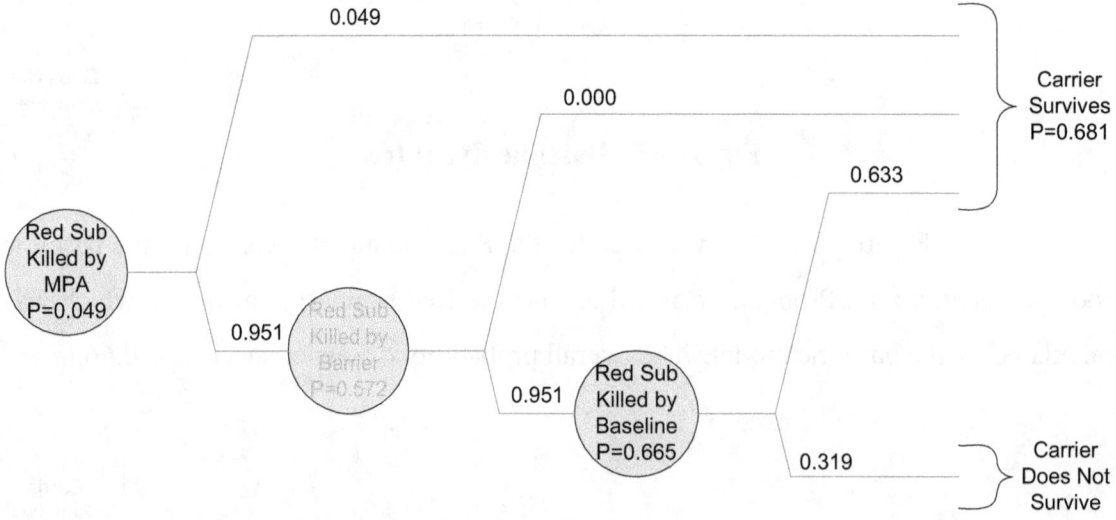

Figure 67 - MPA Event Tree

Figure 67 is the event tree for the MPA alternative. This is similar to the barrier event tree, in that two of the three nodes are active. In this case the first opportunity to kill the red submarine occurs outside the OA, in the MPA's patrol area. In this case the Barrier is not present so its node has no bearing on the outcome.

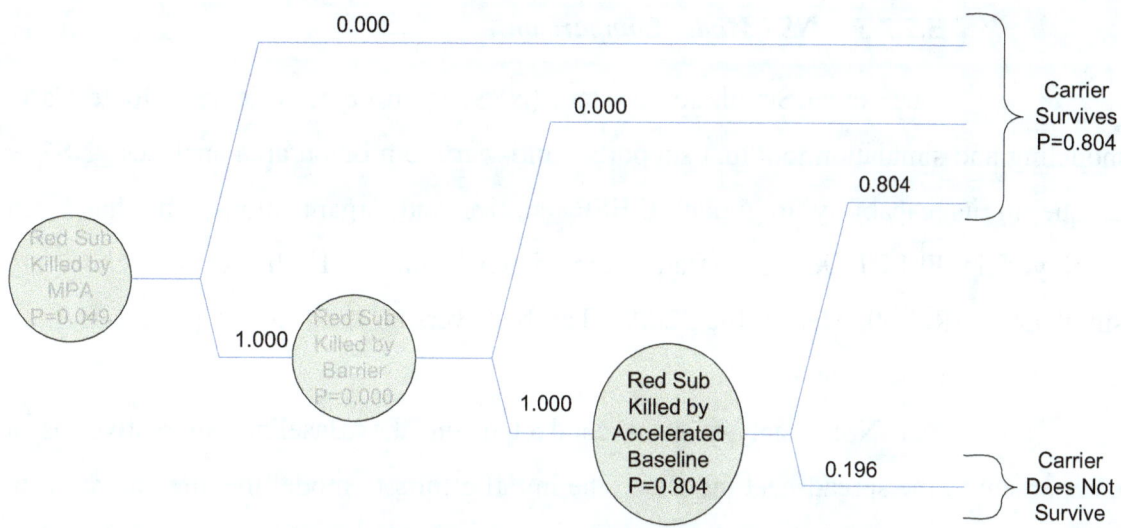

Figure 68 - Advanced Capabilities Build Event Tree

Figure 68 is the event tree for the Advanced Capabilities Build alternative. Like the baseline event tree it only has one active node. However, it uses the improved probability of kill calculated by the Advanced Capabilities Build model.

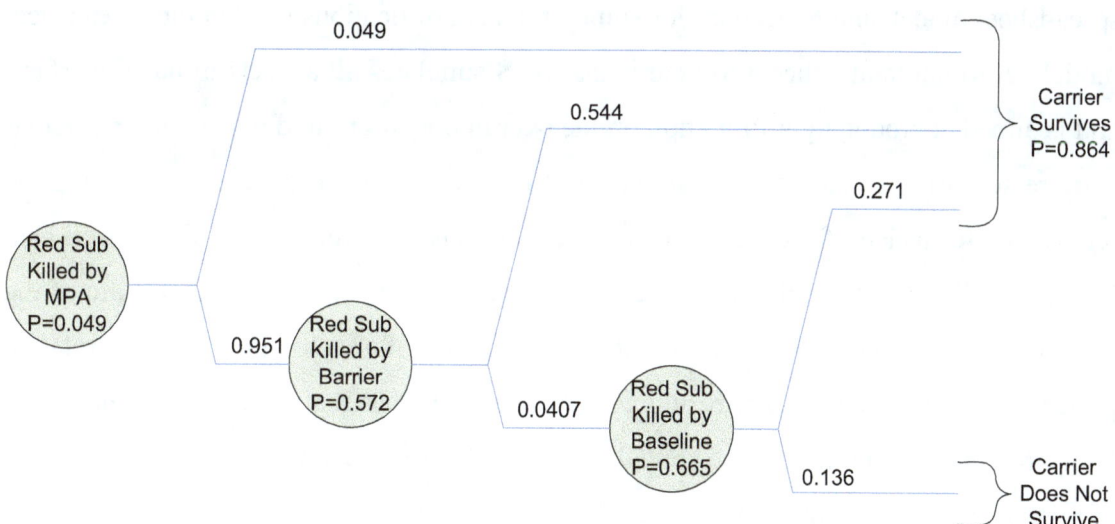

Figure 69 - Barrier Plus MPA Event Tree

Figure 69 is the event tree for the Barrier plus MPA alternative. It uses all three nodes.

3.2.2.5 NSS Model Comparison

The Naval Simulation System (NSS) is an object oriented Monte Carlo modeling and simulation tool that supports multi-warfare mission area analyses. NSS is unique in its capability to model C4ISR entities and organizations, and has been employed in FLEETEX, Fleet Battle Experiments, and in High Level Architecture simulations. [Ref 60, Metron Inc., 2002] The NSS version used in this project used an unclassified database.

An NSS analysis was conducted on the Baseline alternative as a comparison to the spreadsheet models. The initial efforts to model the alternatives with NSS were unsuccessful because the DDGs were 100% effective at preventing Red submarines from attacking the carrier, which conflicted with more credible stakeholder analysis results and other research conducted during the problem definition phase.

For the comparison with the spreadsheet models the NSS unclassified database objects were modified to mimic the performance of corresponding objects in the spreadsheet model, and to account for some of the simplifications used in the spreadsheet model. An important concept to note is that NSS simulates all aspects of naval warfare, and is aimed at producing information on the overall operations and results of a particular warfare scenario. In contrast, the spreadsheet models are aimed only at determining the relative performance of the alternatives under analysis. Therefore only the aspects that impact the differences in alternative performance are modeled, and the models are of the lowest fidelity that allows successful prediction of each alternative's relative performance. This low fidelity results in spreadsheet models that appear quite unrealistic compared to NSS, but in fact the spreadsheet models produce a more accurate prediction of relative system performance.

The Baseline alternative was modeled in NSS as a formation with a CVN (USS Theodore Roosevelt) at the center, three DDGs (based on USS Winston Churchill) at 000, 315, and 045 relative from the carrier at a range of 15,000 yards and a CG (USS Port Royal) at 180 relative, 15,000 yards. The CVN patrolled a 22.5 nm x 22.5 nm box at 15 knots, with the other ships in the formation maintaining their formation positions. Restricting the CVN to a 22.5 nm square box prevented the other ships of the formation from leaving the 30 nm square box. The Red submarine was modeled using the SS KILO object in the NSS database. The Red submarine was assigned a 100 nm square box as a patrol area, to allow the submarine to approach the CSG from any direction.

A number of changes were made to the NSS objects to provide more realistic results, and to incorporate the same simplifications that were incorporated in the spreadsheet model. The NSS scenario was setup to use low resolution sensor models. This was done to prevent sonar performance from being modeled using the radar equation. While the radar equation sonar performance model is workable, the effort required to derive radar parameters from sonar parameters is beyond the scope of this project. The following changes were made to the NSS unclassified database to make it comparable to the spreadsheet model:

- The maximum detection range of the SQS-53 sonar on the DDG/CG ships was reduced to 7500 yards, and the probability of detection for each glimpse interval was reduced to 0.5. These parameters are based on the results of the sonar equation based spreadsheet sonar detection model.
- The speeds of all ships in the NSS model were changed to match the speeds used in the spreadsheet model.
- Changed the KILO maximum tactical response speed to five knots to match the speeds used in the spreadsheet model.

NSS was used to run a Monte Carlo simulation of the Baseline alternative. The Monte Carlo simulation consisted of 999 iterations. At the end of each iteration NSS recorded whether the CVN had been destroyed or damaged, and reported the percentage of total iterations that resulted in each condition. These two conditions are mutually exclusive in NSS, so their sum gives the percentage of iterations that resulted in the CVN being hit by the submarine's torpedo. This sum is considered equivalent to the CVN being killed in the spreadsheet model. Therefore, subtracting the sum of the CVN damaged and CVN destroyed percentages from one gives the probability of CVN survival.

Table 6 - NSS Modeling results

CVN Damaged	3%
CVN Destroyed	0.3%
CVN Survives	96.7%

Table 6 presents the results of the NSS modeling. The NSS model produced a much higher probability of carrier survival than the Baseline spreadsheet model (96.7% vs. 66.5%). This disparity occurred even though the NSS model was adjusted to match, as much as the NSS's architecture would allow, the assumptions and performance parameters of the spreadsheet model. Prior to the adjustment the NSS model produced a 100% probability of carrier survival.

The NSS results are contradicted by the results of the stakeholder analysis, which indicated a significant submarine threat against US aircraft carriers. Validation of the ASW aspects of NSS are beyond the scope of this project, but would be a worthwhile research project in the future.

3.2.3 Operational Suitability

From the modeling and analysis standpoint operational suitability consists of Operational Availability (Ao) and Reliability (Re). Operational Availability (Ao) is defined as the percent of mission time that a system is able to provide the required operational mission functions. Ao is calculated as [Ref 61, Office of CNO, 2003]:

$$Ao = \frac{Uptime}{(Uptime + Downtime)} \qquad \textbf{Equation 19}$$

A system is in an Upstate when the system is capable of performing all of the required operational mission functions. The amount of time that a system is in an Upstate is called Uptime. A system is in a Downstate when the system cannot perform one or more of the required operational mission functions. Time that a system is in a Downstate is called Downtime. A failure that causes system Downtime is defined as an operational mission failure (OMF).

An engagement is a specific period of time within a mission. Engagement Reliability (*Re*) is the probability that a system can complete an engagement without an OMF. The *Ao* and *Re* model is comprised of electrical components. Electrical components are best modeled using an exponential distribution. Therefore, *Re* is calculated as [Ref 61, Office of CNO, 2003]:

$$Re = e^{-\left(\frac{t}{\text{Mean Time Between Operational Mission Failure (MTBOMF)}}\right)}$$ **Equation 20**

Where t is the engagement duration

$$MTBOMF = \frac{\text{Total Mission Time}}{\text{Total number of OMFs}}$$ **Equation 21**

The ASW Operational Availability (*Ao*) and Engagement Reliability (*Re*) Model is a simulation model utilizing the Naval Sea Systems Command (NAVSEA) Tiger Version 8.21.42 Availability and Reliability Computer Program within the Naval Supply Systems Command (NAVSUP) Readiness Based Sparing (RBS) Workstation Version 5.1.

Tiger is a Monte Carlo Simulation program that calculates system *Ao* and *Re* using input information that consists of the system configuration, component reliability, maintainability and logistics constraint information and the Operational Mission Profile. Component criticality is also incorporated.

3.2.3.1 *Process*

Components that provide the operational mission functions critical to support ASW Operations were identified for each system alternative. Reliability Block Diagrams (RBDs) were prepared to show operational success paths among all critical components of the system. The purpose of the RBD is to show the various series-parallel block combinations (paths) that result in system success. Reliability and maintainability information was collected for every component in the RBD and is provided in the following sections of this report.

Components that do not provide operational mission functions critical to support ASW Operations were not included in this model. These components were assumed to be reliable.

The ASW System is required to support a 14 day mission and, within this 14 day mission, the ASW System is required to support a 6 hour ASW engagement. The 14 day mission time was a stakeholder requirement. The 6 hour engagement time was derived from the amount of time it would take an enemy submarine to travel across the 30 x 30 nm OA traveling at 5 knots. The Operational Mission Profile of each system alternative is different; therefore the Operational Mission Profile will be further detailed when discussing each system alternative RMA model.

This information was collected for each system alternative and used as input into the Tiger model. It was assumed each ASW system alternative had a full compliment of weapons, supplies and personnel required to perform the operational mission functions critical to support ASW Operations at the start of the mission.

Each Tiger simulation follows this sequence

1. Time to fail "t" is calculated for each equipment (block in the reliability bock diagram) using the following equations. The equipment time to failure values are assumed to have an exponential distribution about the equipment mean time between failure (MTBF).

$$Re = e^{-\left(\frac{t}{MTBF}\right)} \quad \textbf{Equation 22}$$

or

$$t = -\ln(R) \times MTBF \quad \textbf{Equation 23}$$

'R' is a random number between zero and one selected by Tiger from a pseudorandom number string. MTBF is an input parameter provided in the tables below for all critical equipment included in the model. Equipment in the Tiger model can be placed in one of three states during a simulation phase: 1) Off 2) 'On but not Critical' 3) 'On and Critical'. There is no effect on *Re* and *Ao* when equipment is turned off. When equipment is turned off in a phase TIGER assumes a 0% failure rate. This disallows a failure occurrence by this equipment and does not contribute toward system downtime for *Ao*. When equipment is turned 'On but not Critical', TIGER allows the equipment to fail, but a failure does not cause an OMF, therefore, no system downtime is added. If the equipment is not repaired and the timeline transitions to a phase where that same equipment is now deemed critical, an OMF may occur at the start of that phase; depending on the configuration of the equipment in the system (see step 2). When equipment is 'On and Critical', equipment can fail causing a system OMF; depending on the configuration of the equipment in the system (see step 2).

2. The equipment times to fail are arranged in chronological order. Times to fail beyond the mission duration are ignored. At the first equipment time to fail Tiger determines whether the failure will drive the system to an Up state or a Downstate. If the equipment is a single point of failure the system would then be in a Downstate and the failure would be classified as an OMF. If the equipment is part of a redundancy, the system may be in an Up state if the redundant path is available. This failure would not be classified as an OMF. If the equipment is repairable, and there is a spare part available to make the repair, the equipment is repaired. A new equipment time to fail is calculated for the equipment when the repair is completed. The total time to repair the system from an OMF is Downtime; this includes the mean time to repair (MTTR) and the mean logistics delay time (MLDT). MLDT refers to the amount of time needed to acquire the spare part from storage after the part

was requested. In the ASW model repair was not allowed on any outboard items for the duration of the 14 day mission. For repairable inboard systems the MTTR is provided in the tables below. A 2 hour MLDT time was assumed for all repairable systems.

3. If the first failure resulted in a system Downstate, Tiger treats all of the time accumulated from the start of the simulated mission to the first equipment time to fail as system Uptime. The time accumulated to make the equipment repair is system Downtime. Upon repair and restoration of the system, the time accumulated to the next equipment time to fail is Uptime.

4. At the next equipment time to fail Tiger determines whether the system is in an Up state or a Downstate. Tiger checks whether any previous failures are still being repaired which could impact redundancy shown in the RBDs. The equipment repair is made based on the conditions stated in step 2, and a new equipment time to fail is calculated for the equipment when the repair is completed.

5. Tiger is keeping track of the Onboard Replacement Parts (OBRPs) that are being "consumed" as failures occur. If there are no more repair parts available to make a repair and an OMF occurs, the equipment is retained in a Downstate for the remainder of the simulated mission. In the ASW model a full compliment of OBRPs was assumed for repairable systems.

6. This process is repeated at each equipment time to fail until the mission duration time is met.

7. At the end of this simulated mission the Uptime and Downtime are calculated for this simulated mission.

8. Tiger then repeats the above simulation sequence until it has performed the number of simulated missions specified in the Tiger Input File. Nine-thousand nine-hundred and ninety nine (9999) simulated missions were conducted in the ASW model. The large number of simulations is run to achieve a statistical sample that suitably represents the equipment failure occurrence within the allocated mission time.

9. When all of the simulated missions are performed the Uptime from all of the simulated missions is added to obtain the Total Uptime, and the Downtime from all of the simulated missions is added to obtain the Total Downtime. The *Ao* is then calculated using Equation 19.

10. The total simulated mission run time is divided by the total number of OMFs to calculate MTBOMF as stated in Equation 21. *Re* is then calculated using Equation 22.

The percent of the 14 day ASW mission time that each system alternative is able to provide the required operational mission functions, *Ao*, is provided in the following sections of the report.

The probability that each system alternative can complete the 6 hour ASW engagement without an operational mission failure, *Re*, is provided in the following sections of the report.

3.2.3.2 Baseline System RMA Model

Components in the Baseline system that provide the operational mission functions critical to support ASW Operations are provided in the table below. The Baseline System RBDs are provided in Figure 70.

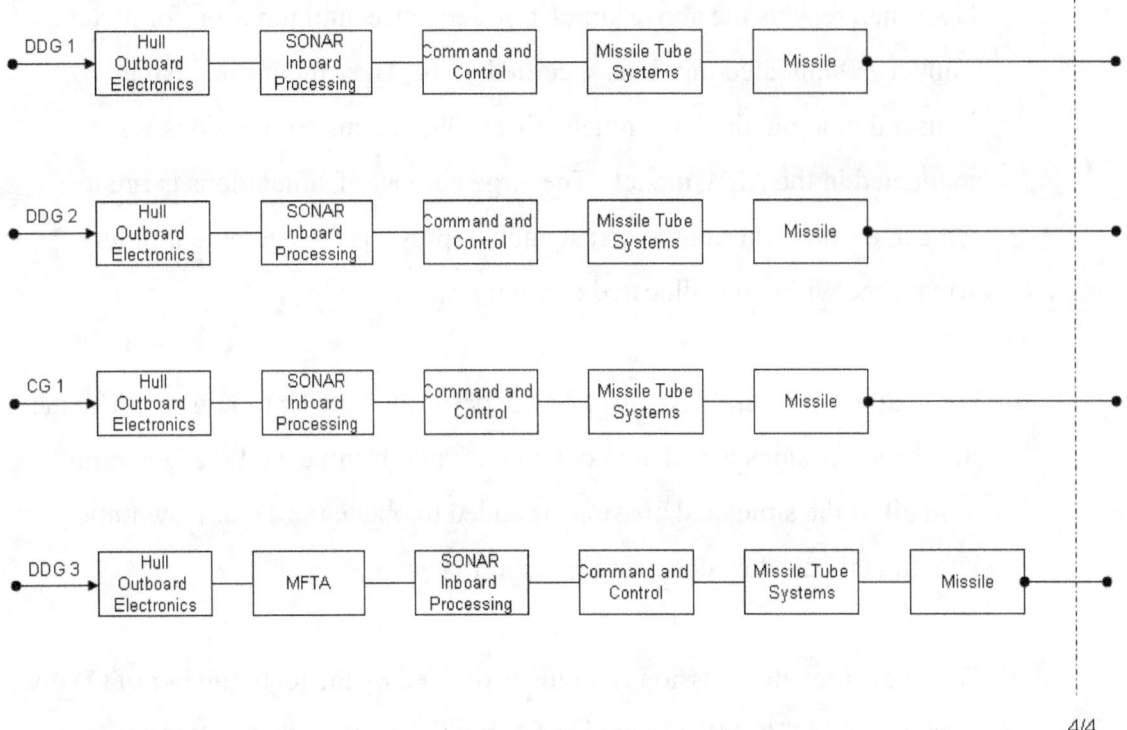

Figure 70 Baseline System RBDs

Table 7 - Baseline RMA Data

Component	MTBF	MTTR	Source
Hull Outboard Electronics	13,022 Hours*[1]	Not Repairable During Mission	[Ref 62, Moreira, 2007]
MFTA	8712 Hours*	Not Repairable During Mission	[Ref 63, Lomba and Nashold, 2007]
SONAR (SQQ-89) Inboard Processing	225 Hours*	65 minutes	[Ref 64, Silveria, 2008]
Command and Control System	216 Hours*[2]	2 Hours	[Ref 65, NAVSEA PMS 425, 2005]
Missile Tube Systems	3598 Hours*[3]	1 Hour	[Ref 66, Pettus, 2005]
ASROC Missile	35,040 Hours	Not Repairable During Mission	[Ref 67, Theunissen and Holbrook, 1998]

*The actual MTBF values for these systems are classified. The MTBF provided is a representation of the systems' performance, however, for classification reasons, the actual values are not provided. The actual values are provided in the pertinent references.

Notes:

1. The SQQ-89 Hull Outboard Electronics failure rate was not available. The system that best resembles the SQQ-89 is the new VIRGINIA Class LAB Array. While both arrays are cylindrical, the LAB array contains more elements than the surface ship cylindrical array, thereby having a slightly more optimistic failure rate, however it is expected that the actual design requirements for both will be equivalent in actual operation.

2. The failure rate of the Combat Control system on the DDGs/CG Surface Combatant was not available; therefore the failure rate of a submarine Combat Control system was used. The reliability of these two systems is expected to be similar because these systems are highly analogous, consisting of COTS hardware equipment consoles, software components certified to the same standards and similar weapons interface hardware.

3. The failure rate of the DDG/CG Surface Combatant Missile Tube Systems was not available; therefore the failure rate of the SSGN Missile Tube Systems was used. This is a conservative approach because the Missile Tube System on a SSGN is exposed to more extremes of pressure and temperature due to the nature of the submarine operations. This is expected to lead to a higher failure rate for the SSGN tomahawk canister loaded missiles. Thus, the reliability for the surface launch systems is likely to be understated.

The Hull Outboard Electronics failure rate is a summation of the following components: Hydrophones and Bottles. The Hull Outboard Electronics failure rate is an effective failure rate which takes into account allowable loses of components due to a permissible decibel reduction in signal loss (the amount of reduction allowable is not provided for classification reasons).

The SONAR Inboard Processing failure rate is a summation of the following components: Signal Conditioning, Beam Forming, Signal Processing and Displays.

The Missile Tube Systems failure rate is a summation of the following components: Missile Tube System, Missile Tube Gas System, Missile Tube Hydraulics and the Canister.

This Baseline System resides on 4 DDG/CG Surface Combatants that are used continuously throughout the 14 day ASW mission. All 4 DDG/CGs are required continuously for the duration of the 14 day mission. The Hull Outboard Electronics, MFTA, SONAR Inboard Processing, Command and Control System and the Missile Tube Systems are in an 'On and Critical' state for the duration of the 14 day mission. The Missile is in a low-powered 'On but not Critical' state for all but one hour of the 14 day mission. During this time the missile is still subject to failure however, the failure rate of the missile was significantly reduced. The Missile is in an 'On and Critical' state for one hour of the 14 day mission.

Maintenance was not allowed on the Hull Outboard Electronics, MTFA or the Missile at any point during the 14 ASW mission. If a failure did occur, the system would remain in a Downstate until the end of the 14 day mission. Maintenance was allowed on all other systems. However, any maintenance activity that was conducted contributed to system downtime. The DDG/CG was assumed to be equipped with a full compliment of spare parts and personnel required to complete maintenance actions.

3.2.3.3 Maritime Patrol Aircraft (MPA) System Alternative RMA Model

Components in the MPA system alternative that provide the operational mission functions critical to support ASW Operations are provided in the table below. The MPA system RBDs are provided in Figure 71.

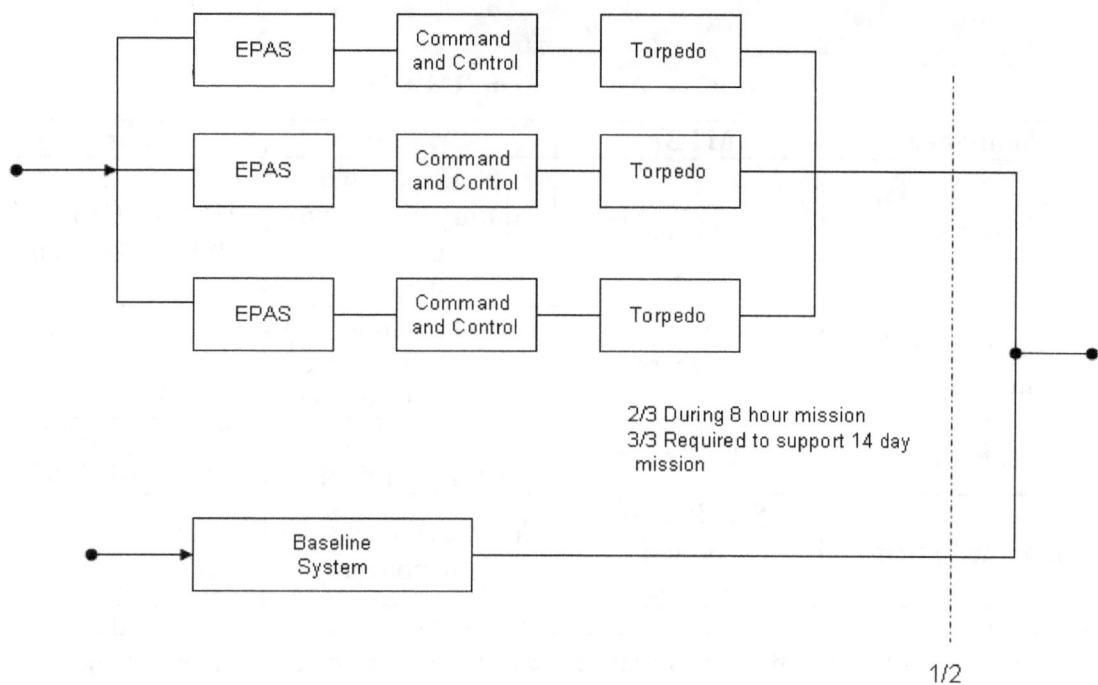

Figure 71 - MPA System RBDs

Table 8 - MPA System RMA Data

Component	MTBF	MTTR	Source
EPAS	400 Hours[1]	Not repairable during flight time 30 minutes On Station	[Ref 68, Office of USDAT&L, 2001]
Command and Control System	216 Hours*[2]	Not repairable during flight time 3 Hours in station	[Ref 65, NAVSEA PMS 425, 2005]
Torpedo	135 Hours*	Not Repairable During Mission	[Ref 69, NAVSEA PMS 404, 1998]
Baseline System	See Baseline System Components	See Baseline System Components	
*The actual MTBF values for these systems are classified. The MTBF provided is a representation of the systems' performance, however, for classification reasons, the actual values are not provided. The actual values are provided in the pertinent references.			

Notes:

1. The EPAS system is not built yet. The ATFLIR (Advanced Targeting Forward-Looking Infrared Pod) system most closely resembles the EPAS system both in the functionality provided and the projected equipment to be used. Therefore, the failure rate of the ATFLIR was used for the EPAS system.

2. Submarine Command and Control (C2) system failure rate values were used for the C2 system on the Airframe. This is a conservative estimate since the C2 system on a submarine is substantially more complex than that on the airframe.

The EPAS, Command and Control System and the Torpedo reside on a MPA. The endurance of the MPA is such that it can only support an 8 hour mission. Three MPAs are used per day to support the 14 day ASW mission. Two MPAs will be in flight at the same time; the first MPA will be in the operations area and the second will be traveling to the operations area to relieve the first. Therefore, two MPAs are required to support an 8 hour mission. The EPAS and Command and Control Systems are in an 'On and Critical' state for the 8 hour MPA mission. The Torpedo is in an 'Off' State for all but one hour of the 14 day mission. Maintenance is not allowed on any system during flight time. If a failure occurs on the MPA during the mission, another MPA can replace it, however the system will remain in a Downstate until the second MPA arrives in theater (a 2 hour transit time from station to the operations area was assumed). Every 8 hours a new MPA arrives and the component operating modes remain the same.

All systems are in an 'Off' state while on station waiting to return to operation. During this time maintenance can be conducted without impacting system Ao and Re. If a system has not completed maintenance before it is required to return to operation the system is considered in a Downstate until maintenance is complete.

The torpedo is in an 'On and Critical' state for one hour during the 14 day ASW mission.

The Baseline system is a redundant system in the MPA system alternative model. The Baseline system is described in the 'Baseline System RMA Model' section of this report.

3.2.3.4 Barrier System Alternative RMA Model

Components in the Barrier system alternative that provide the operational mission functions critical to support ASW Operations are provided in the table below. The Barrier system RBDs are provided in Figure 72.

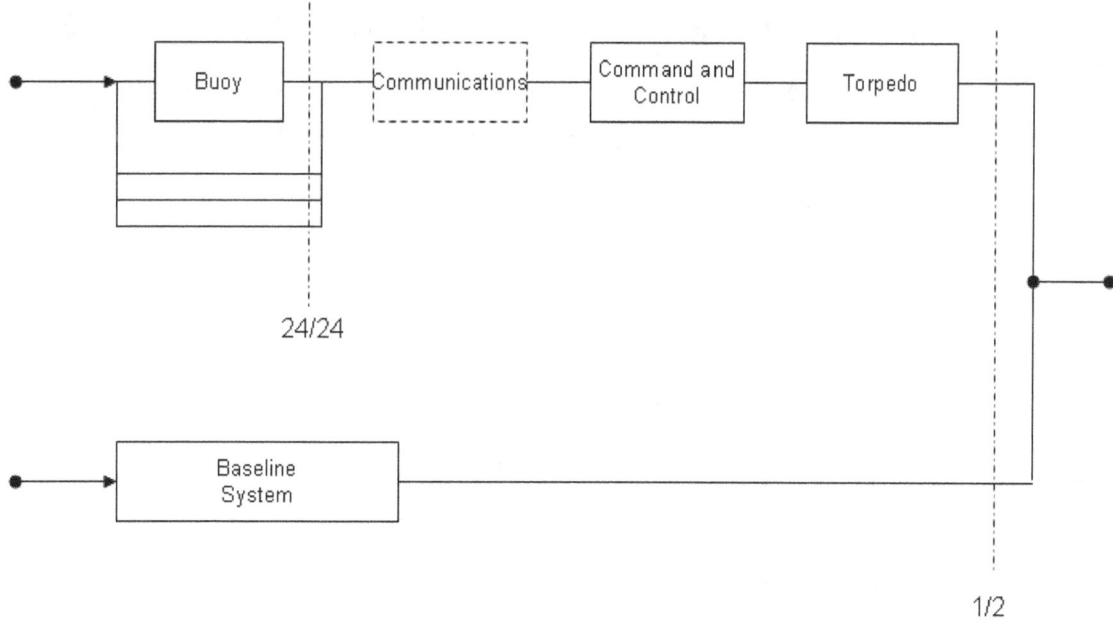

Figure 72 Barrier System RBDs

Table 9 - Barrier System RMA Data

Component	MTBF	MTTR	Source
Buoy	9,600 Hours	Not Repairable During Mission	[Ref 70, Lumpkin and Pazos, 2004]
Communications link	N/A	N/A	N/A
Command and Control System	720 Hours	2 hours	[Ref 71, Volkert, 2005]
Torpedo	135 Hours*	Not Repairable During Mission	[Ref 69, NAVSEA PMS 404, 1998]
Baseline System	See Baseline System Components	See Baseline System Components	
*The actual MTBF value for this system is classified. The MTBF provided is a representation of the system's performance, however, for classification reasons, the actual value is not provided. The actual value is provided in the pertinent reference.			

A Satellite is assumed to be used as the communication link between the Buoys and the LCS. The reliability of Satellite components is unknown. Therefore, it is assumed that the Satellite is always available and that the buoys are always in a position to communicate with it.

The failure rate provided for the buoy takes into account failures due to transmission loss, buoys that have run aground or have been picked up by fishing vessels etc. The buoys in this system alternative will be replaced every two days; therefore, transmission loss is the only failure mode that the buoys will be subjected to. Hence, the failure rate used is a conservative estimate.

Twenty-four (24) Buoys are utilized in this system alternative. To maintain adequate detection all 24 buoys are required to be operational. Due to ocean activity it is necessary for the LCS to frequently repopulate the perimeter with buoys. Buoys are required to be replenished at a maximum rate of once every 6 hours and at a minimum rate of once every two days. An RMA model was constructed to represent each of these operational mission profiles. The latter represents a more demanding situation for the buoys. Therefore, a conservative approach was taken which uses the second operational mission profile to represent the Barrier system alternative.

Buoys are constantly replenished and never retrieved. Therefore, 24 buoys are required to support a two day mission and 7 sets of 24 buoys are required to support the 14 day ASW mission. The buoys are in an "On and Critical' State for the two day duration. No maintenance is allowed on the buoys. If a buoy fails, then the system remains in a Downstate until the buoy is replenished. The operational modes remain the same for each set of buoys in use.

The Command and Control System resides on the LCS. The LCS can support the 14 day ASW mission continuously. Therefore, the Command and Control system on the LCS is in an 'On and Critical' state for the duration of the 14 day ASW mission in order to process the data sent by the buoys. Maintenance is allowed to be conducted on the Command and Control system; however, any maintenance that is conducted contributes to system Downtime. The LCS was assumed to be equipped with a full compliment of spare parts and personnel required to complete maintenance actions.

The Torpedo is in an 'Off' State for all but one hour of the 14 day mission. The torpedo is in an 'On and Critical' state for one hour during the 14 day ASW mission.

The Baseline system is a redundant system in the Barrier system alternative model. The Baseline system is described in the 'Baseline System RMA Model' section of this report.

3.2.3.5 ACB System Alternative RMA Model

The ACB system alternative provides the same functionality as the Baseline System, thereby, utilizing similar components. The only known difference in components between the Baseline System and the Advanced Capabilities Build system is three additional MFTAs.

The Advanced Capabilities Build RMA model was established by modifying the Baseline system model with three additional MFTAs. The Advanced Capabilities Build system RBDs are provided in Figure 73.

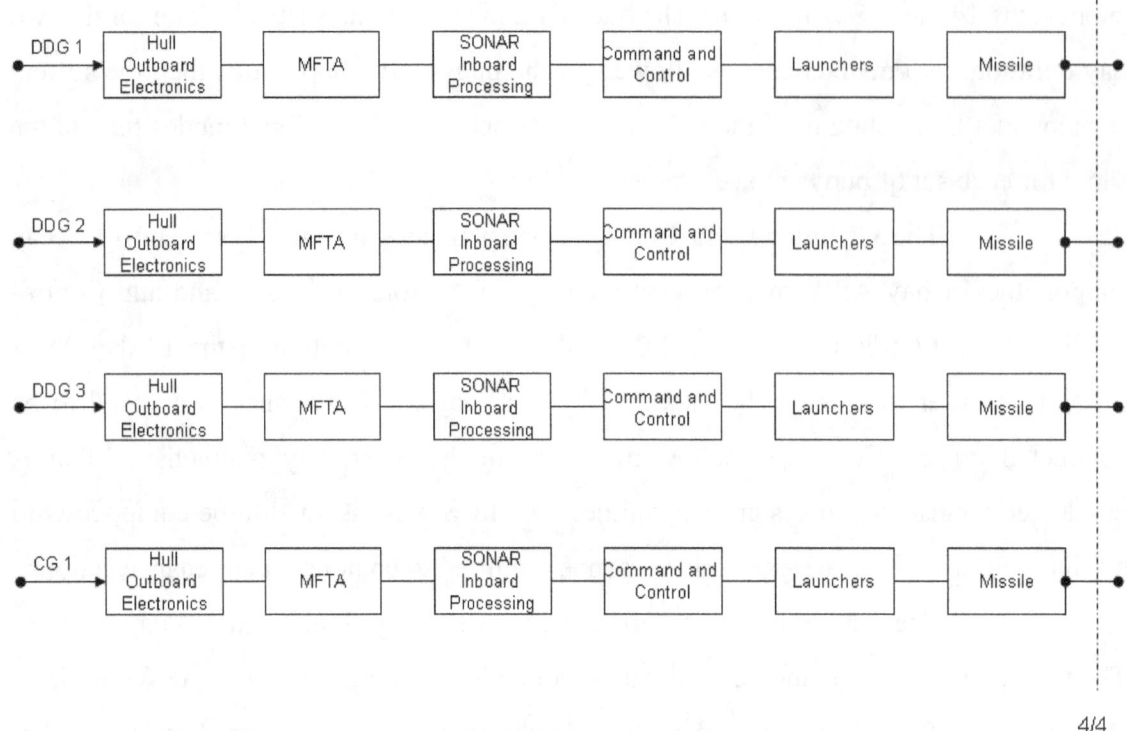

Figure 73 - ACB System RBDs

The MFTAs are in an 'On and Critical' State for the duration of the 14 day mission. The MFTA is an outboard component, therefore, no maintenance was allowed on the MFTA during the mission. The operational mission profile, failure rates and operating modes of the remaining components are consistent with the Baseline System alternative RMA model.

3.2.3.6 *Barrier with Advanced Capabilities Build Alternative RMA Model*

The Barrier with Advanced Capabilities Build System Alternative consists of the Barrier System Alternative used in redundancy with the Advanced Capabilities Build System Alternative.

The Barrier System Alternative RMA model consisted of the Barrier System Alternative used in redundancy with the Baseline System. The Baseline System becomes the Advanced Capabilities Build System with the addition of three MFTAs.

Therefore, the Barrier with Advanced Capabilities Build System model was created by modifying the Baseline portion of the Barrier System Alternative RMA model with three additional towed arrays. The operational mission profile, failure rates and operating modes are consistent with the Barrier System Alternative RMA model.

3.2.4 Modeling Results

Table 10 contains the results of the Operational Effectiveness and Operational Suitability Modeling. The individual operational effectiveness models were run, and their results integrated using the event trees described previously. The results of the Baseline and Barrier models warrant further discussion and are addressed in detail below.

Table 10 - Integrated Modeling Results

Alternative	Carrier Survival	Operational Availability	Reliability
Baseline	0.665	0.820	0.802
Barrier	0.857	0.989	0.991
MPA	0.681	0.995	0.987
ACB	0.804	0.774	0.803
ACB plus Barrier	0.916	0.985	0.990

3.2.4.1 Baseline Modeling Results

The spread sheet model, described above, was executed utilizing a Macro which created a family of Monte – Carlo replications of the Detection – Track – Engagement simulation. For each iteration of the model the resulting engagement analysis worksheets were combined and then analyzed to determine whether the threat submarine was able to successfully engage the CVN prior to being hit by a surface launched ASROC weapon. The ScoreCard worksheet in the WorkBook was utilized to capture the results of an ensemble of 25 engagement analysis, each of which exhibits different results due to the randomization of the starting position of the opposing force submarine and the random fluctuations of the active and passive signal excess parameters.

Figure 74 shows the results of one scorecard worksheet for a family of 25 engagement scenarios. The yellow table indicates if the threat submarine was successful (column = TRUE) or if the CSG surface ships were successful (column = FALSE). Also indicated are time of torpedo engagement, range to the CVN at torpedo engagement and the torpedo run for that engagement.

SS vs. CVN		Range	Bearing	Torp Crse	Torp Run
TOF	11910	12542.38	13.48463	153.7249	9823.203
TOH	12346.52				
SS Win?	TRUE				
DDG1 vs. SS					
TOF	13680				
TOH	13712				
					Run Model
DDG2 vs. SS					
TOF	14490				
TOH	14506				
DDG3 vs. SS					
TOF	14580				
TOH	14597				
CG1 vs. SS					
TOF	999999				
TOH	17564				
			Count	**Percent**	
		Red Win	8	32.0	
		Blue Win	17	68.0	

Run Number	**SS Win?**	**TOF**	**TOH**	**Range**	**Bearing**	**Torp Crse**	**Torp Run**
1	TRUE	11700	12143.71	12710.33	13.40	152.87	9985.01
2	TRUE	3870	4312.84	12685.00	14.64	154.09	9965.47
3	FALSE	2040	2471.32	12173.71	-14.92	107.08	9706.21
4	FALSE	2550	2993.17	10100.74	-10.95	76.00	9972.85
5	FALSE	2010	2444.68	11963.32	-14.70	102.01	9781.85
6	FALSE	2640	3077.80	12519.35	-14.98	110.03	9851.97
7	FALSE	2880	3316.69	11487.32	-14.09	94.31	9827.00
8	FALSE	2970	3408.42	12186.21	-14.80	103.92	9865.90
9	FALSE	3270	3713.09	9215.99	-8.30	66.63	9971.11
10	TRUE	4350	4793.07	13445.02	12.76	170.33	9970.60
11	TRUE	11850	12284.93	12588.21	13.68	155.82	9787.29
12	FALSE	1830	2264.21	11528.83	-14.24	95.79	9771.07
13	FALSE	2280	2723.04	10024.16	-10.75	75.21	9969.81
14	FALSE	2520	2961.86	10477.39	-11.96	80.46	9943.23
15	FALSE	2700	3134.35	11941.70	-14.69	101.82	9774.22
16	TRUE	3210	3653.18	12511.39	-14.92	107.13	9973.07
17	FALSE	1830	2273.53	12368.80	-14.83	104.57	9981.01
18	FALSE	1980	2416.61	11885.10	-14.58	100.00	9825.11
19	FALSE	3780	4214.36	11708.76	15.00	141.31	9774.63
20	FALSE	12030	12466.00	12430.39	13.27	151.56	9811.35
21	TRUE	3420	3863.99	12418.50	-14.85	105.18	9991.31
22	TRUE	3870	4312.10	12294.74	14.93	147.60	9948.82
23	FALSE	11700	12143.38	12707.73	13.42	153.02	9977.63
24	FALSE	11490	11928.95	12812.26	13.90	158.31	9877.84
25	TRUE	11910	12346.52	12542.38	13.48	153.72	9823.20

Figure 74 - ScoreCard worksheet example

After verifying that the spreadsheet model performed as expected through numerous validation runs, conducted while varying controlled parameters (fluctuation standard deviation, source level, detection threshold, target strength, acoustic signature level, initial range and bearing of opposing submarine), the analysis team executed ten series of 25 engagement ensembles and evaluated the results.

The bar chart shown in Figure 75 tabulates the results of these 10 runs. A data analysis tool in Excel was then used to generate descriptive statistics for these results. The results indicate, as shown in Figure 76, that the Carrier Strike Group was successful in defeating (hence Carrier survival) the enemy submarine in 66.5% of the engagements, with a standard deviation of 10.77. These baseline results provide the key measure of effectiveness (Aircraft Carrier Survival) as indicated in the Objectives Hierarchy analysis. Finally, the ScoreCard worksheets are contained in Appendix F.

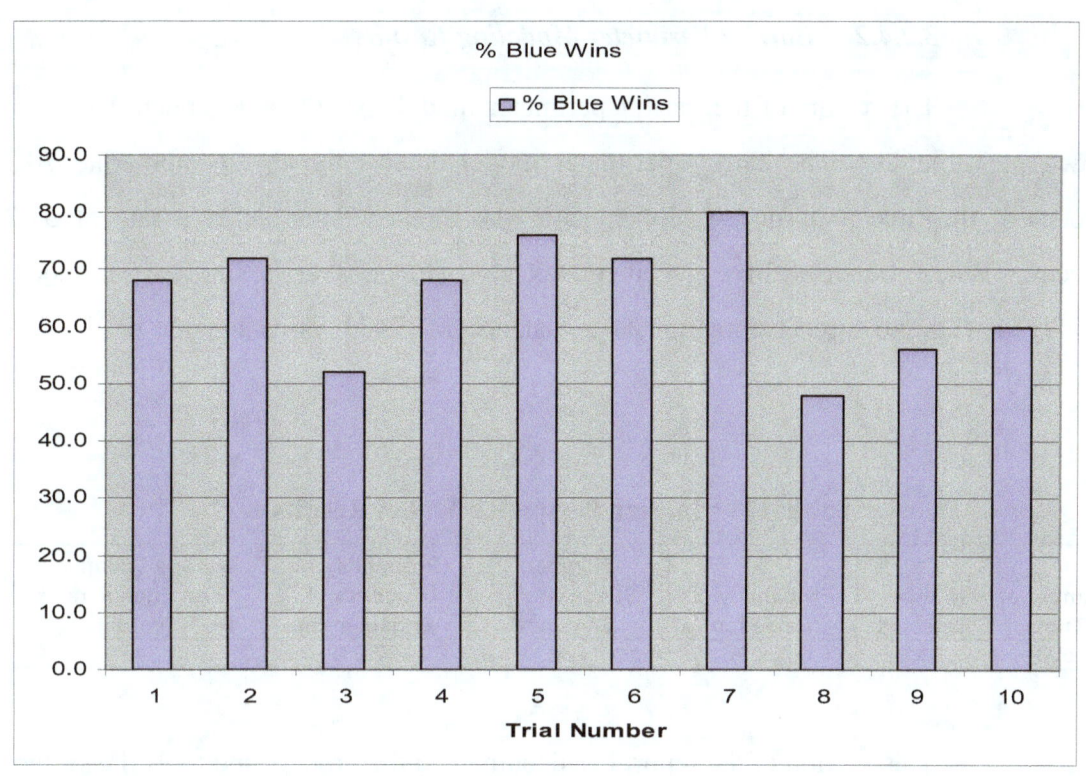

Figure 75 - Results of 10 sets of 25 Ensemble Engagements

Run	Psurv
1	60.0
2	80.0
3	88.0
4	68.0
5	56.0
6	72.0
7	52.0
8	68.0
9	56.0
10	68.0

Column1	
Mean	66.5454545
Standard Error	3.24839439
Median	68
Mode	68
Standard Dev	10.7737054
Sample Variance	116.072727
Kurtosis	0.14579054
Skewness	0.66097373
Range	36
Minimum	52
Maximum	88
Sum	732
Count	11

Figure 76 - Results and Descriptive Statistics for Baseline

3.2.4.2 Barrier Perimeter Modeling Results

The results of the barrier perimeter model for 500 independent trials are shown in Table 11. The barrier perimeter model detects the threat submarine 70.2 percent of the time and successfully engages the threat submarine at a rate of 57.2 percent. When a successful engagement takes place, on average the barrier model initially detects the threat submarine at a distance of 5,437 yards outside of the OA boundary.

Table 11 – Barrier Perimeter Model Results

Number of Trials	Number Detected	Probability of Detection	Number Successfully Engaged	Probability of Successful Engagement	Average Distance of First Engagement (yards)
500	351	70.2%	286	57.2%	5437

This section of the report has documented the process and tools the system engineering team utilized to produce results needed to support the decision phase of the SEDP. The report describes the current baseline system the Navy operates to satisfy the Effective Need, and identifies 13 alternative candidates that are evaluated to determine if any of them can contribute to more effectively satisfying this need.

Using key feasibility measures the team identified three distinct alternatives having potential to contribute to a more effective solution to the protection of the CSG from submarine threats. The team has used models and historic data to generate measures of performance for operational effectiveness and operational suitability. The Decision Making phase of the systems engineering process will seek to apply utility scoring functions to this information and combine it with estimates of cost and risk for each option to support stakeholder decision making processes. These utility functions will assist in determining the degree to which any of the candidate solutions quantitatively dominate the others in the decision space of the stakeholder.

4 DECISION MAKING

In the previous chapters, four significantly different alternatives are presented in order to satisfy the stakeholders' requirements for improved ASW. In addition, the baseline, current Program of Record (POR) or "do nothing" alternative is presented to provide a frame of reference allowing a comparison to judge improvement provided by the alternatives. These improvements are considered to be the Utility of the solution: the most benefit afforded to the stakeholders in addition to the benefit provided by the current Program of Record.

Through Alternative Scoring (including the formation of a Decision Matrix, conduct of a Sensitivity Analysis, comparison of System Life Cycle Costs, and comparison of associated Risks), the four alternatives were compared, resulting in identification of the best solution when compared to the remaining alternatives.

4.1 ALTERNATIVE SCORING

Alternative Scoring was used to compare the four proposed alternatives (baseline, Maritime Patrol Aircraft (MPA), Barrier, and Advanced Capabilities Build, as well as the combination of Barrier and Advanced Capabilities Build) with respect to multiple objectives and multiple evaluation measures, including Value and Cost Modeling. Value Modeling was used as a decision theory approach to accommodate the Stakeholders' preferences in terms of value or utility. An Additive Value Model applied the Stakeholders' value preferences to convert 'raw' performance results into a weighted evaluation. Results of Cost Modeling were then considered in concert with Value Modeling in order to support Stakeholder consensus on alternative effectiveness.

4.1.1 Decision Matrix

Because this project was intended to examine and recommend improvements to Anti-Submarine Warfare effectiveness, system utility was determined by the design team to be improvement over the existing baseline system. The greater the improvement to the existing baseline system, the more utility and therefore more value would be realized for the stakeholders. In this way, the baseline system was normalized to provide zero utility, and the respective value score of the alternatives were determined by calculating the delta or difference from this normalized value.

The Decision Matrix was arrived at by first creating a Raw Data Matrix, consisting of raw data scores. This matrix utilizes the output of the modeling and simulation effort, providing values in the form of percentages for the Key Metric of Carrier Survival. Availability and Reliability percentages were arrived at through reliability modeling and are included in the Raw Data Matrix as well. The Raw Data Matrix is shown in Table 12.

Table 12 - Raw Data Matrix

Evaluation Measure	Alternatives				
	Baseline	ACB	Baseline + Barrier	Baseline + MPA	ACB + Barrier
Carrier Survival P_{surv}	0.665	0.804	0.857	0.681	0.916
Ao	0.820	0.774	0.995	0.989	0.985
Re	0.802	0.803	0.987	0.991	0.990

Considering that the utility score for the baseline system is the basis for improvement through application of the alternative systems, a required range of effectiveness was determined. Using the baseline system Raw Data score from the modeling, simulation and reliability determination efforts, these scores were determined to be the lower limit acceptable and the upper limit of effectiveness as 100%. Any alternative that achieved a value score lower than the score achieved by the baseline, would provide no value to the stakeholders. The required range of effectiveness matrix is shown in Table 13.

Table 13 - Required Ranges of Effectiveness

Required Ranges of Effectiveness		
Carrier Survival	0.665	1.0
Ao	0.820	1.0
Re	0.802	1.0
	low	high

Global weights as provided in the Objectives Hierarchy were then utilized for each of the competing systems to be evaluated, as well as the baseline system. Probability that the ASW system prevents enemy launch of an effective weapon against the aircraft carrier within the CSG was a system effectiveness measure given a global weight of 90%. Protection of the high value aircraft carrier was considered to be the most important objective of the system and if this was not realized on a consistent basis, then the system would prove to be less than useful. Contributing to the overall effectiveness of the system were the key metrics of detecting the enemy submarine outside the range of his offensive weapons, localization and tracking of the enemy submarine target to allow for follow on actions, and classification which would ensure that the target being tracked is in fact an enemy vessel thereby avoiding a friendly fire situation. These key metrics are evaluated in the modeling of the alternative scenarios whereby the model predicts an effectiveness score based on the outcome of the modeled scenario.

Secondary to the objective of protecting the Aircraft Carrier was a system suitability measure for a trustworthy system. It was assigned a global weight of 10%. It was considered important for the system to "perform as advertised". The system must enable increased persistence (considered to be a measure of high reliability, Re) and exhibit decreased downtime (Ao). A system that was extremely effective, but not available, would have limited value as a whole.

The final decision matrix was determined by considering the values of the alternatives' Raw Data Scores, as well as the range of effectiveness scores. The range of effectiveness normalized the Raw Data Scores to zero, thereby generating a Value Score that represents the total value relative to the baseline system. It should be pointed out that for the Advanced Capabilities Build the availability value score is a negative number. This indicates this value is less than the comparative value generated by the baseline system. Technically this occurred due to the increased number of towed arrays used in this alternative. Failure rates are additive terms, therefore the increased number of components lead to an increased failure rate and therefore a lower availability value. The Decision Matrix is shown in Table 14.

Table 14 - Decision Matrix

Evaluation Measure	Global Weight	Alternatives				
		Baseline	ACB	Baseline + Barrier	Baseline + MPA	ACB + Barrier
Carrier Survival	0.90	0.00	41.49	57.31	4.78	74.96
Ao	0.05	0.00	-25.56	97.22	93.89	91.67
Re	0.05	0.00	0.51	93.43	95.45	94.95
TOTAL VALUE SCORE		0.00	36.09	61.11	13.77	76.79

Based on the importance, or weight of each system objective and the degree of value to which each alternative system would provide toward accomplishing that objective, the decision matrix indicates which system will provide the highest degree of Total Value. The ACB + Barrier system received the highest Total Value Score. This indicates that the ACB + Barrier system provides the most total system value.

4.1.2 Sensitivity Analysis

The Total Value Scores in the decision matrix were generated based on a number of critical assumptions in our design effort, to include various system performance parameters for both the proposed CSG assets and the enemy diesel sub, procurement and operational cost parameters of these systems, and also the global weights that our group assigned to the evaluation metrics. If any of these assumptions prove to be flawed, the results of our research could be incorrect, so it is therefore appropriate to conduct sensitivity analysis on these assumptions. Due to time constraints we focus our sensitivity analysis on a single assumption, which is the global weights.

Essentially, the values chosen for the global weights may make a difference in which alternative system provides the highest total system value. If the global weights were to change, one alternative system may then be favored over another. Sensitivity analysis considers the affects on decisions if the global weights were to change.

Sensitivity analysis was conducted for each evaluation measure on all top system level objectives. This process involves varying the weight of one evaluation measure while keeping the ratio of the remaining evaluation measures to the remaining weight the same and the sum of the global weights equal to one. One evaluation measure was evaluated at a time. Global weights were varied from 0 to 100% to determine the net effect on the Total Value Score. These numerical results are provided in Table 15 through Table 17.

Table 15 - Sensitivity Matrix Global Weight 1, Carrier Survival

System Objectives	Global Weight	Alternatives				
		Baseline	ACB	Baseline + Barrier	Baseline + MPA	ACB + Barrier
Carrier Survival	1	0.00	41.49	57.31	4.78	74.96
Ao	0	0.00	-25.56	97.22	93.89	91.67
Re	0	0.00	0.51	93.43	95.45	94.95
TOTAL VALUE SCORE		*0.00*	*41.49*	*57.31*	*4.78*	*74.96*

Table 16 - Sensitivity Matrix Global Weight 1, Ao

System Objectives	Global Weight	Alternatives				
		Baseline	ACB	Baseline + Barrier	Baseline + MPA	ACB + Barrier
Carrier Survival	0	0.00	41.49	57.31	4.78	74.96
Ao	1	0.00	-25.56	97.22	93.89	91.67
Re	0	0.00	0.51	93.43	95.45	94.95
TOTAL VALUE SCORE		*0.00*	*-25.56*	*97.22*	*93.89*	*91.67*

Table 17 - Sensitivity Matrix Global Weight 1, Re

System Objectives	Global Weight	Alternatives				
		Baseline	ACB	Baseline + Barrier	Baseline + MPA	ACB + Barrier
Carrier Survival	0	0.00	41.49	57.31	4.78	74.96
A_o	0	0.00	-25.56	97.22	93.89	91.67
R_e	1	0.00	0.51	93.43	95.45	94.95
TOTAL VALUE SCORE		*0.00*	*0.51*	*93.43*	*95.45*	*94.95*

Graphically, the sensitivity analysis is shown in Figure 77 through Figure 79. These figures show the best system alternative for each evaluation measure at all possible global weights. The results of sensitivity analysis conclude, that for all global weights, the ACB + Barrier System Alternative provides the greatest value toward accomplishing the carrier survival and the increased persistence system objectives. There exists for the objective of decreased downtime (A_o) a point at which the Maritime Patrol Aircraft (MPA) is equally valuable as the ACB + Barrier System Alternative. This occurrence is known as a Point Of Indifference (POI). The POI for decreased downtime occurs at a global weight of 0.75. Previous to, or ahead of the POI determines which alternative provides greater value, which in this instance is the Barrier System Alternative. A reasonable "Rule of Thumb" indicates that if the POI is within 10% of the original global weight for the evaluation measure being evaluated, then it is considered sensitive. Therefore, by definition, this global weight is not considered to be sensitive (Global Weight for decreased downtime is 5.0% while the POI is 75%. This difference is clearly greater than the 10% criteria to be considered sensitive).

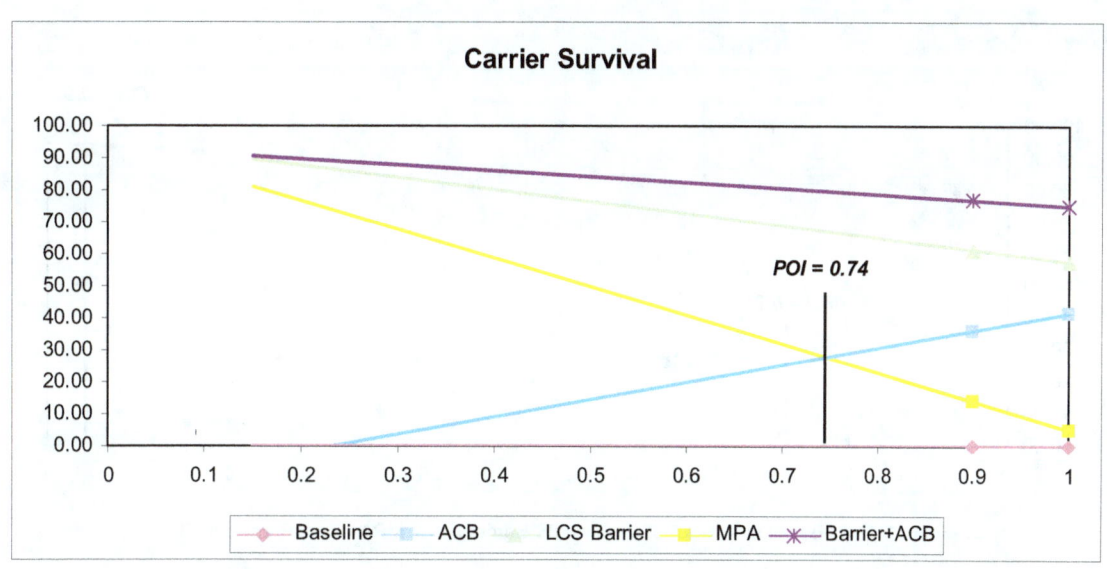

Figure 77 - Carrier Survival Sensitivity Analysis

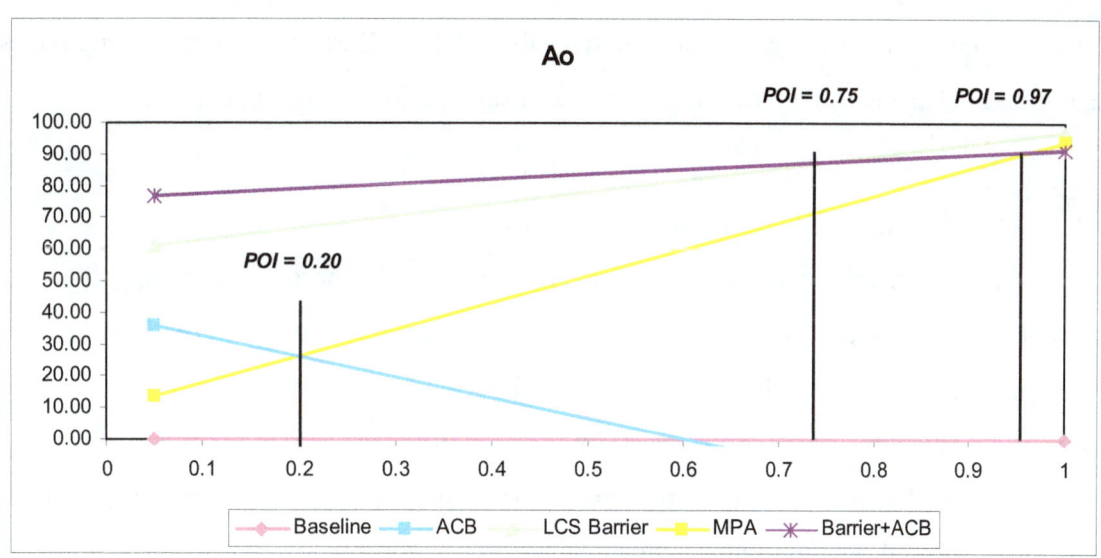

Figure 78 - Availability Sensitivity Analysis

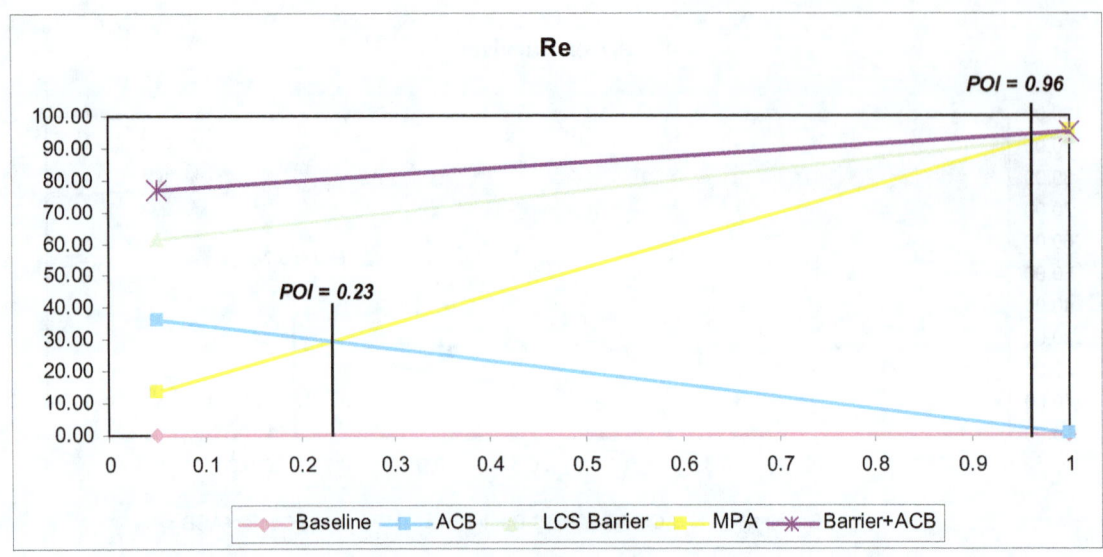

Figure 79 - Reliability Sensitivity Analysis

Sensitivity Analysis reveals that no global weights are considered sensitive and reaffirms the results of the decision matrix; the ACB + Barrier System Alternative is recommended as the system to provide the most satisfaction to the stakeholders.

4.2 COST ANALYSIS CONSIDERATION

In support of recommendation development for the best value among the four alternatives, other sections documented the total value score for each alternative based on modeling results and weighting values from the value hierarchy. This section of the report will review the cost analysis performed and present the cost modeling results. The results will be discussed and presented in a graphical format. Refer to Appendix H for additional material related to the cost analysis.

For each alternative, costs are estimated for four categories over a 25-year lifecycle period. The four cost categories are design, production, operation, and disposal. In order to provide a fair cost comparison over the 25-year period, a net present value (NPV) analysis will be implemented to transform the yearly costs over time into a single dollar value. Note that all costs are considered to be relative to the costs for the baseline

CSG alternative. In other words, the cost information shown below is referenced to the CSG alternative and is considered to be relative to the CSG program of record.

The cost estimation methodology employed in determining the LCCP for each alternative was based on the following three techniques:

- Researched references including a documented program plan and or funding profiles
- Where specific cost references were not available, an analogous system was used for comparison adjusted accordingly to fit the system description.
- If no analogous system existed, the team worked with subject matter experts to estimate costs based on previous experience.

The concept behind NPV is that it represents the total lifecycle cost of a given alternative adjusted to current year dollars. To calculate the NPV for an alternative, Equation 24 is used:

$$NPV = \sum_{n=1}^{N} \left[\frac{FV}{(1+k)^n} \right]$$

Equation 24

Where, FV is the future dollar value for year n, k is the discount rate, and N is the total number of years. The NPV is the sum of the yearly discounted cash flows over the timeframe of interest.

A cost model for each alternative was constructed to identify the cost to design, produce, operate, and dispose each of the systems. A common model and set of assumptions and constraints was used to ensure comparable cost model results. The overall assumptions and constraints include:

- 25-year lifecycle
- Calculations assume the support of one CSG for 40 14-day missions
- Operation costs includes personnel costs

- Discount rate *k* of six percent
- Costs for all categories are considered to be relative to CSG baseline program of record

Table 18 shows the NPVs for each alternative relative to the CSG baseline program of record. A lifecycle cost profile (LCCP) for each alternative (excluding the CSG baseline alternative) was generated and are shown in Figure 80 [Ref 73, Department of the Navy Fiscal Year 2007, 2007] [Ref 74, Department of the Navy Fiscal Year 2009, 2008] [Ref 75, Department of the Navy Fiscal Year 2007, 2006] through Figure 82. [Ref 76, PEO IWS, 2005] [Ref 77, Under Secretary of Defense, 2007] [Ref 78, O'Roarke, 2006] The LCCP profiles graphically represent the non-discounted costs each year for all four cost categories.

Table 18 – NPVs for Alternatives Relative to CSG Baseline

Alternative	NPV ($M)
CSG Baseline	0.0
CSG Advanced Capabilities Build	112.2
MPA	89.3
Barrier	696.7

The NPVs for the ACB and MPA alternatives are of a similar magnitude, however the Barrier alternative is shown to have a significantly higher NPV. The primary driver for this separation is attributed to the operational costs of the buoy replenishment segment of the Barrier alternative. Refer to Appendix H for specific cost details and assumptions for the three alternatives.

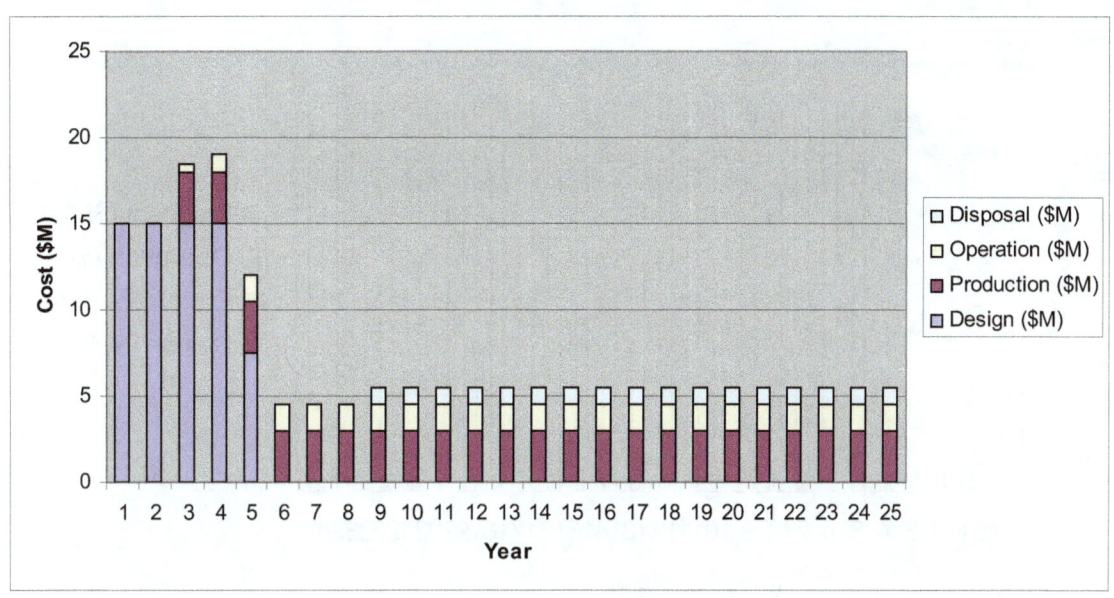

Figure 80 – CSG Advanced Capabilities Build Alternative LCCP

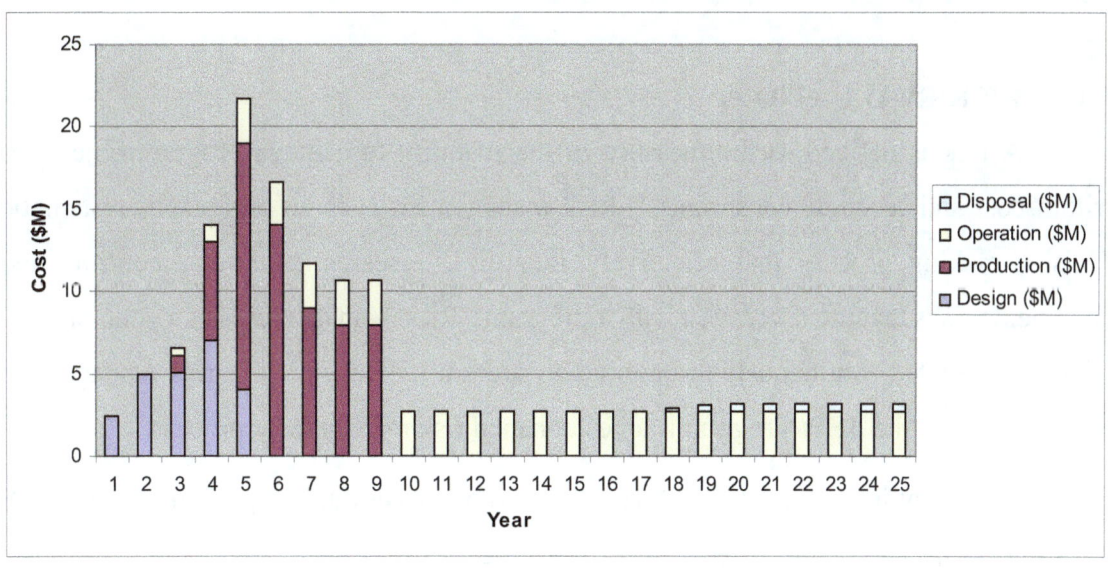

Figure 81 – MPA/EPAS Alternative LCCP

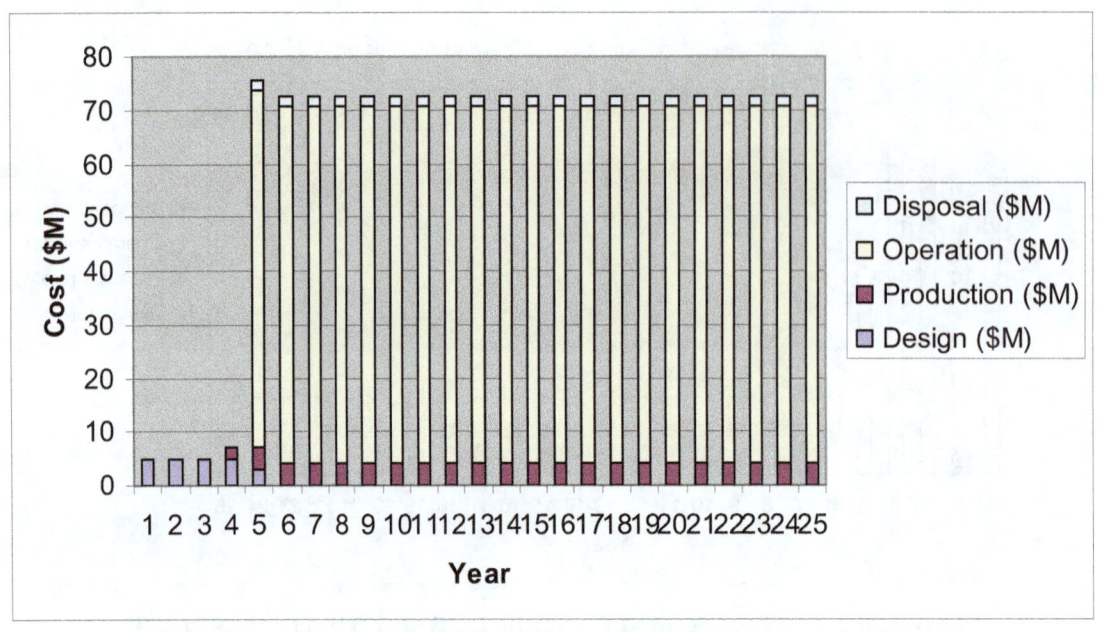

Figure 82 - Barrier Alternative LCCP

4.3 RISK EVALUATION

A risk is defined as the measure of the inability to achieve program objectives within cost and schedule constraints. Risk management is as an organized, systematic decision-making process that effectively identifies, assesses, monitors, controls and documents risks that are associated with a program. Risk Management is a cyclic process which is executed continuously throughout a program's lifecycle. The risk management process used by the ASW Program is an established risk management process.

Risks that impact either the ASW Program or successful completion of the MSSE Capstone Project were identified. Risks were identified using such techniques as: best judgment, lessons learned, negative trends, forecasting etc.

Every risk event has both a likelihood of occurring and a potential adverse consequence. These attributes were assessed and analyzed in order to quantify each risk identified. The likelihood that the risk event would occur was rating on a scale from 'A' to 'E'. A level 'A' rating indicates a remote possibility that the event will occur. A level 'E' rating indicates a near certainty that the event will occur. The consequence of the event occurring is rated on a scale from '1' to '5'. A level '1' rating indicates a minimal or no impact to the program. A level '5' rating indicates an unacceptable impact to the program.

Risks were then plotted on a risk matrix. A risk matrix is a pictorial representation of risk which clearly displays risk priority based on the likelihood and consequence of each risk. The green, yellow and red sections of the risk matrix denote low, medium and high priority risks, respectively. A sample risk matrix is provided below.

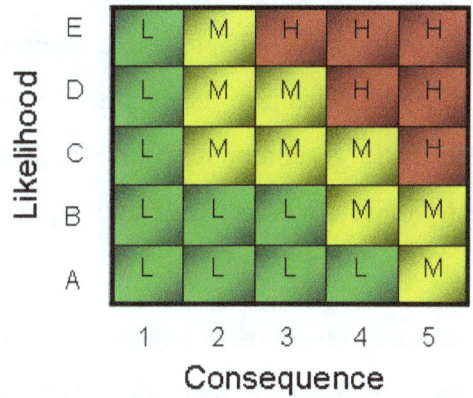

Figure 83 - Representative Risk Matrix

Low priority risks may cause minimal program impact. Minimal oversight is needed to ensure risk remains low. Medium priority risks may cause some program disruption. Mitigation plans are required and may need to be executed. High priority risks may cause major program disruption. Mitigation plans are required and must be executed. Mitigation plans were constructed for all risks and were implemented based on risk priority.

This risk management process was performed continuously throughout the MSSE Capstone project. Previously identified risks were continuously tracked and evaluated for adequacy of mitigation plan. Risk status was reevaluated and mitigation plans were changed as necessary. New risks were identified and controlled using this same process.

All risks were documented and are provided in the following subparagraphs. Project and program risks are segregated. Project risks are related to the successful completion of the MSSE program and therefore exist in the same capacity for all alternatives. Over the course of the MSSE Capstone Project these risks have been mitigated and all have been retired. Project risks are provided in Table 5, Appendix G for reference. Program risks are dependent on the implementation of a specific alternative. Program risks will be evaluated to compare system alternatives regarding risk. Note that, since the Baseline System will be used in each system alternative the Baseline Risks apply to all system alternatives although they are only displayed once under 'Baseline System'. Additionally the system alternative titled Barrier with Advanced Capabilities Build Alternative consists of the Barrier System Alternative used in conjunction with the Advanced Capabilities Build Alternative. Therefore, a separate risk assessment was not conducted for the Barrier with Advanced Capabilities Build Alternative; the risks associated with this system are a compilation of the risks associated with (and documented under) the Barrier System Alternative and the Advanced Capabilities Build Alternative.

Three risk categories were considered for each system alternative: 1) Performance Based Risks. 2) Cost Based Risks. 3) Schedule Based Risks. Program risks are provided by category in Figure 84, Figure 85, and Figure 86 and described in Table 19, Table 20, and Table 21. Table 22 provides the total number of low, medium and high priority risks associated with each system alternative.

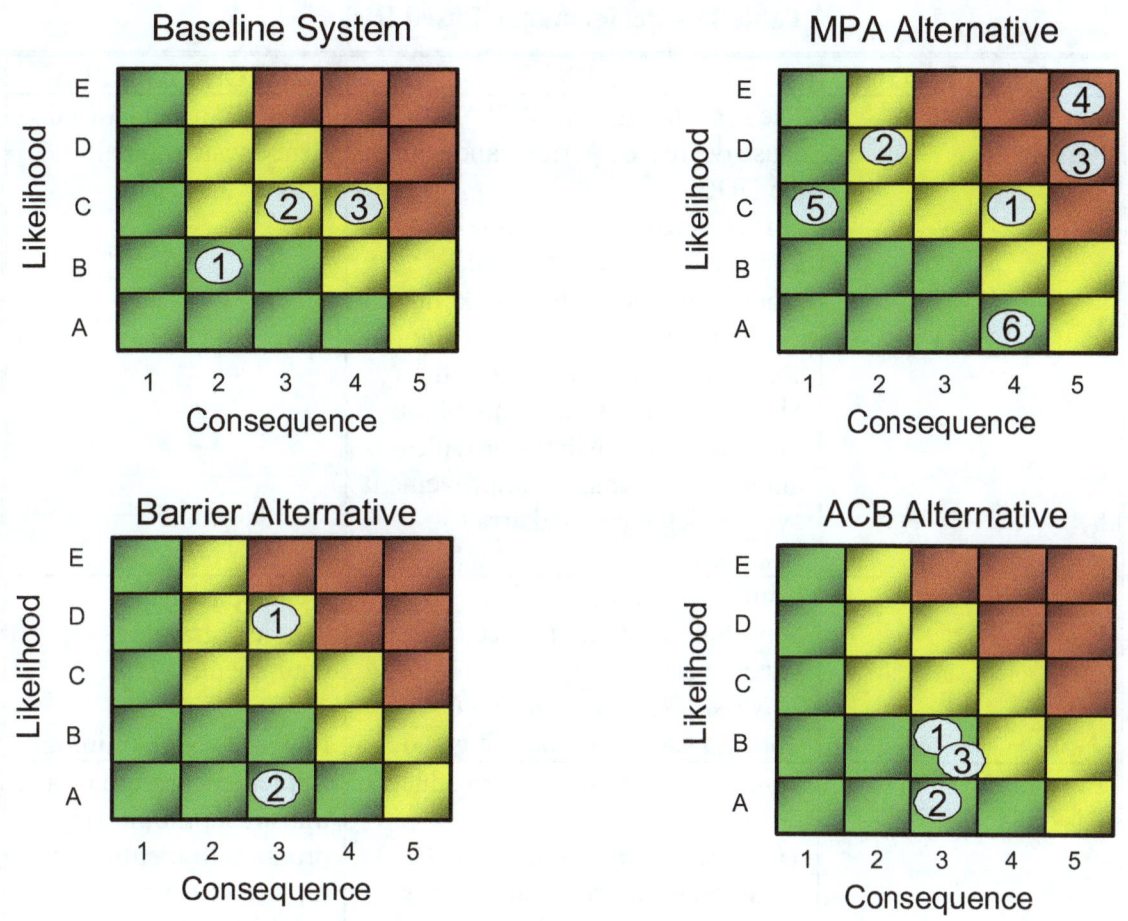

Figure 84 - Performance Based Program Risks

Table 19 - Performance Based Risks

IDENTIFICATION	ANALYSIS	MITIGATION PLAN
Baseline System Risk 1	The schedule risk of MFTA would cause decreased performance on the DDG. *This risk was assessed at a B2.* The MFTA is close to final production; therefore the likelihood of a schedule delay is low. The consequence is low because the MFTA is only used on one of the four ships. The MFTA provides minimal performance improvement over the legacy towed array system.	Use the current Towed Array system on all ships.
Baseline System Risk 2	Insufficient at sea training opportunities could reduce overall system performance. *This risk was assessed at a C3.* This risk can easily be mitigated.	Develop realistic synthetic training equipment. Increase at-sea training.
Baseline System Risk 3	Risk of aging/failing of transducers on hull. *This risk was assessed at a C4.* This issue is currently being seen on other Platforms. This affect would decrease source level, effect directivity index, and reduce bearing and range measuring accuracy.	Implement a more robust transducer monitoring program to identify and replace sensors exhibiting decreased performance.
Maritime Patrol Aircraft (MPA) Alternative Risk 1	The alternative requires that a MPA be deployed continuously in support of the ASW mission. There is a risk that there is a gap in the MPA availability for the ASW mission due to other in theater MPA requirements. *This risk was assessed at a C4.* We may not be able to control the availability of the MPA. If the MPA is not continuously available this alternative will experience a performance degradation.	This is a consequence of overall theater commanders strategic planning. Mitigation is outside of our scope.

IDENTIFICATION	ANALYSIS	MITIGATION PLAN
Maritime Patrol Aircraft (MPA) Alternative Risk 2	There is a risk regarding the distance of CSG operating area from nearest MPA base. *This risk was assessed at a D2.* CSG operating area location is not predictable. If the CSG operating area is far from the nearest base the MPA time on station would be reduced due to transit time.	Allocate more aircraft for adequate coverage.
Maritime Patrol Aircraft (MPA) Alternative Risk 3	Risk of weather related impacts. *This risk was assessed at a D5.* Weather severely impacts EPAS. For example the system does not operate well in fog, or at nighttime. Under these conditions, performance will be degraded.	Use other sensors available to P3 however reduced performance would result. The only additional mitigation would be a redesign.
Maritime Patrol Aircraft (MPA) Alternative Risk 4	Risk of the detection ability of EPAS. *This risk was assessed at a E5.* EPAS cannot detect a target that is below a certain depth. If the opposing force submarine does not enter the required depth threshold they will not be detected.	This is a limitation of system. Cannot Mitigate
Maritime Patrol Aircraft (MPA) Alternative Risk 5	Risk that a P-8 acquisition delay may cause a performance degradation. *This risk was assessed at a C1.* Based on current DoD acquisition performance a delay is possible. Consequence low.	The P-3 aircraft can be used as a mitigation without a reduction in performance capability or endurance.
Maritime Patrol Aircraft (MPA) Alternative Risk 6	Risk that the system does not perform as expected. *This risk was assessed at an A4.* The system has already gone through a number of years of satisfactory testing.	Use traditional sensor types resulting in reduced performance.

IDENTIFICATION	ANALYSIS	MITIGATION PLAN
Barrier Alternative Risk 1	Risk that the barrier may drift faster than expected. *This risk was assessed at a D3.* There is a high likelihood of unknown barrier movement due to unknown ocean activity. This would cause the formation to be broken and detection would incomplete.	More frequent repositioning/relaying of buoys.
Barrier Alternative Risk 2	Risk that buoys planned for use do not meet projected performance values. *This risk was assessed at a A3.* These sensors are close to final production therefore system performance should be understood prior to IOC. If the buoys do not perform as expected either acoustic performance or intermittent communications would affect the early warning capability of the barrier and overall performance would be reduced.	Utilize a greater number of buoys and robust communications.
Advanced Capabilities Build Alternative Risk 1	The schedule risk of MFTA would cause decreased performance on the DDG. *This risk was assessed at a B3.* The MFTA is close to final production. Therefore the likelihood of a schedule delay is low. However, in this alternative the MFTA is used on all the ships. Therefore, the consequence of the MFTA unavailability is higher in this system alternative than the Baseline System.	Use the current Towed Array system on all ships.
Advanced Capabilities Build Alternative Risk 2	Risk that the system does not perform as expected. *This risk was assessed at an A3.* The MFTA is close to final production; therefore, system performance should be fully characterized prior to IOC. If the MFTA does not perform as expected, the detection performance would be impacted. .	Use the current Towed Array on all 4 DDGs in place of the MFTAs. This is the configuration of the Baseline System, therefore, performance would degrade but not below the Baseline System performance

IDENTIFICATION	ANALYSIS	MITIGATION PLAN
Advanced Capabilities Build Alternative Risk 3	No appreciable gain in overall detection performance or reduction in "detect to classify" latency. *This risk was assessed at a B3.* Based on results from the submarine ARCI program, there is a high potential for performance gains to be reached by the 2013 timeframe. If gains not realized system would be as good as baseline system	Use the Baseline System

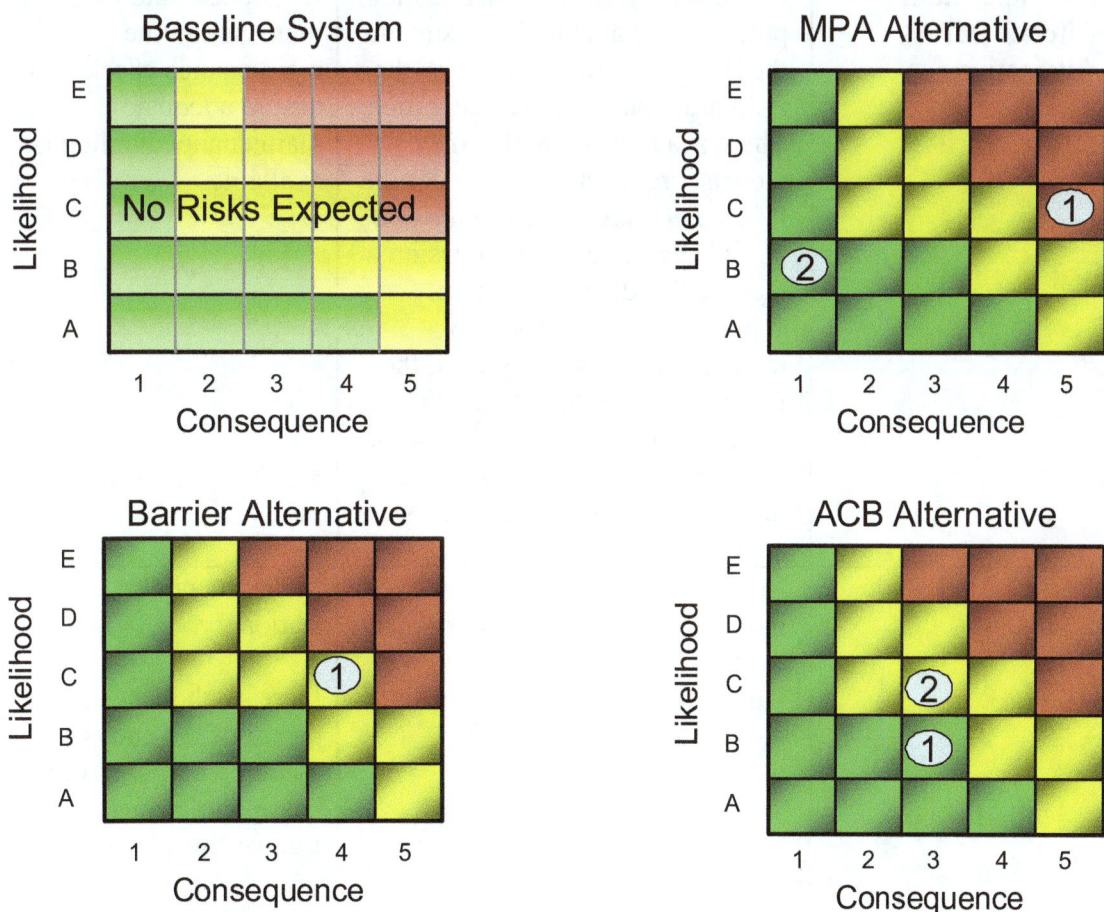

Figure 85 - Cost Based Risks

Table 20 - Cost Based Risks

IDENTIFICATION	ANALYSIS	MITIGATION PLAN
Baseline System Risk 1	No risk expected	
Maritime Patrol Aircraft (MPA) Alternative Risk 1	Risk that the EPAS System may have development cost growth. *This risk was assessed at a C5.* A new system will most likely see increased cost. This may lead to program cancellation if development cost exceeds the Nunn-McCurdy threshold.	Early mitigation is to rigorously manage cost. If risk is realized traditional sensor types could be used but would result in reduced performance.
Maritime Patrol Aircraft (MPA) Alternative Risk 2	Based on current DoD acquisition performance a delay is possible in the P-8 acquisition, therefore, the P-3 would be used as a mitigation. There is a risk is that this may increase maintenance costs for the P-3. *This risk was assessed at a B1.* Using the P-3 for a mission that the P-3 does not currently conduct might increase P-3 maintenance cost. However, the P-3 is sufficient to conduct the Battle Group Operations mission, and therefore only a minor increase in maintenance cost is anticipated.	If fallback onto P-3, increase routine maintenance checks and ensure adequate maintenance funding is available.
Barrier Alternative Risk 1	Risk of the cost of the buoys over the lifecycle. *This risk was assessed at a C4.* Many buoys will be required to continuously recycle the barrier over the mission.	Make the buoys stationary. Increase the detection power of the buoys so that they do not have to be repopulated as frequently.

IDENTIFICATION	ANALYSIS	MITIGATION PLAN
Advanced Capabilities Build Alternative Risk 1	Risk that the MFTA program is not funded adequately to achieve the required performance when it is needed. *This risk was assessed at a B3*. The MFTA is building upon an established successful process, therefore the likelihood of this risk occurring is low.	Use the current Towed Arrays on all platforms.
Advanced Capabilities Build Alternative Risk 2	Risk that a continuous funding stream is not available to support the research and development needed to develop the required technologies. *This risk was assessed at a C3*. This has a Medium probability of occurring as the surface ship side has been slow to fund a continuous R&D effort to support an equivalent Advanced Processing Build Structure equal to the version used by the submarine sonar programs.	Use baseline system; investigate potential submarine technologies for transition

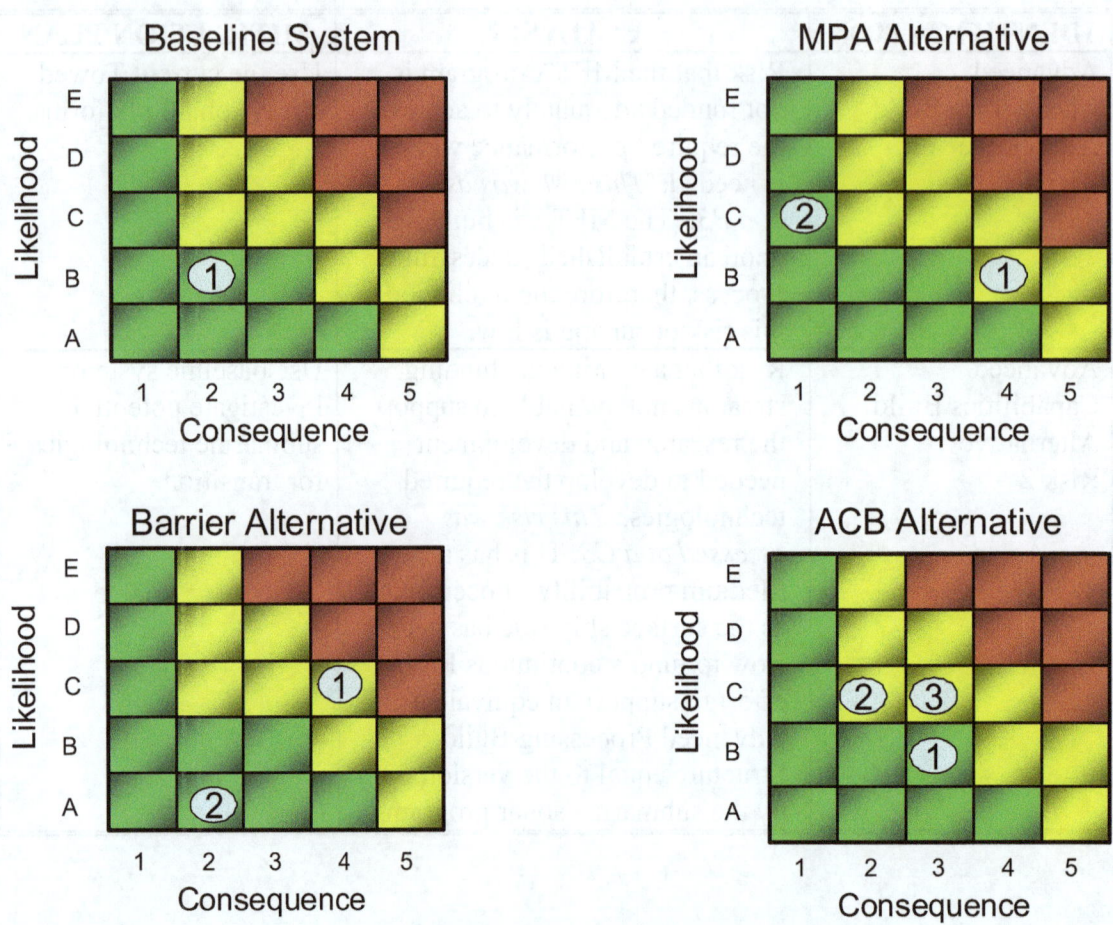

Figure 86 - Schedule Based Risks

Table 21 - Schedule Based Risks

IDENTIFICATION	ANALYSIS	MITIGATION PLAN
Baseline System Risk 1	Risk that there is a MFTA schedule delay. *This risk was assessed at a B2.* The MFTA is close to final production; therefore the likelihood of a schedule delay is low. The consequence is low because the MFTA is only used on one of the four ships. The MFTA provides minimal performance capabilities in the Baseline System.	Use current Towed Array for all platforms.
Maritime Patrol Aircraft (MPA) Alternative Risk 1	Risk that the EPAS program falls behind schedule. *This risk was assessed at a B4.* Development has already started.	Ensure that EPAS development is managed effectively to minimize schedule impact.
Maritime Patrol Aircraft (MPA) Alternative Risk 2	Risk of a P-8 acquisition delay. *This risk was assessed at a C1.* Based on current DoD acquisition performance a delay is possible. Consequence low. The P-3 aircraft can be used as a mitigation without a reduction in performance capability or endurance.	Use P-3 aircraft. No performance degradation expected.
Barrier Alternative Risk 1	Risk that there is insufficient production of DWAD assets. *This risk was assessed at a C4.*	Use fewer buoys in barrier.
Barrier Alternative Risk 2	Risk of infeasible logistics of carrying, deploying and underway replenishment of DWADS on LCS. *This risk was assessed at an A2.*	Use fewer buoys in barrier.
Advanced Capabilities Build Alternative Risk 1	Risk that there is a MFTA schedule delay. *This risk was assessed at a B3.* The MFTA is close to final production. Therefore the likelihood of a schedule delay is low. However, in this alternative the MFTA is used on all the ships. Therefore, the consequence of the MFTA unavailability is higher in this system alternative than the Baseline System.	Use current Towed Array on all ships

IDENTIFICATION	ANALYSIS	MITIGATION PLAN
Advanced Capabilities Build Alternative Risk 2	Risk the ship modernization availabilities cannot support fielding plan. *This risk was assessed at a C2.* Is the install schedule such that all required platforms can be updated in time to support Battle Group Operations?	Prioritize advanced development installation for carrier strike group deployers.
Advanced Capabilities Build Alternative Risk 3	Risk that new technologies will not be available in time to support scenario timeline. *This risk was assessed at a C3*	Transition to partial capabilities that may be ready

Table 22 - Summary of Risks by System Alternative

	Low Priority	Medium Priority	High Priority
Baseline System	2	2	0
Maritime Patrol Aircraft (MPA) Alternative	4	3	3
Barrier Alternative	2	3	0
Advanced Capabilities Build Alternative	5	3	0
Barrier with Advanced Capabilities Build Alternative	7*	6*	0*
* Barrier with Advanced Capabilities Build Alternative risks are a compilation of the risks associated with the Barrier Alternative and the Advanced Capabilities Build Alternative.			

4.4 CRITICAL ASSESSMENT OF ALTERNATIVES

In order to provide a recommendation to the decision maker of the alternative that will provide the most satisfaction to the stakeholders, the design team considered for each alternative the Total Value Score and the Life Cycle Cost. This created a cost-value comparison for each alternative in which the system that "cost less and did more" could be identified, as well as alternatives that would be clearly dominated by other alternatives. This weighing of Life Cycle Cost against the Total Value Score of the alternatives is known as a Cost Benefit Analysis (CBA). Graphic illustration of the Life Cycle Cost versus Total Value Score is shown in Figure 87.

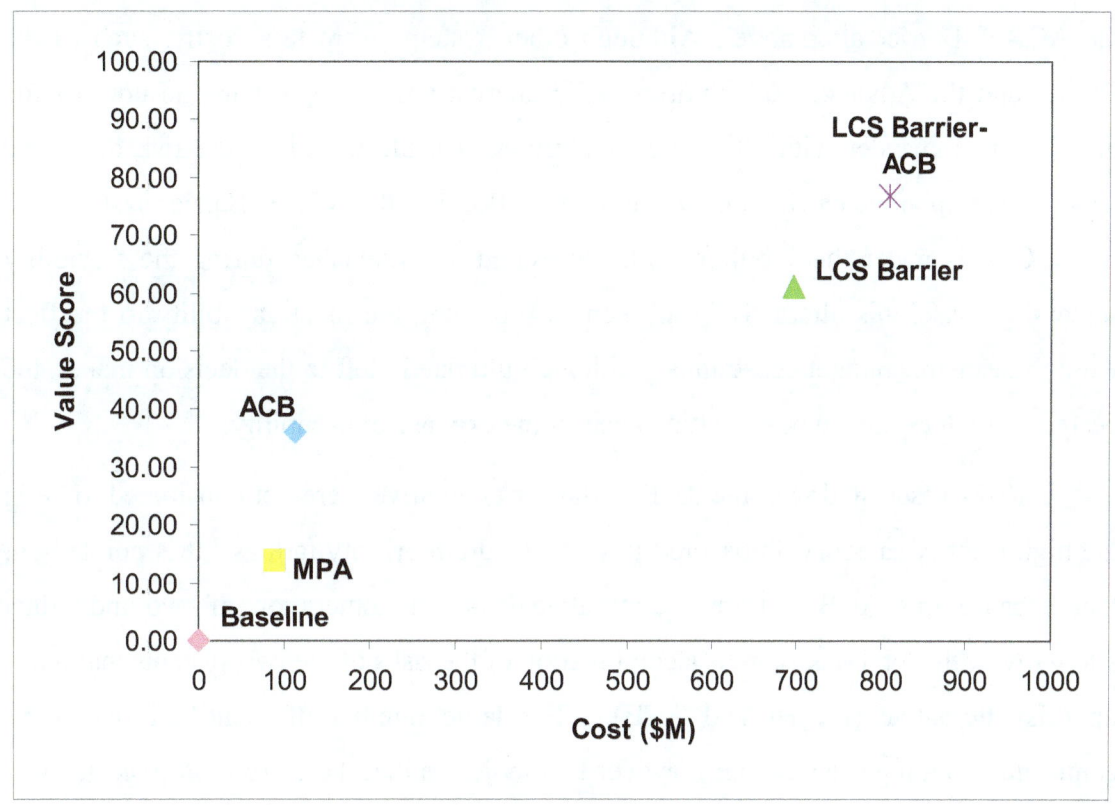

Figure 87 - Cost-Benefit Analysis Plot

From the Cost-Benefit analysis plot, improvement in performance (Value Score) over the baseline is clearly evident, as the baseline is normalized to the origin of the plot. Each alternative is an improvement over the baseline; however the amount of improvement comes with increasing cost. The Advanced Capabilities Build alternative shows a performance gain of nearly 162% over the MPA/EPAS alternative for a relatively low cost increase of 26%. This represents a "good trade" in which a major performance increase is gained through a relatively low cost increase. In this particular case, the design team concluded that the MPA/EPAS alternative was dominated by the Advanced Capabilities Build alternative and was not considered further.

In reviewing the effective need statement: "An improved ASW system is needed to protect carrier strike groups from enemy attack through effective, timely, and precise engagement by providing tactically significant detection, localization, tracking, and classification of quiet acoustic threat submarines in challenging environments", the design team considered that the system that clearly was most able to meet this need was the ACB + Barrier alternative. Although other systems were less costly, such as the Barrier and the Advanced Capabilities Build alternatives, these systems do not provide the CSG Commander with all of the capabilities possible to reduce the risk of enemy engagement upon the carrier high value target. Because the ACB + Barrier system Life Cycle Cost is under the 1 billion dollar threshold as established during the feasibility screening phase, this alternative was seen as providing the most capability to the fleet within reasonable budget constraints. Although ultimately left to the decision maker, the design team does not advocate cutting costs at the expense of capability.

Risks associated with the ACB + Barrier alternative were not considered to be in the high priority category, but scored low and medium priority ratings. It is pointed out that because this ACB + Barrier alternative is a conglomeration of two individual alternatives, the total risk score is a combination of the risks of the two systems that make up this alternative (Barrier and ACB). The large number of identified risk items contributes to a high risk rating; however this indicates that there are more risk items to manage vice areas of high risk within the alternative.

The information provided during the Decision Making phase of the systems engineering process is utilized to allow the selection of the most satisfying solution for acquisition. The effort applied during the systems engineering process has also identified a number of areas for further investigation. These areas, along with known limitations of the process and tools utilized by the systems engineering team are discussed in the final section of this report.

5 CONCLUSIONS

5.1 RECOMMENDATION

The System Engineering Team has successfully applied the practices and selected tools of the Systems Engineering Design Process to understand and formalize the needs of the customer. Thirteen (13) possible alternative solutions were developed to meet those needs. Through processes of feasibility screening and decision scoring a best available solution was determined. The identification of Aircraft Carrier Survival during an engagement with enemy submarines as the critical Measure of Effectiveness for the solutions space allowed our team to concentrate on evaluating candidate architectures that support the ASW engagement process, which included detection, decision and weapon engagement.

Pursue LCS Deployed Barrier Solution; Consider Technology to Reduce Total Buoy Costs

The analysis conducted by the systems engineering team has focused on the protection of the CVN while it is conducting aircraft launch and recovery operations as described in the reports scenario and concept of operations description. As illustrated in Chapter 4 of this report, the Advanced Capabilities Build and the LCS deployed Barrier alternatives result in nearly identical operational effectiveness outcomes. However, after combining additional decision criteria such as Operational Suitability metrics and cost through the utility function, we have demonstrated that the Advanced Capabilities Build alternative suffers from the impact of inadequate reliability due to the reliance on the towed array system component. Therefore, the systems engineering team recommends that the customer pursue the development and fielding of the LCS deployed Barrier capability.

In considering this option, the customer should be aware that a significant Life Cycle cost driver for this solution is the production rate required for the active sonobuoys. The sonobuoy inventory driver is the need to reseed the field due to buoy drift from ocean current effects. Potential mitigations for this cost driver might include investigation of "station keeping" technologies that would allow the buoys to remain in place for a significantly longer period of time.

Consider Also Pursuing ACB Approach to Improve Operational Effectiveness

Due to the critical nature of the CVN protection measure of effectiveness, the system engineering team would also recommend that the costumer consider a course of action that includes pursuit of both the Barrier capability and the Advance Capabilities Build solution. The team makes this recommendation in recognition of the relatively low cost of Advanced Capabilities Build solutions made available through the ACB approach and the improved performance provided by these two system alternatives acting in parallel as a layered defense approach to providing protection against submarine torpedo attack on the aircraft carrier.

5.2 KEY ASSUMPTIONS

The systems engineering team acknowledges that key assumptions were required to allow the project analysis to be completed in a timely manner. These key assumptions should be considered by the decision maker when assessing the completeness of the recommendations, and caution should be used in accepting the conclusions of this academic analysis for the extremely complex mission area of ASW. Additionally, future research should consider varying these assumptions to determine their significance in the design and analysis of an ASW system in support of carrier operations. The key assumptions are outlined here for the customer.

The Potential Performance Contribution of a Self Defense Function Was Not Investigated. As discussed in Chapter 3 of this report, the Self Defense function represents the ability to defeat a submarine launched torpedo. If it is possible to successfully design and build this capability it has the potential to contribute significantly to the overall probability of CVN survival during torpedo attack. In fact, if a 100%

effective torpedo defense capability could be produced the CVN would be rendered immune from risk of submarine torpedo attacks.

Perfect Torpedo Performance Assumed. Due to the limitations associated with modeling and simulation tools available to the systems engineering team the decision was made to model torpedo performance as 100% effective for launches within the torpedo maximum range. The systems engineering team understands that the probability of torpedo successfully acquiring, homing and detonating on a target is not 100%, however the team did not have a defendable model for threat torpedo performance nor an unclassified performance model or data for U.S. torpedo inventories. Assuming that the probability of success for either U.S. or adversary torpedoes is roughly equivalent these limitations should not affect the overall effectiveness models. The inclusion of a failure probability for the torpedoes would require significantly more advanced modeling tools that include submarine and carrier strike group behavior following torpedo launch and subsequent re-engagements.

No Attack by Submarine on CVN Screen Units. The modeling tools available did not support the analysis of attack by the enemy submarine on the Cruiser/Destroyer screening assets. This limitation is likely to result in more successful attacks by U.S. forces on enemy submarines than might be realistically expected for the baseline and Advanced Development approaches. A significantly more sophisticated modeling tool, which allows use of a successful submarine torpedo launch against a screen escort to be used as a localization and attack cue for the remaining ASW assets would be required to quantitatively assess the actual impact of allowing attack by enemy submarines on screen assets.

Threat Behavior Model Limited. The enemy submarine behavior is modeled as a "kill or be killed" tactic as described in section 3 of this document. This behavior, where the threat submarine aggressively pursues the CVN until successfully establishing a torpedo launch position, is likely to result in increased opportunities for the CVN screen assets to detect and engage the enemy submarine. In addition, the modeling approach did not allow for consideration that the enemy submarine might pursue an attack upon the AOE logistics support ship.

Contribution to Submarine Attrition by Theater Assets. The scoping of scenario and CONOPS that was necessary for our problem domain analysis precluded consideration of the contribution that might be made by systems that support attrition of enemy submarines before they arrive at the designated operating area. Further consideration should be given to such system solutions in the future, as they have the potential to significantly reduce the expected number of enemy submarine engagements incurred by the CVN strike group.

Ramifications of False Alarms. For simplification purposes, the models did not consider the ramifications of false alarms for either detection or classification. Additional work could be performed to produce detection operation curves for false alarm rates versus recognition threshold setting. Also an investigation into resource limitations and complications related to false alarms would provide additional insight and modeling realism.

5.3 LIMITATIONS

The systems engineering team identified several limitations during the execution of the Systems Engineering Development Process. Application of this methodology to an actual analysis and design problem would require that these limitations be overcome. Limitations and constraints in our process included:

- Report Classification Level. The systems engineering team elected to maintain this report at an unclassified level. This was done to facilitate team collaboration from home, make use of the BlackBoard facilities at NPS and also to allow for periodic unclassified reviews with our thesis advisors. While this is not seen as a major impact on the execution of the Systems Engineering Development Process, it will affect the actual outcomes that might be achieved using classified reference material for CONOPS, scenarios, system component performance and cost.
- Modeling and Simulation Tools. The Systems Engineering Team would have liked to have a modeling tool or frame work that would enable the

full-spectrum analysis of ASW operations which would support an analysis of fleet level movements and behaviors down through the application of sonar system performance in simulated environments. This tool would need to support use from remote sites to support use by both the distance learning projects as well as potentially program support activities conducted by NPS staff and students. Availability of this tool set would enable more emphasis on tool tailoring vice tool/model development.

- Access to Actual Performance and Cost Data. Several of the components utilized by the alternative solutions are still in the development stage so that the actual results of developmental and operational test have not yet been vetted or published. In addition performance data for many of the mature components is classified. These concerns apply to the cost as well as performance data. For these systems the team drew upon our experience with analogous systems in conjunction with the limited published data for our analysis. The team believes that our estimates have sufficient accuracy to not degrade the fidelity of the analysis.

APPENDIX A

NAVAL POSTGRADUATE SCHOOL

MONTEREY, CALIFORNIA

Improved Anti-Submarine Warfare (ASW) Effectiveness
Project Management Plan
MSSE Capstone Project

By

James Broadmeadow	Nguyen Nguyen
Francis Dziekan	Patrick Roach
Francis Frantz	Jeffrey Sammis
Rodney Gudz	Scott Santos
Patrick Kelley	Kenneth Silveria
Shawn Kennedy	Cullen Smith
Christine Moreira	Kirk Volk
	Steven Wright

Approved for public release; distribution is unlimited

APPROVAL SHEET
For
MSSE CAPSTONE –
Improved Anti-Submarine Warfare (ASW) Effectiveness
PROJECT MANAGEMENT PLAN

APPROVED BY: _____ **DATE:** _____
Advisor, Dr. Eugene Paulo

APPROVED BY: _____ **DATE:** _____
Advisor, Mr. Mark Rhoades

REVIEWED BY: _____ **DATE:** _____
MSSE (DL) Academic Associate, Dr. Cliff Whitcomb

REVIEWED BY: _____ **DATE:** _____
MSSE (DL) Program Manager, Dr. Wally Owen

REVIEWED BY: _____ **DATE:** _____
Systems Engineering Department Chair, Dr. David H. Olwell

THIS PAGE INTENTIONALLY LEFT BLANK

REPORT DOCUMENTATION PAGE			Form Approved OMB No. 0704-0188
Public reporting burden for this collection of information is estimated to average 1 hour per response, including the time for reviewing instruction, searching existing data sources, gathering and maintaining the data needed, and completing and reviewing the collection of information. Send comments regarding this burden estimate or any other aspect of this collection of information, including suggestions for reducing this burden, to Washington headquarters Services, Directorate for Information Operations and Reports, 1215 Jefferson Davis Highway, Suite 1204, Arlington, VA 22202-4302, and to the Office of Management and Budget, Paperwork Reduction Project (0704-0188) Washington DC 20503.			
1. AGENCY USE ONLY *(Leave blank)*	**2. REPORT DATE** October 2007	**3. REPORT TYPE AND DATES COVERED** Technical Report	
4. TITLE AND SUBTITLE: Improved Anit-Submarine Warfare (ASW) Effectiveness Project Management Plan			**5. FUNDING NUMBERS**
6. AUTHOR(S) Newport MSSE Cohort			
7. PERFORMING ORGANIZATION NAME(S) AND ADDRESS(ES) Naval Postgraduate School Monterey, CA 93943-5000			**8. PERFORMING ORGANIZATION REPORT NUMBER**
9. SPONSORING /MONITORING AGENCY NAME(S) AND ADDRESS(ES) N/A			**10. SPONSORING/MONITORING AGENCY REPORT NUMBER**
11. SUPPLEMENTARY NOTES The views expressed in this report are those of the author and do not reflect the official policy or position of the Department of Defense or the U.S. Government.			
12a. DISTRIBUTION / AVAILABILITY STATEMENT Distribution Statement (mix case letters)			**12b. DISTRIBUTION CODE**
13. ABSTRACT (maximum 200 words) N/A			
14. SUBJECT TERMS			**15. NUMBER OF PAGES**
			16. PRICE CODE
17. SECURITY CLASSIFICATION OF REPORT Unclassified	**18. SECURITY CLASSIFICATION OF THIS PAGE** Unclassified	**19. SECURITY CLASSIFICATION OF ABSTRACT** Unclassified	**20. LIMITATION OF ABSTRACT** UL

NSN 7540-01-280-5500

Standard Form 298 (Rev. 2-89)
Prescribed by ANSI Std. 239-18

LIST OF KEY PERSONNEL

Key Stakeholders

Director USW NUWC: ....Peter Herstein

IWS 5 Chief Engineer: .... Colleen Cannon

NUWC UDNS Lead: .... Joseph Monti

Technical Director NWDC: .... Wayne Perras

Fleet Representative: .... TBD

NUWC Chief Engineer: .... Steve Jette

Capstone Project Advisors

NPS Advisor .... Eugene Paulo

NPS Advisor .... Mark Rhoades

NUWCDIVNPT MSSE Capstone Project Team Key Personnel

Program Manager .... Steven Wright

Deputy Program Manager .... Patrick Kelley

Systems Engineer/Architect .... Scott Santos

Information Management Lead .... Patrick Roach

Information Management Deputy .... Kirk Volk

Working Integrated Product Team Leaders .... TBD

TABLE OF CONTENTS

1	INTRODUCTION	191
2	OBJECTIVES	192
3	PROGRAM	192
	3.1 PROJECT PHASES	192
	3.2 SYSTEMS ENGINEERING DESIGN PROCESS	193
	3.2.1 Problem Definition	193
	3.2.1.1 Needs Analysis	*193*
	3.2.1.2 Value System Design	*194*
	3.2.2 Design and Analysis	194
	3.2.2.1 Alternatives Generation	*195*
	3.2.2.2 Modeling and Analysis	*195*
	3.2.3 Decision Making	196
	3.2.3.1 Alternative Scoring	*196*
	3.2.3.2 Presentation for Decision Makers	*196*
	3.3 RISK MANAGEMENT PLAN	196
	3.4 DELIVERABLES	197
4	ORGANIZATION	197
5	POLICY	198
	5.1 DECISION MAKING POLICY	198
	5.2 INDIVIDUAL POLICY	199
	5.3 OPERATIONAL POLICES	200
	5.4 INFORMATION MANAGEMENT POLICY	200
6	STANDARD	203
7	SCHEDULE	203
	7.1 MILESTONE SCHEDULE	204
8	LIST OF REFERENCES	205
9	INITIAL DISTRIBUTION LIST	206

LIST OF FIGURES

Figure 1 - IPT Structure 198
Figure 2 - Project Timeline 203

1 INTRODUCTION

This document details the Project Management Plan (PMP) to be utilized by the Newport Cohort of the Naval Postgraduate School (NPS) Master of Science in Systems Engineering (MSSE) Capstone Project. The team will apply a formal Systems Engineering Design Process (SEDP) to evaluate the current needs, identify potential capability gaps, develop requirements and assess alternatives. Elements of the project's phases, schedule, organization and methodologies are detailed herein.

The project topic is an assessment of Improved Anti-Submarine Warfare (ASW) Effectiveness. The initial problem statement is derived from the *"Chief of Naval Operations' Anti-Submarine Warfare Concept of Operations for the 21st Century"*, which documents high level goals, challenges and the future environment for 21st Century ASW operations. As stated in the concept of operations, the near term the goal is to, *"maximize our undersea advantage anywhere in the world by leveraging advances in acoustic processing, data collection and sharing, communications, collaborative real-time planning, reachback support, rapid maneuver, and precision engagement"*. In the long term the key goal is to, *"build on these advances to fully leverage an integrated network of sensors coupled to stand-off weapons, thereby maximizing our advantages in persistence, speed, and precision as the conceptual framework for our future"*.

In response to the shifting strategic environment, NUWC's Technical Director has announced a working vision for NUWC centered on Next Generation Undersea Warfare – the theater-level warfare-from-under-the-sea capabilities that effectively support and enable networked Joint forces to be expeditionary, adaptable, and responsive, allowing them to perform a broad set of missions and tasks in support of the nation's defense strategy. Our project will conduct and report on our SEDP of this call to improve ASW operations.

2 OBJECTIVES

The objectives of the Improved ASW Effectiveness program is to implement the techniques in a systems engineering methodology to address the overarching need to improve ASW effectiveness in tomorrow's battlespace including operations near-land, with the need to establish area control in a congested, chaotic environment, and facing adversaries with every advancing levels of technological sophistication. We will implement the SEDP and the associated principles to refine the problem statement, synthesize potential solutions, evaluate them based on Measures of Effectiveness and Performance using analytic and simulation based tools, establishing the requirements necessary to produce a design baseline. The scope of the program will be to complete the first three phases identified in the Systems Engineering Design Process (SEDP), to include needs analysis, analysis of alternatives, and provide a feasible solution.

3 PROGRAM

The overall program will follow the SEDP as a systematic approach to developing the design framework through the program lifecycle. A phased approach will address the key tenets to the SEDP methodology, Problem Definition, Design and Analysis, and Decision Making in a logical progression. Coupled with this process will be a robust Risk Management plan acting as a continuous check and balance tool for evaluating each alternative. The following sections provide details on this methodology including a listing of planned deliverables and their place within the overall program timeline.

3.1 PROJECT PHASES

The program will be comprised of individual project phases tailored to meet requisite objectives of the overall program. The first project phase will focus upon problem definition necessary to establish a functional hierarchy that succinctly captures the stakeholder needs with measurable objectives. The second project phase will conduct design and analysis necessary to explore and establish feasible alternatives, with sufficient modeling and sensitivity analysis to ensure optimal design alternatives. The final project phase will cultivate decision making artifacts necessary to make informed decisions on what constitutes a best-value solution, including both technical and cost considerations.

3.2 SYSTEMS ENGINEERING DESIGN PROCESS

The SEDP will be implemented to provide a design framework and methodology for exploring candidate alternatives necessary to meet the project goal, including SEDP artifacts organized to clearly convey results for informed decision making. The project timeline is shown as Figure 2. Detailed dates associated with the schedule are in Section 7.1

3.2.1 Problem Definition

During Problem Definition the SEDP will focus upon interdisciplinary methods for defining a vision of what constitutes a trustworthy system, in terms of meeting the stakeholder needs through value system design. Issue formulation, analysis and interpretation will be applied to define the problem space, employing various analytical methods to broaden creativity and reduce predisposition and bias. Problem definition is crucial as it greatly establishes the basis for all subsequent SEDP analysis and evaluation: the 'foundation' of the project. Iteration and periodic Stakeholder reviews will be used to ensure an effective problem definition.

3.2.1.1 Needs Analysis

A Needs Analysis will be conducted to establish an Effective Needs Statement for the project, utilizing many of the following SEDP techniques:

- Stakeholder Analysis – to collate expressed system needs, wants and desires. Analysis may include Affinity Diagramming to organize language information, goals and constraints.
- Input-Output Model Analysis – to scope and bound the problem by defining boundaries of the system and boundary conditions.

- Needs and Constraints Analysis – to garner stakeholder perspective of the 'need' in the context of current conditions, future environment, resources to bring to bear, etc.
- Concept of Operations – to define a stakeholder vision for what the system 'is', a statement of mission requirements, and a description of 'how' the system will be used.
- Functional Analysis – to determine 'what' the system must do, not 'how' the system will function. The functional analysis provides a basis for developing innovative alternatives in follow-on phases. It encompasses system functional composition, and flows among functional components.

3.2.1.2 Value System Design

Value System Design forms the foundation of criterion through which alternatives are assessed and ultimately modeled for suitability and compliance with user needs. The Value System Design will utilize the following SEDP techniques:

- Objectives Hierarchy – to expand the Stakeholder's effective need into a qualitative Value Tree of system functions and objectives, for which evaluation consideration may be applied, and which is defensible and practical.
- Evaluation Measures – to develop specific measures to evaluate how well each bottom-level objective will be met.
- Weighting – to establish Stakeholder preferred weighting among objectives of a Value Tree, resulting in a complete Value Model for comparison of different alternatives.

3.2.2 Design and Analysis

During Design and Analysis the SEDP will employ various analytical, modeling, and simulation methods to expand the design space to allow for a wide range of potential solutions. Iteration and periodic Stakeholder reviews will be used to ensure effective design and analysis.

3.2.2.1 Alternatives Generation

Alternatives Generation will be conducted to arrive at candidate solutions that address the system objectives developed during the Problem Definition Phase. Alternatives Generation will utilize the following SEDP techniques to explore solution alternatives for the system under consideration:

- Organized Brainstorming – to apply group techniques for open exploration of solution elements that address each critical system objective.
- Zwicky's Morphological Box (ZMB) – to gather brainstorming results for objective-elements, and group these into 'alternatives' that address all system objective categories.
- Feasibility Screening – to identify alternatives that meet all system constraints, and hence are feasible, with feasibility criteria based on system objectives and Stakeholder feedback.
- Quality Functional Deployment – to ensure customer objectives are matched with technical performance measures and design dependent parameters.

3.2.2.2 Modeling and Analysis

Modeling and Analysis will be performed to approximate performance attributes of alternatives under consideration. Modeling will be used to represent or describe an important property of a system to be brought into being, or to analyze a system already in existence. The purpose for Modeling is to provide insight relative to the specified alternatives, better understand system relationships and required data, and ultimately assist in making informed decisions. Economic Modeling may be developed as well, to support follow-on Decision Making (e.g., life cycle cost profile).

Optimization can be applied to systematically determine the 'best' result for an objective that satisfies all constraints, while Sensitivity Analysis determines the robustness of the results.

3.2.3 Decision Making

During the Decision Making Phase the SEDP not only considers objective results, but also subjective attributes relative to the alternatives under consideration. In terms of subjective qualities, attribute-scales will be developed in concert with Stakeholder preference to provide clear and meaningful methods for ranking.

3.2.3.1 Alternative Scoring

Alternative Scoring compares alternatives with respect to multiple objectives (often competing) and multiple evaluation measures, including Value and Cost Modeling. Value Modeling is a decision theory approach that can accommodate a Stakeholder's preferences in terms of value and risk. An Additive Value Model applies Stakeholder value preferences to convert 'raw' performance results into a weighted evaluation. Results of Cost Modeling can then be considered in concert with Value Modeling to support a Stakeholder consensus on alternative effectiveness.

3.2.3.2 Presentation for Decision Makers

Decision Making can employ various techniques to characterize alternatives in a manner that facilitates informed decisions. Provided deliverables should clearly convey alternative performance, risk, and cost, including all key attributes required by the Stakeholders. The SEDP will capture all preceding decisions leading up to any major event on the project.

3.3 RISK MANAGEMENT PLAN

A Risk Management plan will be established and maintained throughout the program lifecycle identifying, analyzing, managing, and mitigating both program and project risks and their status as they change with time. Program risks are defined as those risks associated with the Improved Anti-Submarine Warfare (ASW) Effectiveness Program, for example a change in system requirements. Project risks are defined as those risks associated with the successful completion of the Newport cohort NPS MSSE Capstone Project, for example a schedule slip caused by unexpected travel.

Risks will be assigned and described in two dimensions: likelihood of occurrence and program consequence. Numerical assessment methods may be used to characterize program attributes, for example system reliability. Any risk determined to have either a medium or high impact will be assigned appropriate risk mitigation. Advisors and other important project stakeholders will be regularly informed of risk status.

3.4 DELIVERABLES

Several deliverables will be provided to the capstone project advisors. These deliverables include this PMP, the project proposal, the in-progress review presentation materials, the final report and associated presentation, and any models developed during the course. These deliverable products will be provided via Blackboard®.

4 ORGANIZATION

The Newport cohort will be organized into Working Integrated Product Teams (WIPTs) that are headed by a WIPT lead. Each WIPT lead is a member of the Overarching-Level Integrated Product Team (OIPT) that is headed by the Program Manager (PM).

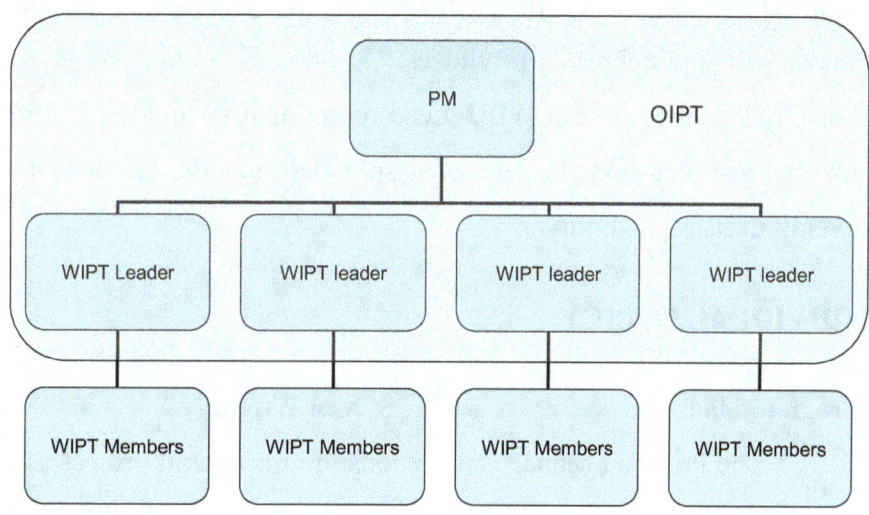

Figure 1 - IPT Structure

WIPTs will be established as necessary to meet program objectives within each program phase. As an WIPT completes its assigned tasking the WIPT lead will report to the OIPT and members will be reassigned as necessary. The OIPT is responsible for identifying the WIPT requirements throughout each project phase.

5 POLICY

5.1 DECISION MAKING POLICY

All decision making will be performed by Integrated Product Teams (IPT) either at the Overarching-Level (OIPT) or the Working-Level (WIPT). Therefore, issues will be discussed in a small group environment, and final decisions will be made and promulgated by the appropriate IPT. This policy will circumvent the inefficiency related to large group dynamics. The general decision making procedure will be as follows:

1. Strive for consensus as the first option. The PM or IPT Lead will determine whether or not consensus can be reached. While the WIPT focus upon issues

within their purview, they also support the OIPT for overarching and policy issues.

2. If no consensus can be reached, then the IPT decides by group vote; the IPT leader will hold tiebreaker privileges.

3. For OIPT decisions each WIPT Lead representative and the PM must be present for majority decision: in case of a split decision the OIPT Lead or PM holds overall decision authority.

5.2 INDIVIDUAL POLICY

Program Manager   Steven Wright

The Program Manager is responsible for overall project coordination. He acts as the final decision arbiter and assigns tasking. He is the primary point of contact with NPS faculty and staff, as well as the OIPT Lead.

Deputy Program Manager   Patrick Kelley

The Deputy Program Manager assists the program manager in his assigned tasking. He assumes the full responsibility and authority of the PM when absent due to work or travel commitments.

Lead Systems Engineer/Architect   Scott Santos

The Lead Systems Engineer (LSE) is responsible for project integration, ensuring that the outputs of the individual IPTs are compatible with each other and address overall system requirements. The LSE is responsible for ensuring that team efforts adhere to SEDP principles. The LSE's architecture responsibility is to ensure that the overarching architecture directly addresses all of the system requirements.

Information Management Lead   Pat Roach

The Information Management Lead is the primary person responsible for establishing and maintaining Blackboard® folders and content to facilitate information sharing among team members. The Information Manager is responsible for maintaining version control of all products.

Information Management Deputy   Kirk Volk

The Information Management Deputy is responsible for assisting the Information Management Lead in maintaining the file sharing system and providing alternate access to the system in the leads absence.

WIPT Leads

WIPT Leads are responsible for overall coordination of their IPT tasking and reporting progress to the PM and LSE. WIPT Leads serve as standing members of the OIPT.

Individual Team Members

All team members are responsible for executing assigned tasking in a complete and timely manner. Full participation at team meetings is expected.

5.3 OPERATIONAL POLICES

- IPTs will set up a meeting location and schedule. Routine weekly meetings are expected.
- The PM will call for full team meetings as required.
- Minutes will be taken documenting all IPT and full team, meetings and posted on the file sharing site. Recording responsibilities will rotate among team members.
- Artifacts will be produced with a standard set of software tools to be accessible by all team members.

5.4 INFORMATION MANAGEMENT POLICY

SEDP artifacts will be maintained in the Newport Project Files section of the SI0810 Blackboard®. The Blackboard® site will contain three main folders:

- Deliverables – Items that are required to be delivered to NPS as noted in Section 3.4
- Controlled – SE products that are produced and used throughout the life of the project.
- Reference – contains raw data and reference material that will not change over the life of the project.

Controlled items are produced by the appropriate WIPT and submitted for approval by the OIPT. Once approved the items are moved to the Controlled folder by the Information Manager.

Changes to items in the Controlled folder will be processed through the same path as an original product.

Controlled Items
- Input/Output Models
- External System Diagram
- Concept of Operation
- Objectives Hierarchy
- Functional Hierarchy
- Functional Flow Diagram
- N2 Diagram
- Statement of Effective Need
- Alternative Architecture Diagrams
- Models
- Model input and output data
- Lifecycle Planning
- Lifecycle cost estimates
- PMP
- Proposal
- Final Report
- Presentations
- Sensitivity Analysis
- Alternative Scores

Reference/Items
- Stakeholder Inputs
- Affinity Diagrams
- Brainstorming Results
- Meeting Minutes
- Standards
- Bibliography

6 STANDARD

Individuals are expected to arrive to each team meeting prepared to discuss the topic at hand. This requires prior research and planning at the individual level. Individuals who cannot attend a team meeting are expected to review the meeting discussions, major decisions and/or actions assigned prior to the following meeting.

Individuals will be required to support their appropriate WIPT. Each WIPT will decide how the work will be divided within their group. Each individual is expected to provide their assigned tasking. The WIPT lead responsibility will be rotated among cohort members.

Noncompliance with these expectations will be deemed as unacceptable performance. As a class, we will conduct periodic anonymous evaluations of each other in order to identify non-contributors and rectify the situation.

7 SCHEDULE

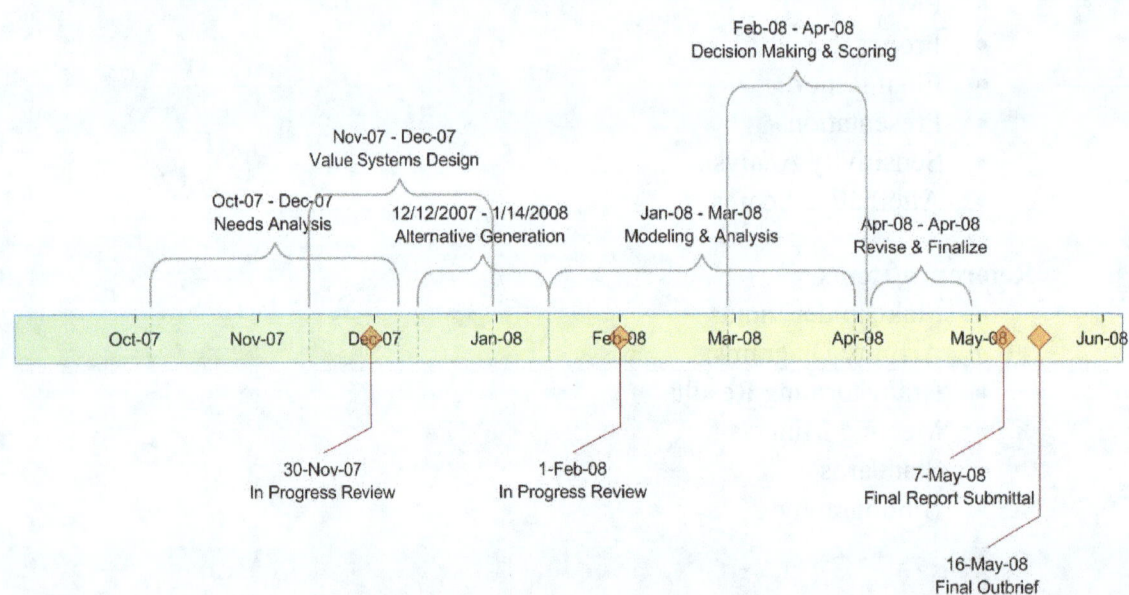

Figure 2 - Project Timeline

7.1 MILESTONE SCHEDULE

                                                                    Start/Finish

Stakeholder Requirements: -- 5 Oct / 26 Oct

CONOPS: -- 19 Oct / 26 Oct

Scenarios: -- 19 Oct / 2 Nov

Finalize Problem Statement: --- 26 Oct / 2 Nov

Functional Analysis: -- 2 Nov / 30 Nov

Functional Flow Diagrams: --- 9 Nov / 16 Dec

System Decomposition: --- 16 Nov / 7 Dec

Value Systems Design: --- 16 Nov / 21 Dec

1st In Process Review: --- 30 Nov

Measures of Effectiveness: -- 7 Dec / 21 Dec

Alternative Generation: -- 14 Dec / 18 Jan

Modeling and Analysis: -- 11 Jan / 28 Mar

2nd In Process Review: --- 1 Feb

Decision Making and Scoring: -- 29 Feb / 4 Apr

Finalize/ Revise: -- 4 Apr / 25 Apr

Final Out briefing: -- 16 May

8 LIST OF REFERENCES

1. Anti-Submarine Warfare Concept of Operations for the 21st Century, By Chief of Naval Operations.

2. Buede, Dennis M. (2000), The Engineering Design of Systems – Models and Methods, John Wiley & Sons, Inc., New York NY.

3. Sage, Andrew P. & Armstrong, James E. Jr. (2000), *Introduction to Systems Engineering*, John Wiley & Sons, Inc., New York NY.

4. Forsberg, Kevin PhD, Mooz, Hal, & Cotterman, Howard (2005), *Visualizing Project Management – Models and Frameworks for Mastering Complex Systems* 3rd Edition, John Wiley & Sons, Inc., New York NY.

5. Paulo, Gene PhD., Naval Post-Graduate School, SI4007 – *Fundamentals of Systems Engineering* - Course Notes 1st Quarter 2006

6. D.F McCormick, Speech to the National Defense Industry Association Undersea Division, Groton, CT, September 2005.

9 INITIAL DISTRIBUTION LIST

1. Dudley Knox Library
    Naval Postgraduate School
    Monterey, California

APPENDIX B

Newport MSSE Cohort Team Member Professional Background:

NUWC, Div NPT NPS MSSE Team	Professional Background
Jim Broadmeadow	A mechanical engineer for 13 years at NUWC in the Payload Integration and Launcher Systems Department. Primary focus was on the development and integration of Unmanned Undersea Vehicles onto submarines, now coordinating technical efforts associated with Launcher systems on the new VIRGINIA Class submarines.
Frank Dziekan	Electrical Engineer with 19 years at NUWC in various positions for Surface Ship and Submarine Sonar programs including current position as Lead Systems Engineer for the AN/BQQ-10(V). Have also served as ASW Technical Advisor for the CNO (Surface Warfare N863) as part of NUWC Field Team
Jim Frantz	An Electrical Engineer with 22 years experience at NUWC working in the Combat Systems Department for various Submarine Acquisition Programs. Prior assignment with the Submarine Program Management office for Submarine Combat Systems, PMS425 has lead to the current assignment as Combat Control System, AN/BYG-1 System Engineer.
Rodney Gudz	A Mechanical Engineer with 14 years experience in mechanical design and analysis, currently supporting the Submarine Imaging Technical Design Agent primarily Virginia Class Photonics Mast.
Patrick Kelley	Patrick Kelley is currently assigned as the System Command's Technical Warrant Holder for Integrated Undersea Warfare. Mr. Kelley's duty station is NUWC Division Newport, where he is a member of the Undersea Warfare Combat Systems Department staff. Previous assignments have included Commander, Submarine Pacific Fleet and NAVSEA Advanced Systems Technology Office.
Shawn Kennedy	An electrical engineer with 12 years experience at NUWC providing digital signal processing and algorithm development support for undersea ranges. Also five years in private industry developing real-time multi-threaded software to control CD and DVD replication equipment.
Christine Moreira	Mathematician with 4 years experience at NUWC in the USW Combat Systems Department. Currently performing Reliability,

	Maintainability and Availability predictions for VIRGINIA Class Systems.
Nguyen Nguyen	An Electrical Engineer graduated from UTEP in 1988. Employed by Naval Undersea System Center in 1991. Experience at NUWC included Acoustic Device Countermeasure testing and Advanced Countermeasure Development. Currently responsible for building target models for Weapon Analysis Facility at Torpedo Systems Department.
Pat Roach	5 years US Navy service in submarines. 20 years contractor and government systems engineering experience in submarine and surface ship launchers, torpedoes, missiles, and combat control systems.
Jeff Sammis	21 Years as government contractor and employee, involved in all facets of surface ASW combat system development. Currently working as Lead Systems Engineer for a Foreign Military Sales (FMS) variant of the SQQ-89 ASW Combat System.
Scott Santos	A Mechanical Engineer with 22 years experience in submarine weapons systems, mainly as a member of the Fleet Failure Analysis Team. Currently responsible for coordinating the efforts of Failure Analysis and In-Service Engineering onsite representatives at the Intermediate Maintenance Activities.
Kenny Silveria	18 years at NUWC. Currently (last 2.5 years) the AN/SQQ-89(V) Lead System Engineer (LSE) working in support of PEO IWS5B. 8 years prior was the ARCI Lead External Interface Engineer.
Cullen Smith	A Mechanical Engineer with 9 years of experience in Submarine imaging and communications systems. Currently working on the Common Submarine Radio Room on Trident and VIRGINIA Class Submarines and also the development of a new non-penetrating periscope for the VIRGINIA Class.
Kirk Volk	An electrical engineer with 19 years experience at NUWC as systems engineer in support of acquisition and development of RF communications systems, optical sensors, and ATE.
Steve Wright	Electrical Engineer With 22 years at NUWC Working in the Combat System Department, Performing System Engineering Roles on Submarine Combat Control System Acquisition Programs.

APPENDIX C

STAKEHOLDER QUESTIONAIRE

Our design team developed a stakeholder questionnaire in order to establish a standard set of interview elements for query of each stakeholder. The questionnaire was composed of questions intended to facilitate discourse that could help characterize the stakeholder needs, while encouraging stakeholder creativity. The questionnaire also facilitated interview of stakeholders who proved difficult to reach in terms of their remote proximity or schedule, allowing timely initial query when stakeholder audience was a premium, and increasing productivity for subsequent interview with these respondents. After some early trial and iteration on survey questions, the following became the basis of our stakeholder questionnaire:

- What are some of the major limitations the US Navy is currently facing in defeating SSK, e.g. Functional, Logistical, etc.?

- What types of technologies are currently needed to more effectively keep an SSK from impeding US Aircraft carrier operations?

- From a system standpoint, what are some challenges facing our ability to detect, identify and defeat SSK?

- What would be some important features of a system devised to protect US Aircraft carriers from SSK?

- What are some systems or processes (current or future) that are (may prove to be) effective in detecting / deterring SSK?

- Define a successful ASW mission (major characteristics associated with a successful mission).

➢ What are the main areas (ports, choke points, channels, open water, etc.) of concern for defeating SSK?

➢ What improvements can be made in the decision making process (Automation, operator training, etc.)?

➢ What do you see as the greatest challenge in modern ASW?

➢ Without any consideration of current limitations (technologies, political, cost, etc.), define your vision of a "perfect" ASW system

Early stakeholder feedback indicated quest for improvement in undersea warfare equated to a desire for ASW improvement, and the questionnaire was designed to further explore the spectrum of stakeholder ASW needs.

APPENDIX D

STAKEHOLDER RECOMMENDED RESEARCH

In addition to stakeholder interviews, the design team also conducted significant research so as to better characterize the problem space and facilitate stakeholder needs concurrence. Various source materials were consulted as part of this research, including those references suggested by stakeholders as germane subject-matter. Below is an example of materials that were consulted as part of the initial needs analysis research:

- Undersea Distributed Networked Systems (UDNS), Jun 2007 – Unclassified NUWC brief on a systems engineering based framework for developing UDNS. The UDNS concept is to support geographically dispersed sensor, command & control, and influencer systems that are networked to generate an aware, flexible and agile system focused on the operational mission of the group or force of systems. Included an epitome of Fleet needs in an ASW context.
- CNO ASW CONOPS, May 2007 – Unclassified Chief of Naval Operations (CNO) point paper providing a high level CONOPS of ASW in the 21st century. Provides an overview of the operating environment, near and far-term ASW initiatives, force attributes, development priorities, and way-ahead ASW principles and associated capabilities.
- Next-Generation Undersea Warfare and UDNS, Jan 2007 – Unclassified NUWC technical report that presents the rationale, implications, and perceived advantages for next-generation USW, whereby distributed networked systems is deemed a key enabler. Challenges in engineering a distributed networked system, co-evolved with war fighter CONOPS, is also addressed.
- Cooperative Strategy for 21st century Sea Power, Oct 2007 – Unclassified CNO paper describing significance (what & why) of the maritime strategy, the strategic imperatives, the core capabilities for strategy implementation, associated priorities and opportunities, and recognition of undersea warfare as an essential contributor.

➢ Global ASW CONOPS – Secret CONOPS identifying a framework for Full Spectrum ASW (FSASW), comprised of operational/tactical layers, tailored per Rules of Engagement (ROE) and environment. Applied to illustrative scenarios, the framework is a guide for both DOTMLPF & Technical development initiatives (e.g. across Planning, RDT&E and Acquisition Lifecycles).

➢ Naval Warfare Publication (NWP) 3-21, Feb 2007 – Secret publication addressing Fleet Antisubmarine Warfare (e.g. doctrine, Tactics/Technique/Procedures).

APPENDIX E

NEEDS RESEARCH DOCUMENTATION

All resulting Needs Analysis language information from both stakeholder interviews and materials research were captured in an electronic worksheet format (i.e. Microsoft Excel) to ensure the information was suitably recorded and documented for traceability. **Figure 3** denotes the worksheet format utilized to record stakeholder questionnaire results, whereby any compound stakeholder reply was broken down into individual needs elements which are identified as original needs. **Figure 4** denotes the worksheet format utilized to record research data acquired from each specific information source, whereby "yellow sticky" references were documented as original needs.

#	Question	Stakeholder #1	Stakeholder #2
1	*What are some of the major limitations the US Navy is currently facing in defeating SSK, e.g. Functional, Logistical, etc.?*	Understanding Red capability and tactics. Understanding what additional Red capability does to US and allies plans. Taking advantage of non US assets.	Training/operator proficiency in applicable environments
	*Breakdown of stakeholder answers into **Original Needs**:*	Understanding Red capability and tactics.	Training/operator proficiency in applicable environments
		Understanding what additional Red capability does to US and allies plans.	
		Taking advantage of non US assets.	
2	*What types of technologies are currently needed to more effectively keep an SSK from impeding US Aircraft carrier operations?*	Shallow water track and trail upon leaving port. ISR tools to say when departure is happening	Any technology that will support active or passive detection at tactically significant ranges.
	*Breakdown of stakeholder answers into **Original Needs**:*	Shallow water track and trail upon leaving port.	Any technology that will support active or passive detection at tactically significant ranges.
		ISR tools to say when departure is happening.	

Figure 3: Needs Analysis Questionnaire Data (sample)

Document:	System Engineering Based Framework For Developing Undersea Distributed networked Systems (UDNS)
Reference:	Presented by UDNS Tech Lead
Document Type:	PowerPoint Presentation
Document Classification:	Unclassified
Synopsis:	Summary of NUWC efforts in this arena

Requirement No.	Status	Document Reference	Data Element (Stakeholder Input)	"Yellow Sticky"
1	OK	UDNS Brief	Provide Enhanced Situational Awareness	Provide Enhanced Situational Awareness
2	OK	UDNS Brief	ProvideFaster Engagement Chain Timeline (Time)	Provide Faster Engagement Chain Timeline (Time)
3	OK	UDNS Brief	Provide Increased Engagement Effectiveness (Probability)	Provide Increased Engagement Effectiveness (Probability)
4	OK	UDNS Brief	Need to Relieve Platforms to Conduct Other Tasking	Need to enable ASW capable Platforms to concurrently Conduct non-ASW Tasking.
5	OK	UDNS Brief	Need to Reduce Risk to Forces	Need to Reduce submarine threat to ASW Platforms
6	OK	UDNS Brief	Need to make all sensor data available to all warfighters. (Data not currently currently shared among users. Sources must forward data to known recipients.)	ASW information and data needs to be available to all ASW nodes

Figure 4: Needs Analysis Research Data (sample)

APPENDIX F

MODELING SCORECARDS

Scorecard results for Baseline System.

Scorecard 1

SS vs. CVN		Range	Bearing	Torp Crse	Torp Run
TOF	11910	12542.38	13.48463	153.7249	9823.203
TOH	12346.52				
SS Win?	TRUE				
DDG1 vs. SS					
TOF	13680				
TOH	13712				
DDG2 vs. SS					
TOF	14490				
TOH	14506				
DDG3 vs. SS					
TOF	14580				
TOH	14597				
CG1 vs. SS					
TOF	999999				
TOH	17564				
				Count	Percent
			Red Win	8	32.0
			Blue Win	17	68.0

Run Number	SS Win?	TOF	TOH	Range	Bearing	Torp Crse	Torp Run
1	TRUE	11700	12143.71	12710.33	13.40	152.87	9985.01
2	TRUE	3870	4312.84	12685.00	14.64	154.09	9965.47
3	FALSE	2040	2471.32	12173.71	-14.92	107.08	9706.21
4	FALSE	2550	2993.17	10100.74	-10.95	76.00	9972.85
5	FALSE	2010	2444.68	11963.32	-14.70	102.01	9781.85
6	FALSE	2640	3077.80	12519.35	-14.98	110.03	9851.97
7	FALSE	2880	3316.69	11487.32	-14.09	94.31	9827.00
8	FALSE	2970	3408.42	12186.21	-14.80	103.92	9865.90
9	FALSE	3270	3713.09	9215.99	-8.30	66.63	9971.11
10	TRUE	4350	4793.07	13445.02	12.76	170.33	9970.60
11	TRUE	11850	12284.93	12588.21	13.68	155.82	9787.29
12	FALSE	1830	2264.21	11528.83	-14.24	95.79	9771.07
13	FALSE	2280	2723.04	10024.16	-10.75	75.21	9969.81
14	FALSE	2520	2961.86	10477.39	-11.96	80.46	9943.23
15	FALSE	2700	3134.35	11941.70	-14.69	101.82	9774.22
16	TRUE	3210	3653.18	12511.39	-14.92	107.13	9973.07
17	FALSE	1830	2273.53	12368.80	-14.83	104.57	9981.01
18	FALSE	1980	2416.61	11885.10	-14.58	100.00	9825.11
19	FALSE	3780	4214.36	11708.76	15.00	141.31	9774.63
20	FALSE	12030	12466.00	12430.39	13.27	151.56	9811.35
21	FALSE	3420	3863.99	12418.60	-14.85	105.18	9991.31
22	TRUE	3870	4312.10	12294.74	14.93	147.60	9948.82
23	TRUE	11700	12143.38	12707.73	13.42	153.02	9977.63
24	FALSE	11490	11928.95	12812.26	13.90	158.31	9877.84
25	TRUE	11910	12346.52	12542.38	13.48	153.72	9823.20

Scorecard 2

SS vs. CVN		Range	Bearing	Torp Crse	Torp Run
TOF	12120	12558.64	13.14057	150.3467	9956.457
TOH	12562.44				
SS Win?	FALSE				
DDG1 vs. SS					
TOF	1800				
TOH	1871				
DDG2 vs. SS					
TOF	14400				
TOH	14414				
DDG3 vs. SS					
TOF	14340				
TOH	14365				
CG1 vs. SS					
TOF	999999				
TOH	17565				
				Count	Percent
			Red Win	7	28.0
			Blue Win	18	72.0

Run Number	SS Win?	TOF	TOH	Range	Bearing	Torp Crse	Torp Run
1	FALSE	15690	16132.83	13309.51	-14.97	124.12	9965.22
2	TRUE	3750	4194.28	12074.22	12.77	140.27	9997.82
3	TRUE	11550	11984.23	12741.07	14.04	159.90	9771.70
4	FALSE	2250	2689.68	10194.49	-11.40	77.89	9894.20
5	FALSE	2430	2859.29	10261.70	-12.15	81.41	9660.50
6	FALSE	2040	2483.99	11177.75	-13.29	87.97	9991.17
7	TRUE	3960	4393.97	12085.92	14.92	147.90	9765.78
8	FALSE	2130	2566.37	11753.20	-14.44	98.15	9819.85
9	TRUE	3510	3952.27	9521.60	-9.35	70.04	9952.52
10	TRUE	3720	4160.36	11621.10	8.21	128.64	9909.51
11	TRUE	11490	11926.09	12770.60	13.99	159.30	9813.48
12	FALSE	11610	12046.07	12780.91	14.01	159.57	9813.02
13	FALSE	2850	3287.01	11576.37	-14.20	95.41	9834.27
14	TRUE	4020	4449.67	12457.55	14.43	156.98	9668.96
15	FALSE	1890	2328.48	12392.24	-14.93	107.37	9867.32
16	FALSE	3000	3436.35	11503.42	-14.13	94.66	9819.22
17	FALSE	1980	2421.84	11219.62	-13.46	89.15	9942.92
18	FALSE	3060	3500.93	9247.02	-8.56	67.43	9922.30
19	TRUE	12450	12888.56	12407.58	13.05	149.46	9869.04
20	FALSE	2430	2868.24	10090.34	-11.22	77.12	9861.79
21	FALSE	8400	8839.79	13755.15	-14.43	144.71	9896.66
22	FALSE	9570	10014.19	12783.60	-14.41	112.81	9995.66
23	FALSE	2070	2511.35	11984.54	-14.55	99.56	9931.87
24	FALSE	2910	3347.82	10876.36	-13.02	86.20	9852.31
25	FALSE	12120	12562.44	12558.64	13.14	150.35	9956.46

Table 1

SS vs. CVN		Range	Bearing	Torp Crse	Torp Run	Run Number	SS Win?	TOF	TOH	Range	Bearing	Torp Crse	Torp Run
TOF	2640	9959.899	-11.0679	76.48634	9789.953	1	TRUE	12150	12587.48	12478.92	13.28	151.70	9844.65
TOH	3075.045					2	TRUE	12240	12682.86	12533.47	13.05	149.55	9965.93
SS Win?	TRUE					3	FALSE	1770	2208.80	11461.00	-13.97	93.22	9874.51
						4	FALSE	2100	2542.01	10224.05	-11.34	77.63	9946.64
DDG1 vs. SS						5	FALSE	12030	12472.59	12586.97	13.20	150.87	9959.69
TOF	5430					6	TRUE	2670	3113.69	12801.70	-15.00	112.20	9984.56
TOH	5452					7	TRUE	3870	4309.43	12686.93	14.51	155.96	9688.53
				Run Model		8	TRUE	3420	3863.96	12498.98	-14.90	106.54	9990.59
DDG2 vs. SS						9	TRUE	12210	12649.34	12456.02	13.11	150.03	9866.62
TOF	8190					10	FALSE	2160	2604.26	11746.13	-14.17	95.11	9997.31
TOH	8231					11	TRUE	12450	12893.97	12504.43	12.91	148.25	9990.83
						12	TRUE	4710	5153.96	13594.88	12.05	174.08	9990.54
DDG3 vs. SS						13	FALSE	2730	3169.48	12078.19	-14.69	101.75	9899.74
TOF	13740					14	TRUE	3660	4099.92	12106.08	-8.70	112.89	9899.60
TOH	13769					15	TRUE	4470	4912.35	13488.78	12.41	172.25	9954.35
						16	FALSE	1890	2333.23	11902.78	-14.40	97.65	9974.22
CG1 vs. SS						17	FALSE	1860	2298.45	12268.73	-14.86	105.27	9866.62
TOF	999999					18	FALSE	2520	2958.75	10004.11	-10.96	76.04	9873.24
TOH	17565					19	TRUE	4080	4517.22	12932.24	13.93	162.18	9838.95
						20	FALSE	11400	11842.31	12913.95	13.91	158.39	9953.52
				Count	Percent	21	TRUE	3840	4284.19	12709.48	14.65	153.84	9995.84
			Red Win	12	48.0	22	FALSE	2490	2927.93	9587.81	-9.84	71.75	9854.87
			Blue Win	13	52.0	23	FALSE	2370	2804.61	10193.93	-11.69	79.20	9780.22
						24	FALSE	2550	2988.28	11362.53	-13.84	92.11	9862.73
						25	TRUE	2640	3075.04	9959.90	-11.07	76.49	9789.95

Table 2

SS vs. CVN		Range	Bearing	Torp Crse	Torp Run	Run Number	SS Win?	TOF	TOH	Range	Bearing	Torp Crse	Torp Run
TOF	12150	12422	13.17076	150.6325	9837.806	1	FALSE	11550	11991.16	12686.77	13.51	153.97	9927.62
TOH	12587.17					2	FALSE	2820	3254.77	9914.79	-10.96	76.06	9783.82
SS Win?	TRUE					3	FALSE	15720	16159.92	13100.02	-14.89	121.28	9899.57
						4	FALSE	2790	3231.39	12999.85	-14.95	117.86	9932.64
DDG1 vs. SS						5	FALSE	11550	11990.31	12787.63	13.77	156.82	9908.45
TOF	13500					6	TRUE	4500	4943.38	9634.22	12.29	102.88	9977.62
TOH	13531					7	TRUE	2250	2694.32	13306.43	-14.77	123.40	9998.60
				Run Model		8	TRUE	12180	12617.32	12417.54	13.15	150.44	9841.11
DDG2 vs. SS						9	TRUE	4530	4973.79	13534.87	12.40	172.31	9966.85
TOF	14400					10	FALSE	3120	3562.02	12425.74	-14.89	106.22	9946.99
TOH	14414					11	FALSE	2850	3288.97	12410.90	-14.93	107.45	9878.31
						12	TRUE	3990	4430.54	12913.59	14.18	159.75	9913.69
DDG3 vs. SS						13	FALSE	1920	2358.85	11163.75	-13.49	89.40	9875.67
TOF	14580					14	FALSE	2970	3409.61	11989.14	-14.60	100.34	9892.71
TOH	14600					15	FALSE	2610	3052.60	12155.12	-14.68	101.61	9959.97
						16	FALSE	2460	2894.31	11637.50	-14.37	97.28	9773.42
CG1 vs. SS						17	TRUE	4230	4673.02	13335.29	13.22	167.48	9969.45
TOF	999999					18	FALSE	2910	3352.01	12316.96	-14.82	104.42	9946.71
TOH	17566					19	FALSE	2610	3054.04	11573.85	-13.94	92.91	9992.36
						20	FALSE	2820	3255.89	11282.13	-13.82	91.87	9809.03
				Count	Percent	21	FALSE	3120	3562.61	9281.89	-8.56	67.43	9960.12
			Red Win	8	32.0	22	FALSE	11430	11871.75	12861.31	13.84	157.55	9940.95
			Blue Win	17	68.0	23	FALSE	3120	3559.92	9204.72	-8.49	67.21	9699.60
						24	FALSE	3090	3525.87	11834.54	-14.55	99.55	9808.53
						25	TRUE	12150	12587.17	12422.00	13.17	150.63	9837.81

Table 3

SS vs. CVN		Range	Bearing	Torp Crse	Torp Run	Run Number	SS Win?	TOF	TOH	Range	Bearing	Torp Crse	Torp Run
TOF	2220	13042.37	-14.9518	117.6464	9972.163	1	FALSE	2130	2573.84	11747.65	-14.19	95.29	9987.81
TOH	2663.142					2	FALSE	3090	3527.34	9807.59	-10.51	74.26	9841.51
SS Win?	TRUE					3	FALSE	3060	3503.07	10443.45	-11.81	79.77	9970.52
						4	FALSE	2850	3291.50	10377.97	-11.74	79.45	9935.18
DDG1 vs. SS						5	TRUE	3840	4279.45	11770.87	14.99	140.07	9889.18
TOF	5700					6	TRUE	12420	12859.30	12495.50	13.20	150.92	9885.76
TOH	5730					7	FALSE	15660	16103.16	13346.21	-14.98	124.78	9972.69
				Run Model		8	FALSE	8130	8571.91	13857.79	-14.20	148.03	9944.55
DDG2 vs. SS						9	FALSE	2250	2687.68	12860.80	-14.96	117.17	9849.22
TOF	6210					10	FALSE	11820	12261.60	12725.06	13.56	154.55	9937.54
TOH	6228					11	FALSE	12030	12473.55	12609.76	13.19	150.77	9981.32
						12	FALSE	2190	2624.89	11395.55	-14.03	93.72	9786.38
DDG3 vs. SS						13	FALSE	2010	2444.36	10381.27	-12.15	81.40	9774.60
TOF	13350					14	FALSE	3420	3861.45	9423.44	-9.10	69.19	9934.09
TOH	13391					15	TRUE	3750	4191.64	12454.73	11.44	146.93	9938.37
						16	FALSE	2010	2451.55	10965.48	-13.01	86.16	9936.39
CG1 vs. SS						17	FALSE	2400	2833.30	11345.53	-14.01	93.60	9750.78
TOF	999999					18	FALSE	1890	2330.08	12164.63	-14.75	102.84	9903.15
TOH	17565					19	FALSE	1920	2355.91	10652.57	-13.06	86.49	9809.43
						20	FALSE	2460	2899.98	9392.57	-9.10	69.19	9901.03
				Count	Percent	21	TRUE	12360	12801.06	12570.08	13.26	151.45	9925.39
			Red Win	6	24.0	22	FALSE	2430	2871.09	12047.77	-14.62	100.61	9925.92
			Blue Win	19	76.0	23	FALSE	2010	2447.46	12116.69	-14.77	103.23	9844.31
						24	TRUE	2580	3015.04	12469.50	-14.99	110.58	9789.95
						25	TRUE	2220	2663.14	13042.37	-14.95	117.65	9972.16

Table 1

SS vs. CVN		Range	Bearing	Torp Crse	Torp Run		Run Number	SS Win?	TOF	TOH	Range	Bearing	Torp Crse	Torp Run
TOF	2880	11267.58	-13.8852	92.45953	9757.421		1	FALSE	11520	11957.67	12732.01	13.82	157.31	9849.10
TOH	3313.599						2	TRUE	12210	12646.27	12383.02	13.14	150.34	9817.54
SS Win?	FALSE						3	FALSE	2670	3105.98	11473.37	-14.10	94.38	9811.10
							4	FALSE	2190	2629.04	12594.86	-14.99	110.79	9879.86
DDG1 vs. SS							5	FALSE	2070	2511.83	12406.95	-14.88	106.03	9942.75
TOF	4830						6	FALSE	2310	2738.95	11466.51	-14.34	96.89	9652.88
TOH	4858						7	FALSE	1890	2327.43	12166.03	-14.81	104.04	9843.56
					Run Model		8	FALSE	2550	2983.97	10047.76	-11.36	77.73	9765.68
DDG2 vs. SS							9	FALSE	1980	2413.32	10914.86	-13.30	88.04	9751.23
TOF	2130						10	TRUE	4260	4703.65	13150.53	13.86	162.78	9983.71
TOH	2152						11	FALSE	2100	2541.83	12057.23	-14.61	100.45	9942.64
							12	FALSE	11850	12291.13	12600.14	13.32	152.07	9926.89
DDG3 vs. SS							13	FALSE	3330	3769.71	9229.73	-8.59	67.52	9894.92
TOF	2430						14	FALSE	2280	2717.57	12798.14	-14.98	115.83	9846.89
TOH	2437						15	FALSE	2010	2445.48	11338.18	-13.92	92.75	9799.73
							16	TRUE	4230	4671.00	9193.97	11.35	95.64	9924.03
CG1 vs. SS							17	FALSE	8190	8628.89	13760.80	-14.22	147.78	9876.59
TOF	999999						18	FALSE	11760	12202.55	12821.71	13.71	156.11	9958.89
TOH	17568						19	FALSE	2880	3321.89	10462.54	-11.92	80.29	9943.99
							20	FALSE	11760	12199.37	12575.85	13.38	152.64	9887.36
				Count	Percent		21	TRUE	3300	3737.18	9614.90	-9.97	72.21	9838.04
			Red Win	7	28.0		22	FALSE	2550	2984.84	10141.99	-11.55	78.56	9785.43
			Blue Win	18	72.0		23	TRUE	4080	4518.38	12982.55	13.89	162.53	9865.08
							24	FALSE	2850	3279.70	9843.55	-11.08	76.55	9669.57
							25	FALSE	2880	3313.60	11267.58	-13.89	92.46	9757.42

Table 2

SS vs. CVN		Range	Bearing	Torp Crse	Torp Run		Run Number	SS Win?	TOF	TOH	Range	Bearing	Torp Crse	Torp Run
TOF	2040	11398	-13.7987	91.73353	9919.031		1	FALSE	2370	2803.63	10623.80	-12.72	84.43	9758.09
TOH	2480.781						2	TRUE	3990	4427.44	12762.56	14.30	158.54	9843.90
SS Win?	FALSE						3	FALSE	2100	2543.99	13313.67	-14.75	123.88	9991.24
							4	FALSE	2010	2451.84	13050.68	-14.93	118.74	9942.90
DDG1 vs. SS							5	FALSE	11700	12140.29	12690.03	13.57	154.61	9908.10
TOF	960						6	TRUE	2490	2933.44	13299.72	-14.74	123.95	9978.81
TOH	999						7	FALSE	2850	3283.39	10700.39	-12.88	85.41	9752.69
					Run Model		8	FALSE	2280	2717.92	12893.97	-14.95	117.77	9854.71
DDG2 vs. SS							9	FALSE	3000	3444.28	11928.67	-14.40	97.62	9997.74
TOF	1380						10	TRUE	4110	4551.16	9166.15	11.27	95.04	9927.55
TOH	1394						11	FALSE	2160	2601.70	10362.09	-11.69	79.22	9939.67
							12	FALSE	8400	8830.91	13480.06	-14.42	144.92	9696.89
DDG3 vs. SS							13	FALSE	2250	2692.79	10281.72	-11.43	78.06	9964.31
TOF	2040						14	FALSE	2310	2753.04	12776.99	-15.00	112.09	9969.99
TOH	2063						15	FALSE	12540	12982.79	12610.46	13.24	151.26	9964.34
							16	TRUE	3000	3442.43	12063.08	-14.60	100.29	9956.07
CG1 vs. SS							17	FALSE	2220	2662.75	10362.53	-11.64	78.96	9963.40
TOF	999999						18	FALSE	9480	9924.00	12762.26	-14.39	112.54	9991.46
TOH	17566						19	FALSE	2250	2691.66	12988.09	-14.96	117.40	9938.87
							20	FALSE	11790	12222.82	12561.65	13.76	156.62	9739.91
				Count	Percent		21	FALSE	2640	3073.48	10613.70	-12.70	84.35	9754.79
			Red Win	5	20.0		22	TRUE	12210	12653.17	12567.88	13.11	150.10	9972.69
			Blue Win	20	80.0		23	FALSE	3420	3864.20	12418.13	-14.85	105.08	9995.92
							24	FALSE	3120	3562.62	9950.29	-10.58	74.52	9960.38
							25	FALSE	2040	2480.78	11398.00	-13.80	91.73	9919.03

Table 3

SS vs. CVN		Range	Bearing	Torp Crse	Torp Run		Run Number	SS Win?	TOF	TOH	Range	Bearing	Torp Crse	Torp Run
TOF	4200	13159.1	13.58658	164.9289	9917.261		1	TRUE	4020	4456.57	12737.80	14.30	158.56	9824.18
TOH	4640.702						2	TRUE	2910	3352.86	12802.34	-15.00	112.70	9965.73
SS Win?	TRUE						3	TRUE	4110	4549.70	13080.34	13.73	163.82	9894.68
							4	FALSE	2730	3172.07	10349.96	-11.64	78.99	9948.01
DDG1 vs. SS							5	FALSE	2850	3291.05	10829.86	-12.76	84.71	9925.08
TOF	7980						6	FALSE	2460	2902.39	11133.10	-13.28	87.92	9955.36
TOH	7999						7	TRUE	4050	4490.95	13024.24	13.97	161.80	9922.74
					Run Model		8	TRUE	2310	2748.39	12996.21	-14.90	119.90	9865.31
DDG2 vs. SS							9	TRUE	4020	4462.14	9216.80	11.35	95.62	9949.69
TOF	6270						10	TRUE	3750	4183.32	11673.49	13.02	138.80	9751.14
TOH	6292						11	FALSE	2790	3190.30	11476.31	-14.99	110.64	9008.04
							12	FALSE	2370	2808.14	9956.18	-10.87	75.67	9859.64
DDG3 vs. SS							13	TRUE	2430	2873.78	12795.47	-15.00	112.04	9986.43
TOF	5460						14	TRUE	2910	3351.76	12927.05	-14.98	115.97	9941.01
TOH	5485						15	TRUE	4380	4822.52	13327.93	13.19	167.68	9958.09
							16	TRUE	11790	12233.25	12713.49	13.44	153.24	9974.50
CG1 vs. SS							17	FALSE	2580	3019.70	9280.37	-8.75	68.06	9894.68
TOF	999999						18	TRUE	3150	3591.67	12500.13	-14.93	107.68	9939.03
TOH	17568						19	FALSE	2370	2809.76	13153.27	-14.79	122.94	9896.04
							20	FALSE	2250	2687.80	9560.73	-9.76	71.49	9851.97
				Count	Percent		21	TRUE	4680	5124.08	13452.82	12.87	169.70	9993.33
			Red Win	13	52.0		22	TRUE	2820	3259.22	12485.92	-14.96	108.67	9883.90
			Blue Win	12	48.0		23	FALSE	2190	2633.23	12065.93	-14.58	100.01	9974.12
							24	FALSE	3150	3590.69	9881.80	-10.51	74.24	9917.06
							25	TRUE	4200	4640.70	13159.10	13.59	164.93	9917.26

Table 1

SS vs. CVN		Range	Bearing	Torp Crse	Torp Run	Run Number	SS Win?	TOF	TOH	Range	Bearing	Torp Crse	Torp Run
TOF	2970	10536.38	-12.5173	83.32648	9763.688	1	FALSE	3030	3465.74	9955.31	-11.01	76.26	9805.65
TOH	3403.877					2	TRUE	3930	4368.55	12653.30	14.52	155.80	9868.90
SS Win?	FALSE					3	TRUE	2640	3081.74	12911.76	-14.98	115.65	9940.52
						4	TRUE	4110	4550.21	13057.63	13.83	162.98	9906.27
DDG1 vs. SS						5	TRUE	4680	5123.32	13478.88	12.63	171.08	9976.16
TOF	2520					6	FALSE	1890	2327.85	10915.50	-13.09	86.67	9852.99
TOH	2525					7	TRUE	11730	12169.34	12588.76	13.41	152.95	9886.64
					Run Model	8	TRUE	11790	12231.89	12714.32	13.52	154.12	9944.05
DDG2 vs. SS						9	FALSE	3060	3503.66	10226.46	-11.25	77.24	9983.80
TOF	1830					10	FALSE	3300	3735.57	9662.48	-10.21	73.11	9801.70
TOH	1859					11	TRUE	2700	3140.16	9338.79	-8.91	68.58	9905.08
						12	TRUE	2910	3348.87	12388.78	-14.92	107.12	9875.99
DDG3 vs. SS						13	FALSE	2850	3292.33	11861.88	-14.38	97.41	9954.00
TOF	2850					14	TRUE	3750	4173.00	11772.46	11.97	144.46	9518.84
TOH	2883					15	FALSE	9720	10163.60	12717.29	-14.34	111.98	9982.49
						16	FALSE	3060	3495.96	11726.78	-14.42	97.93	9810.66
CG1 vs. SS						17	FALSE	2760	3203.38	13236.53	-14.82	122.27	9977.57
TOF	999999					18	TRUE	12780	13224.17	12501.14	12.89	148.06	9995.29
TOH	17569					19	FALSE	11580	12016.81	12644.44	13.69	155.86	9629.64
				Count	Percent	20	TRUE	11610	12044.39	12619.93	13.78	156.92	9775.13
			Red Win	11	44.0	21	FALSE	3000	3439.50	12259.02	-14.83	104.62	9890.19
			Blue Win	14	56.0	22	FALSE	2880	3313.65	11473.03	-14.18	95.22	9758.51
						23	FALSE	1920	2361.73	11475.33	-13.88	92.41	9940.50
						24	FALSE	11460	11901.94	12826.22	13.76	156.62	9945.02
						25	FALSE	2970	3403.88	10536.38	-12.52	83.33	9763.69

Table 2

SS vs. CVN		Range	Bearing	Torp Crse	Torp Run	Run Number	SS Win?	TOF	TOH	Range	Bearing	Torp Crse	Torp Run
TOF	2460	9676.862	-9.90372	71.98365	9923.468	1	FALSE	2190	2628.03	11978.88	-14.63	100.83	9857.14
TOH	2900.978					2	TRUE	4590	5032.78	13476.54	12.55	171.49	9964.02
SS Win?	FALSE					3	FALSE	2490	2928.58	10712.06	-12.65	84.04	9869.62
						4	FALSE	2100	2538.50	11682.62	-14.29	96.34	9867.61
DDG1 vs. SS						5	TRUE	3420	3860.58	9113.76	-8.13	66.10	9914.54
TOF	1860					6	FALSE	11640	12077.33	12625.84	13.62	155.09	9841.32
TOH	1887					7	TRUE	2670	3108.83	12592.21	-14.99	110.85	9875.17
					Run Model	8	TRUE	2430	2872.46	12934.80	-14.98	115.69	9956.85
DDG2 vs. SS						9	FALSE	2220	2658.98	11574.12	-14.13	94.67	9878.47
TOF	6540					10	TRUE	3840	4282.08	12355.04	14.90	148.64	9948.16
TOH	6570					11	TRUE	12150	12587.44	12429.40	13.17	150.63	9843.78
						12	FALSE	2340	2783.95	12680.21	-14.98	109.75	9990.38
DDG3 vs. SS						13	FALSE	2010	2452.84	11467.67	-13.82	91.94	9965.39
TOF	14490					14	FALSE	2370	2803.86	11374.76	-14.04	93.80	9763.27
TOH	14502					15	TRUE	12660	13104.31	12594.39	13.10	149.98	9998.44
						16	FALSE	2460	2903.19	12092.34	-14.61	100.42	9973.17
CG1 vs. SS						17	FALSE	11580	12020.59	12724.01	13.62	155.18	9914.66
TOF	999999					18	FALSE	4320	4764.36	9553.05	12.06	101.02	9999.49
TOH	17567					19	TRUE	3990	4433.52	13029.09	14.13	160.32	9980.75
				Count	Percent	20	TRUE	3930	4372.91	12894.69	14.35	158.00	9967.01
			Red Win	11	44.0	21	FALSE	2100	2541.92	10223.10	-11.34	77.64	9944.61
			Blue Win	15	60.0	22	FALSE	8370	8803.83	13586.58	-14.33	146.22	9762.65
						23	TRUE	11730	12165.28	12632.22	13.76	156.60	9795.14
						24	FALSE	1980	2418.33	12150.99	-14.78	103.39	9863.89
						25	FALSE	2460	2900.98	9676.86	-9.90	71.98	9923.47

Scorecard Results for Advanced Processor Build Option

Scorecard 1

SS vs. CVN		Range	Bearing	Torp Crse	Torp Run
TOF	3000	9416.308	-9.14268	69.34152	9911.035
TOH	3440.425				
SS Win?	FALSE				
DDG1 vs. SS					
TOF	660				
TOH	726				
DDG2 vs. SS					
TOF	4680				
TOH	4735				
DDG3 vs. SS					
TOF	6060				
TOH	6114				
CG1 vs. SS					
TOF	999999				
TOH	17567				
			Count	Percent	
		Red Win	5	20.0	
		Blue Win	20	80.0	

Run Number	SS Win?	TOF	TOH	Range	Bearing	Torp Crse	Torp Run
1	FALSE	12090	12533.69	12596.82	13.15	150.40	9964.62
2	FALSE	2430	2864.50	10467.44	-12.33	82.35	9777.67
3	FALSE	2850	3289.81	9694.42	-10.03	72.45	9897.10
4	FALSE	3570	4011.83	9232.24	-8.45	67.08	9942.58
5	FALSE	15780	16222.40	13133.07	-14.86	120.39	9955.57
6	FALSE	2490	2930.93	11955.47	-14.53	99.30	9922.45
7	TRUE	12300	12740.45	12547.30	13.24	151.33	9911.69
8	TRUE	3990	4421.14	12381.85	14.60	154.70	9701.99
9	FALSE	2820	3255.48	9688.57	-10.29	73.42	9799.70
10	TRUE	2340	2782.32	13336.93	-14.64	126.03	9953.69
11	FALSE	2040	2475.38	10314.52	-11.93	80.36	9797.61
12	FALSE	3030	3471.85	12652.39	-14.98	110.35	9943.16
13	FALSE	4200	4644.01	13094.00	14.02	161.36	9991.67
14	FALSE	2430	2869.45	9654.90	-9.94	72.11	9889.15
15	TRUE	12780	13224.11	12603.36	13.13	150.29	9993.96
16	FALSE	2250	2683.79	10200.38	-11.75	79.49	9761.77
17	FALSE	11520	11957.03	12633.64	13.65	155.47	9834.56
18	FALSE	11670	12106.01	12529.92	13.49	153.77	9811.76
19	TRUE	3810	4246.48	12035.56	14.97	145.84	9822.14
20	FALSE	2700	3134.53	11279.06	-13.87	92.29	9778.36
21	FALSE	12630	13072.40	12535.98	13.09	149.88	9955.55
22	FALSE	2100	2543.32	13316.21	-14.72	124.52	9976.21
23	FALSE	2730	3164.17	9912.26	-10.99	76.18	9770.22
24	FALSE	3210	3648.47	12281.30	-14.86	105.47	9867.15
25	FALSE	3000	3440.43	9416.31	-9.14	69.34	9911.03

Scorecard 2

SS vs. CVN		Range	Bearing	Torp Crse	Torp Run
TOF	4050	8908.183	10.8088	91.78027	9827.518
TOH	4486.714				
SS Win?	FALSE				
DDG1 vs. SS					
TOF	5880				
TOH	5908				
DDG2 vs. SS					
TOF	2070				
TOH	2135				
DDG3 vs. SS					
TOF	14490				
TOH	14504				
CG1 vs. SS					
TOF	999999				
TOH	17565				
			Count	Percent	
		Red Win	4	16.0	
		Blue Win	21	84.0	

Run Number	SS Win?	TOF	TOH	Range	Bearing	Torp Crse	Torp Run
1	FALSE	11820	12256.74	12528.91	13.44	153.28	9828.06
2	FALSE	11730	12169.58	12628.82	13.48	153.69	9892.07
3	FALSE	12120	12557.03	12431.81	13.20	150.94	9834.68
4	FALSE	3300	3739.77	9669.09	-9.96	72.18	9896.33
5	FALSE	11970	12412.94	12615.29	13.24	151.27	9967.59
6	TRUE	4170	4611.72	13134.19	13.75	163.68	9940.20
7	FALSE	2910	3350.70	11386.37	-13.78	91.61	9917.24
8	FALSE	2370	2812.16	13361.88	-14.59	126.96	9949.99
9	FALSE	2820	3255.71	10553.40	-12.46	83.01	9805.03
10	TRUE	4020	4463.46	12980.28	14.22	159.38	9979.26
11	FALSE	11460	11903.93	12641.67	13.67	155.66	9989.81
12	FALSE	11970	12410.65	12633.24	13.42	153.11	9916.13
13	FALSE	2520	2955.98	10865.82	-13.08	86.63	9810.99
14	FALSE	2610	3053.44	11911.53	-14.40	97.69	9978.98
15	FALSE	13170	13614.09	12780.26	13.53	154.18	9993.46
16	FALSE	3180	3623.42	12638.91	-14.97	109.27	9978.46
17	FALSE	1890	2333.98	12354.03	-14.81	104.13	9991.10
18	FALSE	2370	2814.14	13333.65	-14.73	124.32	9994.61
19	FALSE	2640	3079.84	10253.07	-11.53	78.50	9897.79
20	TRUE	3840	4281.14	12587.95	14.69	153.21	9927.15
21	TRUE	3990	4427.93	12790.32	14.27	158.81	9854.88
22	FALSE	3780	4217.79	12171.83	14.93	147.55	9851.77
23	FALSE	2250	2691.90	12270.74	-14.79	103.72	9944.23
24	FALSE	2730	3171.85	9659.13	-10.37	73.72	9943.11
25	FALSE	4050	4486.71	8908.18	10.81	91.78	9827.52

Scorecard 3

SS vs. CVN		Range	Bearing	Torp Crse	Torp Run
TOF	2610	11601.77	-14.2166	95.58182	9845.443
TOH	3047.51				
SS Win?	FALSE				
DDG1 vs. SS					
TOF	2280				
TOH	2313				
DDG2 vs. SS					
TOF	2130				
TOH	2147				
DDG3 vs. SS					
TOF	1200				
TOH	1245				
CG1 vs. SS					
TOF	999999				
TOH	17567				
			Count	Percent	
		Red Win	6	24.0	
		Blue Win	19	76.0	

Run Number	SS Win?	TOF	TOH	Range	Bearing	Torp Crse	Torp Run
1	TRUE	4110	4548.51	13032.77	13.76	163.55	9867.85
2	FALSE	11550	11991.95	12807.65	13.72	156.19	9945.31
3	FALSE	3270	3711.63	12458.92	-14.91	106.98	9938.07
4	FALSE	1890	2332.39	12635.62	-14.98	109.75	9955.22
5	FALSE	3180	3622.39	12163.12	-14.69	101.62	9955.16
6	FALSE	11550	11991.80	12963.60	14.04	159.92	9941.91
7	FALSE	11550	11991.98	12776.26	13.65	155.46	9945.91
8	FALSE	11460	11893.15	12619.02	13.86	157.74	9747.32
9	FALSE	2550	2992.58	10250.91	-11.37	77.78	9959.50
10	FALSE	8310	8748.49	13737.87	-14.29	146.73	9867.47
11	TRUE	2340	2780.16	13046.49	-14.90	119.85	9904.98
12	TRUE	2970	3413.23	9130.86	-8.00	65.70	9974.10
13	TRUE	4170	4612.05	13084.39	13.90	162.38	9947.65
14	FALSE	11940	12379.01	12564.01	13.37	152.61	9879.18
15	TRUE	3720	4157.28	12151.46	5.54	136.29	9840.26
16	FALSE	3060	3503.65	9210.33	-8.24	66.45	9983.62
17	FALSE	8280	8718.95	13752.04	-14.29	146.70	9877.85
18	FALSE	2820	3262.24	10635.94	-12.29	82.15	9951.83
19	FALSE	2550	2987.66	11346.04	-13.84	92.11	9848.70
20	FALSE	2220	2653.91	11717.77	-14.48	98.60	9764.37
21	TRUE	4140	4580.93	13062.05	13.88	162.61	9922.41
22	FALSE	2670	3112.22	10592.08	-12.20	81.65	9951.51
23	FALSE	2430	2871.77	13202.16	-14.80	122.63	9941.39
24	FALSE	11640	12075.17	12576.87	13.64	155.40	9792.76
25	FALSE	2610	3047.51	11601.77	-14.22	95.58	9845.44

Table 1

SS vs. CVN		Range	Bearing	Torp Crse	Torp Run		Run Number	SS Win?	TOF	TOH	Range	Bearing	Torp Crse	Torp Run
TOF	2670	10726.06	-12.6994	84.33564	9859.178		1	FALSE	11670	12108.80	12643.74	13.56	154.53	9874.47
TOH	3108.121						2	FALSE	2610	3049.52	9512.42	-9.50	70.57	9890.58
SS Win?	FALSE						3	FALSE	8370	8813.28	13901.20	-14.19	148.09	9975.29
							4	TRUE	3750	4175.87	11614.72	12.66	140.87	9583.58
DDG1 vs. SS							5	FALSE	4560	5004.07	13442.74	12.91	169.44	9992.96
TOF	1920						6	FALSE	8490	8924.72	13637.66	-14.15	148.67	9782.69
TOH	1938						7	FALSE	2550	2992.61	9590.98	-9.54	70.69	9960.22
					Run Model		8	TRUE	3720	4158.63	12200.22	5.48	136.44	9870.74
DDG2 vs. SS							9	FALSE	3060	3496.18	11078.24	-13.46	89.18	9815.42
TOF	1620						10	FALSE	2400	2831.18	11961.61	-14.78	103.54	9702.95
TOH	1653						11	FALSE	3000	3439.70	12421.86	-14.92	107.28	9894.82
							12	FALSE	1950	2388.76	11606.02	-14.18	95.19	9873.63
DDG3 vs. SS							13	FALSE	1920	2362.24	11935.22	-14.47	98.50	9951.85
TOF	1830						14	FALSE	3990	4433.42	9147.50	11.09	93.78	9978.48
TOH	1868						15	FALSE	2490	2924.68	9667.80	-10.28	73.38	9781.82
							16	FALSE	3840	4283.91	12738.55	14.61	154.52	9989.41
CG1 vs. SS							17	FALSE	2400	2836.39	10294.47	-11.83	79.86	9820.30
TOF	16980						18	FALSE	2520	2960.54	10679.71	-12.48	83.11	9913.57
TOH	17039						19	FALSE	2370	2808.75	11066.94	-13.33	88.23	9873.36
							20	FALSE	2730	3167.44	10539.91	-12.34	82.37	9843.81
				Count	Percent		21	FALSE	12360	12803.20	12502.96	12.96	148.68	9973.57
			Red Win	3	12.0		22	FALSE	2610	3050.66	11901.42	-14.48	98.62	9916.25
			Blue Win	22	88.0		23	TRUE	13560	14003.97	12734.86	13.44	153.25	9990.84
							24	FALSE	12330	12769.00	12467.48	13.16	150.49	9879.03
							25	FALSE	2670	3108.12	10726.06	-12.70	84.34	9859.18

Table 2

SS vs. CVN		Range	Bearing	Torp Crse	Torp Run		Run Number	SS Win?	TOF	TOH	Range	Bearing	Torp Crse	Torp Run
TOF	2580	9428.002	-9.4899	70.52252	9807.525		1	FALSE	3030	3471.85	9524.53	-9.39	70.17	9943.01
TOH	3015.825						2	FALSE	2820	3260.82	9286.91	-8.70	67.88	9919.91
SS Win?	FALSE						3	FALSE	1980	2424.07	12249.76	-14.73	102.44	9993.13
							4	FALSE	2520	2956.60	11106.67	-13.50	89.40	9824.89
DDG1 vs. SS							5	FALSE	3180	3621.34	9817.24	-10.29	73.40	9931.62
TOF	1080						6	FALSE	3720	4150.31	11538.25	7.47	130.89	9683.44
TOH	1115						7	FALSE	11670	12107.99	12572.36	13.46	153.45	9856.22
					Run Model		8	FALSE	11850	12290.92	12695.51	13.54	154.32	9922.14
DDG2 vs. SS							9	TRUE	3750	4189.98	12286.94	11.84	145.08	9901.13
TOF	1170						10	FALSE	2640	3078.90	11761.82	-14.37	97.30	9876.65
TOH	1218						11	FALSE	11580	12019.44	12897.37	14.04	159.99	9888.87
							12	FALSE	2430	2868.36	12795.06	-14.99	115.26	9864.50
DDG3 vs. SS							13	FALSE	15810	16252.87	13047.49	-14.77	118.34	9966.07
TOF	600						14	FALSE	3030	3473.83	12268.68	-14.75	102.84	9987.75
TOH	678						15	TRUE	3990	4429.89	9015.77	10.93	92.62	9899.08
							16	FALSE	4230	4664.29	13068.76	13.24	167.36	9773.07
CG1 vs. SS							17	TRUE	4470	4912.61	13324.86	13.21	167.53	9960.16
TOF	16980						18	FALSE	3390	3832.84	12479.17	-14.91	106.74	9965.43
TOH	17039						19	FALSE	3510	3953.12	12334.58	-14.81	104.21	9971.63
				Count	Percent		20	FALSE	2520	2961.69	12227.30	-14.76	103.12	9939.61
			Red Win	5	20.0		21	TRUE	2940	3377.19	12208.30	-14.84	104.85	9838.25
			Blue Win	20	80.0		22	FALSE	2910	3351.54	10595.54	-12.24	81.88	9936.11
							23	FALSE	13050	13493.06	12779.99	13.59	154.84	9970.36
							24	FALSE	2610	3052.44	9558.90	-9.45	70.39	9956.36
							25	FALSE	2580	3015.83	9428.00	-9.49	70.52	9807.52

Table 3

SS vs. CVN		Range	Bearing	Torp Crse	Torp Run		Run Number	SS Win?	TOF	TOH	Range	Bearing	Torp Crse	Torp Run
TOF	11730	12707.58	13.4068	152.9359	9980.516		1	TRUE	4170	4609.08	13151.50	13.46	165.88	9880.85
TOH	12173.51						2	FALSE	2250	2693.43	10764.63	-12.51	83.28	9978.70
SS Win?	FALSE						3	FALSE	2370	2809.42	10231.93	-11.51	78.37	9888.53
							4	TRUE	12750	13192.96	12576.90	13.15	150.42	9968.14
DDG1 vs. SS							5	FALSE	2970	3405.59	9550.44	-9.88	71.89	9802.32
TOF	5130						6	FALSE	8220	8655.97	13672.11	-14.19	148.09	9810.88
TOH	5180						7	TRUE	12480	12920.41	12459.39	13.04	149.45	9910.61
					Run Model		8	FALSE	8310	8753.91	13923.66	-14.17	148.40	9989.46
DDG2 vs. SS							9	FALSE	2190	2633.53	11857.60	-14.34	96.90	9981.00
TOF	5850						10	TRUE	11790	12229.55	12634.50	13.50	153.84	9891.42
TOH	5911						11	FALSE	11700	12132.60	12506.74	13.65	155.49	9734.87
							12	FALSE	9330	9771.92	12773.59	-14.49	113.76	9944.64
DDG3 vs. SS							13	FALSE	1950	2386.02	12150.96	-14.82	104.44	9811.99
TOF	13980						14	FALSE	8460	8898.74	13763.58	-14.15	148.64	9873.20
TOH	14007						15	TRUE	13140	13583.13	12756.22	13.54	154.26	9971.99
							16	TRUE	4140	4578.75	13094.88	13.60	164.79	9873.25
CG1 vs. SS							17	FALSE	1920	2363.64	11372.74	-13.64	90.48	9983.45
TOF	17280						18	TRUE	12120	12562.51	12567.42	13.16	150.50	9957.93
TOH	17333						19	FALSE	2670	3112.26	11990.69	-14.53	99.29	9952.28
				Count	Percent		20	TRUE	2370	2814.15	13114.87	-14.93	118.64	9994.83
			Red Win	8	32.0		21	FALSE	2100	2538.47	12094.78	-14.73	102.44	9867.13
			Blue Win	17	68.0		22	FALSE	3720	4158.49	11949.32	6.65	133.26	9867.41
							23	FALSE	2010	2443.79	11216.33	-13.80	91.72	9761.73
							24	FALSE	2280	2722.86	10177.61	-11.17	76.91	9965.72
							25	FALSE	11730	12173.51	12707.58	13.41	152.94	9980.52

Table 1

SS vs. CVN	Range	Bearing	Torp Crse	Torp Run	Run Number	SS Win?	TOF	TOH	Range	Bearing	Torp Crse	Torp Run
TOF	3210	9508.843	-9.51583	70.61229	9882.86	1	FALSE	2190	2630.09	10457.08	-12.01	80.71	9903.41
TOH	3649.173					2	TRUE	12180	12622.76	12551.11	13.10	149.99	9963.52
SS Win?	FALSE					3	TRUE	4350	4792.14	13420.12	12.74	170.42	9949.71
						4	FALSE	2010	2446.25	11359.91	-13.92	92.77	9816.99
DDG1 vs. SS						5	FALSE	1890	2332.28	12165.65	-14.70	101.91	9952.69
TOF	2130					6	FALSE	2790	3231.19	10851.90	-12.80	84.93	9928.25
TOH	2160					7	TRUE	2250	2693.52	13295.67	-14.75	123.77	9980.76
					Run Model	8	FALSE	2610	3046.93	11160.63	-13.57	89.97	9832.45
DDG2 vs. SS						9	TRUE	12330	12774.31	12542.01	12.98	148.85	9998.40
TOF	5190					10	FALSE	8400	8830.51	13478.25	-14.36	145.82	9687.93
TOH	5232					11	FALSE	1950	2386.52	11241.90	-13.73	91.14	9823.25
						12	FALSE	2520	2951.99	9831.59	-10.91	75.84	9721.16
DDG3 vs. SS						13	TRUE	12870	13311.96	12588.75	13.24	151.30	9945.68
TOF	3000					14	TRUE	11550	11990.88	12700.49	13.56	154.46	9921.32
TOH	3069					15	FALSE	2370	2803.15	10765.29	-13.03	86.26	9747.36
						16	TRUE	2640	3081.06	13100.15	-14.88	120.52	9925.40
CG1 vs. SS						17	FALSE	2340	2783.83	12790.78	-15.00	111.92	9987.56
TOF	17430					18	FALSE	2760	3197.07	9405.97	-9.34	70.00	9835.48
TOH	17481					19	FALSE	11850	12290.67	12593.09	13.33	152.20	9916.58
						20	FALSE	2250	2690.97	10780.56	-12.67	84.16	9923.23
				Count	Percent	21	FALSE	2820	3256.14	10782.47	-12.91	85.58	9814.54
			Red Win	7	28.0	22	FALSE	12060	12502.79	12582.75	13.17	150.66	9964.25
			Blue Win	18	72.0	23	FALSE	12180	12615.92	12429.50	13.27	151.58	9809.69
						24	TRUE	12690	13129.88	12413.31	12.97	148.78	9898.65
						25	FALSE	3210	3649.17	9508.84	-9.52	70.61	9882.86

Table 2

SS vs. CVN	Range	Bearing	Torp Crse	Torp Run	Run Number	SS Win?	TOF	TOH	Range	Bearing	Torp Crse	Torp Run
TOF	3990	9036.584	10.82291	91.87906	9963.633	1	FALSE	2700	3142.10	11199.67	-13.41	88.82	9948.63
TOH	4432.763					2	FALSE	12570	13011.90	12548.36	13.15	150.46	9944.33
SS Win?	FALSE					3	FALSE	2610	3049.38	11931.12	-14.55	99.56	9887.58
						4	TRUE	2430	2872.33	13334.86	-14.65	125.96	9953.86
DDG1 vs. SS						5	FALSE	2370	2813.16	12061.98	-14.58	99.98	9972.53
TOF	1290					6	FALSE	3780	4214.34	12289.72	14.79	151.32	9774.18
TOH	1334					7	FALSE	3270	3713.57	12529.72	-14.92	107.26	9981.83
					Run Model	8	FALSE	8340	8782.86	13843.39	-14.47	144.11	9965.75
DDG2 vs. SS						9	FALSE	2010	2449.18	11590.36	-14.14	94.82	9882.98
TOF	1860					10	TRUE	3750	4185.36	11608.97	13.28	137.11	9797.03
TOH	1921					11	FALSE	2340	2783.82	13258.44	-14.81	122.50	9987.36
						12	FALSE	2070	2509.85	12784.97	-15.00	114.12	9898.04
DDG3 vs. SS						13	TRUE	12390	12832.80	12540.99	13.08	149.73	9964.47
TOF	14400					14	TRUE	12420	12862.87	12512.11	13.00	149.08	9966.11
TOH	14415					15	FALSE	12000	12441.27	12563.26	13.23	151.17	9930.02
						16	FALSE	11670	12104.77	12568.04	13.65	155.46	9783.66
CG1 vs. SS						17	TRUE	2850	3289.82	9166.07	-8.36	66.82	9897.47
TOF	10680					18	FALSE	11430	11867.61	12686.33	13.73	156.29	9847.61
TOH	10739					19	FALSE	2850	3287.87	10120.24	-11.32	77.54	9853.43
						20	FALSE	3030	3466.94	9569.65	-9.85	71.78	9832.58
				Count	Percent	21	FALSE	1920	2355.97	11009.07	-13.35	88.38	9810.69
			Red Win	5	20.0	22	FALSE	2400	2839.40	12339.15	-14.88	106.01	9887.87
			Blue Win	20	80.0	23	FALSE	8460	8903.70	13917.25	-14.17	148.44	9984.62
						24	FALSE	1890	2328.97	11785.31	-14.40	97.61	9878.39
						25	FALSE	3990	4432.76	9036.58	10.82	91.88	9963.63

Table 3

						Run Number	SS Win?	TOF	TOH	Range	Bearing	Torp Crse	Torp Run
TOH	3586.833					2	FALSE	15840	16279.28	12692.77	-14.48	113.68	9885.20
SS Win?	FALSE					3	FALSE	2310	2753.01	10973.27	-12.95	85.82	9969.26
						4	FALSE	2580	3022.04	9217.41	-8.38	66.87	9947.42
DDG1 vs. SS						5	FALSE	2310	2751.34	11532.35	-13.98	93.29	9931.62
TOF	2370					6	FALSE	1980	2415.15	11488.03	-14.15	94.88	9792.40
TOH	2394					7	FALSE	2970	3411.98	12825.37	-15.00	113.67	9946.10
					Run Model	8	FALSE	2280	2719.78	12332.03	-14.87	105.70	9896.57
DDG2 vs. SS						9	FALSE	2670	3103.42	10456.39	-12.37	82.52	9753.42
TOF	3450					10	FALSE	11820	12258.43	12652.57	13.60	154.97	9866.15
TOH	3515					11	FALSE	2340	2779.27	9910.98	-10.68	74.90	9884.97
						12	FALSE	2580	3020.00	12682.09	-15.00	111.95	9901.37
DDG3 vs. SS						13	FALSE	2130	2572.85	12974.01	-14.98	116.30	9965.52
TOF	13800					14	FALSE	3120	3561.56	12270.19	-14.80	103.87	9936.57
TOH	13824					15	TRUE	2490	2930.76	13183.79	-14.79	122.96	9918.57
						16	FALSE	12720	13159.69	12444.28	13.06	149.56	9894.51
CG1 vs. SS						17	TRUE	3990	4426.22	12581.22	14.53	155.70	9816.48
TOF	999999					18	FALSE	2160	2600.71	11790.56	-14.35	97.02	9917.50
TOH	17568					19	TRUE	2820	3258.73	9410.37	-9.24	69.66	9872.91
				Count	Percent	20	FALSE	11490	11929.36	12785.14	13.83	157.40	9687.10
			Red Win	3	12.0	21	FALSE	4080	4524.00	9381.54	11.66	98.00	9991.49
			Blue Win	22	88.0	22	FALSE	11760	12200.20	12630.85	13.45	153.34	9905.93
						23	FALSE	15810	16252.54	13104.90	-14.83	119.72	9958.55
						24	FALSE	2190	2623.65	11573.25	-14.31	96.62	9758.52
						25	FALSE	3150	3586.83	9628.11	-10.03	72.44	9830.19

SS Win?	FALSE					3	FALSE	11910	12351.17	12643.90	13.41	153.01	9927.71
						4	FALSE	8550	8988.50	13672.80	-14.60	141.79	9867.68
DDG1 vs. SS						5	FALSE	2730	3170.03	12598.87	-14.98	110.33	9902.08
TOF	2220					6	FALSE	2460	2899.39	10822.04	-12.83	85.10	9887.75
TOH	2245					7	FALSE	3930	4372.29	12829.03	14.42	157.08	9953.11
				Run Model		8	TRUE	4800	5242.32	13566.50	11.89	174.84	9953.63
DDG2 vs. SS						9	FALSE	13440	13882.79	12695.31	13.43	153.12	9964.32
TOF	2040					10	FALSE	2670	3111.95	10747.43	-12.55	83.50	9945.42
TOH	2054					11	FALSE	2070	2513.15	10984.81	-12.97	85.92	9972.31
						12	TRUE	3840	4280.68	12217.60	14.94	146.96	9916.71
DDG3 vs. SS						13	FALSE	11610	12045.27	12561.60	13.61	154.98	9795.07
TOF	2430					14	FALSE	15750	16191.52	13238.81	-14.95	123.37	9935.75
TOH	2441					15	FALSE	11730	12168.77	12605.69	13.48	153.70	9873.76
						16	FALSE	1830	2273.12	12494.73	-14.91	106.88	9971.58
CG1 vs. SS						17	FALSE	3210	3644.96	10364.04	-12.07	81.04	9787.97
TOF	10470					18	FALSE	3750	4192.45	12456.41	11.51	146.61	9956.50
TOH	10520					19	FALSE	11850	12293.14	12668.88	13.34	152.32	9972.11
			Count	Percent		20	FALSE	2280	2720.34	10525.90	-12.15	81.42	9909.11
		Red Win	3	12.0		21	FALSE	2070	2510.66	10364.33	-11.76	79.52	9916.39
		Blue Win	22	88.0		22	FALSE	2580	3020.81	10278.34	-11.54	78.53	9919.70
						23	FALSE	11670	12111.68	12851.22	13.82	157.36	9939.36
						24	TRUE	2220	2663.85	13413.75	-14.59	126.98	9988.19
						25	FALSE	2670	3103.17	11180.34	-13.77	91.46	9747.74

APPENDIX G

MSSE Capstone Project Risks

ASW project and program risks were identified using the risk management process. Project risks are related to the successful completion of the MSSE Capstone Project. Over the course of the MSSE Capstone Project these risks have been mitigated and all have been retired. Project risks are provided below for reference purposes. ASW program risks are described in section XX of this report.

Table 5. MSSE Capstone Project Risks

IDENTIFICATION	ANALYSIS	MITIGATION PLAN
1. Classification – Risk that our report is classified	I. This risk was assessed at an A5. There is a low likelihood that classified material will be included in this report. Classification levels are clearly defined and everyone working this project has been made aware of the importance of not including classified material. However, if this report is classified our NPS Capstone advisors will not be able to read it which is an unacceptable consequence. II. Our final report is not classified. *Therefore, this risk is retired.* There is no need to further mitigate.	I. Our mitigation will be to take steps to insure no classified material is included in this project. Mitigation Plan has been Implemented and is Ongoing.
2. Scope- We are at risk of selecting too large a scope and making it impossible to finish the project in the allotted time or forcing us to address it to shallowly.	I. This risk was assessed at a C3. There is a moderate chance of our project scope being too large, however we will still be able to apply the Systems Engineering principles that we have been taught thus completing our ultimate objective. II. Project scope was narrowed, however, remained at level that we did not have to address the topic too shallow. We longer feel that project scope is a risk. *Risk reassessed and retired.*	I. Take a realistic look at the time we have available and what we can accomplish with our resources. Begin immediate down scope. Mitigation Plan is being executed currently. After the down scope is complete this risk will be reassessed and tracked.

223

IDENTIFICATION	ANALYSIS	MITIGATION PLAN
3. Product Direction- Risk that a single stakeholder may drive the direction of the project	I. This risk was assessed at a B4. There is a low likelihood that interference will occur, however, if this event does occur it may cause our project to not meet graduation requirements or not satisfy the needs of all stakeholders II. Risk has not appeared during alternative generation and preceding efforts. *Risk reassessed and retired.*	I. All stakeholder input will be considered, however, we will use our own judgment to decide how to proceed. Execution not yet needed.
4. New modeling tools techniques- Using new modeling tools and the NPS remote lab is a potential risk due to lack of experience.	I. This risk was assessed at a B2. There is a fairly low likelihood that we will not be able to familiarize ourselves with these new tools. If this does occur, there are existing modeling tools that we are familiar with that can be used. II. This risk was realized during the modeling phase of the System's Engineering Process. The consequence however was reduced due to implementation of the mitigation plan which is use of other sufficient modeling tools. This risk was reassessed at a C1. III. Mitigation Plan was continuously followed. Following this mitigation plan allowed modeling to be completed. *This risk has been retired.*	I. A team has been assigned to begin familiarizing themselves with the NPS remote lab and the associated new tools. Mitigation Plan has been Implemented and is Ongoing. II. Continue using alternate modeling tools, while attempting to use the NPS remote lab.
5. Misinterpreting/ Inadequate Stakeholder Requirements- This potential risk represents the situation where the amount of responses received from the stakeholder questionnaire is not adequate to proceed. Additionally there exists the risk of misinterpreting the stakeholder responses that were received.	I. This risk was assessed at a D4. There is a fairly high likelihood that all stakeholder requirements have not been incorporated. The consequence of this is that the system would not perform as required by users/stakeholders and this would be a high severity issue. II. Mitigation Plan was followed and the team feels confident that relevant stakeholder inputs are being addressed appropriately. This risk was reassessed at an A4. III. Mitigation Plan was continuously implemented throughout the MSSE Program. Stakeholder requirements were successfully interpreted and stakeholders are satisfied. *This risk has been retired.*	I. Mitigation is to make another round of stakeholder follow-up calls/emails. Gather constant stakeholder feedback Mitigation Plan has been Implemented and is Ongoing. II. Low priority monitoring will continue.

IDENTIFICATION	ANALYSIS	MITIGATION PLAN
6. Schedule to Complete – There is a risk that insufficient time remains to complete all required tasking and deliverables prior to need date.	I. This risk was assessed at D5. There is a high risk that the amount of work remaining will result in a shortfall of deliverables by the provided need dates. II. *This risk will retired with the completion of MSSE Program.*	I. Additional time/effort being implemented by team members, including assistance covering areas that are currently lagging behind the schedule pace. More frequent IPT meetings and reading sessions to be planned.

APPENDIX H

Detailed Cost Information

As previously discussed, costs are estimated for the alternatives for four categories over a 25-year lifecycle period. The four cost categories are design, production, operation, and disposal. All cost components are presented below and key cost assumptions and elements are discussed. All costs are relative to a single baseline CSG and assume two 14-day missions per year during the 20-year in-service timeframe. Also, one fundamental cost assumption is all cost estimates are for a production quantity of one alternative over the twenty-five year timeframe.

Figures H-1 through H-3 display the cost data in a matrix format. The yellow columns of data correspond to cost estimate inputs generated by the systems engineering team. The two orange columns are calculated spreadsheet values based on the four input data columns and correspond to the total undiscounted yearly costs and present values, respectively. The numbers in the green spreadsheet cells represents the single NPV for each alternative using a discount rate of six percent.

The accelerated development cost numbers (Figure H-1) are scaled appropriately to support one CSG. The design costs in year number five include testing. The relatively low operational costs are due to the fact that new personnel are not required and the systems are very similar in operation as compared to the CSG baseline.

The cost numbers for the MPA alternative are shown in Figure H-2. Key assumptions and values are listed below:

- A quantity of 10 units are procured to support one CSG and this quantity is reflected in both the production, disposal, and operation costs.

- Aircraft, aircraft operational costs, and related personnel are assumed to be part of a standard CSG and are not included in the MPA costs.

- Yearly operational costs during the 20-year in-service lifecycle includes $1.5M for logistics, maintenance and repair of $50K per unit, and personnel training at $700K.

- Disposal costs start after the 15-year service life.

Figure H-3 contains the barrier alternative cost information. These numbers are based on the following:

- LCS design and production is assumed to be paid for by a different program of record and are not included in the barrier alternative costs. However the barrier alternative does include LCS operational costs ($5M/year) and associated LCS mission package personnel (12 workyears/year at a rate of $125K/workyear) in support of the two 14-day missions per year.

- The cost per buoy is $20K.

- Assuming two 14-day missions per year and a six hour buoy replenishment rate, approximately 3,000 buoys are used each year in operation. This accounts for $60M of the $66.5M yearly operational costs and greatly influences the overall operational cost.

- Due to the expendable nature of the buoys, the cost to produce the buoys which are used during missions is shown under the operation category as opposed to the production category. The $4M yearly production costs indicate fixed costs which are required to manufacture the buoys as opposed to the cost of the buoys themselves.

Year	Design ($M)	Production ($M)	Operation ($M)	Disposal ($M)	Undiscounted Sum ($M)	Present Value ($M)
1	15.0	0.0	0.0	0.0	15.0	14.2
2	15.0	0.0	0.0	0.0	15.0	13.3
3	15.0	3.0	0.5	0.0	18.5	15.5
4	15.0	3.0	1.0	0.0	19.0	15.0
5	7.5	3.0	1.5	0.0	12.0	9.0
6	0.0	3.0	1.5	0.0	4.5	3.2
7	0.0	3.0	1.5	0.0	4.5	3.0
8	0.0	3.0	1.5	0.0	4.5	2.8
9	0.0	3.0	1.5	1.0	5.5	3.3
10	0.0	3.0	1.5	1.0	5.5	3.1
11	0.0	3.0	1.5	1.0	5.5	2.9
12	0.0	3.0	1.5	1.0	5.5	2.7
13	0.0	3.0	1.5	1.0	5.5	2.6
14	0.0	3.0	1.5	1.0	5.5	2.4
15	0.0	3.0	1.5	1.0	5.5	2.3
16	0.0	3.0	1.5	1.0	5.5	2.2
17	0.0	3.0	1.5	1.0	5.5	2.0
18	0.0	3.0	1.5	1.0	5.5	1.9
19	0.0	3.0	1.5	1.0	5.5	1.8
20	0.0	3.0	1.5	1.0	5.5	1.7
21	0.0	3.0	1.5	1.0	5.5	1.6
22	0.0	3.0	1.5	1.0	5.5	1.5
23	0.0	3.0	1.5	1.0	5.5	1.4
24	0.0	3.0	1.5	1.0	5.5	1.4
25	0.0	3.0	1.5	1.0	5.5	1.3
NPV						112.2

Figure H-1 – CSG Accelerated Development Alternative Cost Matrix

Year	Design ($M)	Production ($M)	Operation ($M)	Disposal ($M)	Undiscounted Sum ($M)	Present Value ($M)
1	2.4	0.0	0.0	0.0	2.4	2.3
2	5.0	0.0	0.0	0.0	5.0	4.4
3	5.1	1.0	0.5	0.0	6.6	5.5
4	7.0	6.0	1.0	0.0	14.0	11.1
5	4.0	15.0	2.7	0.0	21.7	16.2
6	0.0	14.0	2.7	0.0	16.7	11.8
7	0.0	9.0	2.7	0.0	11.7	7.8
8	0.0	8.0	2.7	0.0	10.7	6.7
9	0.0	8.0	2.7	0.0	10.7	6.3
10	0.0	0.0	2.7	0.0	2.7	1.5
11	0.0	0.0	2.7	0.0	2.7	1.4
12	0.0	0.0	2.7	0.0	2.7	1.3
13	0.0	0.0	2.7	0.0	2.7	1.3
14	0.0	0.0	2.7	0.0	2.7	1.2
15	0.0	0.0	2.7	0.0	2.7	1.1
16	0.0	0.0	2.7	0.0	2.7	1.1
17	0.0	0.0	2.7	0.0	2.7	1.0
18	0.0	0.0	2.7	0.2	2.9	1.0
19	0.0	0.0	2.7	0.4	3.1	1.0
20	0.0	0.0	2.7	0.5	3.2	1.0
21	0.0	0.0	2.7	0.5	3.2	0.9
22	0.0	0.0	2.7	0.5	3.2	0.9
23	0.0	0.0	2.7	0.5	3.2	0.8
24	0.0	0.0	2.7	0.5	3.2	0.8
25	0.0	0.0	2.7	0.5	3.2	0.7
					NPV	89.3

Figure H-2 – MPA/EPAS Alternative Cost Matrix

Year	Design ($M)	Production ($M)	Operation ($M)	Disposal ($M)	Undiscounted Sum ($M)	Present Value ($M)
1	5.0	0.0	0.0	0.0	5.0	4.7
2	5.0	0.0	0.0	0.0	5.0	4.4
3	5.0	0.0	0.0	0.0	5.0	4.2
4	5.0	2.0	0.0	0.0	7.0	5.5
5	3.0	4.0	66.5	2.0	75.5	56.4
6	0.0	4.0	66.5	2.0	72.5	51.1
7	0.0	4.0	66.5	2.0	72.5	48.2
8	0.0	4.0	66.5	2.0	72.5	45.5
9	0.0	4.0	66.5	2.0	72.5	42.9
10	0.0	4.0	66.5	2.0	72.5	40.5
11	0.0	4.0	66.5	2.0	72.5	38.2
12	0.0	4.0	66.5	2.0	72.5	36.0
13	0.0	4.0	66.5	2.0	72.5	34.0
14	0.0	4.0	66.5	2.0	72.5	32.1
15	0.0	4.0	66.5	2.0	72.5	30.3
16	0.0	4.0	66.5	2.0	72.5	28.5
17	0.0	4.0	66.5	2.0	72.5	26.9
18	0.0	4.0	66.5	2.0	72.5	25.4
19	0.0	4.0	66.5	2.0	72.5	24.0
20	0.0	4.0	66.5	2.0	72.5	22.6
21	0.0	4.0	66.5	2.0	72.5	21.3
22	0.0	4.0	66.5	2.0	72.5	20.1
23	0.0	4.0	66.5	2.0	72.5	19.0
24	0.0	4.0	66.5	2.0	72.5	17.9
25	0.0	4.0	66.5	2.0	72.5	16.9
					NPV	696.7

Figure H-3 - Barrier Alternative Cost Matrix

LIST OF REFERENCES

[1] Admiral Gary Roughhead, General James T. Conway, Admiral Thad W. Allen, "A Cooperative Strategy for the 21st Century Seapower," Presented at the International Seapower Symposium, Newport, Rhode Island, October 2007.

[2] CNO ASW Task Force, "ASW CONOPS for the 21st Century", Downloaded 2007 from; http://www.navy.mil/navydata/policy/asw/asw-conops.pdf.

[3] Donald F. McCormack, NUWC DIVNPT, Technical Director, "Pacing The Threat," National Defense Industrial Association, Undersea Warfare Division, Spring 2007, Number 21.

[4] Grace Jean, "Diesel-Electric Submarine, The U.S. Navy's Latest Annoyance," *National Defense* April 2008.

[5] Eugene P. Paulo, Course Notes for SI 4007 "Fundamentals of Systems Engineering", Naval Postgraduate School, 2006 (unpublished).

[6] Sage, A. P., and Armstrong, J. E., *Systems Engineering and Systems Engineering Management*, Wiley, New York, 2000.

[7] Benjamin S. Blanchard and Wolter J. Fabrycky, *System Engineering and Analysis,* Pearson Prentice Hall, New Jersey, 2006.

[8] Buede, D. M., *The Engineering Design of Systems*, Wiley, New York, 2000.

[9] John F. Reh, "Pareto Principle – The 80-20 Rule," downloaded 2007 from http://management.about.com/cs/generalmanagement/a/Pareto081202.htm.

[10] OPNAV Cross Functional Board Survey Response 10/29/2007.

[11] COMPACFLT Survey Response 11/6/2007.

[12] Joseph M. Monti, "System Engineering Based Framework for Developing Undersea Distributed Networked Systems (UDNS)", presented at the UDNS NDIA Conference NUWC, Newport, RI, February 2007.

[13] NUWC Chief Technology Officer Survey Response 10/26/2007.

[14] NUWC USW Combat Systems Department Survey Response 11/5/2007.

[15] Commander U.S. Fleet Forces Command, "Global Anti-Submarine Warfare Concept of Operations," 2006.

[16] NUWC Military Detatchment Survey Response 11/7/2007.

[17] Raymond J. Christian, "Next-Generation Undersea Warfare and Undersea Distributed Networked Systems," NUWC Technical Report 11790, Jan 2007.

[18] W. Huges, *Fleet Tactics and Coastal Combat*, Naval Institute Press, Annapolis, MD, 2000.

[19] NUWC Chief Engineer Survey Response 10/30/2007.

[20] NUWC Ranges, Engineering, and Analysis Department Survey Response 11/5/2007.

[21] United States Navy, "The US Navy Aircraft Carriers: The Carrier Strike Group," *US Navy Today,* Downloaded Oct 2007 From http://www.navy.mil/navydata/ships/carriers/powerhouse/cvbg.asp.

[22] Pike, John et al, *Battle Group Composition*, Downloaded Nov 2007 from http://www.globalsecurity.org/military/agency/navy/batgru-composition.htm.

[23] Jane's Fighting Ships, REF - *Nimitz Class (CVNM)*, Jane's Fighting Ships, Downloaded March 2008 from http://www8.janes.com/JDIC/JDET/documentView.do?docId=/content1/janesdata/yb/jfs/jfs_3526.htm@current&pageSelected=&keyword=CVN&backPath=http://jdet.janes.com/JDIC/JDET&Prod_Name=JFS&activeNav=http://www8.janes.com/JDIC/JDET

[24] United States Navy Carrier Fact File downloaded May 2008 from http://www.navy.mil/navydata/fact_display.asp?cid=4200&tid=200&ct=4.

[25] United States Navy S-3 Viking Fact File Downloaded May 2008 from http://www.navy.mil/navydata/fact_display.asp?cid=1100&tid=1500&ct=1

[26] Jane's Fighting Ships, *Sikorsky S-70A/H-60*, Jane's Helicopter Markets and Systems, Downloaded March 2008 from http://www8.janes.com/JDIC/JDET/documentView.do?docId=/content1/janesdata/binder/jhms/jhms5021.htm@current&pageSelected=&keyword=MH-60&backPath=http://jdet.janes.com/JDIC/JDET&Prod_Name=JHMS&activeNav=http://www8.janes.com/JDIC/JDET

[27] Jane's Fighting Ships, *Sikorsky SH-60/MH-60/S-70B Seahawk and Aegean Hawk/S-70C(M) Thunderhawk*, Jane's Naval Weapons Systems, downloaded April 2008, from http://www8.janes.com/Search/documentView.do?docId=/content1/janesdata/bin

der/jnws/jnws0846.htm@current&pageSelected=allJanes&keyword=sh-60&backPath=http://search.janes.com/Search&Prod_Name=JNWS&

[28] Jane's Fighting Ships, *AN/SQS-53*, Jane's Underwater Warfare Systems, downloaded May 2008 from
http://www8.janes.com/JDIC/JDET/documentView.do?docId=/content1/janesdata/yb/juws/juws0147.htm@current&pageSelected=&keyword=SQS-53&backPath=http://jdet.janes.com/JDIC/JDET&Prod_Name=JUWS&activeNav=http://www8.janes.com/JDIC/JDET

[29] United States Naval Reserve Intelligence Program, "Ready-for0Sea Handbook, Module 2" Downloaded 23 November 2007 from;
http://www.fas.org/irp/doddir/navy/rfs/part00.htm

[30] Jane's Fighting Ships, *Ticonderoga Class: Guided Missile Cruisers (CGHM)*, Jane's Fighting Ships, downloaded March 2008 from
http://www8.janes.com/JDIC/JDET/documentView.do?docId=/content1/janesdata/yb/jfs/jfs_3530.htm@current&pageSelected=&keyword=Ticonderoga&backPath=http://jdet.janes.com/JDIC/JDET&Prod_Name=JFS&activeNav=http://www8.janes.com/JDIC/JDET

[31] Jane's Fighting Ships, *RUM-139A Vertical Launch ASROC (VLA)*, Jane's Underwater Warfare Systems, downloaded May 2008 from
http://www8.janes.com/JDIC/JDET/documentView.do?docId=/content1/janesdata/yb/juws/juws0453.htm@current&pageSelected=&keyword=RUM-139A&backPath=http://jdet.janes.com/JDIC/JDET&Prod_Name=JUWS&activeNav=http://www8.janes.com/JDIC/JDET

[32] Jane's Fighting Ships, *Arleigh Burke Class (Flights I and II): Guided Missile Destroyers (AEGIS) (DDGHM)*, Jane's Fighting Ships, Downloaded March 2008 from
http://www8.janes.com/JDIC/JDET/documentView.do?docId=/content1/janesdata/yb/jfs/jfs_3532.htm@current&pageSelected=&keyword=AEGIS&backPath=http://jdet.janes.com/JDIC/JDET&Prod_Name=JFS&activeNav=http://www8.janes.com/JDIC/JDET

[33] United States Naval Reserve Intelligence Program, "Ready-for0Sea Handbook, Module 2" Downloaded 23 November 2007 from;
http://www.fas.org/irp/doddir/navy/rfs/part00.htm

[34] Jane's Fighting Ships, *Los Angeles Class (SSN)*, Jane's Fighting Ships, Downloaded March 2008 from
http://www8.janes.com/JDIC/JDET/documentView.do?docId=/content1/janesdata/yb/jfs/jfs_3523.htm@current&pageSelected=&keyword=Los_Angeles_Class&b

ackPath=http://jdet.janes.com/JDIC/JDET&Prod_Name=JFS&activeNav=http://www8.janes.com/JDIC/JDET

[35] Jane's Fighting Ships, Seawolf Class (SSN), Jane's Fighting Ships, Downloaded March 2008 from
http://www8.janes.com/Search/documentView.do?docId=/content1/janesdata/yb/jfs/jfs_3522.htm@current&pageSelected=allJanes&keyword=tank&backPath=http://search.janes.com/Search&Prod_Name=JFS&keyword=

[36] Jane's Fighting Ships, Virginia Class, Jane's Underwater Warfare Systems, Downloaded April 2008 from
http://www8.janes.com/JDIC/JDET/documentView.do?docId=/content1/janesdata/yb/juws/juws0029.htm@current&pageSelected=&keyword=Seawolf_Class&backPath=http://jdet.janes.com/JDIC/JDET&Prod_Name=JUWS&activeNav=http://www8.janes.com/JDIC/JDET

[37] United States Navy P-3 Orion Fact File, Dowloaded May 2008 from
http://www.navy.mil/navydata/fact_display.asp?cid=1100&tid=1400&ct=1

[38] Jane's Fighting Ships, *Lockheed P-3 Orion*, Downloaded May 2008 from
http://www8.janes.com/Search/documentView.do?docId=/content1/janesdata/yb/jfs/jfs_3926.htm@current&pageSelected=allJanes&keyword=P-3%20Orion&backPath=http://search.janes.com/Search&Prod_Name=JFS&

[39] Jane's Fighting Ships, Janes Underwater Warfare Systems Downloaded May 2008 from
http://www8.janes.com/Search/documentView.do?docId=/content1/janesdata/yb/juws/juws0023.htm@current&pageSelected=allJanes&keyword=MGK-400&backPath=http://search.janes.com/Search&Prod_Name=JUWS&

[40] Jane's Underwater Warfare Systems, downlaoded 3 May 2008 from
http://www8.janes.com/Search/documentView.do?docId=/content1/janesdata/yb/juws/juwsa017.htm@current&pageSelected=janesReference&keyword=china%20submarine&backPath=http://search.janes.com/Search&Prod_Name=JUWS&

[41] Jane's Naval Weapon Systems, downloaded 3 May 2008 from
http://www8.janes.com/Search/documentView.do?docId=/content1/janesdata/binder/jnws/jnws0203.htm@current&pageSelected=allJanes&keyword=tank&backPath=http://search.janes.com/Search&Prod_Name=JNWS&keyword=

[42] Nate Orme, "Army Catamaran Hauls Equipment Double-Time," *American Forces News Service*, 8 September 2003, Downloaded March 2008 from
http://www.defenselink.mil/news/newsarticle.aspx?id=28513

[43] Douglas Sample, "Navy Shows Off Next-Generation Vessel," *American Forces News Service*, 4 April 2004 Downloaded March 2008 from
http://www.defenselink.mil/news/newsarticle.aspx?id=26931

[44] Director Operational Test and Evaluation, "Fiscal Year 2006 President's Budget Operational Test and Evaluation, Defense (OT&E, D) Appropriation, Feb 2005.

[45] Stephen Trauth, James Barbara, Patrick Papa, Christine Maluchnik, Donald Paskulovich, Kerry Riese, Ralph Pallotta, "Army Transformation at Sea: The New Theater Support Vessel," *Military Review*, Nov-Dec 2005, Page 51-56.

[46] Military & Aerospace Electronics, Dec. 2006, Downloaded Apr 2008 from
http://mae.pennnet.com/articles/article_display.cfm?article_id=280765

[47] Defense Technical Information Center (DTIC), OSD RDT&E Project Justification (R2a Exhibit), Program Element Number: 0603648D8Z – Joint Capability Technology Demonstrations, Downloaded April 2008 from
www.DTIC.mil/decriptivesum

[48] Federation of American Scientists, P-3 Orion, Dec 1999, Downloaded April 2008 from http://www.fas.org/man/dod-101/sys/ac/p-3.htm

[49] John Pike, P-8 Aircraft, 2007, Downloaded April 2008 from
http://www.globalsecurity.org/military/systems/aircraft/p-8.htm

[50] John Pike, LCS, 2006, Downloaded April 2008, from
http://www.globalsecurity.org/military/systems/ship/lcs.htm.

[51] Assistant Secretary of the Navy for Research Development and Acquisition, "The Navy Unmanned Undersea Vehicle (UUV) Master Plan", November 2004.

[52] John Pike, AN/UQQ-2 Surveillance Towed-Array Sensor System (SURTASS), Downloaded April 2008 from
http://www.globalsecurity.org/intell/systems/surtass.htm

[53] Roger Gentry, SURTASS LFA: Technical Background & Marine Mammal Scientific Research Program, downloaded April 2008 from
http://www.nmfs.noaa.gov/pr/pdfs/acoustics/surtass_background.pdf

[54] Jane's Information Group, Jane's All The World's Aircraft, Downloaded May 2008 from
http://www8.janes.com/Search/documentView.do?docId=/content1/janesdata/yb/jawa/jawa1458.htm@current&pageSelected=allJanes&keyword=SH-60%20procurement%20cost&backPath=http://search.janes.com/Search&Prod_Name=JAWA&#toclink-j0010120164736

[55] Jane's Fighting Ships, Jane's All The World's Aircraft, Downloaded May 2008 from http://www8.janes.com/Search/documentView.do?docId=/content1/janesdata/yb/jawa/jawa1458.htm@current&pageSelected=allJanes&keyword=SH-60%20procurement%20cost&backPath=http://search.janes.com/Search&Prod_Name=JAWA&#toclink-j0010120164736

[56] Airliners.net, N791LM, 2006, Downloaded May 2008 from http://www.airliners.net/search/photo.search?aircraft_genericsearch=Lockheed%20Martin%20P-791&distinct_entry=true

[57] NUWC Keyport MSSE Cohort (Roy Agpaoa, Matthew Cawley, Chad Cossey, Jose Galvan, Alan Giang, Joseph Hanchinamani, Jeffrey Ikeda, John Kenney, Lance Magnusson, Christopher Martinez, Mike Newberry, Eldridge Raymond, John Rykala, Jason Watts, Micheal Wood), *Hybrid Airship Multi-Role (HAMR) Anti-Submarine Warfare (ASW) Mission Capability*, NUWC Keyport MSSE Cohort Capstone Project, Naval Post Graduate School, June 2008

[58] Mike Green, Course Notes for SE 3122 "Naval Weapon System Technology", Naval Post Graduate School, 2007. (unpublished).

[59] Joe Hall, Course Text for ES 300/310 "Naval Weapon System Technology", Naval Post Graduate School, 2006.

[60] Metron Inc., "Analyst Guide for the Employment of the Naval Simulation System (NSS v3.3)," Prepared by Metron Incorporated, for Space and Naval Warfare Systems Command, PMW-153 and Chief of Naval Operations, 31 August 2002.

[61] Office of the Chief of Naval Operations, "Operational Availability Handbook A Practical Guide for Military Systems, Sub-Systems and Equipment," OPNAVINST 3000.12 A, Department of the Navy, Washington D.C, 02 September 2003

[62] Christine Moreira NUWCDIVNPT 2524, "VIRGINIA Class Large Aperture Bow (LAB) Array Operational Availability (Ao) and Reliability Requirements Generation," white paper, December 2007. CONFIDENTIAL DOCUMENT

[63] John F. Lomba and Daniel Nashold, "Performance Specification for the Multi-Function Towed Array (MFTA) (U)," NUWC-NPT Technical Document 11,795, March 2007. CONFIDENTIAL DOCUMENT

[64] Prepared by Kenneth Silveria NUWCDIVNPT 1551 for the IWS5B Program Office, "AN/SQQ-89(V) Undersea Warfare Requirements Functional

Specification Document Build 2," PEO-IWS5B-SQQ-89A(V)-PSPEC-B2-001-R1, May, 2008. SECRET DOCUMENT

[65] NAVSEA PMS 425, Test and Evaluation Master Plan (TEMP) Revision 3, for Combat Control System AN/BYG-1(V), Annex E, No. 234-11, 12 May 2005.

[66] Norm Pettus, Analysis conducted by Norm Pettus, Electric Boat Corporation, Groton CT. Documented in: Christine Brown NUWCDIVNPT 2524 for the PMS 398 Program Office, "Ohio Class Guided Missile Submarine (SSGN) Operational Availability (Ao) Status Report (U)," 30 September 2005, CONFIDENTIAL DOCUMENT

[67] Daniel J. Theunissen and R. Owen Holbrook, "Effects of Environment and Aging Upon Missile Reliability," Proceedings Annual Reliability and Maintainability Symposium, 1998

[68] Office of the Under Secretary of Defense For Acquisition, Technology & Logistics, "Report of the Defense Science Board Task Force on Options for Acquisition of the Advanced Targeting POD and Advanced Targeting FLIR POD (ATP/ATFLIR)," Washington, D.C., February 2001

[69] NAVSEA PMS 404, XWS 20880-1 System Performance Specification Torpedo Mk48 ADCAP Modifications, Revision A dated 11 May 1998.

[70] Rick Lumpkin and Mayra Pazos, "Lifetime Statistics of Most Recent Drifter Deployments (2002-2003)," Global Drifter Program/ Drifter Data Assembly Center, NOAA/AOML, Miami, Florida, DBCP-20, Chennai, India, October 18-22, 2004

[71] R. Volkert, SPAWARSYSCEN PMS 420, "Requirements for the Littoral Combat Ship (LCS) Flight 0 – Spiral Alpha Anti-Submarine Warfare (ASW) Mission Package," Revision 2.41 1100000000-2.41-0236, 15 September 2005.

[72] US Department of Defense, "Program Budget Decision 753," December 2004, Downloaded Oct 2007 from http://www.missilethreat.com/repository/doclib/20041200-DOD-pbd753budget.pdf.

[73] Department of the Navy Fiscal Year 2007 RDT&E Budget Item Justification for Advanced Processing Build, February 2007, Downloaded April 2008 from http://www.globalsecurity.org/military/library/budget/fy2007/navy-peds/2007-0603561n.pdf

[74] Department of the Navy Fiscal Year 2009 Budget Estimates, Justification of Estimates February 2008, Research, Development, Test & Evaluation, Navy

Budget Activity 4, Downloaded April 2008 from
http://www.finance.hq.navy.mil/fmb/08pres/rdten/RDTEN_BA4_book.pdf

[75] Department of the Navy Fiscal Year 2007 Budget Estimates Submission, Justification of Estimates February 2006, Other Procurement, Navy Budget Activity 2, Downloaded April 2008 from
http://www.finance.hq.navy.mil/fmb/07pres/PROC/OPN_BA2_BOOK.pdf

[76] Program Executive Office Integrated Warfare Systems Brief for CNO's ASW Offsite (Draft), March 2005

[77] Military Composite Standard Pay and Reimbursement Rates Fiscal Year 2008, Office of the Under Secretary of Defense Memorandum, April 19, 2007

[78] Navy Littoral Combat Ship (LCS): Background and Issues for Congress, CRS Report for Congress, Ronald O'Roarke, August 2006

[79] World Wide Shipping Lanes Image, downloaded April 2008 from
http://images.google.com/imgres?imgurl=http://news.nationalgeographic.com/news/2007/06/images/070628-human-footprint_big.jpg&imgrefurl=http://news.nationalgeographic.com/news/2007/06/070628-human-footprint.html&h=249&w=461&sz=59&hl=en&start=4&tbnid=NLxmfTpZQ7EqKM:&tbnh=69&tbnw=128&prev=/images%3Fq%3Dglobal%2Bshipping%2Blanes%26gbv%3D2%26hl%3Den%26sa%3DG'

[80] Robert J. Urick, Principles of Underwater Sound 3rd Edition, Peninsula Publishing, California, 1983.

[81] Personal Computer Interactive Multi-Sensor Trainer (PCIMAT) Version 5.0, 2006

[82] NUWC Director Undersea Warfare, Brief to OPNAV N4, 2006

[83] Fleet Forces Command, SONAR 101 Brief, May 2006

[84] Enterprise Carrier Strike Group Image, downloaded April 2008 from
http://www.strategypage.com/military_photos/military_photos_200658221841.aspx

INITIAL DISTRIBUTION LIST

1. Defense Technical Information Center
    Ft. Belvoir, Virginia

2. Dudley Knox Library
    Naval Postgraduate School
    Monterey, California

3. Dr. Eugene Paulo
    Naval Postgraduate School
    Monterey, California

4. Mark Rhoades
    Naval Postgraduate School
    Monterey, California

5. Steven Wright
    Naval Undersea Warfare Center Division (Code 2522)
    Newport, RI

www.ingramcontent.com/pod-product-compliance
Lightning Source LLC
Chambersburg PA
CBHW082032300426
44117CB00015B/2448